ingland, not even the roads. It seems to me that this shameless & benighted government of ours would gladly institute a rain of terror. They have tried by every means in their power to terrify me into cowed submission — but in this they have failed I do assure you.

14. In due course the two summonses were delivered & against Cape & hill, and as you know the first case was heard by Biron at Bow St on Friday Nov. 9th. That case was hotly defended by us. We had about 40 witnesses, all eminent men & women of good will; all prepared to swear that my book was not obscene, and to give their carefully considered reasons for thinking that the book should circulate in England. We had doctors male & female, men of science, Educationalists, clergy, journalists, & of course a great number of my fellow authors. We had also some prominent book sellers who had purchased the W of L for their shops — and for their circulating libraries only after first having read it, mark you, only after having read it. And now we must leave the government for a time & consider the legal procedure. Not one of our witnesses was admitted by Sir Charles Biron, who would listen to no one but inspector Prothero, the policeman. Inspector

Radclyffe Hall's handwritten notes for a lecture on the trial of *The Well of Loneliness*, given to Southend Young Socialists, 25 January 1929 (Alessandro Rossi-Lemeni)

THE TRIALS OF
RADCLYFFE HALL

Also by Diana Souhami

Gluck: Her Biography
Gertrude and Alice
Greta and Cecil
Mrs Keppel and Her Daughter

THE TRIALS OF RADCLYFFE HALL

Diana Souhami

Weidenfeld & Nicolson

LONDON

First published in Great Britain in 1998
by Weidenfeld & Nicolson

© 1998 Diana Souhami
The moral right of Diana Souhami to be identified as the author
of this work has been asserted in accordance with the
Copyright, Designs and Patents Act of 1988

A CIP catalogue record for this book is available
from the British Library.

ISBN 0 297 81825 2

Typeset by Selwood Systems, Midsomer Norton

Set in Monotype Sabon

Printed in Great Britain by Butler & Tanner Ltd,
Frome and London

Weidenfeld & Nicolson

The Orion Publishing Group Ltd
Orion House
5 Upper Saint Martin's Lane
London, WC2H 9EA

TO SHEILA

I have felt awkward about what to call Radclyffe Hall. Christened Marguerite, she preferred to be known as John. Neither seemed quite right and Radclyffe Hall sounds like a residential college. I have slipped from one name to another with attempted nonchalance.

Radclyffe Hall was dyslexic. In quotation from her manuscripts and letters I have kept her idiosyncratic spelling.

To avoid cluttering the text with footnotes sources of quoted material are given at the end of the book by page number and opening phrase. These notes start on page 384.

Contents

CONTENTS

ILLUSTRATIONS

Radclyffe Hall, May 1934 (*Hulton Getty Picture Collection Ltd, London*)
Una Lady Troubridge by Romaine Brooks, 1924 (*National Museum of American Art, Washington, DC/Art Resource NY*)
Radclyffe Hall, 1936 (*Harry Ransom Humanities Research Center, University of Texas*)
Evguenia Souline, circa 1934 (*Joan Slater*)
Radclyffe Hall with Fido, circa 1939 (*C Magrini, Harry Ransom Humanities Research Center, University of Texas*)

Private Matters

In January 1998 the British government released into the public domain papers about the ban, seventy years earlier, of Radclyffe Hall's novel *The Well of Loneliness*. My book was in manuscript but I was keen to see this new material. Radclyffe Hall and her solicitor Harold Rubinstein had kept all notes, letters and transcripts about the trial, but I wanted to find out what the law makers and enforcers had written in private to each other.

At the Public Record Office London I saw this new release. More pieces of the jigsaw fitted into place. The quality of bigotry of Stanley Baldwin's government was there in memoranda. It surprised me to see that this bigotry was endorsed by the post-war Attlee government too. Many files though were empty and marked 'retained by the Home Office'. I phoned their Record Management Services and asked why. I was told the material was sensitive, that it was not in the public interest for it to be released and that to do so would impede national security.

In an incredulous letter I explained that it was important to me to see these papers. 'Even if they add detail', I said, 'as I suspect they do, to evidence of homophobia and manipulation of the law by that particular administration, is it in the public interest, at this stage, for such details to be withheld?' The Department replied that it would look again at the extracts. Two months later I received a letter. The material was being retained 'in the interests of national security'. The matter, I was told, would be reviewed in 2007.

I suspected these private memoranda would inspire scorn. All the evidence I had showed that the Home Secretary of the time Sir William Joynson-Hicks, the Lord Chancellor Lord Hailsham, the Director of Public Prosecutions Sir Archibald Bodkin, his deputy Sir George Stephenson, the Chief Magistrate Sir Chartres Biron, the Attorney General Sir Thomas Inskip, were determined to secure a conviction and ban this book. They manipulated the law to this end and to avoid any process that might serve the interests of the defendants.

Lesbianism was not to be mentioned. The subject was inadmissible. Radclyffe Hall referred to a 'conspiracy of silence'. It is taking a long time to break this silence. I wrote to the current Home Secretary Jack Straw, to the Chancellor of the Duchy of Lancaster, to my constituency Member of Parliament Karen Buck. I asked them to help me get sight of these papers. I am indebted to them, to James Cornford, to Andrew Ecclestone at the Campaign for Freedom of Information and to Anya Palmer at the Stonewall lobby for gay and lesbian rights.

A week before my book went to press I was allowed to see the contentious papers. I was pleased to amend my text. I now include details of how the Home Secretary issued warrants to the Post Office requiring them to intercept mail addressed to the book's Paris publisher, of how he squashed opposition from the fair-minded Chairman of the Board of Customs Sir Francis Floud, and of how the Director of Public Prosecutions schemed to indict the London publisher Jonathan Cape and the book's distributor Leopold Hill.

This saga apart, I am full of thanks for help given me over access to source material. I am grateful to Alessandro Rossi-Lemeni, son of the opera singer Nicola Rossi-Lemeni. In his basement in Rome were two trunks containing Una Troubridge's diaries from 1931 to 1943, autobiographical pieces by Radclyffe Hall, her lecture notes, and fragments of unpublished manuscripts.

In the autumn of 1996 I worked on these papers in a Rome hotel in a room with a terrace that looked out over the roofs of the old city. Future researchers will have formal access to them. They have now been shipped to the Harry Ransom Research Center at the University of Texas. They form an important addition to their Radclyffe Hall collection. The Center already held her letters to Evguenia Souline with whom she fell in love in 1934, and all papers concerned with the American trial of *The Well of Loneliness*. My thanks to the librarians there and in particular to Pat Battle.

Alessandro Rossi-Lemeni also enabled me to retrieve 140 more of Una's diaries lost from view for the last fifteen years in a house in Kent. They date from 1943 and are crucial to understanding the events surrounding the death of Radclyffe Hall. These diaries too will soon go to Texas.

In her will Una appointed Horatio Lovat Dickson, a director of the

Macmillan publishing house, as her literary executor. He wrote a biography of Radclyffe Hall in 1975 then gave the research papers he had inherited to the Canadian National Archive, Ottawa. These include more of Una's diaries, her other writings, Radclyffe Hall's personal and business letters and much relating to the English trial of *The Well of Loneliness*. The executorship has passed to Horatio Lovat Dickson's son Jonathan. I am grateful to him and to his agent A. M. Heath & Co. Ltd. for their help and for permission to quote from copyright material.

Cara Lancaster, great-granddaughter of Mabel Batten, Radclyffe Hall's first love, has inherited her diaries, letters and papers. She kindly let me study these and use quotation from them.

IMy thanks to Joan Slater and Monica Still. They have amassed an impressive archive over the past decade. Their knowledge of the life and works of Radclyffe Hall is huge. They organised a memorial fund to restore and maintain her catacomb vault at Highgate Cemetery. She now has an oak coffin, and candles light her private altar. Joan has written an as yet unpublished biography of her. She generously let me make use of her research papers.

In the long haul of writing I have depended on the encouragement and editorial inspiration of Rebecca Wilson, publishing director at Weidenfeld. My thanks to her and to my agent Georgina Capel for her support, advice and flair.

All thanks too to my friend Naomi Narod. She always expects my books to be bestsellers and casts them for stage and screen with in my view remarkable perspicacity.

MARGUERITE

I

The Fifth Commandment

On a summer day in 1884 a blue-eyed four-year-old with ash blonde hair walked with her English nurse in the old cemetery in West Philadelphia near her grandmother's house. It was quiet there, the day was clear, she could smell boxwood, pine and new-mown grass. She walked on a gravel path littered with tiny shells, which she stopped to collect. There were high trees to her right, an avenue ahead and, to her left, bare grass, mounds of earth and new graves.

A small group wearing black came towards her across the grass. A woman among them, tall with a long veil and gloves, seemed to stare at her. Two of the men carried between them a white wooden box. The group stopped by a freshly dug hole beside which was a mound of earth. They lowered the box into the hole and a man began shovelling in earth. At the sound of the earth hitting the box, the woman jerked back. The movement made the girl think of her mechanical bear on its green baize stand at home in London. The woman bent over the hole in the ground then raised her face and screamed. She seemed to scream at the sky, the trees, the man shovelling earth and the little girl out with her nurse.

Consolation for such ontological terrors was not on offer to Marguerite Radclyffe-Hall from her mother whom she feared and despised: 'Always my mother. Violent and brainless. A fool but a terribly crafty and cruel fool for whom life had early become a distorting mirror in which she saw only her own reflection.'

In two unpublished autobiographical pieces, *Forebears and Infancy* and *Michael West*, in letters and in fictional allusion in her novels, she defined her mother as grasping, violent and capricious. 'I cannot,' she said, 'keep the fifth commandment.' Home for a child, she averred, should be a refuge, a place of affection and kindness. Hers was 'bereft of security' and haunted by the feeling that something was wrong. 'I pity those whose memories of home have been rendered intolerable as have mine. They and I have lost a great sweetness in life.'

The mother of her fantasy was religious and peaceful. 'A woman one would long to protect while coming to in turn for protection.' The mother she had, Mary Jane Hall, 'late Sager formerly Diehl', was attracted and attractive to rakish men and had startling mood swings. She gave birth on 12 August 1880 to a daughter she had tried to abort, whom she never liked and to whom the acutest insult she could fling was, 'You are like your father.' Not an ounce of the child's blood, she said, came from her. The girl was Radclyffe through and through. Her hands, nose, temper and perversity were the curse of the father, the devil incarnate.

This birth took place in England in a house called Sunny Lawn at Westcliff, Bournemouth. 'Sunny Lawn' God Help Us, Radclyffe Hall wrote:

> A night of physical passion and then me, born solely of bodily desire, of animal impulse and nothing more. For I cannot believe those parents of mine could ever have known the love of the spirit. Nor did I bring peace into that distracted home by drawing their warring natures together. Quite the contrary. At the time of my birth a deadly quarrel was raging.

She learned of this quarrel from her mother. Her parents parted for ever a month after her birth. Her father, Radclyffe Radclyffe-Hall, known familiarly as Rat, the man whom she so resembled, whose blood alone flowed in her veins, was, so she heard, a degenerate who beat and abused his wife, chased her round the house with a pistol, had sex with the servants and threw a joint of cold lamb at the cook.

Mary Jane Sager met him in Southport, Lancashire in 1878. She was travelling with his cousin, James Reade, who had settled in New Orleans when he married her aunt. He had gone to America from Congleton, Cheshire, where his family owned silk mills. He was in Southport visiting family and recovering from a back injury – he had been thrown and kicked by a horse.

Mary Jane had an aspirational regard for the English gentry. She was twenty-seven, widowed and dissatisfied at living with her mother in Philadelphia. In her teens she had run off with and married a young Englishman, Wallace Sager, who died of yellow fever. The Halls, their cousins and uncles the Reades, Martins and Russells, were conservative gentry who had ladies for wives. 'They believed in God, upheld the Crown and supported the Church of England.' They were clergymen, factory owners, teachers, doctors. Portraits showing their sidewhiskers, stiff clothes and solemn thoughts hung on the library walls of Derwent, a greystone estate with an elm park in Torquay, Devon.

Rat's father, Charles Radclyffe Hall, was President of the British Medical Association and a physician at the Western Hospital for Consumption. He was author of *Torquay in its Medical Aspects* and *Is Torquay Relaxing?* He founded a charitable sanatorium there for the treatment of 'reduced gentlewomen with affected chests'. His career was lucrative, his business acumen shrewd, his nature cautious and thorough and his wife rich in her own right. Esther Westhead when he married her in 1847 was, at thirty-six, a widow with three children – a son and two daughters.

Radclyffe was the only child of her second marriage. He studied law at Oxford but did not qualify. He had a large allowance and no desire to work. He collected mandolins, wrote songs, did magician's tricks, took photographs of the New Forest and waves crashing on rocks and painted landscapes his daughter when adult judged 'too appalling for words'. He hunted, kept horses, and dogs whose names were in the Kennel Club books – French poodles were his favourite breed. He liked travel, owned a yacht and never stayed in one place long.

He wore expensive clothes and diamond studs in his cuffs. Women took up his time. 'I regret to say that his love affairs were seldom in accord with his social position.' He offended his father by a foray into acting under the alias Hubert Vane and a fling in Torquay with a local fisherman's daughter.

He and Mary Jane Sager married at St Andrew's parish church,

Southport, on 2 July 1878 within months of meeting. The ceremony was to legitimize the birth of their first daughter, Florence Maude. Walter Begley, a friend from Radclyffe's student days, a large, shambling clergyman with nervous mannerisms, officiated. The wedding breakfast was held in a hotel. Mary Jane's mother stayed in Philadelphia. The Halls from Torquay and the Reades from Congleton deplored the speed of the alliance, the irregularity of the reception, the uncouthness of Americans, the fisherman's daughter, the scandalous Hubert Vane. In his wedding speech Rat said, 'You've heard of the glorious stars and stripes, well I've married one of the stars may I never deserve the stripes.'

He called himself a painter and wore a green velvet coat, check trousers and a silk bow tie. He sailed with his wife to Philadelphia to meet his in-laws. This honeymoon was not a success: 'They quarrelled in private and they quarrelled before friends in public, they quarrelled before the negro servants, they quarrelled from the moment they opened their eyes. Their scenes were crude, disgraceful and noisy.'

A year later, in 1879, Radclyffe's father died, leaving him a trust income of £90,000. Domestic chaos and divorce were not considerations in Charles Radclyffe-Hall's will. It was a document of propriety with family loyalty and indissolubility at its root. By the terms of it at Radclyffe's death the family capital would pass in turn to his children.

But Radclyffe's marriage was a disaster. It did not so much fail as implode. When Marguerite was born the doctor was unavailable, the nurse was at the chemist and Rat was in bed with the maid. 'When I was born my father was being blatantly and crudely unfaithful. The details were too base to record.' The maid, Elizabeth Sarah Farmer, was ordered from the house by Mary Jane. She moved to London and gave birth to another of Rat's daughters the following year. She registered the child as Mary Ratcliffe Farmer, left blank the box 'Name of Father' and took in needlework to supplement the £200 a year he gave her.

Three weeks after Marguerite's birth Florence, her legitimate baby sister, died. She too had had wide-set blue eyes and ash blonde hair. For the last eight days of her life she also had infected gums, diarrhoea and convulsions. Mary Jane said she died 'by reason of her father's sins' – that she had inherited syphilis from him. Rat left Sunny Lawn never to return.

Mary Jane became hysterical. It was seven weeks before she registered her second daughter's birth. She gave the father's occupation as
Gentleman, left blank the box 'Name of Child', then started court
proceedings. She claimed that a month into the marriage her husband
used violent and abusive language, beat her and in September 1880,
with one daughter dying and another newborn, deserted her. Through
counsel Radclyffe denied the charges. He said her temper was so
violent, her personality so unstable, it was necessary physically to
restrain her.

Mary Jane was granted judicial separation, custody of the child and
substantial maintenance. But socially her life was bleak. She had an
unwanted child and no house of her own. The Halls accused her of
provoking her husband and would have nothing to do with her. There
was nothing for her in Philadelphia, Sunny Lawn was a house of
horrors, she knew no one in London, and English society viewed her
as American, gold-digging and vulgar.

In a gesture of respectability she had her daughter christened in a
Protestant church. 'My mother had me christened Marguerite. She
could not have chosen a more inappropriate name I detested it.' A
Mrs Baldrey, who lived in Bournemouth in a big house with a pine-
tree drive, was godmother. She gave Marguerite a prayer book with an
ivory cover and a Bible with a silver gilt clasp.

Marguerite, the abiding evidence of rash desire, the recipient of her
mother's rage and disappointment, was shunted about for her first six
years. She was assigned to Nurse Knott who dressed her in frills
and curled her hair. She remembered an Atlantic liner, Nurse Knott
vomiting, the bathroom of Grandmother Diehl's Philadelphia home
where the taps gushed hot and cold water and the bath was panelled
in mahogany. And then, on a certain November day, she remembered
standing on the steps of a house in Notting Hill, west London, a glass
window patterned like in a kaleidoscope over the door.

This house was to be home for a while. The woman who owned it
wore black satin. She and Nurse Knott drank tea and talked of their
dislike of Marguerite's mother. Marguerite persisted in enquiring why
and was ushered to bed. On the first-floor landing was more stained
glass: a dragon and St George with a knife. The nurse explained that
the saint was killing the dragon and if Marguerite did not behave he
would come down and kill her too.

Mother was usually absent or suffering a headache or a rage. She wore exotic clothes, smelled of perfume, laughed a lot, but cried more. She played the piano and sang in a high soprano voice. Her moods were unsettling, her temper short. Household problems enraged her. She screeched at the servants, withheld their wages and summarily turned them and their possessions out of the house.

Grandmother Diehl came to stay. To her, Marguerite said she owed her moments of childhood happiness. 'Without her I think I must have died of sheer starvation of heart and spirit.' She had long, coiled-up hair, blue eyes, spoke in a soft drawl and was used to a house without men. Her father had died when she was a child. At seventeen she had married Edwin Otley Diehl, a stockbroker. She had her daughter and two sons, but when widowed at twenty-three took her children to live with her mother.

She called Marguerite sugar plum, which somehow turned into Tuggie. 'To her I was Tuggie til the day of her death.' She took her to matinées, read Dickens aloud, took her shopping at William Whiteleys department store where the green stair carpet was woven with yellow globes of the world. She did not scold and was never unkind. Through her Marguerite said she discovered 'an altogether new sensation ... a sensation that made you discontented unless you were with the person you wanted to be near. A sensation that made you want to look at them and admire them and be praised by them and kissed by them. It was no less a factor than love.'

Her grandmother wrote down her efforts at poems and praised her 'inordinately'. When Marguerite asked why her mother cried and was disliked by Nurse Knott and why her father had gone, Grandmother Diehl, however circumspectly, always tried to reply.

'If she and I could have lived alone I feel that we two would have been content.' Here was the fantasy mother who talked of heaven, God and love, was soft-spoken and attentive and who made her feel worthwhile. But she kept disappearing to America. And between them was Mary Jane Hall. 'The influence of my mother was so potent that it held my grandmother perpetually in chains.'

Mary Jane's tyranny ruled, her ungovernable tempers and ever-changing moods. In the Notting Hill sitting-room she and Grandmother Diehl talked of money, the Case and Radclyffe, a man whom Marguerite associated with all that was worst in the world. It was Radclyffe who prompted her mother's invective. Grandmother Diehl would say, Do be careful, the child is in the room. Mary Jane, in subdued rage, would then spell words out, not speak them. Which exasperated Marguerite, for she was dyslexic – a disability associated with birth trauma – and though she could memorize stories, poems and songs, spelling eluded her and she had difficulty learning to read or write.

Mother's attention was unwelcome. Sometimes she clasped and kissed her, called her her poor, poor little girl, cried into her neck and made the front of her dress wet. Marguerite recoiled, so her mother wept the more and said that even her own daughter did not love her. Then abruptly she would stop and tell Mrs Diehl to get ready to go to the theatre. 'Why Mary Jane,' Mrs Diehl would say, 'you're up and down like a thermometer.' And Marguerite, alone in her room, learned to hate her.

Revenge and venality sustained Mary Jane. The Case went on for years with legal wrangling over custody and money. In an initial decree for separation, granted on 25 February 1882, Rat was ordered to pay £1,250 a year. Mary Jane then took her case to the Chancery division of the court to claim on Marguerite's behalf against the grandfather's will. She delayed divorce fearing Radclyffe might remarry and his father's money pass to other legitimate children. In a second hearing one third of his inheritance was awarded to Marguerite to be administered in trust. Against this settlement Mary Jane's allowance was reduced to £750 a year. This allocation of funds was to cause inordinate bitterness from mother to daughter in later years.

The marriage had been a disaster, its disintegration was cruel. Marguerite was its victim. Mary Jane denigrated her husband and all his relatives and denied her daughter contact with any of them. Marguerite saw her father no more than a dozen times. Another of her abiding fantasies was that life would have been better had she been brought up by the Halls at Derwent.

There were few visitors to her mother's house. Social graces were not demanded of Marguerite nor learned by her. No one troubled much what she did. She had lessons with her nurse in the mornings and a walk in Kensington Gardens. She needed special tuition which she did not receive. She liked to hear stories read aloud, she learned rudimentary arithmetic and to sing and play the piano. But she could not read or write. She stayed confused as to which letter was which.

Without children to play with she invented Daisy, an imaginary friend. She protected Daisy from the stained-glass dragon and played with her in the park. Daisy admired all Marguerite did. Her advent alarmed Nurse Knott, who suggested to Mary Jane that her daughter needed friends.

Told to desist from this game, Marguerite had a temper tantrum and bit her nurse on the hand. Ushered to her mother's bedroom, where her mother was brushing her hair, she refused to say her imaginary friend, her *alter ego*, did not exist. More than a game, it was an exercise in consolation, an endeavour to repair a fractured world. Her father had called her Daisy, and a Marguerite is a genus of daisy. Her mother saw in her face and manner an image of the man she loathed. She pushed her to the bed and beat her with the silver hairbrush. When she had finished she consigned her to the nurse and slammed the bedroom door. 'It was a hard whipping given and received in temper, an unfortunate whipping.' It was one of many administered while her mother was out of control. Its predictable effect was to inspire her daughter with defiance, hatred and rage.

In 1886 Grandmother Diehl returned to Philadelphia. Marguerite was to go for her summer holiday to Marlow-on-Thames with her mother and nurse. Her grandmother would stay on alone for a while in the Notting Hill house, then sail. Marguerite pleaded with her to take her too. Her grandmother cried, bought her a caged canary called Pippin and told her to be a comfort to her mother.

'Life all at once became blank, empty, awful.' Marguerite was separated from the only person she loved. Mother, with her beatings and exhortations, was best avoided. Father, the worst person in the world, had disappeared. Her mother said she was like her father, ergo she was bad.

She retreated inwards, was solitary, watchful, strange. She did not know how to play with children, trust a parent or how to feel safe. In the inchoate world of childhood, responses were formed by her and reactions made. She took into her feelings all that happened, sought control of her world, made emotional equations, disturbed connections, that echoed on into the books she was to write and the adult life she chose. Dark forces informed her early years. Abandonment elided with insecurity, hatred of her mother with aggrandizement of herself. Unfairness called for justice and violence for revenge.

2

Sing, little silent birdie, sing

Marlow provided consolation. Marguerite picnicked in the meadows with her nurse and went boating on the river. 'It was delicious to go to bed in the twilight and to lie there listening to sounds in the garden beneath, the twittering of birds in the trees, the strains of a distant band playing on the deck of a passing steamboat.'

Mary Jane seemed happier. In London, a child and an ever-present mother cramped her style. The Marlow hotel was comfortable and anonymous and Mr Rutland, a young man in white flannels with black curly hair and a red face, took her out at weekends in a smart carriage. Nurse Knott disapproved and nor could Marguerite like him. His visits meant periods of peace and good temper, but he laughed too much and called her a queer little fish.

The holiday ended abruptly. Mr Rutland visited when Mary Jane was with another suitor – a portly one with side whiskers who gave Marguerite chocolates. There were raised voices from Mary Jane's sitting-room and the sound of her tears. The men left hurriedly, Mr Rutland to his carriage, the one with side whiskers to the steam launch on the river. Nurse Knott and the housekeeper were instructed to pack. They were all to leave for London on the afternoon train. In whispers, the servants complained of their employer's tantrums, the unscheduled departure, the hurry and discomfort. The nurse said she would give notice were it not for the child.

On the train, Marguerite questioned her mother. The portly gentleman had, she was told, gone to France. Mr Rutland was not to be mentioned again. Her mother gave the London taxi driver an unfamiliar address. Marguerite asked where they were going and was told to be quiet. She persisted in a keening monotone – Where are we going, I wonder? Where are we going I wonder? – was warned, then hit. They arrived at new lodgings, a small house in Bayswater, and she was sent to bed.

Her mother lived in a chaotic world of impulsive actions, tantrums, resentments and sexual intrigue. Her egotism ruled. Marguerite was conscious of frustration and evasions over issues intrinsic to her own life. To resist her mother and to assert a personality of her own, she developed an implacable obstinacy, a refusal to kowtow or comply.

She particularly disliked her mother's bedroom, where often she was chastised. It had magenta curtains and wallpaper with bunches of pink roses: 'A foolish indefinite sort of room with too many trifles, too many ornaments, too many chairs, too many pictures all inferior, too many colours, too much of everything and too little of anything that really counted.'

On an autumn morning when she was eight she was summoned to it and told that next day she would go to school. She was to be good and make nice friends. Nurse Knott took her to Whiteleys and bought her a black pencil-box with a gold pagoda and Chinamen on its lid, short and long pencils, an Indiarubber, a white bone pen-holder, a tortoiseshell penknife, a brown leather satchel, a shiny black mackintosh, a grey skirt and cotton blouse. They were possessions of promise. That night Marguerite kept them in sight on a chair by her bed.

The schoolroom seemed long. At the far end was a blackboard with a pointer. She was allocated a desk. The head teacher assessed her new pupils to assign them to classes. They began with reading aloud. Marguerite listened to the competence of the other children. As her turn came near, she had a panic attack. 'Even simple words presented insurmountable difficulties.' The text was indecipherable. The teacher commented in surprise that she could not read at all. Tests in writing, geography and arithmetic were all equally incomprehensible, equally humiliating. She was put in the lowest class.

It was a day that stayed with her. Her dyslexia was neither recognized nor understood. The ramifications of it were huge. She was imaginative and from the age of three had been inventing rhymes. But her manner of reading and writing was unpredictable and laborious. She floundered academically. In later years as a writer she was either dependent on lovers to make sense of her spelling, or she dictated to typists. She had difficulty in deciphering her own writing and for years could not use dictionaries. Even after winning literary prizes she hid her original manuscripts and talked of destroying them out of embarrassment over her inability to spell.

Walking home at the end of that first day at school her satchel felt like a ton weight. Her mother asked her how she had got on. All right, she replied. She was rebuked for her diffidence and sent to her room. Problems at school and home made her naughty. Her naughtiness was responded to with beatings and she became withdrawn and asthmatic.

Mary Jane grew more irritable by the day. She was socially isolated. The English climate oppressed her with its winter fogs, sunless days and long black nights. She breakfasted alone by the light of a gasburner. Servants, perpetually hectored, gave notice. There was an atmosphere of exasperation 'like an unpleasant electric current'.

And the Case dragged on. Mary Jane wanted to divorce Radclyffe, get his money and see him punished. She spent afternoons ensconced in the drawing-room with a solicitor or private detective. In 1886 she 'ascertained' that Radclyffe was living at the Norfolk Hotel, Paddington with an unnamed woman. He moved with this woman to a house in Eastbourne. Mr Bowles, manager of the Paddington hotel, agreed to give evidence. Mary Jane sued for divorce on the grounds of adultery. The decree was granted in November 1887, seven years after the separation. Dispute over alimony and custody continued.

One afternoon in 1887 when Marguerite came home, her mother was arguing with a fair-haired man in a tweed suit and white spats. His voice was dictatorial. He kissed Marguerite and smiled at her. He was Radclyffe Radclyffe-Hall, her father. His invisibility had proved another problem at school. She had not known how to explain it and it was one more issue to mark her out as strange. 'She knew that she would like to have a father. She had been to tea with other children once or twice. Apparently they all had fathers ... A father seemed to give one a certain importance in the world she noticed.'

One girl's father was a colonel in the army. Another's was a mayor with a gold chain and fur on his gown. Another's drove to the city each morning in a green phaeton with grey horses. Marguerite admitted that she did not know what her father did and could not remember having seen him. She was teased. One wag, who had seen Hall above a sweet shop in the Portobello Road, suggested this was his occupation.

Excited by evidence of a real father, his smile and blue eyes, she hoped to see him more. He gave her a boat to sail on the Round Pond in Kensington Gardens. He promised a cream-coloured pony that never materialized. He invited her to stay with his mother in Devon and to learn to horseride.

Mary Jane wept and said she would see her daughter dead and buried rather than let her near Esther Hall, who had insulted her and accused her of ruining her son's life. The scene ended with Radclyffe slamming the front door in rage. His subsequent efforts to see Marguerite were blocked. She was told he was wicked and that she should say he was dead.

She had imagined 'a kind, self-satisfied, important father like the other children had'. Instead, there was Radclyffe who swept into her life then disappeared, leaving confusion behind him. But she kept faith with her fantasy. Thoughts of him and of the kind of life she imagined she might have had with him stayed with her as wistful regrets.

She thought other children were talking about her and laughing at her behind her back. Her personality fragmented into aspects of the family psychodrama. She thought that, had she been Radclyffe's son, he might have stayed or taken her with him. Her mother was proof of how unsatisfactory it was to be female. In later years she played at being faithful husband, protective mother, indulgent lover, then subverted these roles like a troubled child.

The decree absolute for the divorce was made on 4 December 1888 by Sir Charles Parker Butt, a high court judge at the Royal Courts of Justice in the Strand. Marguerite was ten. Her father was found guilty of 'adultery coupled with cruelty to the petitioner'. The case was written up in *The Times* and the *Telegraph* and his name blackened. He sailed to France in his yacht after this finding. He sent Marguerite a signed photograph of himself in hunting clothes, which she kept on her desk. She blamed her mother for his absence. 'She it was who had driven father from the house with bitter angry words.'

Mary Jane Hall set about repairing her own social position. She wanted marriage. Her daughter was an encumbrance and proof of emotional failure. Her past, in society's terms, was littered with indiscretions. 'The men who came to the house did not often bring their wives or sisters.' She wooed her singing teacher, Alberto Antonio Visetti, known as 'the Maestro'. Her voice was off-key and her capacity for practice poor, but she was pleasure-loving and dramatic and he fell for her.

Flamboyant, mercurial, half-Italian, Visetti was forty-three and had a reputation as a ladies' man. As far as Mary Jane knew, he was unmarried. He was a founding professor of the Royal College of Music in London and a respected teacher. Photographs of his successful students lined his studio walls: Louise Kirkby-Lunn, Muriel Foster, Keith Faulkner. He had studied at the Milan Conservatoire, had played duets with Charles François Gounod, written a life of Verdi and a three-act opera, *Giselda*.

A maverick character given to status fantasies, 'a touch of "the grand manner" went with his every word and action'. He claimed his father had been an Italian landowner with a castle in Salano, Dalmatia (in fact, he was the village organist). He said he had received music scholarships from the governments of Austria and Italy and a knighthood from the King of Italy and that he was attached to the court of Napoleon III.

He had wide-set brown eyes, a straight nose, closely clipped beard and dapper clothes. Mary Jane was impressed by the glamour of his artistic reputation, his smart clientele, his innumerable love affairs and broken engagements. 'She felt as she mounted the altar steps that she did so over the prostrate form of countesses, marchionesses and duchesses. This man, or better still this lion, was seemingly chained at last. The end of the chain was firmly held in her ridiculously small hand.'

She wanted social position from this, her third marriage. She wanted a salon, parties and invitations. Visetti was expansive, generous and well paid by the standards of the day. He earned fifteen shillings an hour teaching at the College, had private pupils and was conductor and director of the Bath Philharmonic Orchestra. Madame Maria Visetti, as she now called herself on her visiting cards, assumed the air of a patron of the arts and 'held forth confidently on subjects of which she knew little'.

Marguerite, told of the forthcoming marriage only months after her parents' divorce, was bewildered. She had met Visetti twice. You'll have a real father now, her mother said. Marguerite insisted Radclyffe Radclyffe-Hall was her real father. She was told not to mention his name and that he was dead. Is he really dead, is he under the earth, she asked. I wish he were, her mother replied.

Sent with Nurse Knott to Sidmouth in Devon, Marguerite lodged for three months with a fisherman's family while her mother and Visetti went to Bruges for their marriage and honeymoon. Marguerite described herself as 'seething with surprise and resentment', 'heavy with rage and bewilderment' that her mother should have saddled her with this ersatz father and deprived her of her real one. She resolved 'never to admit the interloper for one moment into her heart'. She wrote a letter to Radclyffe asking if she could come and live with him, but did not know where to send it.

Again the countryside consoled, the Devon town, the long tree-lined road from the station, the cliffs, rough sea, the rocks and sand. 'It was a place to dream in, all dappled sky and waves and fishing boats with brown spray-flecked sails.' She then joined her mother and stepfather in Bruges, where Visetti was organizing a music festival. She spent most of the time in bed with chronic asthma.

When they returned to London they settled in Visetti's large house in Earl's Court, 14 Trebovir Road. Grandmother Diehl came over from Philadelphia to complete the family. The house was elegant. The drawing-room had a polished oak floor and panelled walls. In a corner stood a black harpsichord, there were plants in copper jars, a goldfinch in a large cage. Madame Visetti imposed her taste: a carpet, nick-nack tables, photographs in silver frames, pink cushions, a pink brocade cover for the harpsichord. She spared his studio. Specially built, it filled what had been the back garden and had a domed skylight, teak floor, a performance platform with a balustrade of blue and gold, a Bechstein grand piano, an organ, high mirrors and long low divans. 'Here then the great man held his famous operatic classes. Hither came shoals of soulful young aspirants among whom were a few who in the not very distant future would become famous on the boards of Covent Garden.' Here, too, the great man seduced a succession of his students. His marriage was a cover. It gave him the semblance of respectability, but he made no adjustment to his former life.

His sexual overtures were directed at his ten-year-old stepdaughter, too. She told no one of his behaviour until she was in her thirties and living with Una Troubridge, who was to be her partner for twenty-nine years. To her she recounted 'in a voice devoid of emotion' details of Visetti's 'improper advances'. They 'made quite an impression on his

unhappy little victim', Una said. After Radclyffe Hall died, Una wrote
a biography of her. In the first draft she referred to 'the sexual incident
with the egregious Visetti' but omitted this for publication, 'lest we
have psycho analytic know alls saying she would have been a wife and
mother but for that experience'.

The paragraph that followed this deletion described a 'pathetic'
photograph:

> A faded shiny carte-de-visite obviously taken to exploit the 'paternal'
> affection of Alberto Visetti. John [as Marguerite was later to call herself]
> a very thin, bony little girl of about ten, very unbecomingly dressed and
> with all the appearance of an unloved child, standing awkwardly beside
> the seated Visetti, already getting rather portly, the epitome of smug self-
> satisfaction and conceit.

This 'interloper', whom she had resolved never to let into her heart,
forced his attention on her body. In adult life she referred to Visetti as
'my disgusting old stepfather'. For herself, she never had any sexual
impulse toward a man.

The Visetti marriage turned into another travesty of family life.
Madame Maria Visetti was as violent as Mrs Mary Jane Hall. One of
Visetti's pupils spoke of her 'belabouring' Marguerite round the head
and pulling her hair. Nurse Knott was dismissed when she criticized
her for leaving marks on her daughter's body. Marguerite was bereft.
'Nottie had become part of my life. Partings hold much that is tragic
in them.'

'For the sake of companionship', in adolescence Marguerite was sent
to Mrs Coles' school at the end of the road. It was popular with
actresses. Mrs Patrick Campbell's daughter Stella went there, Ellen
Terry's daughter Edy Craig and the Vanbrugh sisters, Violet and Irene.
Marguerite was often in trouble, ill and absent. She recorded 'inflam-
mation of the lungs', 'a good many painful poultices', 'days spent at
home, days spent in bed and always missing the pantomime at Christmas. There seemed a fatality about it.'

Her spelling, as ever, put her to shame. One teacher made a point of
reading out her mistakes in class. ' "Now I wonder what this word can
be" she would drawl then spell it letter by letter as I had spelt it.' The
only success she remembered was a prize – from the Royal Society for
the Protection of Cruelty to Animals – a certificate and book for a

story about kindness to animals. Animal suffering was an abiding concern in her life. She identified with their helplessness. She had pets, the canary Pippin, a pug dog Joey, an Airedale Yoi. And grandmother 'gave all she had in circumstances that were none too easy'.

Despite the tensions, life was privileged materially and artistically. The studio and house at Trebovir Road were filled with students. There were standards of excellence, expectations of achievement, careers carved through talent and work. There was music all day from ten in the morning. Marguerite said she wished, when she opened the front door, to be greeted sometimes by a sound other than singing.

Music helped her dyslexia. She improvised songs on the piano and her grandmother wrote down the words. On her own assessment these verses showed 'not a vestage of talant'. They were about 'Joey', 'Moonbeams', 'The New Year' – 'Oh innocent year your life's begun, Who knows the sin 'ere you are done.' But she was encouraged. Her grandmother paid for their printing. Aged fourteen, Marguerite gave them as Christmas presents. Signed 'Marguerite Toddles' and dedicated to the composer of light operas Sir Arthur Sullivan, they were doggerel laced with despair:

> Sing, little silent birdie, sing,
> Why do you sit so sad?
> For now is born the baby spring,
> And all things should be glad.

Sullivan told her mother that Marguerite 'had ink in her blood'. He taught counterpoint at the College and was Marguerite's trustee. Another visitor, Arthur Nikisch, conductor of the Berlin Philharmonic Orchestra, hearing her improvise at the piano, said she should be trained at the Leipzig Conservatoire. She believed that 'had she wished she could have become a really great musician'. 'Proximity of opportunity', she said, blunted her musical career.

Maria Visetti grew disaffected with her new husband. Visetti kept a carriage with two horses, a groom, housekeeper and maids. Parties at Trebovir Road were frequent and lavish. Dvořák, Tchaikovsky and Elgar were guests. The family took cures and the waters at Homburg and Bagnoles, spent summers at music festivals in Italy, Dresden, Prague, Bayreuth. But Visetti's friends spurned Maria and viewed his marriage as a disaster. 'They did not like her kittenish flirtation any

more than they liked her assumption of intellectual superiority ...
Politics, literature, science, painting and even music, she gave her
opinion on all these with startling decision and a paralysing lack of
understanding.'

Maria Visetti fretted at her unpopularity. She raged at his infidelities
and accused him of humiliating her in front of the servants and of
bringing his mistresses into her house. He called her nagging, manipulative and destructive and said she was ruining his career. He had a
way of pushing the end of his moustache into his mouth when agitated.
His hands shook and he would go white with rage. She threatened
scandal and said she would leave him. In their scenes he smashed the
china and called her abominable and a devil. Both were profligate and
spent beyond their income. There was a constant spectre of debt and
they siphoned off money from Marguerite's trust fund for their own
use.

Marguerite hated them both, retreated inward and nurtured grandiose ideas of her own importance. 'She knew she was different and at
times it worried her. She tried to look this difference in the face, to
grasp it and to give it a name, but it invariably eluded her. Whatever it
was lay hidden out of sight within the depths of her innermost being.'

She viewed herself as misunderstood and special. Her room at the top
of the house, long with low panelling, became a setting for solipsistic
withdrawal. She kept her possessions in obsessive order, unlike her
mother who left everything lying around. On a wall she hung a large
wooden crucifix. The image of the martyr with the crown of thorns
and driven nails, she felt, applied to herself. She imbued this room with
a mix of religiosity, artistic ambition and sexual desire. At her desk she
struggled with her poems and bits of prose – a description of a face in
a crowd, or of a ship sailing.

Alone a great deal, she fantasized about being 'a jeaneous' and a
lover. 'I can scarcely remember the first time I fell in love. I think I was
a lover even from my mother's womb.' She got by without parental
affection but always pined with desire for some girl or woman – her
piano teacher or a girl in a silk dress. Her mother, to whom she said
something of these desires, told her she was perverted.

In later years she took characterizations for her novels from her
formative years: daughters who are victims but who long for a life
elsewhere; mothers like leeches; weak, shadowy fathers. And beyond
these doomed characters she imagined a God who chose those who

suffered, a mother who was gentle and loving, a dignified father of noble blood.

From her real mother, father and stepfather she learned the controlling power of sex – the passions it aroused, the anxieties and fears, its financial underpinning, its manipulations and betrayals, the way it could be used to create and spoil lives. From adolescence on, she added to the family drama with her particular portrayal of it too.

3

Come in kid

In her teens, Marguerite hung about the room next to Visetti's studio where students met before and after lessons. It became her hunting ground. She heard them sing arias by Wagner, Verdi, Mozart and linked these 'passionate declarations of love to their flustered faces'. Her 'ardent temperament', she said, 'wallowed in an atmosphere of false emotion, of sensation called up at will to suit a role'.

Ardent wallowings took different forms. Sometimes it was Visetti and a favoured pupil, once she saw two girls kiss but more often it was a girl and a young man. Talk of liaisons and conquests fired her imagination:

> I came to realise that the desires which had tormented my childhood and which I was told by my mother were wicked, were merely the usual feelings that animated most of my fellow beings, were indulged in as a matter of course and pandered to as the essentials of an artistic temperament. This was a great revelation and one which filled me with excitement.

She emerged from childhood seeking more complex consolation than kisses and chance caresses, though the desires that tormented her had been ordinary enough. They were to do with love and pleasure. But she wanted to free herself from the web of her mother's malice and to kiss and hold hands with girls.

When she was fifteen she pushed up the sleeve of a student in a silk dress and kissed her arm. The girl laughed, seemed apprehensive but interested, so Marguerite kissed her on the lips. She 'repeated the exercise at every opportunity' – until the girl left to study in Paris.

Visetti's star pupil, a soprano Agnes Nicholls, called her 'a queer little kid'. Marguerite told her to shut up, felt embarrassed and went to her room. Visetti favoured Agnes Nicholls and promoted her career. He taught her for five years. 'Next season what a triumph', he would say. They flirted, she chafed him in bad French, he included her in the daily life of the house. She had won a scholarship to the College in 1894 and sung at Windsor Castle, with Queen Victoria in the audience, in Delibes' opera *Le Roi l'a dit*.

She was plump: 'her voluptuous figure appealed to my youth', wrote Marguerite. She had white skin, blue eyes, auburn hair, a large appetite and 'the voice of an angel, unlike any other'. Marguerite contrived to be always at the studio at the time of her lessons. She felt disturbed by her and by 'the look in her eyes. These lessons became the focus of my existence. I lived for them, like the victim of a drug.'

By turns, Agnes Nicholls ignored and claimed her. If Marguerite flattered her, she appeared indifferent. If she flirted with the girl in the silk dress, Agnes became proprietorial, sent her on errands, gave her presents or told her to come and sit beside her. 'And when I did sit by her she would sometimes slide her hand down where mine lay between us and I think it amused her to see the little shiver that her touch produced for she would bend forward to watch my face at such moments.'

Radclyffe Hall was intrigued by the compulsion and power of sex. This first adventure held components of domination, jealousy, manipulation and of humiliating Visetti. She still sought flirtations in the anteroom but it was Agnes Nicholls whom she wooed. 'Her music and her thrilling voice stirred my passion unendurably ... I longed to dominate her, to hurt her, to compel her, to kiss her mouth.'

Agnes Nicholls was to become a star. She won the College gold medal and at twenty was singing solo in concert halls and at music festivals. Marguerite went to all her recitals, waited for her in the artists' room, held her bouquets, cloak and throat spray. She absorbed the aura of performance and fame, the 'stagy compliments' of other artists, 'the hysterical outpouring' of young fans, the 'bold flirting' of young men.

She felt like her 'special property'. After concerts they drove to Agnes's home in Putney. Marguerite sat close in the carriage, held her bare arm under her cloak, was her escort and swain. Agnes talked of herself. She lived, Marguerite said, in a world of her own creation. One night she was the prima donna, her career assured, wooed by men from the peerage. The next she was a failure, ungifted and without prospects. Sometimes she would weep: her performance had been a fiasco, she would never sing again, a top note had failed, the conductor had let the orchestra drown her voice, the music reviewer from *The Times* was there, he would give her a bad notice next day. At other times, she would brag of how she had amazed the audience that night, and could have sung for ever, had Marguerite seen Lord so and so – she could marry him if she liked but would not sacrifice her career for a man.

Marguerite was swept along:

> I bobbed like a cork on the torrent. I could neither steady Agnes nor myself being only seventeen. I wept with her, rejoiced with her and grew daily more under her influence. If my people disliked this friendship they were too eager to pander to the star pupil to say so. Moreover I'm sure they looked on it as quite innocent which indeed it was at this time. It certainly interfered with my studies and developed in me an unwholesome craving for excitement.

Agnes Nicholls lived with her mother. Her father had managed a drapery business in the Midlands. He died leaving unexceptional funds. There was enough for her brother to go to Oxford and for her to study music. Alberto Visetti, proud of his tutelage, made no charge for her lessons and she was paid for her concerts. But she affected the airs of a *grande dame*, boasted of whom she knew, used French phrases, gestured in an affected way and was ashamed of her family, though she resented criticism of them.

Marguerite began to perceive herself as a suitor. She assumed a masculine chic and found that women responded to her. 'They were even inclined to love me a little or at least to let me make love to them. This I did on every occasion and occasions were not lacking among my stepfather's pupils.'

Agnes Nicholls encouraged other flirtations, but kept her own hold secure. And Marguerite grew more enamoured of her singing. 'I believe the girl's in love with her voice,' Mrs Visetti said. 'And it was so. I would have tramped half the world over to hear that perfect organ, so strong, thrilling, chaste and pure. To this day I cannot hear it unmoved.' But it was not just that perfect organ, strong and thrilling. Nor was Marguerite's interest chaste and pure. It was the prospect of sex that obsessed her thoughts, made her tramp from home and neglect her studies.

Diversion from this hot pursuit occurred in October 1898 when she was eighteen. Her father died of tuberculosis. He was forty-nine. She and Grandmother Diehl were called to the Station Hotel, Paddington. Radclyffe Radclyffe-Hall had intended to winter at Cannes. He was thin and feverish with a chronic cough. He wanted to know about her studies and aims in life. He advised her to choose a speciality and stick with it, not spread herself thin as he had. He told her she was good-looking and asked her to send him a photograph of herself. He also told her that she would inherit his estate.

Marguerite did not see her father again. In Paris, a doctor advised him he was too ill for his journey to the sun. He turned back and died at the Lees Hotel, Folkestone, on 24 October. His death was 'markedly lonely and tragic', Marguerite said. An unknown person registered it and on the certificate misspelt his name and got his age wrong.

His will was administered by Walter Begley, his sole executor, the clergyman who had officiated at his wedding. Begley then took a protective interest in Marguerite. She questioned him about her father's life, wanting to find a connection to herself, to counter her mother's denigration and refusal ever to let her meet his family. 'I only feel that I have missed something, some experience that I was meant to have that my father could have given', she wrote.

In his will, Radclyffe left a diamond ring and an annuity of £100 to his and the housemaid's daughter Mary Ratcliffe Farmer, all his mandolins and unpublished musical compositions to a Victoria Holloway who lived in Battersea, his paintings, books, pictures and sketches to Walter Begley. All the family money, by the terms of his own father's cautious will, was to pass to Marguerite when she was twenty-one. Until then, she was to draw a generous allowance. It was a large inheritance for 1898, some £100,000. 'There were some things I shall never forget and my sudden independence was one of them ... I was free, free to go where I liked and do what I pleased, or at least so I fondly imagined. But in this I was reckoning without two reactive elements.'

These elements were her mother and Agnes Nicholls. Mrs Visetti became vicious with envy. Lavish with money whatever its source, she felt this fortune by rights was hers. She was determined to benefit from it. Marguerite resisted her and rows ensued. 'I had no intention of allowing my mother to handle my estate and she had every intention of doing so.' The first row was over the capital the divorce court had initially awarded Mrs Visetti which she had foregone to ensure Marguerite's inheritance but now wanted to claim. The second was about the way she and Alberto Visetti had spent thousands of pounds of Marguerite's maintenance fund on themselves.

Marguerite turned to Agnes Nicholls who now seemed always to be at the house. 'She had grown essential to my existence', Marguerite wrote. Agnes was Alberto's prodigy, had lessons with him daily and he defended all she did and said. She joined the family on visits to Pontresina in Switzerland with Arthur Sullivan, a winter music festival in Dresden, a festival in Prague with Dvořák. Mrs Visetti resented her presence and influence but Agnes tried to act as go-between for her and Marguerite. She appealed to each of them to see the other's point of view.

Marguerite wanted independence and to travel abroad. Mrs Visetti asked Walter Begley to forbid her to leave home until she was twenty-one. Agnes Nicholls supported this. When Marguerite asked why, she cried, accused her of wanting to break their friendship and kissed her on the mouth. Marguerite felt 'pleased, revolted, terrified and a sense of being trapped. From that moment I felt that Agnes and I shared a secret. In many subtle ways she made it evident that she felt this too. There was a great bond between us and I grew less restless and more content to remain at home.' Sex and money made a potent mix. She was no longer just the queer little kid. She was rich, which was power in itself.

That winter, Agnes Nicholls had late lessons at Trebovir Road. She was the last pupil of Visetti's day and he often invited her to dinner. If the weather was cold he feared it might harm her voice and he insisted she stay the night. Marguerite thought Agnes manoeuvred these invitations. 'I used to watch for a certain look in her eyes across the dinner table. I never failed to find it there. It was a strange look, half warning, half invitation. Then I would grow restless glancing continually at the clock, waiting for the hour when we would say goodnight and part outside my door.'

Their rooms were opposite at the top of the house. The moment for which Marguerite waited was when they paused on the landing and said awkward goodnights. She wanted 'the thousand sweet intimacies' that she supposed lay behind Agnes's closed door. 'I wanted to possess her and ignorance gave a sharper edge to my desire.' She wrote of the pleasure of 'those weeks spent hovering on the brink', waiting on the landing, listening, watching the light under the door.

It took manoeuvring to get from hovering on the brink to between the sheets. They went out together, identified with lovers in the park, the themes of songs and operas. 'The end came suddenly without any warning.' After a matinée and tea in town, Agnes returned to Trebovir Road for dinner. There was dense fog, so she stayed the night. At the top of the house she and Marguerite parted without the usual hesitancy. Agnes closed her bedroom door. Marguerite undressed, 'seized with a sense of elation'. On the landing she paused, looking at the strip of light under the door. 'Come in kid,' said Agnes and then, when Marguerite got into bed with her, 'you ridiculous child why didn't you come before?'

4

The pearl necklace she gave me

Marguerite left Trebovir Road when her inheritance came within her control. Her mother attacked her for going out with Agnes Nicholls. She pulled her hat and a clump of hair from her head, called her vile, filthy, corrupt, depraved, against nature and against God and hit Grandmother Diehl when she intervened.

Money was more incandescent than sex. Assessing her finances with a solicitor, Marguerite found the Visettis had overspent on her trust fund by £12,000. She challenged them, said her education had been a patchy affair of cheap governesses and that she did not see how her inheritance had been spent to benefit her.

Mrs Visetti was provoked by it all. Her machinations over the Case had backfired. Radclyffe's daughter, whom she despised by virtue of his paternity, had scooped the lot and was reluctant to give her any. From then on Mrs Visetti made many financial demands. Marguerite dealt with these crisply but with no particular generosity. She used money to control her mother, made her an annual allowance of between £200 and £300 and called her to account as to why she should give her more.

She leased a house in Church Street, Kensington, near the Gardens and Hyde Park. She moved in with her grandmother, furnished the place with antique oak furniture and the oil paintings of her father's forebears and used it as a base for adventure and travel.

The affair with Agnes Nicholls petered out. Independence made Marguerite less tolerant of the *patois* French and affected gestures, or less consumed with interest in her lover's vocal cords. As Una Troubridge was to put it, 'the Lord had not designed her to be a satellite'. Agnes Nicholls went on to sing at Covent Garden – her debut in 1901 was as the Dew Fairy in Humperdinck's *Hansel and Gretel*; she had a long association with the Sadler's Wells Opera, and Edward Elgar and Hubert Parry wrote parts especially for her in their choral works. She married the composer and accompanist Hamilton Harty. They had a successful musical partnership but the marriage failed. In later years Marguerite took other lovers to hear Agnes Nicholls sing Brünnhilde and Sieglinde at Covent Garden.

With money, freedom and her sexual orientation clear, Marguerite changed her image. She preferred to be known as Peter, a sobriquet that did not stick. She swept her hair back from her face, wore tailored clothes, wide-brimmed hats and plain but expensive jewels. She was opinionated and vulnerable. There was a humourless directness about her, an inability to dissemble, to be other than she was or to see another's point of view. Her solemn, misspelt prose was childlike, riddled with clichés and written in a rounded, backward-sloping hand. She collected stamps, rode horses, hunted foxes, kept dogs and budgerigars.

Unmistakeably lesbian, she was not going to pretend a passing interest in men. 'Man is vile to her and I believe that is why she will never marry', the novelist Violet Hunt wrote of her. Eighteen years older than Marguerite, Violet Hunt was the author of *Tales of the Uneasy* and *The Wife of Altamont*. A friend of Henry James and a lover of H. G. Wells, she was famed for her Pre-Raphaelite looks and, later, for a scandalous affair with the writer Ford Madox Ford.

She was a neighbour of Marguerite's in Campden Hill, Kensington. Marguerite adored and wooed her:

Perhaps even now you are thinking me impertinent as you read this letter. I can't help it Violet, I must risk that. If I can't always say the things I am feeling when we are together it is because you have built a brick wall around yourself and I must not venture to get inside it. No doubt you have many good reasons for wanting it to be there. I have never met anyone who could so repulse affection as you can in your own sweet way. If you are angry with me what can I say except that I am so fond of you?

I will never bother you to read this sort of thing again.

'She loved me so hotly poor darling', Violet Hunt wrote. 'She used to write and say that I erected a brick wall between her and me. Why brick, I would say nervously, but I knew. I was always full of someone else. And I wear the pearl necklace she gave me . . .'

Marguerite locked in to attraction then wooed with determination. What she wanted she felt she should have. Her lovers had no money of their own. She used hers for seduction, allowances and gifts. She bought her way into their beds. If one spurned her she fixated on another. Caught in a family psychodrama, some were related to her mother. They seemed to form links in a transference chain. Her mother scorned Visetti for not providing for her in the style she desired. Using her father's fortune, which her mother coveted but was denied, Marguerite controlled her lovers and punished her mother with the money at her command.

In her early twenties, at her great-aunt Mary's house in Knightsbridge, she met Jane Randolph, her mother's cousin. She viewed her with a conqueror's eye:

I had never seen anything so fascinatingly slender and so adorably ugly as the woman who stood before me . . . Her shoes were perfectly cut I noticed and her ankles clad in transparent black silk stockings. Her whole body conveyed an impression of suppleness . . . But it was her face that was the most arresting thing about her for it was so frankly ugly. Oval in shape with a rather large mouth, projecting teeth, a blunt nose and pale blue eyes set far apart and masses of chestnut hair wound round a small head and you have one of the more perfect examples of the fascination of personality that some plain women possess.

Jane Randolph was ten years older than Marguerite. She lived in Washington, had three children, two boys and a girl and a husband on business in London. She liked England, stylish clothes and a good time and was sailing home in a fortnight.

I wondered angrily about her husband and utterly resented his possession of her. I said as much and she laughed. O Bob she said, he's not too bad, he's only rather a bore at times and he's dog poor, that's the worst of him.

It was not the worst of him from my point of view. Possibly the only thing in his favour.

Marguerite was undeterred by husbands. She invited Jane Randolph to the theatre, then saw her each day for what remained of her stay: 'She was quite a new type of woman to me, completely at her ease.' On Jane's last day in England they rode together in a carriage in Richmond Park. It was a spring evening and the park looked pretty in the setting sun. Marguerite seized the moment and her cousin:

> I was tongue tied and could only glare helplessly into her pale eyes. She turned a calm face toward me and did not resent my grip on her arm ... 'I know' she said in her slow southern drawl. 'I guess you needn't tell me because I know.'
>
> 'And if you know' I said angrily 'what in heaven's name are you going to do about it?'

She did what a girl's got to do. Soon after her return to Washington, Jane Randolph's dog-poor bore of a husband dropped dead. Marguerite went out there and provided for her and for her children's education. She bought a car and had a gun and a bulldog called Charlie for protection. They toured the Southern states and 'shared all kinds of youthful escapades'. When Marguerite went into hospital to have impacted wisdom teeth removed, Jane Randolph slept in an adjacent bed.

After a year, Marguerite brought her surrogate family to live with her and Grandmother Diehl in the Kensington house. She also bought Highfield in Malvern Wells, Worcestershire, a large bleak stone house with stables, six acres and uninterrupted views of the Severn Valley. She kept dogs and horses and had her own guns. (Violet Hunt was sardonic about how she *punished* the rabbits.) She described herself as 'free to make my own life, free to go where I please'. Like her father, she was 'mad about hunting' and rode with two packs, the Ledbury and the Old Croom, 'tough sporting packs that it took you all your time to keep up with'.

> Those were carefree days, the pure air, the wide and beautiful landscape, horses, and, although one loved animals not too much imagination when it came to the fox. Cruel and yet intensely alluring ... After a hard day's hunting, a poem dashed off haphazard, because a rhyme was hammering on my brain like a tune.

These poems read as if dashed off haphazard. The countryside

around Malvern figured in them, the hills called Raggedstone, Wind's
Point, Hollybush and Worcester Beacon, the views of the River Severn
and the Wye, the churchyard at Eastnor. Marguerite wrote of kisses,
sunsets, autumn tints, the moon and the pain of love. She hinted
obliquely at trysts and liaisons. Pronouns stayed unrevised and she still
signed herself Marguerite Radclyffe Hall. One, dedicated 'To . . .', spoke
of a dreary cold city that would become like summer 'Decked with
sweet, perfuming flowers' were a certain person there. And 'On the
Lagoon':

> A gondola, the still lagoon;
> A summer's night, an August moon;
> The splash of oars, a distant song,
> A little sigh, and – was it wrong?
> A kiss, both passionate and long.

Wrong or not, she was not going to stop it. On her next visit to the
States, while still living with Jane Randolph, she started a love affair
with another cousin, Dolly Diehl, daughter of her mother's brother
William. Dolly was in her teens and had the familiar fair-haired, blue-
eyed looks of the Diehls. She inspired a more masterful aspect of
Marguerite's muse:

> If you were a Rose and I were the Sun
> What then, little girl, what then?
> I'd kiss you awake when day had begun,
> My sweet little girl, what then?
> I'd waken you out of your valley of dreams
> And open your heart with my passionate beams
> Till you lifted your face to my ruddiest gleams
> My own little girl, yes then.

The passionate beams and ruddy gleams had a sadomasochistic
undertow of domination and compliance. Behind Marguerite's financial
protection was a manipulative view of sex. Jane Randolph remarried –
Harry Caruth, a wealthy Texan. She and her daughter Winifred remained players in the Diehl drama of warped love between mothers
and daughters. For years Marguerite wrote to Winifred about Maria
Visetti's viciousness. Winifred wrote to Marguerite of how unloved she

felt by her own mother Jane. Maria Visetti wrote to Jane of how ill-used she was by Marguerite.

Dolly Diehl danced to the tune of this drama. She went to live with Marguerite and their mutual grandmother in the Church Street house and at Malvern. They travelled in France, Italy and Germany. On the face of it they were cousins with Marguerite the chaperon. But it was a sexual affair with incestuous inflection outside the accepted terms of relationship.

Marguerite drew her lovers into her compulsive inner world with its core of Oedipal revenge. This inner world informed the poems she wrote. In 1906 she paid to have a collection of them published by John and Edward Bumpus of Oxford Street. It was a slim volume, *Twixt Earth and Stars*, dedicated to 'My Inspiration'. She gave her poems elliptical titles: 'You', 'Remember', 'What a Pity'. Behind doggerel and clichés of sunlight and flowers, ran declarations of pain.

> Oh the awful pity of it all,
> That I ever learned to care for you
> That we ever chanced to meet at all
> Since we neither of us could be true.

Her rhymes were simplistic, her psychology complex:

> My love is a bird with a broken wing,
> Alone in a stormy night;
> My love is a lark that forgets to sing
> And dies with the morning light.

Her view of society was received and conventional. Presiding over the world was the benign figure of God the Father, as if from a stained-glass window on the ultimate landing of a rented home.

> And perhaps the Recording Angel
> May wipe out the faults of years
> With the hem of His shining garment
> Grown damp with a sinner's tears

The *Evening Standard* commended her 'sincerity and sweetness', the *Queen* wrote of her 'vigorous, joyous youth, thankful for the right to exist in such a lovely world' and *The Lady* said she had 'real feeling and the power to express it'. No reviewers picked up on the sexual content behind the little rhymes, the possessiveness of the ruddy gleams or that the kisses might be between women. In later years, Radclyffe Hall said she thought the reviewers must all have been fathers 'and thus tolerant of effervescent youth. I was so embarrassingly frank in that volume, my fraicheur and my egotism leave me most amazed – they also make me hot all down my spine . . . Youth is so embarrassingly frank about its own supposed emotions.'

In August 1906 Marguerite and Dolly went to Homburg to see the women's tennis tournaments. The Wimbledon champion, Dorothea Chambers, was playing against a friend of theirs, Toupie Lowther. Toupie – Marguerite called her 'Brother' though her real name was May – had driven herself there on 'execrable' roads in her 40-horse-power Mercedes. She was large, renowned for her lobs and said to have a man's stroke and a man's strength and a temperament 'hopelessly unsuitable to lawn tennis'. She was the daughter of a naval captain and the sister of a Conservative MP. A science graduate and one of the first women to own a motorbike, she lifted weights and was a fencing champion, too. Her affairs with women were stormy and her style flamboyant. She left written instruction for her body after death to be laid out for four days. If, in the view of two doctors, she was still dead, they were to cut her jugular vein, cremate her corpse and strew its ashes to the wind.

Marguerite and Toupie booked in at the Savoy. Also there was another of Toupie's friends, Mabel Veronica Batten. She was with her husband George and her maid Susan Attkins. She was bored. The Savoy was not the dazzling meeting place of ten years past when Edward, Prince of Wales, heir to the English throne, had wooed her in its tearoom and her bedroom. She was now fifty, George was seventy-four. Their rooms were on separate floors. 'Father is quite happy', she wrote to Cara, their only child:

He has found several old men he knows and goes down in the morning on his own to the springs. I went this morning but unless I meet some amusing people I really think I shall not get up regularly . . . Oh you never saw such sporks of people! Not one interesting person have I viewed except a Spanish beauty and an unknown young man who looks like an explorer.

Mabel liked coining words. Sporks were unspeakably dull, poggers were flirtatious, sneevish was an irritable state of mind and poons were thoroughly good sorts and entertaining too. After thirty years of marriage to George, Mabel needed the company of poons. Marguerite arrived at the hotel on 22 August. Here, in Mabel's view, was an undoubted poon. For them both this date would figure as an anniversary for the rest of their lives.

5

Sporks, poggers and poons

Marguerite described herself as 'utterly unstable' and 'in a state of flux' when she met Mabel Batten. She had no settled country, relationship or plan. She divided her time between hunting, travelling and chasing women. 'I was as wax in her hands,' she wrote in notes for an autobiography, 'but those hands were entirely trustworthy. She was to become a spur to my work and from the first my true unfailing inspiration. She was a whole generation older, but of so gay and youthful a spirit, of so balanced, generous and masterly a mind, courteous, kindly and gallant a heart...'

Mabel Batten was a memsahib, a colonial expatriate, for whom marriage had been a financial and social necessity and sexual affairs *de rigueur*. Many men were acquainted with her gallant heart and youthful spirit. She secured their letters in boxes with combination locks. A green leather box opened at 1327, a grey leather one at 365. These letters made no reference to gallantry with women, but showed no fear of adventure. She was scathing about 'elderly virginal scandal-mongering' and 'dowdy second class gossipy old maids'. Used to the warmth of the Indian sun, she loathed the English climate and liked to winter in Morocco, the Canary Islands, or Monte Carlo.

Marguerite noticed that when Mabel and George breakfasted together in the Savoy gardens they had nothing to say to each other. They had married in Simla in 1875 when Mabel was eighteen and George a widower of forty-three. He wooed her with curry paste, pots

35

of honey, three pheasants and a copy of Mrs Gaskell's *Wives and Daughters*. In those days he had called her his chirpy little bird and his sweet unselfish affectionate darling. Together, they had starred in amateur theatricals: *Cut off with a Shilling* and *School for Scandal*. George organized Monday popular concerts at Government House in Simla, coached Mabel's voice and sang duets with her mother, Minnie Hatch. When Mabel said Yes, she would marry him, he sent round four diamond engagement rings and told her to ask her father which she should choose.

Born in Barrackpore, Calcutta, Mabel had travelled as a child to Japan, North Africa and Europe. In her teens she studied music in Bruges and Dresden. Her mezzo-soprano voice proved popular at musical soirées, her rippling laugh, dark blue eyes, 'luxuriant auburn hair', big bust and tiny waist proved popular with men. She knew she was pretty and she expected to be indulged. Her cousin, Una Troubridge, was to say of her, 'She accepted homage as a matter of course. She had always received it.'

Her father, George Cliffe Hatch, was Judge Advocate-General of Northern India. Her two brothers, George and Arthur, were colonels in the army. Of her two sisters, Annie remained Annie Hatch, looked after their mother, had protruding eyes and, as time passed, was short of money. Emma, the eldest, married the Honourable Edward Bourke, fifth son of Richard Mayo, Viceroy of India, who was assassinated in 1872.

Mabel married 'dear old George' without illusion of love. Cara was born in 1876. And George had an unmentioned love child, another daughter. A Bombay scribe wrote to him from time to time on her mother's behalf, asking for money.

George had an unremarkable career in the Bengal civil service. He was Secretary to the Department of Revenue and Agriculture when he wooed Mabel. He feared he would not be enough for his own darling Mab, his little bird of a wife. He feared she had a roving eye: 'I do hope that you do not think me exigent or wanting in trust in you', he wrote soon after their engagement:

> I do darling trust you as much as I love you. In fact I could not do one without the other. When, as in our case, a young girl accepts a man much older than herself the world is always ready to seize any opportunity for making cynical remarks and that is a reason for being more than ordinarily

careful not to give such opportunities and probably it is this fact that
makes me rather sensitive. I feel sure darling that you are perfectly loyal
to me, but ...

The wedding was at Christ's Church, Simla, on 20 November 1875.
On 8 November Queen Victoria's errant son Edward, Prince of Wales
had arrived on a four-month state visit to India with an entourage of
less than respectable friends. It was at a cost of £100,000 to the Indian
government, and more to the British treasury. The Prince's host in
Northern India, Sir John Strachey, Lieutenant-Governor of Bengal, was
married to George's sister. She congratulated Mabel for having found
a kind, affectionate husband. 'You will of course be at Agra when His
Royal Highness is there, and then we shall see a good deal of each
other.'

The Prince of Wales, too, saw a good deal of Mabel. She was one of
the prettiest women around. 'The Prince's tastes are low and childish',
Lady Strachey wrote to her sister-in-law in England:

> He has a perfect mania on the subject of dress ... fresh orders come
> nearly every hour about what the suite are to wear and if a button is
> wrong it is at once noticed and remarked upon. His other tastes are for
> eating and drinking. He is at times thoroughly selfish and inconsiderate
> ... As for his moral character, it is as bad as possible and the respectable
> part of the suite are always in agony lest he misbehave.

As a memento of his misbehaviour with Mabel, he gave her a portrait
of himself set in an amethyst pendant. She flaunted signed framed
photographs of him throughout her house. Their affair continued after
his return to England and on visits to Europe. They met up at Homburg
and for the races at Goodwood and Ascot. He gave her tortoiseshell
combs set with diamonds, an inscribed silver gilt flask, jade ashtrays,
a moonstone brooch. One year at Homburg he gave her a ring, set
with a turquoise heart and tiny diamonds. It was made, he told her,
from his first scarf pin. In his scarcely legible handwriting he wrote
discreet letters to her alluding to the times of their afternoon trysts.

Letters from other prestigious lovers went into Mabel Batten's locked
boxes. Lord Lytton, Viceroy of India from 1876, sent poems. George
benefited from Mabel's popularity. Civil servants improved their pro-
motion prospects when their wives had sagacious affairs. A network
of nepotism linked jobs, spouses, lovers. Lytton made George his

Private Secretary. He thought him incompetent but a cheap option. 'Batten,' he wrote to his wife Edith in 1879, 'is the only civilian of adequate standing whose services can be secured without additional expense to the Government of India.' Lady Lytton disliked George. 'He had such abominable manners and often would get so cocky', she said.

The diarist and poet Wilfrid Scawen Blunt, cousin of Mabel's brother-in-law Edward Bourke and *confidant* to both Mabel and the Viceroy, suspected Lytton gave George the job to manoeuvre himself close to Mabel. 'I warned him of the imprudence and of the opportunity it would give for evil tongues', he wrote in his diary. Security was strict after the assassination of the previous viceroy. Guards at the court were on duty day and night. Mabel could not be smuggled in unobserved. Lytton told Blunt that to his 'chagrin' she 'consoled herself' with his aide-de-camp.

She consoled herself, too, with Blunt and told him of her love affairs and 'those of all Simla'. He called her 'gay, fond of pleasure, quite depraved, but tinged too with romance'. Lytton asked her not to have an affair with Blunt but, in July 1880 (a month before Radclyffe Hall was born), in England for the Goodwood races, she was his guest at Crabbet Park, his ancestral home in Sussex. 'I found her door ajar about 12 o'clock,' Blunt wrote, 'and stayed with her till daylight.'

It was not for long, given the summer solstice, but she inspired a poem from him called 'Butterflies'. Mabel had, he claimed, found no one to satisfy her 'nameless cravings' until Blunt crept into her bed that night:

> Where is the noon can match with thy sunrise?
> Whose is the heart shall win thy constancy?
> Thou with thy foolish loves, mad butterflies,
> What dost thou ask of my sad heart and me?

The answer was, not much. But foolish loves and open doors were more fun than being with George.

She called him Dear Old George and Foxy but did not pretend to find him other than dull. He retired from the Bengal civil service in 1882, brought her and Cara to London, ensconced them in a house at 3 Ralston Street, in a leafy part of Chelsea, and spent much time with fellow old colonials at the Oriental Club in Hanover Square. At home he collected recipes which he pasted into a book and he was particularly fond of acrostics. He 'spent many happy hours working them out'.

Mabel disliked acrostics intensely. She preferred the Count de Mira-fiore, son of the first King of Italy Victor Emmanuel ii, who wooed her with furs, boas and jewels. He gave her an emerald ring that had once belonged to the King of Serbia and a brooch of two diamond tortoises, which she called Sophie and Edward.

London offered wider opportunities than Simla. Mabel played the piano and guitar, coached her voice, sang at salons and private functions and was praised as one of the best amateur lieder singers of her day The composers Fauré, Delius, Elgar and Percy Grainger wrote songs for her. John Singer Sargent did an oil portrait of her as she sang at full throttle. John Koopman and Edward Poynter painted her, too, and editors of the society columns referred to her as 'the April Grand-mother'.

She gave singing lessons, published her own compositions and banked modest royalties from Boosey of Bond Street. Her best known song, 'The Queen's Last Ride', was inspired by the funeral of Queen Victoria in February 1901. It was sung on the first anniversary of Victoria's death by a former student of Alberto Visetti's, Louise Kirkby-Lunn, at the Queen's Hall in a concert conducted by Henry Wood. Mabel's old flame Edward, now the King, presided.

By 1906 Mabel was fifty and plump with a taste for mauve silk housecoats, lace frocks and long earrings. Her scent was specially made from verbena and white lilac by J & E Atkinson of Old Bond Street. She wore stays of heavy pink brocade, was particular for her stomach to appear flat and she always sat erectly. Her once-luxuriant hair was flecked with grey. She tried to henna it, but 'with poor results'. She read through gold or platinum lorgnettes and was slightly deaf.

She slept with a pillow in the small of her back, called her hot water bottles Jones and Charlie, the gold eagle lamp holder above her bed Walter, and a large pear-shaped piece of quartz of which she was particularly fond, The Plump of Peking. She always got up late. She would moue, pout her underlip, say in a little-girl voice, 'Darling I feel sneevish', and give a sidelong glance. She had excessive pairs of shoes, was afraid of bees and wasps, repeated favourite anecdotes and always said 'Bless you' when parting.

Her daughter Cara became extravagantly unconventional. Under the *nom de brosse* Rognons de la Flêche, she painted works of sexual surrealism – mermaids on a fishmonger's slab, nudes in shoes, with whips. She believed in occult forces and did supernatural things with ouija boards, aromas, a rosary and a motor horn. Her husband, Austin Harris, Vice-Chairman of Lloyds Bank and an art collector, was said to weep when he saw the household accounts and to economize by turning off lights even when people were in the room. Cara, not on speaking terms with him, had a live-in lover, Frank Romer, an orthopaedic surgeon. Her children called him Nunkie. Stone deaf in one ear, she used an ear trumpet – a concession to disability Mabel deplored. She kept an orange and blue macaw, which spiced the marital silences with, 'Fuck off you silly bitch.' And she made and scripted ambitious home movies. *The Sun Never Sets: An Epic of Endurance*, filmed on the Isle of Wight, was set in the African jungle. It featured friends in pith hats standing over a tigerskin rug with shotguns. The cat filmed in close-up starred as the lion. *Treason's Bargain* had five acts and 106 scenes. The credits thanked Sibyl, Lady Colefax for providing the elephant, but there was no elephant in it.

Toupie Lowther lost the 1906 Homburg tennis final 6–4, 6–4 to Dorothea Chambers (seven times winner of Wimbledon). On the terrace of the Savoy, Mabel talked with her and Miss Douglas, Toupie's friend of the moment, and with Marguerite and Dolly Diehl. 'Toupie is always very well groomed', Mabel wrote to Cara who lived in Aspenden Hall, Buntingford, Hertfordshire. She thought them all infinitely amusing and not in the least sporkish.

Marguerite discerned in Mabel the motherly recompense she craved. She spoke of her 'natural domination which it never occurred to me to dispute', she elevated her judgement saying she had irreproachable literary taste and was unsurpassed as a critic. Mabel had a languid ease, an accepting indolence and nothing of the rebarbative manner of Mrs Visetti. Here was 'a woman whom one would long to protect while coming to in turn for protection'.

She showed a 'calm unshakeable belief' in Marguerite's literary future. Back in London, she copied out her poems, catalogued them, corrected her spelling and suggested to Robert Coningsby Clarke, composer of 'Mine Are Your Eyes' and 'If She But Knew', that he use them as libretti. 'Very soon it was born in upon me,' Marguerite wrote of Mabel, 'that I must work hard to be worthy of her friendship ... What I am I owe to her. She criticised my work but so justly that I could not feel resentment ... She took me and very gradually proceeded to rub off the sharp and ugly corners.'

For her part, Marguerite wooed with a style Mabel approved – money, poems, jewels and indulgences beyond the means or imagination of George. More than the men of her past, here was a true poon.

But Marguerite was still living with Dolly Diehl, who was financially dependent on her, only nineteen and without London friends. In spring 1907 they all took a holiday in Scotland. Violet Hunt went too. In Edinburgh, at the Royal British Hotel, Violet's room was next to Marguerite's. 'She [Marguerite] used to come and sit on my bed in the clearest coldest Japanese kimono from Liberty with a streak of blue on the collar and her fine sandy auburn hair in a plait ... the decent young girl of twenty five who knew the world in spite of her pigtail and robe of innocence.'

The atmosphere was tense. Marguerite curtailed her stay and went back to Malvern with Dolly. She said she had received letters about trouble with the servants and the groom was anxious about a horse.

She turned more and more to Mabel for kindness, acceptance and calm. She showed her work in hand, poems about the death of her love for Dolly.

> A little shiver crept along my heart
> For you and I were strangers, far apart

In 'Ardour' Mabel learned how 'the new found splendour' of love was for her.

In June 1908 with George and Dolly they rented a house in Sidmouth. This was when 'the seeds were sown of their very deep future friendship', Marguerite wrote. The garden had steps to the beach. They swam each morning, walked by the shore, sat on the rocks and wished they could be alone.

On 12 August, Marguerite's birthday, she and Mabel took an impulsive holiday. They crossed the Channel in a small steamer to Ostend. A passenger, a Mr Brown, forced his company on them. They called him the Brown peril and froze him out. It was their first journey alone and it became a double anniversary in their chronology of important dates. The smart hotels were full. They booked in at a small place, played roulette in the casinos and returned to England as lovers.

Like Violet Hunt, Mabel then wore the pearl necklace Marguerite gave her. But she took this love very seriously. She had no history of lesbian relationship. It needed reconstruction to be acceptable. Visiting Marguerite's London house, she thought how much like the portrait of her great-great-grandfather John Hall, a surgeon, Marguerite looked. From then on Mabel called her John.

More than a fond nickname, this was a symbolic rechristening. It released Marguerite from the hated name her mother had given her and from her discomfort at being a woman. It fed her fantasy and turned her mother's curse into a boast. 'You are Radclyffe through and through, not an ounce of your blood is mine.' By reconstruction she was not the same gender. She was an English squire from a time-honoured family, with horses, hounds and a wife. For Mabel too it defined the partnership in society's terms. It was John who opened the doors, carried the bags, hired the servants and of course paid the bills.

Mabel metamorphosed into Ladye. Her sister Emma married the widowed Earl of Clarendon after Edward Bourke, her first husband, died. Lord Clarendon owned 500 acres of Hertfordshire and War-wickshire and the ruins of Kenilworth Castle. Emma liked to parade the title Lady Clarendon. Ladye spoofed her sister's pretensions and as Ladies are married to Lords let the world know that hers was no marginal partnership, no small-time affair.

John and Ladye they became and put themselves forward to society in the guise they contrived. Ladye praised John's 'positive and emphatic' manner, understood her need for control and commended her financial acumen. But she did not make a macho man of her John. She indulged her childish tantrums, her liking for cocoa and loganberry jam. She complained that all her suits looked alike, urged her to wear 'orna-mental' clothes and told her if she cut her hair short she would not share a house with her.

In autumn 1908 John paid John and Edward Bumpus Ltd to publish *A Sheaf of Verses*. Dedicated to 'Sad Days and Glad Days', she wrote of 'mists of passion' dimming her sight, the fire of kisses, throbbing of pulses, happy couples house hunting – 'where shall we make us a cosy home' – and the 'potent ecstasy' of kissing. Her muse had a comforting breast, submissive lips and delicate hands. John declared her allegiance to Sappho:

> Canst thou forget us who are still thy friends,
> Thy lovers o'er the cloudy gulf of years.

Reviewers saw no unacceptable affections in these poems. Robert Coningsby Clarke, Hubert Bath and Easthrope Martin set them to music to be sung at afternoon teas. The *Daily Express* recommended the *Sheaf* as a Christmas stocking filler and the *Sussex Daily News* said, 'Very few living women poets are at all her equal.'

Ladye spent Christmas with Cara and her grandchildren at Aspenden Hall. John, hunting at Malvern with the Ledbury hounds, fell off her horse Xenophon when jumping a fence. The ground was soft, but she hurt her neck. Thereafter, she and Ladye had many conversations on the 'supposing you had been killed' theme. Ladye pleaded the case of the fox and urged her to give up hunting. John wrote a poem which began:

> I looked on death a moment eye to eye
> And knew him not so swift the vision came
> So hard upon the heels of life, that flame
> And darkness mingled as they passed me by.

Both believed she had been spared the darkness to achieve two goals: literary heights and the love of Ladye. But there was George to accommodate, and Dolly too. George no longer heeded the 'cynical remarks' the world made about his wife. He had prostate trouble, felt old and 'barred from the pleasures of everyday life'. His pension was not good and though his son-in-law Austin Harris looked after his business affairs, he found Margaret, as he felt it right to call her, more than generous with money.

But he was pushed aside. In the summer of 1909 John and Ladye went to the French Riviera and to Alassio where John rented a villa. George hoped to travel out to meet them. To deter him they wrote discouraging letters about the crowds, the heat, the mosquitoes. And then his doctor advised him not to make the journey. 'I fancy he was prompted by some little bird or minx', George wrote to Cara.

He booked in for three weeks at the Pwllycrochan Hotel in Conway Bay, north Wales. He went there with Mabel's maid, Susan Attkins. Each afternoon he walked half a mile with her to the sea and paid twopence for their admission to the pier where they listened to the band. On Saturdays she accompanied him to the hotel dance. Mabel wrote happy letters from the Grand Hotels in Monte Carlo and Lake Maggiore and from Molino di Sopra, John's villa. 'She seems to be enjoying herself', George told Cara.

Dolly Diehl too made other plans. On 19 October 1909, with John as her witness, she married Robert Coningsby Clarke at St Paul's Church, Knightsbridge. They moved to a house in Swan Walk, Chelsea on the bank of the Thames. John went on paying her a monthly allowance, a small price for the freedom to be alone with the woman whom she now called her 'true unfailing inspiration' and her 'reason for all things'.

JOHN

6

John and Ladye

Mabel Batten offered John the stability she seemed to need. It was her art to weave other relationships into the fabric of life with 'darling Johnnie'. 'My dear old George's 78th birthday', Ladye wrote in her diary on 22 January 1910. She took him and their grandchildren to a matinée of *Our Miss Gibbs* then to Rumpelmayers, a fashionable teahouse. Her sister, Emmie Clarendon, was 'frosty' at first. 'Never sends a line. Never wrote to thank Johnnie for an expensively bound copy of her poems.' After a while, she thawed. To Cara, Ladye freely confided her love:

> I find Jonathan delightful to be with. Of course her temper is hotter than tabasco and she is very impulsive but what does that matter? She is true grit all through and a real poon in her outlook on life and is so kind and darling to me. I admire and respect her downright honesty and she is awfully clever too.

John moved with Grandmother Diehl from Kensington to a Chelsea flat in Tite Street, adjacent to Ralston Street where Ladye lived. She breakfasted in Ladye's bedroom; they lunched at the Bath Club and had tea with Dolly Clarke in Swan Walk. They shopped at Harrods or Maples, took a box at the Opera House with the Duchess of Rutland to hear Nellie Melba sing Mimi in *La Bohème* and spent long weekends at Malvern. John bought Ladye a sapphire ring, a necklace of diamonds and emeralds, and supervised Madame Barroche as she fitted her for a black satin evening gown with red crêpe Spanish bows on its lace hem and sleeves.

'Above all else,' John wrote of Ladye, 'I owe her a debt for bringing me into the Catholic church.' God, they believed, had meant them to be together. Ladye had problems with early morning mass, but in her bedroom were a prie-dieu, a shrine with a gilt altar piece, statues of the Madonna and Child and photographs of the Pope. She viewed eternal life and the Lord's benevolence as certainties, liked Gregorian chant, and believed the first three things you asked for in church you usually got.

John was a ready convert. 'The little spiritual ship my grandmother had launched long ago was steered into the quiet harbour.' She joined Ladye for mass, confession and benediction at Brompton Oratory and in private devotions. Her 'faith never wavered'. Both were undeterred by the Vatican's condemnation of same-sex love or the adulterous terms of their match.

They considered themselves blessed and respectable. They were royalists, patriots, Conservatives, Christians, with allegiance to country, God and class. Above all, they were assiduous at having a good time. Their holidays were long and of the sort Ladye adored. Winters in the sun that were a rejuvenation and extravagance George could not provide. In February 1910 they sailed from Southampton in the SS *Burgermeister* for three months in Tenerife. George was despatched with Susan Attkins to Mrs Jefferson in Grantham.

On board ship their cabins, though 'miles away from the ladies' bathrooms', were large. There were storms and John lay clothed, holding her rosary and expecting to die. A young man in a green Homburg and tight trousers assumed they were mother and daughter and wooed John. 'Germans never know when they are not wanted', Ladye wrote to Cara.

In Santa Cruz the weather was perfect. They stayed at the Quisisana Hotel, perched on a cliff up endless steps. In the foyer were palm trees and caged monkeys. They rode on pack mules into the mountains, bought a parrot they called Mr Povey, sang island songs and picnicked overlooking a ravine. Ladye worked on John's poems and read them aloud. Both declared they had never been as happy in their lives before and that this was their one great love. They thought the meaning of the close tie they felt was because they had lived together in a previous incarnation.

For John, it was as if the trials of childhood were past. She was valued, loved, encouraged, needed. On their departure day they watched from the hotel through a telescope for their boat, the SS *Habsburg*, to dock in the port. They sailed on to Lisbon with first-class board in the captain's cabin. They arrived in pouring rain, lunched at the hotel where Byron wrote *Childe Harold*, went to a bullfight, visited monasteries and churches and hired an interpreter to help them buy hats. After a week, with lots of bothers with luggage and the parrot, they travelled on to Paris in the Sud Express.

Such poems as John wrote reflected her love of Ladye and life with her. In London in May she took her next volume to Bumpus. Called *Poems of the Past and Present*, edited, compiled and revised by Mabel, they were about her and dedicated to her. They told of John's root-lessness before meeting her and the fulfilment she had brought. They spoke of Mabel's blue eyes, beloved hands and the flowers and grave-yards of Tenerife. The litany of the Catholic Church became 'A Rosary of Love'.

> By all dead lovers' tears and pains
>   I swear I love thee,
> By all their joys and glad refrains
>   I swear I love thee.
>
> By all the lovers that still live,
>   I swear I love thee,
> By all they take and all they give,
>   I swear I love thee.
>
> By all my youth and passion's might,
>   I swear I love thee
> By all thy beauty and delight,
>   I swear I love thee.
>
> By Love himself, his holy flame,
>   I swear I love thee,
> By those I loved ere thy love came,
>   I swear I love thee.

And so on for fifteen verses. Reviewers gave teatime praise. *The Lady* said 'many fair and gentle thoughts are gracefully expressed by Marguerite Radclyffe-Hall.' The *Daily Express* called her 'a poetess with a very charming gift'. The *Daily News* talked of 'neat statements of the woman's point of view'.

John and Ladye's intimacy was exclusive and the old life faded away. King Edward VII, ill with bronchitis, died at midnight on 6 May 1910. Ladye and John wore black, offered mass for him and watched his funeral procession. John had a miniature of him mounted in a black Wedgwood pendant for Ladye to wear.

Then George became ill. In August he stayed with them at Clifton Cottage, Sidmouth. John composed Spanish songs on her mandolin. 'Her accompaniment is different every time she tries it', Ladye wrote to Cara. Ladye and George sang the vocal parts, 'and the parrot Mr Povey squealed with joy and excitement'. But George was weak on his legs, had swollen ankles and bladder problems, his mind wandered and he put Devonshire cream in his tea.

On 2 October they went with him and Ladye's sister-in-law, Nelly Hatch, to a concert at the Albert Hall where Louise Kirkby-Lunn sang Ladye's setting of John's 'Ode to Sappho'. The next day Mr Povey died, Grandmother Diehl, who was seventy-nine, had a stroke and George sank into delirium. His sister Lady Strachey and Emmie Clarendon sat with him. Dr Pardoe operated on his prostate and a Dr Grosvenor said he 'held out hope'. John divided her time between her grandmother and Ladye.

On 18 October in the early morning Grandmother Diehl died. She had asked to be buried in the family grave in the old cemetery in west Philadelphia. John went with her mother and the coffin to Southampton, saw her and it on to the Atlantic liner, then hurried to Ralston Street. George was rambling and scarcely conscious. He was given intravenous heroin. Ladye held his head and urged him to eat a beaten egg. Kelly, his barber, came to shave him. John, Ladye and Cara went to Westminster Cathedral to pray for him. He died at ten past six in the evening of 24 October.

He was despatched to a chapel of rest in Woking and given a memorial service at St Peter's Church, Eaton Square. The house at Ralston Street, disinfected and left with agents, fetched a high rent as it was coronation year. The solicitor, Mr Johnson, sorted out George's will, investment papers, pension and shares. Ladye benefited by £400 rental income a year, the house and £8,000 capital. As consolation for her bereavement, John bought her a mauve coat and a Pekinese called Fuji and promised her a villa in the sun.

Within a month they and their maids were on their way to the south of France, Alassio, Bordighera, Corsica. They were away six months, a seemly absence. Their itinerary precluded sorrow and Ladye's diaries and letters suggested happy times. With Dolly Diehl married and Grandmother Diehl and George Batten dead, nothing it seemed could now separate her and John from each other and their pledge of eternal love. She wrote of walks in the mountains where the air smelled of pine and eucalyptus, of waves breaking in a sirocco wind, of drives through moors and meadows full of flowers, of their search for a villa for John to buy and of picnics in the sun.

The Bobby Clarkes, as Ladye called them, joined them in Alassio. 'They seem very happy together', she wrote to Cara. 'He looks like a bald cherub. She is much improved in every way and seems now to appreciate Johnnie and all her kindness in a way she never did when she was living with her.' He had a 'wonderful' telescope, and in the garden of the villa by moonlight John and Ladye looked at the stars.

They considered themselves married. John, once the perfect suitor, was now the perfect spouse. In London she leased a large Chelsea flat, 59 Cadogan Square. They furnished it with antique mantelpieces, oak tables, blue Italian pillars for Ladye's bedroom shrine and Dresden china birds. John plied Ladye with presents – a black-and-white bead evening gown, a brocade evening cloak with crimson lining and hood, a black chiffon and voile dress for the afternoons, a diamond safety pin, more strings of pearls.

In Malvern she sold Highfield, which Ladye had thought bleak, and bought the White Cottage, which was thatched and cosy with roses over the porch. 'How I wish you could see this cottage', Ladye wrote to Cara. 'I *know* you would like it as much as you disliked Highfield. It is really very comfy.' She called it 'a perfectly darling big cottage'. It cost £1,500 freehold and was set in the hills. It had a steep sloping garden, beautiful views, a walnut tree with a seat built round it. There was a garage for John's new car, a field for Judy her horse and a separate cottage for two of the servants. Ladye furnished her bedroom with a cream carpet, yellow curtains, an Italian four-poster bed, Indian paintings and portraits of George and Johnnie.

They planted fruit trees and flowering myrtle and had a terrace made. To complete family life, they bought a Yorkshire terrier called Claude, and Otero, a French bulldog. They rescued Rufus, a collie from Battersea Dogs' Home, and acquired a parakeet with clipped wings. John prided herself on her affinity with animals, impulsively acquired them and championed their rights. But she demanded alarming deference and punished them or gave them away if they failed to obey. Claude disappeared into the Malvern Hills when she 'whipped him severely' for running in front of a cart and not coming when called. He was found but wanted nothing to do with her. And the parakeet was judged spiteful and returned to the shop when it took an opportunistic nip from her finger.

Ladye sang John's songs at concerts, arranged their musical settings with Robert Coningsby Clarke and Mr Cuthbert Wynne and prepared her fourth volume of poems, *Songs of Three Counties*, for publication. Socially they mixed with other lesbians of their class who had money and cultural interests. They went to Ethel Smyth's 'suffragette concert', saw 'clever pictures' by Romaine Brooks at the Graphic Gallery and motored with Toupie Lowther to Herstmonceux Castle in Sussex, the estate of her brother, Claude. The Princesse de Polignac, a wealthy patron of the arts, came to tea with her lover Olga de Meyer, wife of the society photographer Adolf de Meyer who had taken Mabel's photograph in 1880.

The wider world only lightly impinged. They deplored the prolonged miners' strike, the scarcity of coal, an exhibition of 'mad futuristic paintings' at the Bath Club and the militancy of suffragettes. 1913 was the year when, on Derby Day, Emily Davison died by throwing herself under the King's horse. In London, suffragettes smashed windows and chained themselves to railings. John wrote and Ladye edited a letter to the *Pall Mall Gazette*:

Sir

Have the Suffragettes no spark of patriotism left that they can spread revolt and hamper the Government in this moment of grave national danger? According to Mrs Pankhurst they are resorting to the methods of the miners! Since when have English ladies regulated their conduct by that of the working classes? But indeed up to the present the miners have set an example of orderly behaviour which the Suffragettes might do well to follow!

I was formerly a sympathiser with the cause of female suffrage, as also were many women who, like myself, are unrepresented, although taxpayers. Women who are capable of setting a revolutionary example at

such a time as this could only bring disgrace and destruction on any
Constitution in which they played an active part.

    Yours, etc.,
      A Former Suffragist

Such worries as they had were domestic. There was the day the
engine of John's car caught fire and the day the water pipes burst. She
and Ladye fussed over each other's safety and health. They nursed sore
throats and avoided draughts. When Ladye had trouble with her teeth,
John painted her gums with tincture of iodine. When she was breathless,
she took her to a heart specialist – he prescribed amyl nitrite. When
John had her haemorrhoids excised, Ladye stayed with her in the
Devonshire Street Clinic in London.

John had the security she said she wanted, the safe harbour of her
fantasy. She was loved and protected with a fortune to spend, servants,
pets, a circle of friends, a flat in town, a house in the country. Reviewers
praised her poems. The pain of childhood was over, the Visettis no
more than ghosts. She fretted when her mother sent a telegram about
financial problems and fretted even more when, with Alberto, she
stayed at the White Cottage. But they left after a few days and it seemed
the past was dead. If some dark magnet had not drawn her, she might
have kept intact all she now had and redefined her life with Ladye's
calmness and ease.

7

If I can fix something for Ladye

In 1912 John was formally received into the Roman Catholic Church. She took the baptismal name of Antonia and chose St Anthony as her patron saint. Bishop Butt confirmed her at Westminster Cathedral. Ladye was her sponsor. Money bought privileges in a number of churches: the personalized pew at the front of the congregation, the inscribed rood, tea with the priest.

They made a pilgrimage to Rome. They stayed in the Grand Hotel de Russie and dined with the Bishop of Nottingham. They went to confession and mass in St Peter's and bought triptychs, gilt angels and an alabaster Madonna. 'Johnnie is pink and happy and delighted with everything and so am I,' Ladye wrote to Cara, 'barring Roman feet which are as bad as Homburg ones. St Peters was more wonderful than ever yesterday ... I adore Italy so that I'm always happy here.'

For a financial consideration, Pope Pius x received them in a 'semi-private audience' at the Vatican. 'Only eight people in a little camera.' He gave them signed pictures of himself, blessed them in a tired voice and looked 'inexpressibly sad and ill'.

They say he suffers agonies of intense gout. He has a very kind face but none of the dignity of the last Pope who loved the pomp and ceremonies which this one is bored by. He is always longing for the sea, can't remember his clothes are white and is always wiping his pen on his soutane.

Ladye endured frailties too. She was overweight, had chest pains, was breathless on exertion and lamented the hills of Tuscany and the stairs in the hotel. She was 'flooding' and found no relief from Dr Dakin's haemorrhage pills and proprietary medicines for 'the change of life'. She disguised her discomforts because they made John anxious. Dolly Clarke joined them for a week. 'She is quite a nice little thing and mad about Rome.' Thirty years younger than Ladye, she was a more sprightly sightseeing companion for John.

And then John became ill with what sounded like glandular fever. Ladye said she had come out of the hot tearooms of the Grand Hotel and did not put on her coat. She was wretched with anxiety. John became irascible with the hotel staff and complained that her room was unhealthy. She decided impulsively to leave Rome for Viareggio then Monte Carlo, though Ladye had hoped to stay for the Ambassador's Ball.

Her attitude to Ladye changed. She was less patient with her pains and limitations. At Viareggio she told her she expected her to housekeep when they returned to England. She complained when they visited a Mrs Brock in a fifth-floor flat and Ladye was carried up the flights of stairs in a chair. Offended by the insinuation of indolence, Ladye became breathless and slept badly. At Monte Carlo John gambled and lost money. Distressed, Ladye mislaid things – her rosary in the casino, the jade button from her ermine tie.

In London, they resolved to be less exclusive and to socialize more. They left a great many visiting cards. They lunched with Sir Edward Elgar, played poker with Ernest Thesiger and had tea at Rumpelmayers with the Princesse de Polignac's sister-in-law, Isadora Duncan. In an endeavour to be industrious, Ladye interviewed cooks and pasted recipes into George's recipe book. To cheer herself she bought a black and mauve lace afternoon frock at Lavenders. She and John went to a lecture by Annie Besant on India and theosophy and were delighted at the good reviews *Songs of Three Counties* received. At the end of the year, at an Arabian Nights ball, Mabel was the Lady of Baghdad, John her Persian slave boy.

But for John the hedonism of this privileged life had palled. She pleaded unchannelled energy and the gulf in their age. In May 1913 she lunched with Phoebe and Oliver Hoare. Phoebe was a close friend of Dolly Clarke. Her husband was the younger son of Sir Samuel Hoare of Sidestrand Hall in Cromer, Norfolk and, like his father, a partner in the family bank of Barnetts, Hoare & Company of Lombard Street. She married him in 1906, the year Radclyffe Hall 'fell head and heart and soul in love' with Mabel Batten. They lived at Gloucester House, Park Lane and had no children. John invited them both to *Tosca* at the Opera House and Phoebe to lunch at the Berkeley. On 15 June they all four went to Ascot. John wore a Fortuny cloak of black and gold.

And then John and Phoebe began to meet alone most afternoons. There was an understanding between them that each had partners to whom they were committed. But it mattered to John that she was preferred to the cuckolded husband, that she succeeded where he failed. For Ladye, the days of grace were over, the great devotion tarnished. For this was an affair, with the usual ingredients of excuses, absence, disappointment and pain.

Phoebe's meetings with John took place on weekdays at Dolly Clarke's house when Oliver Hoare was at the bank. It was more problematic for John. Ladye was always at home. 'I never kept anything from her,' she said after Ladye's death, 'and I never told her an untruth except for once.' Such openness was a mixed virtue. Unattached to a commitment to sexual loyalty, it had a lacerating edge. It meant Ladye was treated to details of John's infidelity.

'Every appointment, every engagement, was made with the proviso "if I can fix something for Ladye"', John said. Such parity assuaged her conscience. Ladye would visit people whom she did not want to see so that John should not feel discomfort or guilt. While Ladye complained of a boring time in Hampstead with Sir Edward and Lady Elgar, John took Phoebe Hoare to dinner and to *Within the Law* at the Wyndham's Theatre. While John lunched with Phoebe at Swan Walk, Ladye lunched with Mrs Draper and Betty Carstairs. Often John brought home a placatory gift – a carved emerald ring, a diamond pin – or made some compensatory gesture when she returned.

Phoebe had the status of mistress. She was an aspect of the construction of the personality of John. When the first Mr Batten was alive, John was the romantic poet, the virile lover, Ladye her perfect woman whom destiny made her meet. After his death, for four years her role was the better husband, provider of an ideal home, 'true grit ... a real poon ... so kind and darling'. She wished to father children. Both declared themselves 'thrilled to the bone', 'wildly excited', when in 1913 Cara became pregnant with her third child. They hoped for a boy. 'Johnnie almost feels like the father', Ladye the grandmother wrote.

Time passed and with an emphasis on domestic comfort the town and country house, the winters in the sun, Ladye became the ideal mother, always there, encouraging of talent, forgiving of wayward behaviour. But John was no longer 'as wax in her hands', nor so kind and darling, nor quite the real poon. Twenty-four years younger, she was more the rake, the *roué*, the Rat, 'blatantly and crudely unfaithful'. But unlike Mary Jane Hall, Ladye kept faith with her man.

The semblance of their life stayed intact. They still went to mass at Brompton Oratory, lunched at the Ritz, dined at the Hyde Park Grill. Both were caught by the Russian craze when the Ballets Russes came to Covent Garden in spring 1913. Ladye acquired a Bakst chiffon dinner gown in scarlet and two shades of purple. They heard the music of Debussy and Stravinsky, saw the dancing of Nijinsky and Karsavina and the set and costume designs of Bakst and Benois.

At Malvern they searched out antiques for the White Cottage – a marble-topped gilt washstand, a bookcase for Ladye's dressing-room. They sang Spanish songs under the walnut tree, went to flower shows, lunched at the Horny Old Arms. Both were inordinately proud when in June a 'very eulogistic' letter about John's poems came from the author and literary critic Sir Arthur Quiller-Couch. And equally proud when 'Desert Love Songs' and 'The Blind Ploughman' were sung at the Queen's Hall on 23 November 1913.

But joy and ease went from their relationship. John lost weight, did no writing, had bursts of temper and violence. Ladye was depressed, had angina attacks and high blood pressure. Her diary, formerly buoyant, became a litany of discomforts and disappointments. Her ankles were swollen, her teeth gave her pain. She hated John being away, was mortified by this betrayal. More and more she lost things – a skunk fur in a taxi, a brooch, then a ring.

On 20 July they dined with Winnaretta Singer – the Princesse de Polignac. She read aloud from her manuscript about travels to Lesbos. 'John very upset afterwards with remords de conscience', Ladye wrote in her diary. 'I get no sleep at all.' *Remords de conscience* did not prevent John from spending the next afternoon with Phoebe Hoare. Or the next and the next and the next. At the week's end she was so tired she fell asleep after dinner, then went to bed at ten. Ladye felt wretched and sat alone, her swollen feet wrapped in damp flannels.

At Malvern in the summer months, John felt confined. She was 'furiously angry' when the dog Otero broke a glass. She beat him. Ladye felt faint in the night and could not sleep. Next day, on 22 August, to commemorate five years since those nights at Ostend, she gave John a diamond pin. 'John seemed all right again and was very loving and made me feel happy.'

It was a fleeting feeling. John then left for Southbourne and a week with Dolly Clarke and Phoebe Hoare. Ladye invited her brother George and his wife Nelly to stay and had a dismal time with them. On the evening of Saturday 30 August, she met John at the station. 'We talked far into the night. I got no sleep till 4 a.m. Felt depressed and breathless.'

Nocturnal talks were salt on wounds. In the morning they missed mass. It rained for a week. Otero, judged unmanageable, was destroyed. Ladye asked John to visit Cara with her. Though John was supposed to feel 'almost' like the father of Cara's expected child, she refused and went again to Phoebe. Then she scuppered the spring holiday plans. They had agreed on Málaga. Ladye loved Spain and was looking forward to it. Now John wanted to go to San Remo, where Phoebe would be at Bel Respiro, her mother's villa. Ladye again lay awake worrying until half past four in the morning.

It was not a situation she could resolve. She had nowhere to turn, no wish to live alone. She was not used to being marginalized. She had always 'accepted homage as a matter of course'. No homage was on offer now and her flirtatious days were done. There was a symmetry in the way she had treated George. She had let him know that though she would not leave him he was too old for her, not sexy and often dull. She had farmed him out to family friends, left him in the care of the maid while she was having fun.

Recession and talk of impending war added to the gloom. The miners' strike dragged on. John and Ladye dined in the library to save coal and had a succession of colds. At Aspenden Hall at Christmas John was uninterested in other guests and dissatisfied with her dressing-room. 'Felt very pleased that this *horrid* year was finished', Ladye wrote in her diary on New Year's Eve. 'Not a happy year and felt delighted when 1914 set in.'

Oliver Hoare wanted this unorthodox affair of his wife's to end. In January 1914 John had an 'interview' with him and Phoebe. Its agenda was not divulged but on 1 February she and Ladye left for a two-month holiday. Away from provocation Ladye felt restored. At the

Sports Club, Monte Carlo, she played roulette and talked to Mrs George Keppel, another lover of the previous King. At Tamaris at the Grand Hotel, she and John had large interconnecting bedrooms and a 'gorgeous view over the sea'. The sun shone, the food was good, she enjoyed their itinerant life and had John's exclusive company. But things were not the same and they were not the couple they had promised to be. Ladye knew, as she copied John's latest eulogies of desire into literacy, that they were not inspired by her:

> Thy beauty burns me as a breath of fire
> When thy hands touch me, all the world is compassed
> Within the limits of their slender whiteness.
> Where may I hide from this destroying rapture,
> From this swift longing that engulfs my being?

Dolly Clarke joined them. She was practically penniless and complained that her husband was 'parsimonious' towards her. John increased her allowance and invited her to live with them in Malvern. They all sailed to Genoa then Florence. It was John's first visit there. 'It leaves Rome far behind', she wrote to Cara. 'It has remained in the middle ages. One feels a strange and yet familiar aura of the 15th and 16th centuries the moment one sets foot in the streets. As I *know* that I lived in the 15th century myself it appeals to me strongly.'

She also *knew* that she was really a man and loved by God. She had the key to preternatural knowledge and hers was an invincible view. She felt an affinity to Florence, ergo she had lived there in a previous life. She was a changeling from another age. What she wrote, who she was, whom she loved, were controlled by a higher power.

More temporally, holiday life frustrated her. Ladye was not enough. John missed Phoebe Hoare and resented being away. Thin and nervous, she criticized all plans and complained of 'superfluous energy' which she could not channel. 'Travelling grows more uncomfortable and expensive every year. I think I simply hate it. What one endures in stuffy trains, filthy hotels and bad food is surprising.'

They got home to a stack of bills and the same domestic grief. Ladye was with Cara on 12 May for the birth of her granddaughter Karen. John was back with Phoebe. At Ascot a Miss Blomfield tried to speak to the King about women's suffrage. Ladye had shingles and could not enjoy the racing. She lunched in one tent with General Upperton and

Major Balfour, John lunched in another with Phoebe.

In London, John caught mumps. She banished Ladye to the Cadogan Hotel, partly to keep her safe from contagion, more out of a desire to be alone. A week later she rented a studio in Tite Street. She said it was a private place to work, but it was also a private place for her tryst.

Politics broke into this impasse like a tidal wave. At the beginning of August Germany declared war on France and Russia. The banks stopped paying out gold and men were mobilized. There were rumours of the requisitioning of trains for troops. London streets were full of territorial soldiers with 'droves' of horses to be shipped to the battle-fields. John wondered if her horse Judy would be wanted. At night the city looked 'sad and unusual' with searchlights and darkened streets.

Bobby Clarke enlisted and Dolly worked for the Red Cross Hospital in Paignton, Cornwall. Phoebe and Oliver Hoare moved to Berkshire. John and Ladye packed up 59 Cadogan Square, leased it to Mr and Mrs Hamilton Bell, sacked the parlour maid and Ladye's personal maid to save money and moved to Malvern.

John talked of turning the White Cottage into a home for wounded soldiers. She said she wanted to enlist, fight and, if needs be, die. 'Had I been able to leave Ladye I would have done war work abroad.' In her mind's eye she was in uniform, shrapnel-scarred and adorned with medals. It was for Ladye she refrained. Or so she liked to think. 'Once, when I suggested going to Serbia, she worked herself up into such a panic that I gave up all ideas of it.'

Foiled and stuck in Malvern, John did what she was best at – told others how to behave. She wrote and printed recruitment leaflets then drove round the town with Ladye distributing them. She scorned an 'odious schoolmaster' who was against his son enlisting and she put up Kitchener's poster 'Your Country Needs You' on the walls of the White Cottage. When a passer-by annotated these, she wrote a fulminating letter to the *Malvern Gazette*: 'What manner of men have we in these parts? Their women should be ashamed of them. Mr M. Radcliffe Hall.'

'Recruiting is going up here', Ladye wrote to Cara on 13 September. 'It is largely due to Johnnie's efforts. She made a really thrilling speech to women at Castle Morton without any notes. It simply poured out with no effort. I was quite taken aback at her eloquence.'

They took clothes for Belgian refugees to the Red Cross and went to lectures on home nursing and bandaging. John gave money and books for wounded soldiers and offered beds for them at the White Cottage. No soldiers arrived. And she and Ladye knitted mittens, socks and mufflers: 'Johnnie knits too beautifully,' Ladye wrote, 'so evenly they look almost machine made. My efforts are much more unprincipled and vague!' Johnnie's efforts were short-lived. Such activities, she said, bored her. Her fantasy was as a frontline hero, not a caring sister, knitting, bandaging and giving comfort to men.

War brought her affair with Phoebe Hoare to an end, separated her from Dolly Clarke, curtailed her first nights at the Opera House and winters in the sun. Stuck in Malvern in Ladye's exclusive company with the daily news of carnage, opportunity seemed to dim. She published a last book of poems, *The Forgotten Island*. Though unrhymed, 'a new departure for me and one in which I took great interest', they were as ever pastoral or about love, its passions, transience and pain. Composed at the piano, or to a tune on her mandolin, designed to be sung by ladies at afternoon recitals or teas, they were suddenly anachronistic in a cruel world and the volume sank without trace.

Then came another trial which precluded the recapture of their happy days. On 21 September John and Ladye went to London to finalize the subletting of their flat. Norman Serpell, their chauffeur, was to drive them to Malvern next day. They had a 22-horsepower Hooper limousine and they piled their luggage – a great deal of it – on its roof. Garry, the maid, travelled with them. They stopped for lunch at the Mitre Inn in Oxford and left at about three p.m. At the Burford crossroads, seventeen miles on, a small car driven by a Mrs Lakin, who was with her sister and niece, crashed into theirs. Serpell was travelling at twenty-five miles an hour, had the right of way and had sounded his horn. Their car smashed into a wall, knocked down one and a half tons of it and scattered the luggage.

The maid was stunned, Serpell hysterical and Ladye seriously hurt. Carried unconscious from the car, she had concussion, head wounds, broken ribs, and damaged vertebrae. She was taken to a Mrs Pigott at Burford Hill House. A Dr Cheattle shaved and stitched her head and Cara's lover, Frank Romer, came from London with two nurses. For ten days she was very ill. On 1 October she was moved by ambulance with John and Dr Cheattle to the White Cottage.

The focus of life then became Ladye's headaches, wounds, temperature, aches and pains. She was in a wheelchair. She could not wear a hat and wound chiffon round her head to hide her shaved hair. John took her to Birmingham hospital to be X-rayed. The cost of doctors, nursing, heat treatments and massage was high.

John built a shrine to the Virgin Mary on the back wall of the White Cottage in gratitude for the sparing of Ladye's life. The priest came and blessed it. And then, with passionate attention to detail, she collected and collated the evidence needed to sue Mrs Lakin: statements made at the time, photographs of the crossroads, the damaged wall and car. She saw her London solicitor, Theodore Goddard, and waited for the trial.

At the White Cottage the ritual was mornings in bed and lunch at one. At three, they set out for Malvern for Ladye's massage and steam bath. They had tea at the confectioner's, returned home at six, then rested until dinner at seven-thirty. John was now trapped. As consolation, she turned to what was to be her life's work – writing prose. She began with short stories. Like her fantasy of self, these had a Messianic edge. Heavily parabolic, cautionary, they aspired to prophetic heights. Written without irony, their illiteracy was stark. Her childish handwriting sloped backwards. Clichés peppered each page. It was as if she chipped her stories out of the stones of dyslexia, cliché and childhood pain.

Their winter holiday was at the thermal baths at Llandudno in Wales. John pushed Ladye's bathchair along the sea front and together they took the spa waters. It was a far cry from the sunny beaches and starlit nights of Tenerife. Back at the White Cottage, Christmas was quiet. John had yet another cold. Ladye wrote to Cara, urging her to get out into the world and to have some fun before her life, like her mother's, became devoid of pleasures. 'Last day of a sad year', she wrote in her diary on New Year's Eve in a shaky, scarcely legible hand. 'Vale 1914.'

8

Roads with no signposts

Ladye read John's stories aloud to visitors to the White Cottage. Ernest Thesiger, invalided home from the trenches of France, heard the first. Called 'Out of the Night', it was about a poet dying of hunger and driven by the 'compelling, devouring vampire of genius' (spelled jeaneous or geanous) to write the greatest religious poem of the century. 'It will go all over the Christian world.' He writes in a prostitute's bedroom. The night is rough, her heart is soft, she takes him in and gives him pencil and paper. The priest she brings to his bedside as he dies gives the poem to a grateful (greatfull) publisher. The prostitute conceals her trade to protect the jeaneous's reputation.

Here was the essential theme of Radclyffe Hall's ambition. The truth must be told and she was there to tell it. She was a genius with a gift from God. Her writing would be disseminated throughout the world. Like Christ, she needed the selfless devotion of a woman to further her martyred art. The conundrum of her chauvinism was that she herself was a woman who cast herself in the male hero's part.

Betty Carstairs stayed at the White Cottage early in 1915. She had tea with Ladye, they did psychical things with swinging amber beads to communicate with dead relatives, then Ladye read her 'The Recording Angel' ('The Rechording Angle') and 'The Career of Mark Anthony Brakes'. Set in a venue favoured by Radclyffe Hall – the gates of paradise – the Recording Angel weighs his clients in the balance and

63

administers capricious justice. A vain woman, uneasily resembling Mrs Visetti, gets pain, poverty and old age as a lesson in compassion. 'Tears will wash her soul.' A dissolute young man with the attributes of Radclyffe Radclyffe-Hall gets absolution because he once saved a boy from drowning and once set a blackbird free. 'Kindnesses are priceless jems in the site of God', the angel, or angle, reminds.

'I always write about misfits', Radclyffe Hall said, the inference being that she always wrote about herself. In 'Mark Anthony Brakes' she intended to write a pioneer piece on race, though the only black people she had come across were servants in her grandmother's Philadelphia house. Brakes acts white 'though in his soul he knew that he sprang from a race of born slaves'. Radclyffe Hall had a parallel predicament with gender. 'Dat chile of ours am destined to be a great man', Brakes's father says. Dat chile 'devours' books, pomades his hair, talks without accent and excels at segregated college. He works as a lawyer. But 'his was a low-class practice entirely among negroes and his heart began to sicken at the futility of his work'.

A white actress, who can afford no better, lets him represent her. Emboldened when he wins her case, he declares his love, asks her to be his wife and says he will give her a cleaner life. 'A cleaner life with a nigger?' she alarmingly responds. 'You just get right out of this – get out will you, you *black nigger* get out!' Something then 'surges up to his reeling brain and down to his feet'. He rapes her – 'gloated over her like a beast over its prey' – then shoots himself.

Radclyffe Hall was no stylist. It was a stark theme for her clumsy prose. It turned into a jumble of unhelpful views on race caught by the assumptions of her time and class. Her interest in Mark Anthony Brakes was sentimental. He, like her, was a misfit, goaded for what he was. And behind this was a raw view of sex that equated with compulsion, rejection and sin.

In 'The Modern Miss Thompson' she was pontifical about women's suffrage (spelled sufferidge). John wanted the vote for herself if not for her servants. As she pointed out, she paid taxes. Her views were from the standpoint of the monied gentry. She and Ladye thought militancy vulgar and a path to civil war. Ladye noted the transgressions of the suffragettes in her diary. She wished, she wrote, they would set fire to each other rather than to churches.

Mrs Visetti had this story read to her. She visited the White Cottage, wanting help with doctors' bills. Miss Thompson, Oxford educated, handsome and severe, shocks her conventional parents with her feminist views. She calls mother 'little mumsy', smokes papa's cigarettes and reads German philosophy in their chintzy rooms. They urge her to marry William Dryden, who earns £10,000 a year. Miss Thompson finds him repulsive. He has fat hands splotched with yellow freckles and is diffident and bald (differdint and balled). At her suffrage meeting 'all eyes are fixed on her'. She aspires to emancipate the human race. The narrator knows 'she is going to lead the movement into a calldrern of seething sex hatred and risentment which will submurge it altogether.'

Ladye edited the stories, had them typed and John sent them off to literary magazines. 'They always came back in my own stamped envelope – I grew to dread my own handwriting', John wrote. These rejections increased her frustration at being marooned in Malvern without diversion. Ladye knew the publisher William Heinemann and asked him to help. They lunched with him on 1 June 1915 at 32 Lower Belgrave Street. John was too shy to talk or even eat: 'But he seemed quite willing to do all the talking and I heard such words of praise that I could scarcely believe my ears.' He commended her narrative skill and original tone and advised her to write a full-length novel. His encouragement gave her focus, though he died in 1920 and it took her a decade to get a novel into print.

She began an autobiography, *Michael West*, a *roman-à-clef*. She changed her own gender, or in her view revealed her true gender, and changed the names of family and lovers, but it was her life, from birth on, that she described and explained. Michael West was the unloved, abused, dyslexic, romantic boy she supposed herself to be. The book was an indictment of her mother and an exercise in self-examination. She took it to the point of meeting Ladye in Homburg, then it petered out unfinished. Ladye complained at the long hours she worked at it and feared she would make herself ill.

Ladye interspersed her diary entries about her aches and pains and John's literary progress with details of the war: Kitchener's appeals for armaments, the deaths of the sons of friends, the *Lusitania* torpedoed off the Irish coast with 1,350 passengers dead. Believing John to be gifted and knowing her to be vulnerable, she tolerated her moods. But she suffered their rows. John's affection for her was not revived by separation from Phoebe Hoare. Ladye was 'too upset to go out' on 20 March 1915 after an argument about the rambling style of her will.

She got the cook and the gardener to witness the document and could not sleep at night.

The war put a stop to shopping treats and sunshine holidays. Both missed metropolitan life. Ladye tried to make light of how seedy she felt, her high blood pressure, angina attacks, wounds, abscesses in her gums and aching teeth – in spring she had seven out under gas. Her ill-health consumed John with anxiety, but made her tetchy too.

On 8 June they motored to Oxford for the court hearing against Mrs Lakin. At the Randolph Hotel John prepared papers until midnight with the solicitor, Theodore Goddard. Next day they hung about the courts, their case delayed by a murder trial. Chance events now gave her ideas for fiction. She began a parable about prejudice called 'Woman in a Crêpe Bonnet'. A man is condemned to death for killing his pregnant girlfriend. A woman waits outside the court wanting a prurient glimpse of the murderer, wanting him to hang. The doors open, he emerges handcuffed, he is her estranged son.

Cross-examined by Mrs Lakin's counsel, John gave clear replies and a consistent version of events. She refuted, with reference to witnesses and photographs, accusations that her car was going at forty-five miles an hour on the wrong side of the road, that it was out of control because of the quantities of luggage on its roof and that she had been abusive to Mrs Lakin. The jury found in her favour and Ladye was awarded unspecified damages. She 'nearly fainted' with relief. With John, she gave thanks in a Jesuit church, went to the cinema, then home and early to bed. For John the courtroom process went beyond the specific case. She sought justice in a quintessential sense. Right, honour and truth must be declared to be on her side. She settled the amount of damages through solicitors, then fired Serpell the chauffeur.

London became safer and she and Ladye reclaimed the flat in Cadogan Square. They shopped at Selfridges, dined at the deserted Carlton Grill, saw an exhibition of war paintings at the Royal Academy and played poker with Ernest Thesiger. Dolly Clarke, back at Swan Walk, was pregnant with her second child. John viewed her, like Mrs Visetti, as a dependant. She feared that the allowance she gave her would prove inadequate, but felt she could not afford more.

At heart John wanted more than this life of teas and trips. Toupie Lowther managed an all-women ambulance unit in France. With the Red Cross she drove wounded soldiers to safety from within 350 yards of German guns. Excitement, fame and romance were elsewhere. John's

stories were returned with standard rejection slips – 'the editor regrets
...' – her poems were little volumes on library shelves; she was thirty-
five; the affair with Phoebe Hoare was over.

1 August 1915 came to feature as an anniversary. The day was sunny.
She and Ladye went to midday mass at Westminster Cathedral, then
lunched at the Berkeley with Ladye's sister whose husband, Lord
Clarendon, had died the previous year. In the afternoon they all went
off to the zoo then back for tea at Emmie Clarendon's house in
Cambridge Square.

Una Troubridge, Ladye's cousin, was there. 'For very good reasons
I was deeply depressed and very lonely', she said of herself. She thought
John good-looking with beautiful eyes and a raffish smile. 'It was not
the countenance of a young woman but of a very handsome young
man.' John was dressed in white, with a small hat with white feathers
that fanned back. She was holding a miniature fox terrier she had
bought the previous week. (It was returned to the breeders when it
developed eczema.) In the evening she and Ladye drove Una home to
her rented flat in Bryanston Street, Marble Arch. They stopped for
supper with her and her mother, Minna Taylor. They talked about
Annie Besant, Christianity and life in other worlds. Una approved of
John's prejudices and religious fervour, 'I had met for the first time in
my life a born fanatic', she later said.

She then began to 'drop in' on John. She was twenty-eight, John
thirty-five, Ladye fifty-eight. They talked of sculpture, literature,
religion, life. Una came for coffee and stayed for lunch, to tea and
stayed for dinner, to breakfast and stayed the night. She described
Ladye as her friend as well as cousin. 'I had always liked and admired
her', she wrote. None the less she had, she said, 'as much consideration
for her or for anyone else as a child of six'. Ladye's chances of a
workable life with the woman she loved ended with the arrival of Una.
Her diary became a catalogue of her own discomforts, Una's intrusion,
John's betrayal.

Una's plight was desperate when she encouraged John's raffish smile
and beautiful eyes. She had venereal disease and an unwanted daughter
from a husband twenty-five years older than herself whom she neither
loved nor liked and whose court martial by the navy the previous
November had been front-page news in the papers.

She had married Captain Ernest Troubridge in 1908 when she was
twenty-one. Her father, Harry Taylor, had died the previous year,

leaving her without money or a home. His estate of under £700 was willed to her mother and scarcely covered his debts. There had been 'great mutual devotion and affinity' between Una and her father. She competed with her mother and elder sister Viola for his affection. She said they were 'like devoted brother and sister', that he was the one in the family who loved her. He called her his 'own sweet little Una' and fretted when she was ill. She called him Harry, admired his height – he was six foot two – his snowy white hair, civility, culture and charm.

In fact, he was improvident with money, away half the year and intellectually unremarkable. For twenty-two years he worked as a Queen's (then King's) Foreign Service messenger. His job was to carry despatches in a bag from the Foreign Office in London to ambassadors in embassies in Teheran, Madrid, Rome, Paris, Berlin, Constantinople and St Petersburg. His annual pay was £300 and he travelled fifty thousand miles a year.

It was a sinecure but nothing more. Una in childhood saw her parents struggle to keep their heads 'just above the waters of really grim privation ... Every unforeseen expense involved days and weeks of anxiety, pinching, scheming and going without necessities.'

Both her parents had aristocratic antecedents and a sense of privileges lost. Minna Taylor was ruled by propriety. She liked to remind the world that the second Baron Castlemaine of Westmeath was her grandfather, that the Florentine families of Tealdi and Vincenzo were cousins, if much removed. She would hire a private carriage while stinting on food. Una despised her for being vain and self-centred and accused her of favouring Viola. John said 'there was no affinity or bond between Una and her mother'. They shared though a desire for money, a ruthless vanity, a concern for status.

From childhood Una remembered rented rooms, her parents' 'unceasing' quarrels, landladies, lamb chops with greasy gravy and then 'a dingy London house with two rooms on each floor and steep stairs in between'. It was the family home at 23 Montpelier Square in Knightsbridge. Summer holidays were spent with an aunt who bred chickens in Hertfordshire or an uncle who owned a dairy farm in Essex. Only when ill was Una indulged. Instead of the grease and shepherd's pie, there was chicken broth and calves' foot jelly, the attentions of a doctor and nurse, a hired carriage and convalescence by the sea. This equating of illness with privilege gave her a lifelong passion for minor ailments and their use to gain attention.

Her father, despite his modest income, financed her artistic ambitions. He was the son of Sir Henry Taylor, diplomat, poet and essayist, and a friend of the painters G. F. Watts, Edward Poynter and Edward Burne-Jones. Una remembered sitting, aged five, on Edward Poynter's knee while he drew pigs and narrated their adventures. She was taught to dance by Mrs Wordsworth at the Portman Rooms and had private piano and singing lessons, though her voice 'had a tendency to wobble and quiver'. When she was thirteen her father paid for her to study at the Royal College of Art. Sculpture was her special subject and she did much-praised statues and busts. She dressed in theatrical clothes, aspired to be a famous sculptor or singer, dropped her given name, Margot Elena Gertrude, and chose Una Vincenzo for its imposing ring.

When he was forty, her father got tuberculosis. He was sent to sanatoriums in Sussex and at Pau in France for the last four months of his life. He died on 5 March 1907, three days before Una's twentieth birthday. She went to Florence to stay with her mother's wealthy relatives, the Tealdis, in their villa Sant Agostino. Like Radclyffe Hall she felt an affinity to the city, to Italy, the Pope and God. She converted to Catholicism to give meaning to her life. 'I came to believe in the survival of the spirit', she said. 'I think I was getting old enough to realise that roads with no signposts sometimes lead nowhere.'

Ernest Troubridge had signposts she recognized: he had white hair, height, age. His forebears were admirals and army men. 'Yield to no difficulties' was the family motto. He had joined the navy and accrued promotions and honours: Captain and Chief of Staff Mediterranean 1907–8; Chief of the War Staff, Admiralty 1911–12; Grand Order of the Rising Sun; Officer of Legion of Honour; Gold Medal of Order of Imtiaz ... His first marriage was to a Canadian, Edith Duffus, in 1891. She died nine years later after the stillborn birth of their fourth child.

Una hoped for a surrogate father. 'Young men failed to interest me which was sad.' What she got was a husband aged forty-six, syphilis, three teenage stepchildren who loathed her, and the blighting of her artistic hopes. Troubridge met her 'by appointment' in London, proposed, then married her in Venice in October 1908. On her marriage certificate, Una gave as her occupation Sculptor. She had a honeymoon in Paris. They stayed at the Hôtel Normande, where Una was 'grievously ill'. Troubridge then sailed to Malta for two years.

In a stark outburst in her diary some twenty-four years later, she wrote of how, had he thought about it, knowing he had syphilis, he would not have deceived a 'pure' girl, and blighted her life with an incurable disease. 'He had no right to marry. Especially to marry a healthy girl young enough to be his daughter. And I should have escaped 14 years of invalidism and its after effects.'

For years she monitored her treatments for this infection: daily visits to doctors, referral to gynaecologists, injections, vaccines and analyses of smears. It made her disgusted with him and herself, hypochondriacal about every symptom of ill-health, rejecting of her daughter, whom she considered tainted like herself, and disdainful of everything to do with sex. 'The physical never mattered to me anyway after the first misery', she wrote when she was fifty-seven.

It was her disposition to do battle and to seem to succeed. She took on the role of marriage as if playing a part. 'Having chosen for my husband a man old enough to be my father I set to work to try to look his age. I shiver when I look back and remember the sweeping black velvets and purple facecloths of that period of altruistic effort.'

Troubridge, a stickler for the proprieties of his position, wanted her compliance. She was the naval officer's wife. She called him Zip and 'my man', lunched on board ship, was a spectator at polo matches between the army and navy and endured tea dances, cricket matches and dull dinners. It was all a charade. 'Troubridge brought me no spiritual development,' she wrote, 'no evolution, no kindness ... I should not have been sidetracked into marrying at all.'

She had an ectopic pregnancy in 1909 then, a year later, after forty-eight hours' labour, gave birth to her only daughter, Andrea. She desperately wanted her to be healthy, but apart from a preoccupation with symptoms of illness and an assiduous watch on the servants, had no desire for relationship with her child. 'Gradually and infallibly, bit by bit, she brought me to the realisation that there was nothing in her whole make-up that was not alien to mine.'

Una spent days in bed with nervous headaches and 'heart attacks'. Nor could she get on with Troubridge's relatives. She wrote of the 'tyranny of kinship'. He housed her, Andrea and his stepchildren at 107 St George's Square in London. The arrangement lasted a hellish year. He then, in November 1912, asked his sister Laura if she would take in his daughter Mary because 'she and Una are like oil and vinegar'.

Laura wrote novels and books on etiquette and thought the modern girl had lost a sense of values. She had kept a family diary of childhood, adored her brother and deplored his domestic problems, but did not feel able to foster his child. Troubridge took a separate house in Durham Place, near St George's Square, for his adolescent daughters and unmarried sisters. His son, Thomas, joined the navy in the Trou-bridge tradition and Una was isolated in a house on her own with Cub, as she called her daughter.

By January 1913, on her sister Viola's recommendation, she was having treatment with a Harley Street psychotherapist, Dr Hugh Crich-ton-Miller, author of *Hypnotism and Disease* and *Treatment by Hyp-notism and Suggestion*. A smooth man, consulted mainly by ladies with money, time and unsatisfactory husbands, Crichton-Miller founded the Tavistock Clinic for Functional Nervous Disorders in London and ran a large private nursing home on his fourteen-acre estate, Bowden House, at Harrow on the Hill. (Viola was unhappily married to a journalist, Maurice Woods. 'It is horribly tragic,' Crichton-Miller wrote of her to Una with less than professional confidence, 'to be sacri-ficed and broken to a thing [her husband] that is all brain and no heart'.)

Crichton-Miller was another father figure, the 'higher power' which Una sought. She paid to find from him the 'evolution, spiritual develop-ment and kindness' her husband failed to provide. He told her she was 'repressing some big complexes' and that her self-confidence would grow when she learned the power of thought control. 'Confidence in yourself is the goal to be aimed at', he said. He wrote to her while she was away, taught her 'self-inducing hypnosis', which she practised in twenty-minute sessions twice a day, hypnotized her into uncon-sciousness for no very clear reason and sent large bills to Troubridge – thirteen guineas a week plus 'incidental expenses'.

Psychotherapy absorbed her in 1913. In her diary she chronicled her 'seances' of loss of consciousness and the psychology textbooks she read – *The Psychology of Suggestion* by William James, *Hypnotism* by Albert Moll. Troubridge sent unhappy letters, asking her to join him in Malta. Which she was in no hurry to do. Happier without him, she did drawings and etchings, took singing lessons, bought a gramophone and sang along to records. She sculpted a head of Nijinsky, who was dancing with the Ballets Russes in London. She saw him in *Sylphides* and *Scheherazade* and he sat for her at the Royal Ballet School in Drury Lane.

She delayed going out to Malta until March 1914. Troubridge met her on his barge and paraded her as the Rear-Admiral's wife. She lunched on board the *Enchantress*, watched him playing polo and dined with ambassadors and their wives. Her respite was to take singing lessons, go to rehearsals and first nights at the Malta Opera House, read *Quo Vadis* in Italian and *Principii Elementari di Musici* by Federico Parisini and do etchings. By the end of the year, she had finished her Nijinsky sculpture, modelled seven heads and done seventy-five drawings. She had heard *The Pearl Fishers* ten times, *Tosca* three, *Rigoletto* twelve and *La Bohème* fifteen.

Troubridge objected to her artistic and intellectual pursuits. He was unimpressed when the *Daily Malta Chronicle* commended her 'cultured voice of remarkable range and sweetness'. He wanted her to focus her life on him and urged her to regard art and singing as 'diversions'. 'I have never really wished you to work at anything that would occupy you away from me', he told her. 'I would much rather you were not engrossed in anything else.'

Marriage to Una proved a trial for him. She was neither deferential nor malleable nor even pleased to see him. Her intellectual energy undermined him and she warred with his family. But the 1914 war proved a greater trial and undermined him more. At its outbreak in August 1914, Winston Churchill was the First Lord of the Admiralty. Troubridge, a Rear-Admiral, was in command of a fleet of armed ships in the Mediterranean. Early in August, he was instructed to intercept two enemy cruisers, the *Goeben* and the *Breslau*. These ships had bombarded ports at Philipville and Bone, escaped, sailed on to Messina and were heading for the Dardanelles.

Troubridge's squadron had four cruisers with nine-inch guns. The two German ships had eleven-inch guns. He aimed to close on them in darkness then fight them at first light. He pursued them on the night of 6 August. He hoped for mist and rain, but the night was clear. By four a.m. he considered that he was too far away from them and that at first light his ships would be in unequal danger from their superior guns. He gave up the chase and returned to the Adriatic.

The *Goeben* and *Breslau* sailed on unchallenged to the Dardanelles. Turkey had joined with Germany against the Allies. Russia's access to the Black Sea was sealed off by these ships. Battles in Gallipoli, Mesopotamia and the Middle East followed with huge loss of life. According to Churchill, the incident brought 'more slaughter, more misery and ruin than has ever before been brought within the compass of a ship'.

An exhaustive inquiry was held, fuelled by Churchill's anger and contempt. Troubridge returned to England in September to give account. Una travelled with him. The papers were full of it and there was a photograph of her in the *Tatler*. Troubridge asked the Admiralty for a trial by court martial in an endeavour to clear his name. 'He did forbear to chase HIGM's ship *Goeben* being an enemy then flying' was the charge. The hearing was from 5–11 November 1914. It was a secret affair, conducted by other admirals and led by Sir Leslie Scott, KC. There were daily sittings, including Sunday. Una took to her bed for the entire proceedings. Troubridge was 'fully and honourably' acquitted of blame. But though technically absolved he lived with the taint of cowardice. It was not a war where rational retreat was commended. Those who were thought honourable died in the fight.

For four months he was not asked to return to his ship or given another appointment. To avoid an imminent question in parliament as to why, Churchill summoned him in March 1915 for an interview. He did not look up from his desk when Troubridge entered, nor did he ask him to sit down. He said, 'Troubridge, I have an appointment to offer you, but as it is in the forefront of the battle, I think you may not care to accept it.'

Una asked her husband how he responded to this insult. 'He said to me, "I am a naval officer and I reminded myself that discipline must be preserved. I told the First Lord that I was ready to accept any appointment that would be useful to my country in time of war."' He was sent to Belgrade to command the forces defending the Danube. It was a post that banished him to obscurity. He never went to sea again 'and he was fanatically a sea sailor'. It was a post, too, that banished him from his wife. If adversity is the testing ground of love, she failed. Months of his enforced company and the social stigma she felt he had inflicted on her played on her nerves and provoked her headaches. Any residual interest she had in him evaporated. She offered no sympathy, no further support. 'Think of my pride', he had said when he asked for trial by court martial. Una thought of herself. His absence gave her space to pursue Radclyffe Hall, a social humiliation to Troubridge that inspired him with rage, called for revenge and barred him from London life.

9

Chenille caterpillars

Ladye chronicled every meeting between John and Una. Her diary was her testimony to the betrayal of trust: 'Una here to breakfast. She lunched with John and saw *The Man Who Stayed at Home*. I took Cara to see *Romance* and we had tea out. Una to dinner as usual. I slept badly and felt very depressed.' John was now 'so changed' towards her. She was always irritable and never wanted to go anywhere alone with her, but wanted to be alone with Una.

This was not, as with Phoebe Hoare, an affair with prescriptive limits, contained by regard for marriage. Una had left Troubridge in all but deed. A determined woman, she wanted to oust Ladye and have John to herself. She was 'completely under the spell of her enthralling personality. All I knew or cared about was that I could not, once having come to know her, imagine life without her.' The Admiralty offered her a passage to Belgrade to join Troubridge. She declined. 'I hate exile from the intellectual and artistic pursuits of London', was her excuse. 'I dread a stagnation that may end in atrophy.' Even Andrea, aged five, was now an encumbrance and an intrusion. Alone with her, Una felt cooped up.

A month after meeting John, in September 1915, she asked Crichton-Miller if he would foster Andrea at Bowden House and see that she went to mass. Crichton-Miller declined. He suggested a Miss Prior, who lived at Roxeth Head nearby:

There are three old ladies, the youngest of whom is about sixty in the shade. There were four recently, the fourth died of excessive senility last summer ... For the last ninety years they have specialised in taking care of Anglo-Indian children ... Their terms might be a little high, but whatever they charge, I think you could be sure of getting good value. They would be enormously impressed by the fact that Andrea was a Roman Catholic and would be more likely to find fault for the fewness of the services attended than for the number of them!

It was a strange environment for a psychiatrist to recommend for a small child. Andrea was passed like an unclaimed parcel to whoever would have her for a while.

To Ladye, John rationalized her infidelity. She assured her she would never leave her – but nor was she going to change. She talked again of 'superfluous energy' and Toupie Lowther's ambulance unit. In late September she took both her and Una to the Watergate Bay Hotel near Newquay in Cornwall. Ladye, unfit for cliff walks and beach games, was left on her own in the hotel. 'Talked till very late with John after we went up to bed', she wrote on 2 October. She dreamed that her eyes were on fire and that while she watched from a river bank John drowned. She woke shouting and bathed in sweat.

In a move that compounded Ladye's insecurities, John sublet both the London flat in Cadogan Square and the Malvern house. The war had reduced her income, but it was her habit to move out of places as impulsively as she moved in. Their furniture went into store and she took a suite of rooms at the Vernon Court Hotel in Buckingham Palace Road. Ladye's bedroom had views over the palace gardens. They were pleasant quarters, but with no sense of home. Una hung her Nijinsky drawings in John's sitting-room.

Ladye still had time with John: shopping at Selfridges, lunch at the Savoy Grill, a matinée of Gladys Cooper in *Please Keep Emily*. They prayed together at the Oratory and Ladye read aloud to her in the evenings. But there was an underlying loss of expectation from the relationship, a revision downward of trust, a death of hope that past happiness would ever come again.

On Ladye's fifty-eighth birthday on 27 October, John took her to lunch at the Ritz. She gave her a travelling cushion, a gift she was to have no occasion to use. A few days later, she took Una on a jaunt to

Taplow to buy her a bulldog called Juno. Ladye lunched alone, feeling 'done up, sad and rotten'.

And then on 29 November John went alone with Una to the White Cottage. They were supposed to compile an inventory of the furniture and contents before the tenant, Mrs Lygon, moved in. They went by train to Malvern, then took a carriage. It was a damp misty day, the house was warm from the anthracite stove burning in the hall. The servants had gone. It was the first time Una had seen the White Cottage. It was the kind of home she had never had and the home she wanted with John. The date was significant, another anniversary:

> I can shut my eyes now & recall the luncheon she had prepared for me – & trying to eat while I summoned my resolution to leave immediately – & all that followed, & in the evening our walking along the valley road to where the lights ended & the hedges began – & so back to the White Cottage with a bond forged between us.

They were both, she wrote, 'breaking troth' to their partners, though troth to Troubridge did not amount to much and she summoned no resolution to leave. She justified herself by her relative youth: she was thirty years younger than Ladye. For Mabel Batten, from the evidence of her diaries, Una's intrusion was a disappointment that compromised her to the core. John perhaps intended an adventure, a respite from boredom, one more conquest on a par with those of her father. She was ambivalent about Una. 'How do I know if I shall care for you in six months' time?' she said. But she gave her a platinum ring engraved with their names and she had fashioned another destructive triangle and incestuous circle.

Una intended that John should care for a lifetime and more. She rented an artist's studio in Tite Street, Chelsea. John was her principal subject. Drawing her and making a sculpture of her were pretexts for being with her all day. She read aloud the manuscript of *Michael West* and all John's short stories. She noted her grandiose ambition, her vulnerability and need for praise. This prose mapped the psychological terrain Una intended to claim.

Una had a fervour to serve. In Florence when she had watched the initiation ceremony of a novice into a closed order of nuns, she had wished she was the girl. She lauded what she saw as subordination of self to the highest power. If she served Radclyffe Hall as disciple and vestal virgin, she could subsume her own personality yet achieve glory. She would also have a lot of money and no responsibility. She liked first nights, travel, 'beautiful clothes and the opportunity for wearing them'. And sexually, after Troubridge, she was through with men. John was a quasi-man without the misery Troubridge's attentions brought.

'London like a Christmas card under deep snow', Ladye wrote as the year came to an end. Relationships were wintry too. On Christmas Eve the three of them went to midnight mass. John gave Ladye a pink, fur-lined Chinese wrap and gold hatpins. Ladye gave her a wristwatch, a prophetic gift, for time was running out. She felt 'depressed and *very* sad'. 'Una spent all New Year's Eve with us till 10.45 pm. John and I saw the troublesome year 1915 out together and both felt depressed. Vale 1915!'

Nor did Ladye hail 1916 as happy or new. For the first week of it, John went with Una to Tunbridge Wells. They booked in at the Wellington Hotel. Ladye sang 'Mother England' at tea parties, lost her fox fur muff, 'lunched and dined alone and slept badly'. It poured with rain, there were gales and a tree came down in the garden of the White Cottage and killed Mr Hooper the gardener.

Rear-Admiral Troubridge arrived in London in February. He had not seen his wife for nine months and wanted her evasions explained. He expected her to meet him at the station but, with a sudden headache and sore throat, she went to bed at the Vernon Court Hotel. He saw at her studio the marble head she was sculpting. He made what he would of her reluctance to be alone with him, her immersion into the life of this woman called John. He dined with them all at the Vernon Court, went without Una to the wedding of his daughter, Mary, and slept at his club. His career seemed uncertain and his pay had been halved.

Una told him she was not going out to Belgrade and that she would stay married but only in name. She reminded him she was still being treated by Crichton-Miller for 'neurasthenia' and by Alfred Sachs for venereal infection. Perhaps to avoid the possibility of divorce, he was received into the Catholic Church on 27 February. Ladye had 'a long and quiet talk' with John about the implications of it all.

Thomas Troubridge, Una's stepson, arrived without warning at the hotel. He urged Una to return to his father, accused her of humiliating him and warned that scandal would rebound on her. She hinted at revelations that would damage him more than forbearing to chase enemy ships.

Tension infected them all. John was 'excessively irritable' with Ladye and harangued her when she was quarter of an hour late arriving at Una's studio. Ladye felt 'too wretched'. John talked of taking Una and Andrea abroad with them as soon as the war allowed and she was gloomy when Dolly's baby, Jacqueline, was born. The atmosphere was 'sad beyond words', Ladye wrote. 'Felt chilled bodily and mentally ... Thought seriously of going to live by myself.'

She was too unwell for humiliation and upheavals. John signed the lease on a new flat at 22 Cadogan Court and decided to sell the White Cottage when the tenant offered to buy it. She and Ladye talked over these plans until one-thirty one morning. John assured her that the new flat was for the two of them, but Una was involved at every stage. '*Wish* I felt stronger and more able to work', Ladye wrote in her diary. Una helped choose the wallpapers, the stove for Ladye's bedroom, John's bed from Barkers. Ladye was offended when, at Una's prompting, John took a room down the corridor as her bedroom, not the one adjacent to her own as she had hoped and they had agreed.

To get away she went for a week to the Grayshott Senacle Convent in Surrey. With a regime of prayer and early nights, spared Una's constant presence and in the company of nuns, she felt better. While she was away, John took Una to Malvern to arrange the sale of furniture from the White Cottage. She wrote Ladye a 'darling but depressed letter' about parting with the place. It had been their shared home for five years.

On 29 April Ladye complained that black specks floated across her eyes as she tried to read. Next day it was 'chenille caterpillars'. Her oculist 'found nothing seriously wrong'. She was tired, breathless and her pulse was 'intermitting' when the three of them supervised moving the furniture from 59 Cadogan Square to 22 Cadogan Court.

On 13 May they all went to a Red Cross concert. They heard pieces by Elgar, and Agnes Nicholls sang 'To the Fallen'. Next day John again took Una to Taplow. Juno the bulldog was not up to par and was to be swapped. Ladye went alone to midday mass then lunched with Cara and showed her the new flat. John and Una were tempted to spend the night in Skindles, a fashionable hotel near Maidenhead. They eventually went back with the new dog to Una's flat. The phone was ringing when they arrived. Ladye was vexed that John was so late for dinner.

John returned reluctantly to the Vernon Court. She vented her anger at Ladye for curtailing her movements and constraining her freedom. Her tabasco temper had a poisonous fire. Ladye rose from the dinner table, complaining of pins and needles down her right side and of acute chest pain. She then collapsed. John could not get their doctor so she phoned Una, who went to the hotel. Ladye had had a cerebral haemorrhage. Next day she scrawled in her diary with her left hand, 'Another stroke'.

For ten days she lay paralysed and speechless. John thought she divined from her eyes and 'inarticulate sounds' a recognition of herself and the desire to say something important to her alone. Aware that Ladye was dying, she craved her forgiveness. She appealed to the doctor to work some alchemy and make her speak. He volunteered an injection of amyl nitrite, but feared it might finish her off. Ladye stayed silent and died on 25 May.

Obituarists in the *Star, The Times,* the *Morning Post* wrote of her fine voice, charms, and friendship with Edward VII. John had her embalmed and on her corpse laid a silver crucifix blessed by the Pope and gold medals of Our Lady of Lourdes and St Anthony. The funeral was on 30 May. A requiem mass was held in Westminster Cathedral. Those attending were listed in *The Times*: 'The French Ambassador, the Dowager Countess of Clarendon, Lord Cecil Manners, Rear Admiral Troubridge, Mrs Austin Harris and her tall young daughter Miss Honey Harris, Mrs George Marjoribanks and Miss Hatch' and many more. Una, though a cousin and friend who 'had always liked and admired her', stayed away.

John spent grandly on the paraphernalia of death. She bought a catacomb chamber the size of a small chapel in Highgate Cemetery. It had pillars and Mabel Veronica Batten chiselled in stone above its cast-iron gate. Inside were four shelves. Ladye's coffin lay on one. Two of the others were reserved for John and Cara. The fourth was 'for the sake of a proper balance'. As the years passed the question of whose remains should be housed in this inner sanctum became the test of intimacy.

The paint was scarcely dry at 22 Cadogan Court. Nothing had been unpacked. John left the Vernon Court and went to stay with Dolly Clarke. Consumed with guilt and grief, she poured out anguished letters to Cara:

I don't understand things ... Because she has gone I am no longer all myself. Some day the riddle will be solved, in the meantime I can only wonder ... How can I ever hope to be happy again, I can only wait and try to live a decent life and to please her word in all things in case I did not always please her before. If I had many faults and sins then perhaps this will be an offering for them. I don't know, I can't see clearly. The only thing I do see is that I must never fail her. From now on no interest shall ever lower her memory for me. There shall not be seen a shadow to come between us. I am waiting for some work to turn up and expect that she will guide me.

In her will, a 'long and conversational document' for which John had criticized her, Ladye voiced fears that after her death Cara and John would feud: 'it would grieve me greatly should they grow less friendly or lose sight of each other when I am no longer on this earth'. Cara, Emmie Clarendon and others close to Mabel were not sympathetic to John's grief. Goodwill toward her was scant. They saw these burial displays as care that had come too late. They wanted Mabel to be buried with George. They had observed and deplored the advent of Una, the way this had spoiled Mabel's life. They believed that the tension this caused contributed to her death. They went back to calling John Marguerite and invitations faded away.

'I have tried to dismiss the outrageous gossip that is unworthy of the devotion of your mother and me', John wrote to Cara. But she could not dismiss her own guilt:

The thing that hurt me when she died was the terrible idea that any peevish words of mine had caused the attack ... I shall never forgive myself that I allowed her to be annoyed over Una's constant presence ... I only hope that my beloved Ladye never thought that any ones wishes except hers were being consulted about our flat.

'Her passing was the shock of my life', she said. 'In losing her I lost a shield between myself and the world.' The loss uncovered old insecurities of abandonment and of that childhood memory of a coffin in the ground. She looked forward to death with 'the certainty of reunion' and said her youth and will to live had died too.

Nor was Una a consolation. She seemed like a malevolent accomplice. 'Her grief was overwhelming and intensified by remorse,' Una wrote. 'She was submerged by an all-pervading sorrow ... She blamed herself bitterly and uncompromisingly that she had allowed her affection for me to trespass upon her exclusive devotion to Ladye, that she had brought me so closely into their home life, thereby marring the happiness of Ladye's last months on earth.'

Una's strategy was to serve and wait. She destroyed her diaries for the years 1915 and 1916, her own evidence of Ladye's humiliation. For herself, she was 'desperately miserable at what looked like an almost total shipwreck of our happy relationship'. John did not now want to see her. There were accusations and rows. Una developed what she called 'an old heart affection' – palpitations and a racing pulse – a sure way to capture the concern, time and attention of the woman whom she was determined to have.

TWONNIE

10

The eternal triangle

Mabel Batten had loved Radclyffe Hall in a devoted way. She compensated her for the miseries of childhood, encouraged her ambition and tolerated her temper. She was punished for her pains. Cara took away her mother's diaries. John asked to borrow the last one 'for a few days'. 'I have a great desire to read it', she said. There, detailed, was her unfaithfulness and the unhappiness it had caused.

She justified herself to Cara, said that she had given the best eight years of her life to Ladye, 'and although other people took my surface interest twice during that time, they never touched my soul or penetrated into my mind'. Una knew the details of this surface interest. There was a complicity between them, a share of guilt and they 'frayed each other's nerves' when they met.

But John could not bear ever to be alone. A night in the unlived-in flat at Cadogan Court was an intolerable reminder. 'The confusion there is past all belief', she wrote to Cara. She stayed with Dolly Clarke and her baby daughter at Swan Walk and at a country house in Purton, Wiltshire.

Una wanted to be with her, even if that meant no more than misery shared. She rented a house at 13 Royal Hospital Road, Chelsea, because it was near Swan Walk. Her 'heart affection' and the threat of its untreated consequences alarmed John, who took her for a week to the Royal Victoria Hotel at Llanberis in Wales. 'It was lonely and beautiful,'

Una wrote, 'and we went to the top of Snowdon and trailed round Caernarvon Castle ... but it was not a success.'

John's thoughts were all of Ladye. She kept her clothes and possessions and did not accept that her death meant extinction. 'She is so very much alive. The idea that such a personality could cease to exist is too absurd.' She spoke of killing herself to be with her, but feared that might confound their chances in heaven. She wanted to reassure her, resume ordinary communication, justify her relationship with Una and be forgiven if she had transgressed.

Wherever Ladye now was John determined to find her. And wherever John now went Una was going to follow. The Church was too philosophical with its ideas of heaven deferred, its exhortations to prayer, piety, submission to the will of the Lord and a long wait before all was revealed. John wanted to get in touch right away.

She paid for the help of a medium, a kind of warden of an extra-terrestrial missing persons bureau. The first they went to, Mrs Scales, was unsatisfactory. She had two lots of triplets and three lots of twins, was unwell, hard up and distracted. She went into a sweaty trance, failed to evoke anyone or thing in the least like Ladye, said 'horrible things', had an attack of 'neurotic mania' and was in both their views 'hysterical with erotic tendencies'.

Una then contacted Sir Oliver Lodge, former President of the Society for Psychical Research. He had a credibility Mrs Scales lacked. He was Principal of the University of Birmingham, a Fellow of the Royal Society and author of various works on lightning conductors, electrons and the universe. His book, *Raymond or Life and Death with Examples of the Evidence for Survival of Memory and Affection After Death*, was selling fast. It went into six editions in 1916. Hundreds of soldiers were being killed each day and it was bought by the bereaved.

Raymond was Sir Oliver's youngest son. He qualified as an engineer but volunteered in September 1914. He became a second lieutenant in the South Lancashire regiment and was sent to Ypres. He was the kind of young man Radclyffe Hall encouraged to enlist with her recruitment speeches and leaflets. His was the active service she said she wanted for herself.

In letters home, Raymond wrote of the 'unending vista' of war, enteric dysentery, dead horses and dead men 'once smelt never forgotten'. He was he said 'pigging it' in the trenches, shot at and shelled. He saw his friends killed by sniper fire; his servant had his leg blown off and his best friend, Fletcher, was hospitalized because his 'nerves were all wrong'. His captain acquired a German helmet and had it cleaned out because 'part of the owner was still inside it'. The German prisoners included an officer aged sixteen 'and student types with spectacles, poor devils I do feel sorry for them'.

'I should think that never in this world before have there been so many men so fed up', he wrote. He asked his father to send morphia tablets because when men got hit in the morning, they had to wait until dark to be moved. He asked for a book about the stars and for some cocoa and he complained of rats and mice. He said he valued his primus stove and stone water jar and that at the war's end he would like a simple room with the view of a garden.

By 6 September 1915 he was sleeping in wet clothes in a dugout swimming with water. 'Great happenings are expected here shortly and we are going to have a share', he wrote. And then his captain sprained an ankle falling from his horse and Raymond was put in temporary command of C Company. 'Hope not for long. Too responsible at the present time of crisis.' A week later he wrote, 'You will understand that I have the Company to look after and we are going into the front line trenches this evening at 5 pm.'

Sir Oliver received the familiar telegram:

The King and Queen deeply regret the loss you and the army have sustained by the death of your son in the service of your country. Their Majesties truly sympathise with you in your sorrow.

Raymond had been hit about midday on 14 September. Telephone wires were cut and no one could get a doctor. He died the next day. Lord Kitchener expressed sympathy too.

Nothing in Raymond's letters sought consolation in the sky. Rather, he inferred that people might behave better on earth. But irrationality was fashionable. War had made life awful. Sir Oliver, like Radclyffe Hall, consoled himself with a notion of paradise where Raymond now resided. To communicate with his son he paid for sessions with mediums. He documented his findings and submitted these to the Society for Psychical Research in Hanover Square.

The Society prided itself on its standards of investigation and research and the status of its members. Among its former presidents were Bishop Boyd Carpenter, Canon of Westminster and Chaplain to the Forces;

Professor Gilbert Murray, author and classics scholar; Lord Rayleigh, Professor of Experimental Physics at Cambridge and Mr Gerald Balfour MP, brother of A. J. Balfour, the Prime Minister from 1902 to 1905.

Sir Oliver's favoured medium was Gladys Leonard of Maida Vale. Through her he met again with Raymond. Sir Oliver ascertained that Raymond was happy, lived in a house 'made from emanations from the earth' and had a girlfriend with long gold hair and a lily in her hand. Raymond regularly visited his parents at the family home, Mariemont, at Edgbaston outside Birmingham. He came at night when they were in bed. 'The air is so quiet then.'

Sir Oliver advised Radclyffe Hall to join the Society and go to Mrs Leonard. He offered a solution to her problem, a way for her to bring guilt, grief and loss into her control. She set about communicating with Ladye with obsessive application. 'The idle apprentice,' Una said, 'was metamorphosed by sorrow into someone who would work from morning to night and from night till morning, or travel half across England and back to verify the most trifling detail.'

Writing was forgotten. Here was her work, the channel for 'superfluous energy', her full-time occupation. Between 1916 and 1920 evidence of Mrs Leonard's 'possession' by Ladye was her overwhelming interest. She and Una went each week, sometimes five times a week. Every session was minuted, typed and analysed. They amassed an archive of paperwork and employed a full-time secretary. Una read aloud about discarnate spirits, mediumistic trances, Ostensible Communicators and Ostensible Possession. John hired a private detective in case Mrs Leonard cheated by unpsychical visits to the Public Record Office. Their findings were collated, analysed and sent for scrutiny to Sir Oliver.

John wanted to get close again to Ladye. Una wanted to usurp Ladye and get close again to John. She went along as recorder, witness, whatever John asked. She was needed at the sessions. It was the eternal triangle. The arrangement assuaged John's conscience. She and Una were together not for pleasure, desire, or themselves, but only to serve Ladye. Una concurred. All she cared about was not to be parted for a morning or a night. Seances with Mrs Leonard had a parallel with hypnosis with Crichton-Miller. Both were a relinquishing of responsibility, a pseudo-submission to a higher power.

Gladys Leonard lived in a three-room basement flat at 41 Clifton Avenue, Maida Vale, west London. She kept her seance room hot and a red light glowed in the window. Mediums, she said, are extremely sensitive, highly strung individuals. Before going into a trance she got pins and needles and felt herself to be swelling to an enormous size. Clear, dry weather was important for 'psychical manifestations'. On foggy days communication from the dead was difficult.

She wrote an autobiography, *My Life in Two Worlds*. In it she posed the question, 'Are Our Loved Ones to be thought of only as Yesterday's Sunbeams?' Her answer was 'a resounding No!' She acquired special powers at the age of eight. A member of the local church died and Gladys had recurring visions of 'radiantly happy people' in green valleys. Happy Valleys, she called them, and was surprised others could not see them too.

In her teens Gladys went to spiritualist meetings where 'discarnate spirits from the other side' manifested themselves through mediums. A fat man with protruding eyes talked in the voice of a girl of seven. A middle-aged woman inhabited by a North American Indian kept giving bloodcurdling howls. On her twenty-seventh sitting Gladys was inhabited by Feda, a thirteen-year-old Indian girl who had apparently married Gladys's great great grandfather then died in childbirth in 1800. Feda told Gladys that together they could do great things.

For money, Gladys worked as a repertory singer and actress. Throat troubles and the extraction of all her teeth impeded her career. She married Mr Leonard who was also an actor with throat troubles and profound deafness in his right ear. Money was short and they made do in a succession of nasty lodgings. In spring 1914 in a spiritualist paper, she advertised private sittings. Three people turned up for the first session. In a trance Gladys saw the murdered King of Serbia holding a bloody cannon ball. Six weeks later war started: 'I understood then the purpose for which I was needed. I was to be used to prove to those whose dear ones had been killed that they were not lost to them and the dead had never died.'

The bereaved, the grief-stricken and the deranged came to her. She had an undoubted facility for saying what they liked to hear. She preferred them relatively sane and well-heeled. Oliver Lodge became a client in 1915 and sent other sitters via the Society for Psychical Research. 'Where would my work have been without Sir Oliver Lodge's help?' Gladys Leonard asked.

In August 1916, John and Una made their way to Maida Vale, determined to meet again with Ladye. Gladys Leonard was wearing a blonde, wavy hairpiece and had applied a lot of face powder. Una had her notebook ready. Mrs Leonard made a noise like the air coming out of an inflatable cushion. She stared and seemed catatonic, then sweated, writhed, clutched Una's shoulder and joggled her arm so that she had difficulty writing. Ladye was possessing Feda and Feda was possessing Mrs Leonard.

Feda talked through Mrs Leonard in a squeaky foreign voice. She said 'pletending' and 'tly' instead of pretending and try. She described Ladye's hair, eyes and dimpled skin. Ladye, it was ascertained, was velly well. Feda explained the topography of the brave new world she was now in. The dead go to a plane, one to seven, that fits their earthly interests. There are 'houses, gardens, meadows, woods, lakes'. Artists paint and singers sing. Ladye was on plane three. Jesus Christ was on plane seven. She had been up to visit him a few times – in a group, or gloop. She lived by herself though her visitors were numerous and she saw George often. He was very well, too. She had a nice home: a stone house with French windows, wide entrance hall, heavy furniture, coloured cushions, a garden with 'heaps and heaps of flowers' and a horse with a soft mouth and 'naughty little ears'. The ground was springy for horseriding; 'You will love it when you come.'

She looked pretty, cheeky and bright and about thirty years old. She kept up her singing and guitar playing. She assured John that she had not suffered when she died. It had only been a little blood clot on the brain. All her disabilities were gone: no high blood pressure or arterial sclerosis. She was not lonely on plane three and thought it the best one for John because of all the dogs and horses. She did a bit of voluntary work in the day among the 'poor souls who had just left their physical bodies', then she went home, took off her clothes and had a lie down.

John found the reassurance, relief and absolution that she wanted. Ladye was alive and well and blooming in a better world. Questions to Feda yielded replies that rendered irrelevant guilt or grief. Ladye forgave her any carelessness or neglect before that fateful brain haemorrhage; nothing could interfere with their eternal life together. In a few years they would be reunited 'like a needle to a magnet'. (Una butted in that she wanted to die too if John was to 'go over' soon.)

Una was now marginalized and punished daily. If Ladye had endured jealousy because of Una's constant presence, Una, in the nature of triangles and nemesis, was to have her measure of it meted out. She became witness and scribe to a relationship of incomparable consummation. Earthbound, Ladye had seemed wheezy, pleasant, indolent. Now she was infallible and still in love with John, or 'Twonnie' as Feda called her.

'Hold your face to one side Twonnie, she wants to kiss you', Feda said to John. Ladye caressed Twonnie, advised, admonished and expressed concern and undying love. She worried about her haemorrhoids, her nose going red in the cold, acidity in her stomach and the disgraceful way she swore. And she could see Una's fibroids and told her to get them sorted out. Una wrote it all down. If she was slow with her note taking, John was sharp and told her to abbreviate more.

Sometimes Una got waspish. She asked how she could be expected to take sensible notes with Feda grabbing on to her arm so hard. She was less than respectful when Feda's writhings caused Mrs Leonard's hairpiece to singe on the electric fire. And she admitted to 'an unpleasant little shock' when Feda's vocabulary reflected Mrs Leonard's social position not Mabel's. The ethereal Ladye now said 'of ten' pronouncing the t. In her Kensington days Ladye, of course, said 'orphan'. Feda referred to corsets where Ladye wore stays and to 'back premises', a term unknown to her class. 'Twonnie' irritated Una, too. 'Feda I must tell you it's Johnnie, not Twonnie', she said. 'Ladye wants you to call her by the right name.' But Mrs Leonard's psychic tolerance had its limits: 'Johnnie is a boy's name. Twonnie is very much nicer', she replied.

The sessions were for John not Una. She paid to fabricate life. It was as if Ladye had sneaked off on a world cruise and now John had tracked her down. 'I expect you're much happier on your side than we are here', John said. She feared Ladye could not understand her own 'awful earth grief', her agitation and sleepless nights. Why had she left in a way that was such an awful shock to her? 'Doesn't she know I want to join her?' she asked Feda. Did she receive her prayers? Didn't she know that she loved her more intensely than was bearable? 'Does she love me more than anyone else?' she enquired.

'Silly question', Feda replied. 'There is more in our love than has ever been between two women before.' Ladye would rejoice were Twonnie to join her. Meanwhile she suggested she go to a friend of Mrs Leonard's, a Mr Humely, for relaxation and breathing exercises. His charges were reasonable. She gratefully received Twonnie's prayers, which went first to the seventh plane then came down to her. She had 'passed over' both because 'the sands had run out' and for the sake of

Twonnie's evolution and spiritual development. She had left 'the core of herself' with her. She did not want Twonnie to go over that fateful stroke again and again. She should live for the present and have a good time with Una.

This became a recurring theme. Mrs Leonard knew her trade. Ladye, it seemed, now more than commended John's relationship with Una. She thought the three of them made a 'wonderful combination'. Una must carry the torch and look after Twonnie. Ladye was more than occupied on plane three, what with horseriding, gardening and day trips to Jesus. She told John and Una to go off on holiday together, that it gave her a fillip if they had a good time.

It had not been quite like that in the Vernon Court Hotel. 'Lunched and dined alone and slept badly', was Ladye's lament then. Nor was it quite what John wanted to hear. Did Ladye not realize that she was living the rest of her life in memory of her, that life had no meaning without her? Yes, Ladye knew that. Ladye knew everything.

Una wanted to know if Ladye was glad that she too was 'so fond of Twonnie'? Yes, Feda replied, but she must not show her fondness slavishly. And when someone whose name perhaps began with T was around, she should try to conceal fond feelings.

> *Una*: Tell my Ladye she's got to help me to take care of Twonnie.
> *Feda*: She says yes she wants that. She puts her in your charge.
> *Una*: Tell her I am honoured and will do my best.
> *Feda*: She says she's afraid you hardly appreciate the magnitude of your task. It will be perfectly awful sometimes. Terrible.
> *Una*: Tell her I'll stick to it all right.

Ladye thought Troubridge's absence was 'the best thing all round'. She was more conformist these days and wanted appearances upheld. When Una had her hair cut short and the nape of her neck shaved, Ladye fingered it and gave an ethereal shudder. She preferred Una's 'medieval fashion' of plaited knobs over the ears. She again warned John never to cut hers. She would not speak to her if she did.

Behind the idiocy of it all was the terror of an abandoned child. Like a child, Radclyffe Hall turned shadows into substance, imagined a fantasy mother who would always love her and a fantasy world that was always safe. A wafer could become the flesh of Christ and Gladys Leonard, Ladye.

Radclyffe Hall could, as she chose, recreate the world. Death was life, she was a man and reality was in her control. Events could not 'render it intolerable'. Her perfect woman was always there, mother, lover, friend, 'the woman one would long to protect while coming to in turn for protection'.

Boundaries blurred between now and then and between herself and Una. The drama of psychic possession in Maida Vale had a parallel in Chelsea. John merged eternally with Ladye and Una merged into John. John's psychical research notes were all about Ladye. Una's diary was for and about John. If John left her supper, went to the dentist, had a cold, bought a sweater, Una noted it down.

It became unclear which of them was hearing Ladye rapping on the wardrobe and why Una should want to know about it quite as much as John. They wrote up notes together, instructed the typist and read books on other worlds. They planted roses and rhododendrons by the Highgate mausoleum. Only John's temper tantrums drew a temporary sharp divide. 'J very depressed & in vile temper. Not a nice evening and I cried much after I was left alone', was an aggrieved diary entry of Una's in February 1917. When Una mis-set the alarm clock, John's fury was 'almost too miserable to bear'. When she left their notes at Mrs Leonard's, John 'raged with fury and distress'. But mostly Una did what was wanted and John's dependency grew. After the storms she was sweet, '& I just love her anyway', Una wrote. And John, who had a dependent heart, felt gratitude. 'Where would I be without my Squiggie', she said and meant.

Living in separate quarters was inconvenient for their work. But sharing a house might seem to exclude Ladye and there was Trou-bridge's leave to consider. When they worked late at Una's house, John stayed the night. If it was Swan Walk, Una slept on a couch. And then John caught measles and Dolly Clarke feared for her baby. John stayed with Una, who nursed her. In gratitude, John gave her a sapphire and diamond ring and then a feather eiderdown and 'a lovely model gown' from Sheba's of Sloane Street. And she added a codicil to her will bequeathing all clothes and personal things to her. 'It meant *so* much to me', Una wrote.

It meant even more to her that they should share a home. On 15 February 1917 her landlady, Mrs Gregory, told her to be out of the house in Royal Hospital Road by noon. She objected to lesbian goings-on. Una found 42 St Leonard's Terrace nearby. John helped her settle in but left at ten p.m. 'Very much depressed at new start in another squalid little lonely abode, but one must just do one's best and go on. I am very, very tired', Una wrote in her diary.

In spring John braved the flat at Cadogan Court, leased for herself and Ladye. She needed Una's constant presence and support. They transcribed their notes, took meals together, walked the dogs. Una again moved to be close by. She signed a lease on an unfurnished house at 6 Cheltenham Terrace. John bought two Cromwellian oak chairs and an oak refectory table for it. When there was an air raid in July, Una ran into the street to look for John, who that night told her she loved her very much.

Una wanted to stay with her for all eternity. She knew the strength that lay in seeming weak, the power her acquiescence held. John always worried when Una was ill. Knowing John read her diary, Una teased for sympathy: 'I often wonder how one can go on living feeling as ill & done in as I do. And I sometimes wonder if anything really bad is the matter. I never seem to be out of pain of some kind.'

If Ladye found eternal devotion by dying, then so would Una. She too saw floating caterpillars as well as sparks of light. 'Heart attacks', colitis, cystitis, headaches, were all recorded along with the gusts of wind, the bumps and bangs that were communications from Ladye. Looniness cocooned their lives. Una felt 'so dematerialised' she could neither speak nor eat her lunch. She was five foot five but weighed seven stone. The 'puffs of air' she felt on her hands called for appraisal by Crichton-Miller. She complained of feeling 'odd & restless & uneasy as if someone were trying to get at me'.

She and John began to communicate telepathically, had identical thoughts about the canary, stoked the fire when the other was about to do it. Una hummed the tune that was in John's mind. Andrea, on a rare visit from boarding school and foster care, caught their mood. She told her mother she 'had seen Our Lord Our God sitting on her pillow in the night'. John chain-smoked Dunhill cigarettes and in the drawing-room at Cadogan Court saw Ladye sitting on the sofa in a petticoat doing up a shell-pink blouse. In April 1917 she said that psychical research was the only thing that mattered to her and that her life's work was to become a medium.

11

A very grave slander

Communicating with Ladye had its dull side. She was fixed up in the ultimate Grand Hotel, was well and loved John more than ever, but the relationship lacked life. Sessions with Gladys Leonard took a different tack.

Radclyffe Hall hoped to publish her research in the journal of the Society for Psychical Research. The Society required 'evidential proof' of the existence of the dead. Its members needed to show that they had subjected their hypotheses to empirical tests.

For Radclyffe Hall, the emphasis shifted from grief about Ladye to documenting what she was up to. Daily life revealed her. Her ubiquity took her onto the bookshelves and the ceiling, up the drainpipe, into the tea leaves and the shifting glass. As an earthling, Ladye had loved idleness – hours in bed with milky drinks, hot water bottles and a book. Now she was everywhere. Sortilege evoked her. Una saw her in a large, luminous patch in the shape of a Zulu shield hovering over John's bed. Both heard her scrabbling in the cupboard. She moved cushions in the night. John talked of the 'three of them', a trinity of paranormal interaction.

Their curiosity about Ladye tested Mrs Leonard's ingenuity. In session after session they scrutinized the significance of places beginning with P or people beginning with S, jewellery of a certain colour, random words or phrases, any of which might indicate past or present familiarity with some person or place known to Ladye. The quest was on a par with George Batten's obsession with acrostics which Ladye had so deplored. It was not, historically speaking, the way she had liked to pass her time.

Feda engaged them in 'book tests' to show Ladye's all-pervading powers. Near the top of page 152 of the nineteenth book on the left on a shelf at the height of Una's skirt pocket John would find a message from Ladye. She was led to *Orval*, given to Mabel Batten by its author Owen Meredith. 'Almost though not quite at the top of the page' were the words 'today, tomorrow, yesterday, forever'. Equally successful, supernaturally speaking, was Feda's directive to two-thirds down page 108 of the sixth book from the window on the shelf at the height of John's knee. It was *The Old Curiosity Shop* and John found 'talked of their meeting in another world as if he were dead but yesterday'.

Most of it was hopeless. In Una's flat the twenty-eighth page of the twelfth book from the left, on the shelf level with the window ledge, in the room with the longest shelves, was *Naval Tracts of Sir William Monson volume 2, Navy Records Society, 1902*. All its pages were uncut and the text too tedious to pursue. And the assurance that they would find a message to do with golf on page thirty-six of *The Science of Peace*, which dealt entirely with the sins of Germany in provoking the First War, was perhaps more the fault of Troubridge's reading matter than Mrs Leonard's clairvoyant skills.

In page after page of John's recorded notes, twenty-four archive volumes, she struggled to make correlations that taxed her intelligence and hopes. It was a relief when she was led to *Spirit Intercourse* by H. MacKenzie and there on the title page were the words, 'There is no chance and no anarchy in the universe. All is system and gradation. Every god is there sitting in his sphere.' A relief too when on page thirteen of *First Steps to Nursing: A Manual for Would Be Probationers* she found the lines: 'Even without training this woman is a boon and blessing to her suffering friends in an emergency' – evidence that she had saved Ladye's life in that Oxford car crash.

This quest for Ladye was a full-time occupation. It meant that Una was always with John. She did not claim the central place in her affections; it was enough to have all her time. Once she was foolish enough to be scathing about Ladye's appearance in a photograph on John's desk. Wrath followed and her tears. She did not do it again.

Sir Oliver Lodge invited them in January 1917 to stay at his house in Birmingham. In the evening they sat round an oval table with linked hands. The spirits rapped, the table tilted and the wine glass swirled. John had a nosebleed and went to bed. Lady Lodge grew tired. Alone with Una, Sir Oliver dazzled her with psychical phenomena until one in the morning. 'So *very* interesting & a great & adorable man.'

These psychical pursuits clashed with the doctrine of the Catholic Church. Radclyffe Hall became a bane to priests. Convinced of her own closeness to God, she tested them with Feda, plane three and lesbian love. The Father Confessor at Brompton Oratory was a 'veritable torment' to her. The 'prospect of a break with the church preyed on her mind'. Father Warwick refused to allow a memorial tablet to Mabel Batten on the wall of his church at Malvern Wells. Una went from priest to priest, hoping to find a sympathetic confessor. She called it 'an errand of mercy rewarded by complete failure'. Then Father Thurston, recommended by Oliver Lodge, told Radclyffe Hall that if she kept an open mind about alleged phenomena she was doing no evil. She replied that 'as an educated woman and serious investigator' she would not 'submit herself any longer to tirades on the subject in the confessional'.

Nor could Ladye's daughter Cara accept her mother's posthumous preoccupation with John. Mabel was not tapping on her wardrobe, sitting on her sofa or comforting her in the night. Jealous, she went to see Mrs Leonard. She said that she and her mother had been like sisters whom Radclyffe Hall was now doing all in her power to divide. She asked for sittings with Feda.

Her request was a problem. Gladys Leonard profited from Radclyffe Hall at a guinea a go, plus extras of jewellery, clothes, accommodation expenses and paid holidays. She did not want to lose her most lucrative client. She gave Cara a single session. Deaf and with an ear trumpet, Cara shouted questions about her mother at Feda. Feda writhed and in a tortured voice complained she could make no contact with Ladye. She got through to George Batten instead, who told his daughter to go to a different medium.

Cara felt insulted and fobbed off. Her son Peter had been wounded in France and she was sure her mother would want to console her. She wrote to Una, asking her to use 'tact and good help' against the monopolizing by John of her mother's ghostly time. When that failed she wrote 'disagreeable' letters. She was 'outrageously rude' and there were 'painful scenes'. She made swipes about Crichton-Miller's patients being lunatics, said she had taken a 'spirit photograph' of her mother which she would not let them see and was disparaging about their research endeavours. An attack on Mrs Leonard's 'necromantic practices' appeared in the *Daily Mail*. Someone had tipped the editor off and he sent journalists for a sitting at Maida Vale.

There was gossip and acrimony. Dolly Clarke sided with Cara. She disliked the way Una monopolized John and chased everyone else away. Una called Dolly crude, her hands coarse and her baby immensely fat. And she encouraged John to stop her allowance. Phoebe Hoare sided with Dolly and when Una and John called on her in May 1917, would not see them. She sent an 'insolent' letter, went on holiday with Dolly and spread it about that Una neglected Andrea.

And there was Troubridge. On his summer leave John and Una told him about their commitment to each other through their shared work of psychical research. Afterwards Una felt tired and sick, 'now it was all over'. They had arranged to meet him for lunch at the Savoy next day but he did not show up. They took Andrea to Southbourne for a seaside holiday while he stayed in London. John again told Una she loved her very much.

Troubridge left for Greece on 26 August 1917 with few residual hopes for his marriage. He had disliked Una's interest in singing and sculpture because it took her attention from himself and his children. Now she was in a lesbian relationship with a woman she called John and spent all her time communicating with her dead cousin who had been this woman's lover. It was an outrage and he thought she had gone mad.

Radclyffe Hall's money made it possible for Una to leave him. Troubridge acknowledged that her 'means were very much larger than his own'. In November Una rented a furnished house, Grimston, in Datchet near Windsor. It was in her name though John paid most of the expenses. She told Troubridge it was away from London air raids and safe for Andrea. She did not explain that she lived there with John, that Andrea was fostered out to Ida Temple, a local dog breeder, and that Mrs Leonard had a bungalow nearby.

'Unpleasant letter from T as usual', Una noted in her diary in January 1918. 'Owing to this interest, you have completely dropped your relations and mine', he wrote. 'This interest' was more Radclyffe Hall than psychical research. He knew from his sisters and from Viola and Minna that Una's true passion was not for Mabel Batten's bumps and gusts. He thought Radclyffe Hall was immoral and had lured Una from him and Andrea.

Una did not care what any of them thought. 'Their offence to me was destructive', she wrote of them all. 'They did their utmost to diminish my beloved.' Shared life with John became increasingly hermetic. Socially Ladye had been easy and reparative, Una was sharp and divisive. Nor did Grimston suit John. It was small and she was disturbed by noise. Una had to make the breakfast. There was no space for servants or a live-in cook. And John disliked Andrea staying and the untidiness of her toys. Sometimes she made generous gestures – she bought her a bicycle – but she had no affection for her.

'I've married Ladye and I've married you', John said equivocally to Una in January 1918. They fought more than newly-weds ought. After one bout John had to 'resort to a Ponds compress' and Una bruised her back. Next evening Una read aloud all Ladye's 1916 diary, 'a sad occupation and painful', she said.

They submitted their joint research paper 'On a series of sittings with Mrs Osborne Leonard' to the council of the Society for Psychical Research. The secretary, Isabel Newton, called them 'investigators of whom the Society expects great things'. Radclyffe Hall was asked to read it at a Society meeting. It was over two hundred pages. She read the first part on 31 January 1918 at the Society's rooms in Hanover Square. Gerald Balfour was in the chair. The audience learned how MRH (Marguerite Radclyffe Hall) and UVT (Una Vincenzo Troubridge) had gone anonymously to a medium Mrs Osborne Leonard, how Mrs Leonard went into a trance, her normal voice thrust aside by Feda her Control, herself possessed by an 'Ostensible Communicator from the other side' whose resemblance to MRH's dear friend MVA (Mabel Veronica Batten – the A was to protect her identity) was unmistakeable. Radclyffe Hall told them how Feda described MVA's clothes, hair-do and voice, the houses she and MRH had lived in together, their holidays in Tenerife, the car accident at Oxford, their thermal baths and poetry, the domestic minutiae of their shared lives. She then gave a description of MVA's living arrangements on plane three and evidence of her continued communication with MRH and UVT through raps, book tests, lights on the wardrobe and worse.

After the reading one council member, St John Lane Fox-Pitt of South Eaton Place, pioneer of incandescent lamps for municipal street lighting, left the room in disgust. Apart from him, it was all highly commended. Balfour said Una was the finest recorder he had ever known. For the second half of the paper to be read on Friday 22 March, the Society rented the Steinway Hall and invited the public.

John rehearsed for it with Una. On the day, they breakfasted in bed together, got the ten-fifty train to London, did book tests, then dressed for the lecture at four-thirty. Sir Oliver Lodge was in the chair. Mrs Visetti, Una's mother, Cara, her daughter Honey and Dolly Clarke were in the audience.

John read beautifully, Una said. Isabel Newton called it a flawless paper. It was to be published in the Society's journal and John was nominated for election to the council. Well pleased, she and Una took the train home to Datchet and in the evening cycled to Old Windsor in divine weather on the Sparkbrook bicycles John had bought.

But not all those who heard the paper thought it flawless. Quite a few knew the drama of sex, guilt and jealousy that underpinned it, bleached though it was into pseudo-science. 'Outrageous gossip' was not easily pushed aside. Radclyffe Hall was telling the world about herself and her life with Mabel Batten and Una Troubridge. The mausoleum at Highgate, the pews, plaques and inscribed roods in churches and now this monolithic effort at resurrection testified publicly to the same thing – an outspoken declaration of lesbian love.

In June, Cara complained to Helen Salter at the Society. She said the paper was a pack of lies. Radclyffe Hall was separating her from her mother. Una had abandoned her husband and child and was mentally unbalanced, which was why she was treated by Crichton-Miller. Mabel Batten had resented Una. Quarrelling about her with Radclyffe Hall had precipitated her stroke. Cara wrote an 'infamous letter' to John, who in turn wrote to Oliver Lodge:

> Mrs Salter now has the matter in hand and we believe intends to inform Mrs Harris that she must either put her accusations in black and white and affix her signature thereunto, or else withdraw them, also in black and white, in toto. If she does the former, the matter will be dealt with by our solicitor as it will constitute a very grave slander, but we both pray that she will not compel us to such steps. I can never forget who she is, and Una feels as I do. On several occasions relations of Mrs Harris's have told us that we had no right to encourage her to take an interest in Psychical Research as they considered her unbalanced to the extent of

being mentally deranged … I think her lack of balance and excitability are perhaps the kindest and truest explanation of what she has done … To have to admit such things about the daughter of the most wonderful friend a woman ever had is painful beyond all words.

It was not so painful as to stop Radclyffe Hall making such admissions or from threatening legal action. Cara did not put anything in black, white or in toto, but nor did she withdraw her accusations. Mabel Batten had, in her will, asked them to stay friends. Their loathing for each other lasted a lifetime.

The war ended in November 1918. John looked for a large house for herself and Una. In January 1919 she bought Chip Chase in Hadley Wood, Middlesex, a mock castle, quite outside the financial reach of Troubridge. She arranged for builders to refurbish it. As a gift for Mrs Leonard, she bought Hampworth Cottage at Oakleigh Park nearby. She wanted her medium available for daily sittings.

Troubridge, who had been promoted to 'full Admiral with seniority', arrived that month unannounced at the Datchet house. There was 'an unpleasant scene'. Una refused to see him except in John's presence. They told him of Chip Chase and their plans to live together. He threatened legal action and accused John of having wrecked his home.

Una saw Alfred Sachs, Crichton-Miller and on three consecutive days Mr Hastie, John's solicitor. She provided medical evidence that Troubridge had infected her with syphilis and that as a consequence she suffered neurasthenia for which she needed psychiatric help. Hastie 'thought he could settle things'. He prepared a deed of separation which gave Una custody of Andrea. Troubridge signed this on 8 February. Radclyffe Hall thought he did so 'in the full understanding that should he refuse, the scandal would be made public and Una would sue publicly for a judicial separation'.

Troubridge had received enough adverse publicity. He had no desire for any more of his life to be made public. Nor could he afford litigation. But that same day he made a new will with a clause about Andrea:

In the event of my wife Una Vincenzo Troubridge formerly known as Margot Elena Gertrude Troubridge predeceasing me I appoint my sisters Laura Hope and Violet Gurney to be the guardians of my infant daughter Andrea Theodosia Troubridge during such period or periods as I shall be on foreign service and I direct that my said daughter shall under no circumstances be left under the guardianship or care of Marguerite Radclyffe-Hall.

He hated Radclyffe Hall and thought her influence pernicious. Enraged and humiliated, he intended revenge. But he did not know what to do about Andrea. He could not provide her with a home, but he would sooner she was on the streets than with her. Una countersigned the deed of separation on 10 February. She talked to her mother and sister about it and 'explained' matters to Andrea. 'Great peace and relief upon me', she wrote. 'Deo Gratis.'

Troubridge made another angry move. On Una's birthday, 8 March, a letter arrived that he was now seeking custody of Andrea. John took Una to her own solicitor in Holborn, Sir George Lewis, head of the firm Lewis & Lewis. He told them 'the deed signed by the Admiral was binding'. 'He could not take the child, and his letter was a mere subterfuge written with a view to intimidating Una into making certain statements to his advantage.'

Una made no statements to Troubridge's advantage. She did not see him again. In April she moved with John into Chip Chase. Troubridge agreed to pay maintenance for Andrea who was eight. She was sent to a convent boarding school in Sussex, seventy miles away. Called May-field, the convent was run by nuns who inspired her with a dislike of the Catholic Church. John paid her fees.

Una's legacy of venereal disease depressed her. A succession of doctors failed to cure her. Dr May treated her by some kind of painting of the vaginal wall. He told her she 'would always be sensitive', but three years' extreme care might make her 'relatively sound'. 'I think it so damnably hard on John and an uphill lookout!' Una wrote. Cystitis and discharges figured more in her diary than the joys of desire. Dr Hathaway tried 'electrical treatment'. Alfred Sachs gave her daily injections and vaccines and was forever taking swabs. It all reduced her to tears. 'Oh John is good to me', she wrote in May 1919. 'Where would I be in this terrible trouble without her devotion and friend-ship?'

She resumed hypnosis with Crichton-Miller – once a week on a Monday. These sessions, the seances with Mrs Leonard, endless book tests, evidential proof of Ladye, venereal disease and the stress of separating from Troubridge took its toll. She became phobic and felt unreal. Crichton-Miller wanted her to have psychoanalysis as an in-patient at Bowden House.

John took her there by car at the end of May. Miller asked John not to visit for three weeks and to send only postcards not letters. John told Una she would communicate telepathically. She was writing a paper on this for the Society. And Ladye, she said, would knock on the clinic walls or shine lights in the night.

John disliked Una being controlled by a regime other than her own. Adrift without her, she walked the dogs in the moonlight and 'longed for Squig to see it'. She wrote Squig's diary entries, went alone to Mrs Leonard and suffered the separation. Una had become essential to her and her dependence was acute. Without her the paranormal lost its fascination. She sent peaches, carnations and roses. Una longed to be home. She called her routine 'damned dull' and said Miller 'took loonies' at Bowden House.

While Una was there her mother, Minna, rang John to say Troubridge had been knighted and Una was now 'a Lady'. 'Troubridge has had K added to his threadbare CMG', John wrote in Una's diary on 3 June. Una called it 'a bore' and affected not to care. But she readily dropped her more than threadbare Mrs, embellished the title and assiduously thereafter called herself Una, Lady Troubridge. Servants addressed her as such and it was printed on her visiting cards. She pulled rank though the honour came from a man she despised and whom she had left. If Mabel Batten was a spoof Ladye, she was the real thing. John, too, let the world know that she was partner to Lady Troubridge. It made her more of a Lord.

Una stayed three weeks at Bowden House. On the evening of 20 June she made a scene and demanded to see Miller. He went to her room at half past ten. She told him she had had enough and was leaving in the morning. He was emphatic that she should stay. He told her she needed intensive analysis. 'He went at 11.30 very angry. So was I, but I concealed it which he did not.'

She was up at five-thirty next day 'wildly excited' about getting away. John arrived mid-morning. Una said goodbye to Crichton-Miller. He had, she said, 'recovered *outward* control'. It was the end of the relationship. She did not want such insights as he perhaps might have helped her to find. He, like most of the living inhabitants of their former lives, was discarded. A wrangle over money marked the end of it. John and Una accused him of overcharging on his final account. 'It is my misfortune and not my fault,' he wrote, 'that I have to justify my existence and provide for a wife and family on a time-basis. As I am not a surgeon who gets £1000 for an hour's anatomical dissection, but only a person who tries to talk people well, my time has to be charged for, more or less ... Suppose we split the thing and call it 12 guineas ...'

At Chip Chase Una found everything divine. 'Almost too good to be true that I'm home', she wrote in her diary on 22 June. She did not want again to be parted from John, even for a day. Like Feda from the spirit world with 'ostensible possession', John was the air she breathed and where she lived.

12

A grossly immoral woman

Tongues wagged in the West End men's clubs, the Travellers, the Beefsteak, the Garrick, where the armchairs were large and leather and the whisky flowed. News spread that Radclyffe Hall was a lesbian, a seducer of wives and addicted to sorcery.

Troubridge was in town in January 1920. St John Lane Fox-Pitt told him of the paper Radclyffe Hall had read to the Society for Psychical Research. Troubridge let him know how she had wrecked his private life, broken his home and seduced his wife, who had mental problems because of it all. Lady Troubridge said that 'this spirit business was now her life' and she no longer had concern for him or his occupation. Mabel Batten had been immoral too. She had given favours to numerous men before being lured from her husband by this lesbian.

Radclyffe Hall was recommended for membership of the Society's council. Mrs Eleanor Sidgwick, Balfour's sister, proposed her and a circular gave notice that her election would be on 20 January 1920. Fox-Pitt saw opportunity for reprisal. Troubridge had confirmed his suspicions. Radclyffe Hall was a pervert, a threat to decency and the Society's name. He went to Isabel Newton, the Secretary, and declared:

Miss Radclyffe Hall is a grossly immoral woman. Admiral Sir Ernest Troubridge has recently been home on leave, and has, in my presence, made very serious accusations against her. He said she had wrecked his home. She ought not to be co-opted as a member of the council. I did not like to be hostile to her at first, but my own feelings about her have been confirmed by what Sir Ernest Troubridge told me.

Miss Newton thought his accusations 'risky'. She asked in what way Admiral Troubridge regarded Radclyffe Hall as a 'grossly immoral woman'. 'In every way', Fox-Pitt replied. For one thing, she had lived with the MVA of her paper, who was herself immoral. He said he would oppose this election by all means in his power.

He went to Helen Salter, editor of the Society's journal, and complained to her too:

Miss Radclyffe Hall is a thoroughly immoral woman. She lived for many years with the woman mentioned in the paper which she and Lady Troubridge wrote, a woman who was a most objectionable person. Miss Radclyffe Hall has got a great influence over Lady Troubridge and has come between her and her husband and wrecked the Admiral's home. I am quite determined to oppose her election to the council. If I cannot persuade Mrs Sidgwick to withdraw her proposal of Miss Radclyffe Hall for the council I intend to bring the matter before the council myself and put it strongly so as to carry my point, as she is quite an unfit person to be on the council.

Mrs Salter also asked whether 'immoral' was a dangerous word to use. Fox-Pitt fidgeted then said, 'Admiral Troubridge is not at all afraid of anything, and would be quite willing to make this statement publicly. He would not mind it all coming out. He has faced a Court martial at his own request.'

Radclyffe Hall was summoned and told of Fox-Pitt's words. They were catalytic. Here, demeaned, was her life. She acted with a forcefulness thought to be the prerogative of admirals and lords. She demanded that he withdraw his accusations. He refused. Like others after him, he underestimated her. She said her honour and Mabel Batten's were impugned and she gave the eighteenth-century equivalent of a challenge to a duel. She saw her solicitor, Sir George Lewis, and took out a slander action.

Fox-Pitt and Troubridge went into a tizz. Money gave Radclyffe Hall power to use the law and they knew it. She challenged them to make their accusations public and to justify their prejudice. She had no fear of the court's judgement or publicity from such a case. Had the price been crucifixion or public pillory she would have paid it. She was

not going to be embarrassed into silence. She was a homophobe's
nightmare: dykish, rich, unyielding, outspoken, successful with women
and caring not at all for the small vanities of men. Mabel Batten would
have been placatory, smoothed feathers and soothed tempers. Radclyffe
Hall wanted justice, honour and scruple to resound.

It took six months for the case to come to court. It was heard in the
King's Bench division before the Lord Chief Justice – the Rt Hon. Rufus
Daniel Isaacs – and a special jury. It began at noon on 18 November
and finished at seven-thirty the following evening. Una bought a special
hat for the occasion, a thing with an enormous bow. Radclyffe Hall
wore a discreet cloche and rouched skirt. The public gallery was full,
the press eager.

The story made the front page in most of the papers. 'Society women
and the Spooks' in the *Daily Sketch*; 'Spirit Slander Suit' in the *Daily
Mirror*; 'Lord Chief and the Spiritualist' in the *Evening Standard*. *The
Times* ran twelve columns on it. The photographs told the true story:
Troubridge (though he was not in court) in Admiral's uniform; Fox-
Pitt in top hat and tails; Radclyffe Hall in mannish jacket; Una, the
erstwhile admiral's wife, now with bobbed hair and monocle. The
unethereal eye could see that here were mortal passions: unconventional infidelity, jealousy, prejudice and pride.

Radclyffe Hall's counsel was Sir Ellis Hume-Williams, barrister and
Unionist MP. Fox-Pitt he said had made

> as horrible an accusation as could be made against any woman in this
> country. The words used by the defendant could only mean that the
> plaintiff was an unchaste and immoral woman who was addicted to
> unnatural vice and was consequently unfit to be a member of the council
> of the Society for Psychical Research.

It was hard to find a law to apply to sexual immorality between
women. Homosexual men were criminalized for 'acts of gross
indecency'. But there was nothing on the statutes for lesbians, gross or
decent. Men made the laws for their own convenience. The Lord Chief
Justice said he was unsure whether the word 'immoral' in this case
came within the meaning of 'unchastity' in the Slander of Women Act.
The word unchastity came next to adultery and it might be that both
referred only to immorality between the sexes. His advice to the jury
was that they must satisfy themselves that the defendant had used the

words complained of, and that they were defamatory either as imputing immorality generally, or as imputing 'unnatural offences'. If Fox-Pitt had used such words, he had to prove them to be true, otherwise damages should be awarded to the plaintiff.

'All trials are trials for one's life', said Oscar Wilde. This one ought to have proved historic. It might have been about consensual sex between women and with what moral tenets this should comply. Radclyffe Hall had a litigious mind. She claimed the high moral ground. She wished to defend her right to love Mabel Batten and Una Troubridge. But both her lovers had husbands. And she had loved them both at the same time.

The case that emerged in court was a mess. Subpoenaed for cross-examination by Sir George Lewis, Troubridge wrote denying that he had ever made any allegations about Radclyffe Hall. Whatever Fox-Pitt said, Troubridge *did* 'mind it all coming out'. He was now an admiral and a knight. He had endured humiliation and the downgrading of his career over the escape of the *Goeben*. He did not want a part in a court drama of revelations about his wife's lesbianism, syphilis and spiritualism.

Sir John Fox-Pitt wriggled, equivocated and lied. He conducted – discursively – his own defence without witnesses or corroborating evidence. Had he sought it, wise counsel might have advised him to settle out of court. But he was son-in-law of the ninth Marquess of Queensberry, who had ruined Oscar Wilde. (Fox-Pitt married Queensberry's daughter, Edith, in 1898.) There was family pride in victory over subverters of morality. But he was not adept at using the law. He had previously lost a lengthy suit about the patent of his invention of an incandescent lamp for street lighting. Nor had he much common sense.

Had Fox-Pitt proved gross immorality against Radclyffe Hall for unnatural offences and unchastity with a spirit on plane three and an admiral's wife, he might have added richness to the picture of women's lives. In court he denied the words attributed to him and he denied slander. He claimed he had used the word immoral in a special sense. What he said he meant by immoral was that Radclyffe Hall's paper was scientific rubbish, unworthy of the Society for Psychical Research and that its publication was harmful. Her paper, he said, produced a condition of mind which he considered immoral. He had not meant in any way to infer that her character was immoral.

It was all bluff, bluster and backtrack. If 'grossly immoral' meant authoring twaddle, then few at the Society would escape the dock. The Lord Chief Justice struggled to keep his semantic grasp:

> You say that you used the word immoral only in relation to her work in the society ... You deny that you used the language complained of as implying unnatural vice, unchastity, or sexual immorality. The plaintiff contends that you meant that. Whether you have used language calculated to imply it is a matter for the jury.

Cross-examining Radclyffe Hall, Fox-Pitt dithered and obfuscated. He read out passages from her paper about Mabel on plane three, spirit horses and vibratory houses. He asked her whether Lady Troubridge had been under medical treatment for hysterical phobias and obsessions because of her 'spirit experiences'. Radclyffe Hall denied it. Neurasthenia, she said, had a different cause.

Fox-Pitt: What did you pay the medium?
RH.   A guinea a session
Fox-Pitt: What was the medium called?
RH: Feda.
The Lord Chief Justice: What is Feda?
RH: When a woman goes into a trance she has a different and complex personality. I cannot say what Feda is.
The Lord Chief Justice: Then Feda is Mrs Osborne Leonard in a trance?
RH: Yes.
Fox-Pitt: You consider the paper evidential?
RH: Yes.
Fox-Pitt: It gives evidence of a spirit world?
RH: It purports to do so.
Fox-Pitt: On page 355 there is continual reference to a spirit lady and Feda says: 'She's got a nice complexion, very nice. It isn't a bit wrinkled, it's very smooth. Before she passed on, her cheeks fell in a little bit.' It says the lady's complexion has improved.
RH: Those are Feda's words.
Fox-Pitt: I learn too that MVA has learned to ride a horse.
The Lord Chief Justice: I am groping at present. What is, or was, MVA?
RH: It purports to be a communication from a person after her death.
Fox-Pitt: Then Feda says MVA is so glad there are animals in the spirit world. She used to be afraid of horses but is not now.

RH: I cannot tell you that.

Fox-Pitt: Look at page 452. There are various quotations about a spirit having a bath.

The Lord Chief Justice: How does a spirit bathe? I see later on that the lady has a private bathing pool in the spirit world. You must bear in mind that hearsay evidence is not admissible. (Laughter).

Fox-Pitt: (to his Lordship) This is senseless stuff which many people who read it will think is the product of scientific minds. It is pure rubbish and only gives evidence of incipient dementia.

The Lord Chief Justice: (with astonishment) But you allege against the plaintiff unchastity and sexual immorality.

Fox-Pitt then wanted to refer to a dictionary to support his revised definition of the word immoral.

The Lord Chief Justice: You do not mean by the word 'immoral' anything sexual?

Fox-Pitt: No my lord and I will call evidence to prove it.

The Lord Chief Justice: You are not suggesting that the relationship between the plaintiff and Lady Troubridge led to the separation between the Admiral and his wife?

Fox-Pitt: Who suggested it?

The Lord Chief Justice: Not a spirit in the other world.

Miss Salter told the court that no one on the Society's Committee who read and passed Radclyffe Hall's and Lady Troubridge's paper thought it immoral, subversive or improper. She said she had understood Fox-Pitt's accusations to refer to 'some perversion' between the plaintiff and MVA. Cross-examined by him, she admitted she did not know that in the New English Dictionary, where many columns defined 'moral' and 'immoral', there was no reference to sexual relationship.

Una, when questioned by Fox-Pitt, tried to pull rank and quash any lesbian implications. She appealed to the judge about Mabel:

Una: If his Lordship would allow me I should like to say that in life she occupied a high social position and lived in perfect amity with her husband.

The Lord Chief Justice: How does this affect the case?

Sir E. Hume-Williams: There is an allegation made by the defendant that she was a person of low and immoral character.

The Lord Chief Justice: Her high position in society would be no answer
to the charge that has been made.

Gerald Balfour, cross-examined by Fox-Pitt, was asked if he 'accepted
the meaning of the spirit hypothesis of a discarnate entity'. Balfour
asked the Lord Chief Justice if he had to give his views. His Lordship
replied that were he and the jury kept there ever so many days, they
would not understand what he was talking about. He said he wanted
to hurry matters along because not everyone had for ever to live.

Cross-examined by Sir Ellis Hume-Williams, Fox-Pitt cracked. He
garbled about a conspiracy against him to oust him from the Society.
A conspiracy, he said was 'a breathing together so that lies came out
of their mouths'. He called this the 'junta'. The Lord Chief Justice, a
larky man, enjoyed the nonsense of it, but there was no way he could
focus Fox-Pitt's mind. He brought the case to a conclusion. The jury
was confused. It found that Fox-Pitt had used the words 'grossly
immoral', but thought that he had meant them to apply to Radclyffe
Hall's psychical research paper and not to 'unnatural vice, unchastity,
or sexual immorality'. She was awarded £500 damages with costs.

'Home to a much relieved and happy evening', Una wrote in her
diary. Next day was Saturday and they stayed in bed late together and
read the massive newspaper coverage of the case in *The Times*, the *Daily
Sketch*, the *Daily Mirror*. 'Wealthy spiritualist wins £500 damages in
Slander Suit'; 'Feda and MVA Lady Troubridge's Dead Cousin'; 'Lord
Chief Puzzled'; 'Laughter in Court'; 'Strange Slander Suit'; 'The Spirits
of the Dead', were some of the headlines. John and Una had tea with
the Viscttis, then went on to dinner with Gabrielle Enthoven and
'Brother' – Toupie Lowther. Una said she thought Toupie was a her-
maphrodite. They played the gramophone and John and Brother
danced.

Fox-Pitt did not pay the £500. Radclyffe Hall had cleared her name
in court, but at a price. Publicity was wide but cheap and sardonic.
The press enjoyed the joke of it all, the sexual innuendo, the frolics of
lesbians, the antics of the upper classes with time on their hands. They
did not address Radclyffe Hall's courage in bringing the slander suit,
or any wider issues of sexual politics. The Lord Chief Justice had tried
to steer the court toward some sort of analysis of sexual morality. Fox-
Pitt would have none of it, though his views were clear.

He appealed against the verdict and a retrial was ordered. Sir George

Lewis advised Radclyffe Hall to let things rest. 'It was futile spending so much money and enduring more odious publicity when Fox-Pitt would never pay a penny.' After several adjournments and the passing of time, the case withered away.

Society now knew that Radclyffe Hall was a lesbian. In the mind of the establishment she stood convicted of sexual immorality, gross indecency, unchastity and the rest. Fox-Pitt and Troubridge were two more of the enemies she had made. They were the kind of enemy that lies in wait. She had more than tweaked the tiger's tail. Within months a Conservative MP, Frederick Macquister, proposed that a clause 'Acts of Gross Indecency by Females' be added to the Criminal Law Amendment Act which so sensationally indicted Oscar Wilde. Macquister thought that female morals were declining and that lesbianism threatened the birth rate. His clause was passed by the House of Commons then debated in the House of Lords. Lord Birkenhead warned: 'You are going to tell the whole world there is such an offence, to bring it to the notice of women who have never heard of it, never dreamed of it. I think this is a very great mischief.' The insult of silence on the matter was thought best. Existing laws could be tailored in order to indict.

After the trial, John was ill for a fortnight. Though she liked to appear invincible, she coped badly with stress. Phoebe Hoare wrote that her husband Oliver now forbade her to have anything to do with John. John stayed in bed with Una, who read aloud *Ben Hur, Treasure Island* and *Jekyll and Hyde*. On 17 December Una cropped her beloved's golden hair and made her more of a man. Ladye had liked the softer look, but Ladye had had her day. Christmas brought 'evidential proof' of John's commitment to Una. She said Una could be buried on one of the shelves in the Highgate mausoleum alongside herself and Ladye. 'I feel I can never be *really* unhappy again', Una wrote in her diary. She went to mass and thanked God that such love and a roof over her head were infinitely assured.

RADCLYFFE HALL

13

Octopi

Chip Chase, large, castellated, with turrets and mock battle-ments, was a snook cocked at Troubridge. Una's daily diary entries began 'John and I', the order of merit as understood by both. 'Were we comfortable!' she wrote. Comfort mattered greatly to them. It coloured their vision of paradise. Within months they created what seemed a settled home. They had a maid, a cook, three house servants, two gardeners and a full-time secretary. The antique oak furniture was polished daily with beeswax and turpentine, there were flowers in all the rooms in thick glass vases, log fires burned.

Servants came and went with terrible rapidity. A bilious attack or a burned pudding and they were out within the hour. As one secretary put it, 'Miss Hall had a fiendish temper which was exacerbated by Lady Troubridge, everyone except Lady Troubridge it seemed being in the wrong.' Both had a sharp eye for specks of dust on the Cromwellian clock or the Dole cupboard and a sharp tongue for the housemaid. Tradespeople had to meet exacting standards too. 'It behoved everyone to keep in with the couple as they were good customers and generous!'

John and Una's bedrooms interconnected. They got into each other's beds for reading aloud at night, morning breakfast and the rest, but they slept alone. 'Why in the name of wonder should anyone in any conceivable circumstances wish for a bedfellow', Una wrote. 'Nothing has ever led me to believe that comfortable repose can really be achieved with one's head pillowed upon another's breast or with someone else's head riding upon one's bosom.' And John said that not since she was twenty had she 'wanted to spend a whole night of sleep with a woman'.

Her study was on the ground floor. French windows led to the garden. Files and books, meticulously ordered, lined the walls. She worked at an oak refectory table, on which was a globe of the world, a silver mounted horse's hoof and her seal 'La Verité Me Guide'. In a corner was a shrine to Ladye of a candlelit madonna and burning incense. On the wall was a large crucifix, and a fox's head on an oak shield. By the woodburning fire was John's leather smoking chair and antique pipe rack.

In this cloistered, club lounge setting she started a novel: 'Writing, it was like a heavenly balm, it was like the flowing out of deep waters, it was like the lifting of a load from the spirit, it brought with it a sense of relief, of assuagement.' Its unfortunate title was *Octopi*, its theme a lesbian daughter, denied life by a manipulative mother.

A perception of Mother the Tentacled Monster was rooted in Radclyffe Hall's psyche. Mrs Visetti was the archetype, but cameos glimpsed the world over confirmed the prejudice: the daughter of a clergyman's wife 'withering on the stem' in the Grand Hotel, Tamaris, an elderly daughter fussing over her invalid mother in the Cottage Hotel in Lynton in Devon. Radclyffe Hall construed these relationships as 'unmarried daughters who are unpaid servants and the old people sucking the life out of them like octopi'.

Mrs Ogden, chief octopus in her novel, uses tentacles of sickness and loneliness to bind Joan her daughter to her. She uses too tentacles of sexual possession, for her husband disgusts her. 'Joan's strong young arms would comfort and soothe and her firm lips grope until they found her mother's; and Mrs Ogden would feel mean and ashamed but guiltily happy as if a lover held her.'

The Ogdens live in a stifling house in Seabourne, a one-horse town. Their lives are circumscribed by lack of money, fear of sex and fear of life. Elizabeth Rodney, hired to teach Joan, is a 'new woman', educated and independent, like the Modern Miss Thompson of Radclyffe Hall's unpublished suffragette story. She and Joan fall in love and want to live together, Joan as a doctor, Elizabeth as a teacher. Mrs Ogden's tentacles slither round them. Do you love me, she asks her daughter, who wants to reply, 'I don't love you, I don't want to touch you, I dislike the feel of you – I dislike above all else the *feel* of you.'

Elizabeth waits. Each time Joan is at the point of breaking free, mother strikes. 'I think it is a sin to let yourself get drained dry by anyone', Elizabeth says as Joan disintegrates. 'As quickly as you cut through one tentacle another shot out and fixed on to you.'

In an article written years later for an American magazine, Radclyffe Hall claimed high intentions in writing about Joan Ogden and her kind:

> They wither away for want of self expression and encouragement, because they are too refined, too sensitive, too unselfish, or too timid, or perhaps too noble, to make a stand in defence of their rights as human beings.
> ... I came to the resolution that I would try to bring their grievances out into the light of day; a difficult task, perhaps a presumptuous task, but I felt that it had to be done and that I was the person to do it ... I knew that I was throwing down the gauntlet but in a way this made the book all the easier to write, because I was fighting for others and not for myself.

She liked to remind 'her public', as she and Una came to call them, that she spoke for an underclass and was doing God's work. But the strength of the book was that it was about herself, her precarious identity, her black view of mothers, her alienation from men, her desire to find a compensatory replacement for Mrs Visetti, whom she loathed.

All the imagery in the book is of snares. Joan Ogden's feelings for her mother 'eat into her flesh'. Only with Elizabeth Rodney might she 'break once and for all the chains'. Men are no more than a narrative device. Mr Ogden cheats Joan out of her inheritance then dies to further the plot. Joan and Elizabeth are wooed by emotionally inconsequential brothers: Richard and Lawrence Benson. Elizabeth waits ten years for Joan, then marries Lawrence and goes with him to South Africa. She lives in splendour and kills her dream of life with Joan by 'being busy and hard and quite unlike her real self'. Richard waits twenty years for Joan only to hear her say:

> 'I'm not a woman who could ever have married. I've never been what you'd call in love with a man in my life ... Only one creature could ever have saved me and I let her go while I was still young.'
> 'Do you mean Elizabeth?' he asked sharply.
> She nodded. 'Yes she could have saved me but I let her go.'
> 'God!' he exclaimed angrily ...

In pencil on loose-leafed paper Radclyffe Hall produced misspelt, unpunctuated prose. Without expectations from a publisher or agent, she worked in a sporadic way. She put aside her manuscript because of dog shows, trips to London, visits from Mr Cobden the tailor to fit her brocade smoking jacket, driving lessons from Toupie Lowther in John's new car, Blue Bird.

Ladye's ghost was the main distraction. Next to John's study was an office for psychical research 'where the secretary had her habitat'. There was, said Una, 'plenty of work needing close application; reports that must be so adequate and so accurate that they did not return to us from Sir Oliver; regular sittings with Mrs Osborne Leonard; visits to and from members including a young woman liable without warning to become one of two other personalities.'

The Society, embarrassed by the spooks and lesbians court case, prevaricated about accepting Radclyffe Hall on its council. She threatened more adverse publicity unless they acted fast. They duly elected her, so Fox-Pitt resigned. She and Una then went for a 'members only' week to Fishers Hill near Woking with Gerald Balfour and Mrs Sidgwick. It was a token appearance. Radclyffe Hall found other members' psychical communications entirely dull. She was more interested in a meeting with the composer Ethel Smyth and her dog Pan on the golf links. ('I wonder why it is so much easier for me, and I believe for a great many English women, to love my own sex passionately rather than yours?' Ethel Smyth wrote to her friend Henry Brewster in 1892.) She went to tea with John and Una, then dinner.

Una invited her mother to Chip Chase. It was an invitation calculated to discomfort. Una now had a lifestyle which Minna could only envy. House guests for Una had the status of intruders. She wished to be alone with John. Jane Randolph, once wooed and conquered by Marguerite, braved their daunting exclusivity for a weekend in autumn 1920. Now Jane Caruth and widowed for a second time, she found no chink of space for herself. Una remarked with satisfaction on her heavy jowls, upholstered clothes, her 'cranky, prim and hyper-critical strictures'. Jane Caruth deplored the metamorphosis of Marguerite into John. She disliked her short hair, pipe smoking and Una. 'Great relief getting rid of Jane Caruth', Una wrote in her diary.

On holidays from the St Leonard's convent, Andrea was a bewildered guest. Troubridge wrote 'blustering and offensive' letters about Una's treatment of her. She was met from the train by Miss Maclean, the housekeeper. Her treats were visits to Ladye's mausoleum, mass at Brompton Oratory and shopping at Harrods and Gorringes. When a school report gave her conduct as 'fairly good', she was lectured and questioned before breakfast by her mother and John. The qualification had something to do with a girl called Cicely Coventry. John and Una drove to the convent to see Mother Emmanuel and Sister Theodore. Cicely was then expelled.

Una rejected Andrea because she did not please John. Pleasing John was the measure of all that was acceptable. But John wanted Una's undivided attention. Any mothering was to be for herself. She paid Andrea's school fees and provided her with a room at Chip Chase, but she had no interest in her and did not want her around. Andrea received no encouragement or affection from her, nor was she allowed to oppose her in the smallest way. As the years passed she disliked the perception of her mother as lesbian. It embarrassed her. She worried that she might herself be perceived as 'like that'. She said Toupie Lowther 'gave her the willies' because she was 'so obvious'.

Dogs took precedence over daughters. A former drawing-room at Chip Chase, panelled with wood and fitted with linoleum, became a kennels for griffons and dachshunds. Fitz-John Minnehaha was their prime griffon. His relatives were Pipe of Peace, Atthis, Hankie and Gorgo. John and Una were members of the Kennel Club. They reared and judged the best of the breed and accrued prizes and trophies. Their dogs were a quest for genetic perfection. Those with faults went elsewhere. Prudence, a spaniel, they gave away for being unaffectionate. Olaf, a Great Dane, got sores and was shot on the lawn by the vet. 'Olaf went over', Una wrote in her diary in February 1920. She assumed the whirring sounds she and John heard in the night came from his journey to the spheres.

Theirs was one of the most successful kennels in the country according to an article in the *Queen* titled 'The Fitz-John Dachshunds: The Kennels of Una Lady Troubridge and Miss Radclyffe Hall'. It pictured them, though their names were transposed, with 'Our Dogs' Champions Brandesburton Caprice and Champions Fitz-John Wotan and Fitz-John Thorgils of Tredholt. Caprice was '*the* type breeders should aim for', said the *Queen*.

Ideas of the best of the breed informed Radclyffe Hall's political thinking too. She took the package of Conservative politics, allegiance to the ruling class, inherited status, antipathy to communists and Jews (not her 'one or two really dear Jewish friends' and her solicitor and doctor, but 'Jews as a whole'). It also affected her view of feminists and lesbians. Her friends were ones with money and creative ambition.

It was twelve miles to London. They went by car for Una's daily appointment with Alfred Sachs. They then had lunch with Toupie, tea at the Savoy, or a matinée at the Alhambra. John bought Karma, a parrot, from the Army and Navy Stores and cockatoos from Harrods. She got her pipes and cigarettes from Dunhill and had her hair cropped and waved at Truefitts of Bond Street, hairdresser for gentlemen.

Una bought their books at the Times Bookshop: *Peter Pan*, *Susan Lenox* and the 'shockers' John particularly liked. Five times Una read aloud John's favourite novel, Ford Madox Ford's *Ladies Whose Bright Eyes*. It featured a shining knight who spanned fourteenth century and modern times, spurned bourgeois comfort and extolled love and great adventure. It appealed to John who thought she remembered her own medieval incarnation. It was dedicated to Ford's lover, Violet Hunt, for whom she had once so pined.

It was a pattern for Radclyffe Hall to house herself in style, extensively refurbish, purchase antique furnishings, take on all the paraphernalia and responsibilities of domesticity – servants and pets – get the whole place just so, and then sell up. She moved on impulse then rationalized why: the journey to town was tiring, the area suburban, the house too costly to run, she wanted to be nearer to Toupie and the theatres, she needed the social exposure of London.

At root was a subversion, a restlessness. No house was ever right for long and no home was Derwent, the ancestral manor with herself as heir and squire. She wanted always to be somewhere other than where she was. If it was town it should be country, if it was Paris it should be Florence. 'The minute my house begins to "vamp" me – houses do become vampires – I run from it', she said. 'Somehow the household arrangements of a hotel don't clamour for my attention: that happens only in my own home.'

She had moved into Chip Chase in April 1919. By July 1920 she was wanting to move out. She worried about the cost of running the place and the number of meals the servants ate each day. Hadley Wood, she complained, was no place for a writer to be buried. Above all, she wanted contact with the London lesbian scene. Una, like Mabel Batten, was uprooted whether she wanted to be or not. But she said she did not mind where they went as long as they were together. To prove her point, she wrote for details of a lighthouse for sale off the Cornish coast.

A Mr and Mrs Thomas bought Chip Chase for £5,000 in January 1921. It took a week for all John and Una's belongings to be moved to Taylor's Depository in London. Servants were fired and most of the dogs were kennelled. John and Una rented temporarily a flat at 7 Trevor Square, Knightsbridge by Hyde Park, then in May they moved to 10 Sterling Street nearby.

Alfred Sachs was a walk away. He showed Una her streptococci under a microscope. 'They look rather like inverted commas', she said. His bills were high. For seven months of visits, vaccines and pathologists' reports, John paid him £380 – about as much as Troubridge's annual maintenance.

Now she was writing the novel William Heinemann had urged, Radclyffe Hall wanted a place in London literary life. Her women friends helped forge this. Toupie was a pivotal figure in the London lesbian scene of the twenties. Literary and artistic lesbians gravitated to her house and to another former friend of Mabel Batten's, Gabrielle Enthoven. She was a playwright and theatre historian and gave, according to Una, 'faultless dinner parties'.

At Toupie's salon evenings, Radclyffe Hall talked of her work to the novelists Ida Wylie, May Sinclair and Vere Hutchinson. They were popular writers of the time, independent women who led unconventional lives. Ida Wylie recommended her to the literary agent Audrey Heath, a Cambridge classics graduate who in partnership with a friend, May Drake, had set up in 1919 in an office in Soho. Ida was published by Mills & Boon and wrote novels with titles like *Towards Morning* and *The Silver Virgin*. She described herself as 'violently active in the suffrage movement'. Like Toupie she had done war work in France. When she was ten her father had given her money and encouraged her to travel on her own all over England and the Continent. He married 'from time to time', she said, but she had no connection to his wives.

May Sinclair shared John's belief in psychical phenomena. She too was a feminist and suffragette and served with an ambulance corps in Belgium in the war. She wrote a biography of the Brontës and psychological novels: *The Three Sisters, Anne Severn and the Fieldings*. Vere Hutchinson, author of *Sea Wrack, The Naked Man* and *Thy Dark Freight*, openly dedicated her novels 'with undying love' to her partner

'Budge', a painter of animal portraits, Dorothy Burroughes-Burroughes.

In St James's Park one afternoon, walking the dog, John re-met Violet Hunt. Violet came for dinner the following day, gave John several of Ford Madox Ford's novels and talked of his sexual rejection of her, the money he owed her and the social scandal he had made her endure. She took her and Una to the Orange Tree and the Cave of Harmony, clubs in Soho where lesbians danced together.

They all went to PEN Club meetings, motored to the country, played whist and tennis. At a fancy dress ball of Toupie's, John was Prince Charles Edward, Una La Bohème. Toupie's army unit was there: Joan, Liza, Hilary, Susan, Poppy, Honey, Nelly. Una deplored the way they 'carried on' sexually with each other. 'All between members of the same army unit'.

Through Toupie, John also met Romaine Brooks. She called her a 'very great artist'. Romaine was famous for her monotone portraits and sexual affairs. With money inherited from her American mother, she bought the Villa Cercola in Capri and studios and apartments in Paris, London and New York. She had been the lover of the actress Ida Rubinstein, was the partner of Natalie Barney and admired by the fascist poet Gabriele d'Annunzio, who wooed her with jewels. (Gabrielle Enthoven adapted D'Annunzio's *The Honeysuckle* for the stage. John called one of her canaries Gabriele d'Annunzio.)

In July 1921 Romaine spent a lot of time with John and Una. They lunched at the Savoy, dined at the Prince's Grill, drove to the country, went to *The Beggar's Opera* and talked until late at night. Toupie was enamoured of Romaine. She misconstrued what Romaine called a 'fragile *commencement*' between them and bombarded her with phone calls and letters. Romaine, for her part, was enamoured of John, who 'did not respond'. 'One always feels slightly grateful', John said of the interest shown. Romaine invited her and Una to stay for the summer in her villa in Capri. John talked over the idea with Una until one-thirty one morning. Una was against it. In previous years John might have pursued such a stylish affair, but Mabel Batten's death, her own literary ambition and Una's watchfulness now made her cautious.

14

Octopi and chains

Radclyffe Hall said she had the 'soul of a solitary' and that she spoke for misfits. As a Roman Catholic she deferred to the Pope and the gospel of Christ. She also had inchoate theories about predestination, reincarnation and halloaings from the dead. Hers was a deterministic view, however shifting the detail.

In her fiction and fantasy she was drawn to themes of martyrdom and heroic tragedy. In reality she was never alone, indulged all whims of purchase and travel and took the best suite in all the Grand Hotels. Nothing was too good for her and money gave her power. She was served by hired staff, had ninety-four neckties and lodged her jewels at the bank when abroad. Una was her acolyte at her beck and call, often in the room with her while she wrote.

In summer 1921 they decided to go to Italy. John wanted to work on her book and enjoy the sun. Alberto Visetti was ill with gallstones and she and Una worried that if he died it might spoil their plans. Andrea's vacation was a problem too. Una went to see the Reverend Mother at the convent and Andrea was sent back 'in floods of tears' before the new term began. As cold consolation John posted her a photograph album bought from Whiteleys. Una sent cards from distant towns.

They left London on 1 September. Una loved these journeys: 'the fun of the communicating first class single *wagons lits* with our dogs and all our impedimenta. Breakfast in the dining car, the galettes, croissants and rusks in a basket, the little pots of honey and jam'.

In Paris they ordered a mass for Ladye at the Cathedral of Notre-Dame and searched the dog shops for a perfect griffon. In Genoa at the Hôtel Miramar, Una took to her bed with 'external piles'. At Levanto they swam in the sea and went to the casino where John gambled while Una watched. Romaine again tried to entice them to Capri. Their apartment would look out over terraced gardens, it was secluded, all the furniture in it was made by local craftsmen, they could breakfast on the lawns, the weather was perfect. 'My plans depend somewhat on yours', she said.

John resisted. In Florence Una was triumphant, alone with the only person she cared about, in her favourite city: 'We had both of us visited Florence and loved it in the past, but that was a very different thing from discovering all its joys and beauties in the company we both liked better than any in the world: that of each other.'

Ladye was usurped and Mrs Leonard's mediation neither needed nor desired. They stayed at the Hotel Albion by the River Arno and the Ponte Vecchio. John worked at *Octopi* and Una read each day's work aloud. They admired the bands of Fascisti 'swinging along the streets', went to mass at San Michele, their favourite church, 'adored the frescoes', walked by the Arno in moonlight, drove to Bellosguardo for the views. Una's Italian was fluent, John had with her *The Little Help-Mate in Italy* with such phrases as 'I will wear my green coat and my nankeen pantaloons.' At Christmas they lay in bed listening to the church bells through the open windows. John gave Una a large sapphire ring which from then on she always wore. Una gave John malachite cufflinks.

They were away four months. In a final letter Romaine again regret-ted that they had not gone to Capri but arranged to fetch them from the Hôtel Normande in Paris on 9 January 1922 'in open motor':

> We could lunch together chez moi if you don't mind things done in no usual fashion. I strongly hate servants; see them as little as possible ... Such a thing as a well-trained butler would send me mad. After luncheon to the studio, t'other side of river ...
>
> I do so want you to meet my great friend here Natalie Barney. René de Gourmont wrote his *Lettres à l'Amazone* to her and she has written several volumes of aphorisms and poems. She has an unusual mind of the best quality. We have been reading lately a great deal of Freud, Jung and

D. H. Lawrence (not his novels), also James Joyce the new literary movement which explains and makes one more tolerant of the new art movement. Lawrence's *Classical American Literature* is a philosophical treatise, a chef d'oeuvre and very unlike what the title might lead one to expect, but perhaps you know it.

Natalie Barney was known more for her seductions of women and her flouting of convention than for her aphorisms and poems. She epitomized the sexual candour of Paris between the wars. In her Temple of Friendship in her wild garden at 22 rue Jacob lesbians gathered, 'Paris ones and those only passing through town'. Like Romaine, she was rich, American and in her mid-forties. She organized the Académie des Femmes as a counterpart to the all-male Académie Française. Friday was her salon day when dazzling people gathered. 'I have perhaps got more out of life than it contains', she said of herself when old.

Radclyffe Hall drew courage from women like Romaine Brooks and Natalie Barney with their inherited money, artistic success, intellectual confidence and openness about sex. Through them she moved toward self-expression. But she lacked their ease. In much the same way as she kept a distance from feminism and the suffragette movement, she equated Paris and modernism with gimmick and fashion. Stylistic innovation was not her thing. It was symbolic that she collected old oak even if she did then put it in store. She liked accessible narrative, devotional paintings and portraits of her relatives. The only mould breaker for whom she truly had time was herself. In the Hôtel Normande Una read aloud *The Bible and Early Christianity* and *The Soul of an Animal*.

With Una as her wife, Radclyffe Hall took for herself the old patriarchies. She invaded the domain of men. Her clothes, manners and adopted name asserted their power. She hired and more often fired the servants. She sailed the Channel in a first-class cabin. If men crossed her, she sued them in the male courts. Order and control she perceived as masculine. Even her handwriting, formerly rounded and tilting to the left, now sloped to the right in angular script. When her watch gained one and a half minutes in four weeks, it was returned for its imprecision.

This carapace of attitude shielded the persona attacked by her mother, abandoned by her father and violated by Alberto Visetti.

Vulnerability and the dreaded name of Marguerite she perceived as female. So were friendship, love, feelings and the tyranny of need. The flip side of 'masculine' strength was 'feminine' weakness. Una's sycophancy kept the illusion of control intact, though Una had none of the vulnerability John desired to conceal.

Back in London they moved into 10 Sterling Street. It was a small house and crowded out by the grand piano, eight-foot-long refectory tables, leather Chesterfield and huge bookcases. Neither of them liked the place but it was where throughout 1922 Radclyffe Hall worked daily at *Octopi*. She dedicated it 'to Mabel Veronica Batten in deep affection, gratitude and respect'. Una retitled it *The Unlit Lamp*. Audrey Heath admired it 'enormously' but could not think who would publish it. It rippled with disconcerting themes: lesbianism, incest, revulsion at sex between men and women. It had a narrative force, emotional tension, curious intimacy, but it was not literary, witty, polished or smart.

The editor at Collins read it 'with intense interest' but rejected it. Heinemann were encouraging and regretful, Arrowsmith compared it to Flaubert, Century said No. Una then 'boiled' it and read the shortened version to friends. Audrey Heath sent it to ten publishers. They praised it and hoped someone else would take it. The subject matter troubled them all. Radclyffe Hall, it seemed, was imprisoned by her theme. But she was determined to get into print. Audrey advised her to write, as a first novel, something more marketable, less contentious, to light the way for *The Unlit Lamp*.

Radclyffe Hall came up with *Chains*, a title as vexing as *Octopi*. She wrote it in six months. Dedicated 'To Una, with love', its theme seemed to be that chains of love bite deep. It featured details of their domestic life. A writer with inherited wealth, Hilary/John, and his artist wife Susan/Una, let work lapse because of their relationship. All their energy gets spent on their dachshunds, cars, oak furniture and the rest. In an effort to break these shackles, they move from their country mansion to a London townhouse. They store their things in Taylor's Depository. They dance in the Cave of Harmony, take a trip to Italy, then try to part to find their individual worth as artists.

Romaine was a pivotal character in the story. Even the title came from the artist's mark she used on her drawings – a wing held down by a chain. John resisted any romantic involvement with her in life. In her book she flirted freely. Romaine was Venetia Ford, 'the strange erratic brilliant genius of whom Susan had heard so much in the old days at the Slade'. She paints monotone portraits, has a dominating personality, studios in London and in the rue Bonaparte in Paris and a villa in Capri. She appears at a party:

> One of the women was beautiful with an elusive, inward kind of beauty. Her immense black eyes were set in a face that was technically too long … Her queer little straight nose was too short to be classical … But her mouth was the most perfect thing … the lips folded together in a soft, strong curve, with deep-set shadowy corners. Her skin was brown. She looked sun-tanned and her coal black hair, bobbed very short, was uncompromisingly straight. The face was full of curious defects, defects which seemed to combine together to make a noble and perfect whole; under it and through it and over it there was a veiled persistent glow.

Susan is wooed by Venetia Ford. Hilary goes to Canada to try to write. He is away for thirty pages. Susan knows he is insufferable and egomaniacal but she wants him back: '*His* nerves! *His* pictures! *His* books! *His* priceless old oak! *His* work! *His* freedom!' They reunite in platitudes: 'The stark femininity of all the ages looked out of her eyes into his.' He tells her, 'of all the chains in the world the heaviest chain is love. If we weren't chained we'd just float about like toy balloons. The whole world's a forge. Look at all your painters and writers and clever people. They're all chained up as tight as you please to their talents and struggles to be famous.'

Una corrected and transcribed each day's work. Her tone was there in the occasionally acerbic prose. She read it to Toupie who 'howled with laughter' at recognition of incidents in it. Una delivered the completed manuscript to Audrey Heath in June 1923. By July it was renamed *The Forge* and its thin later chapters padded out. By September John had signed a contract with the publisher J. W. Arrowsmith.

She hoped it would lead the way for her better book, her innovative theme. But she was over the main hurdle. She had an accepted novel, an agent and a publisher who wanted her work. An advance copy of *The Forge* arrived in January 1924. Una read it aloud in bed until two-thirty in the morning. Her occupation now was to build the career and reputation of Radclyffe Hall. She registered with Romeike and Curtice press cutting agency and pasted reviews into an album.

Grief for Ladye had had its day. Una was tirelessly obliging and unstinting in her praise. 'Long hours of my reading, perpetual assurances that what she was writing surpassed all that had preceded it. Reading, correcting, typing and retyping.'

Both talked of the 'Holy Spirit of inspiration' and of Radclyffe Hall as a vessel through whom God was pouring His message. Una shored up her ego against any whiff of criticism, indulged her tendentious narrative and gave her a compensatory place of safety where she was always right, invincible, handsome, immortal, and first. She was a formidable acolyte, an indispensable servant, even if there was the grip of tentacles about her and the clink of chains.

15

How to treat a genius

The Forge was published on 25 January 1924. John and Una spent the day being driven in Phillida, their Buick, to London bookshops to check it was stocked and prominently displayed. For four consecutive days Una then sent postcards advertising its publication.

Tireless for publicity, they too were prominently displayed. They took first-night tickets – centre stalls – for all the West End shows. In a week they went to *Sport of Kings* at the Savoy, *The Claimant* at the Queens, *Morals* at the Little Theatre, *The Way Things Happen, The Fairy Tale*. Photographs of 'the noted author Miss Radclyffe Hall' appeared in *TP's Weekly* and *Popular Pictures*. Assiduous of her image, she wore a black sombrero, a black cape, and diamonds in her cuffs and ears. Una was in the frame in a leopardskin coat, her hair shingled, her nails painted, a monocle screwed in her eye. 'It is pleasant to feel oneself distinguished', Radclyffe Hall wrote in an article 'First-Nighters'. 'Childish perhaps; but we are nearly all children at the bottom of our hearts.' 'First nights,' she said, were 'like the best kind of club.' She was a member, along with Noël Coward, Somerset Maugham, Arnold Bennett, C. B. Cochran, Ivor Novello, defined as successful by the company she kept.

Una called many of these shows 'awful tosh'. They did not now go to classical concerts or to the opera which she had once so loved. Both abhorred the avant-garde. Una described a reading by Edith Sitwell at the Poetry Bookshop as 'a bedlam afternoon of Miss Sitwell shouting down a megaphone'. And John 'barred the reading of good English novels, lest they might affect her own style'. She preferred *Jeremy and Hamlet* and *The Flaming Jewel*.

To spread her name she wrote magazine articles about dogs and old oak furniture, first nights and games of golf. Copy was sent off with publicity photographs by Lafayette and Howard Coster, 'photographer of men'. She took her editor, Newman Flower, to lunch at the Savoy, her agent to lunch at the Berkeley and she and Una dined at the Ivy, the Monte Carlo and the Eiffel Tower. She went to PEN Club meetings and to literary lunches. Audrey drew up the contract for her next novel, *A Saturday Life*, and said an American colleague, a Mr Washburn, would find a New York publisher for *The Unlit Lamp*.

Radclyffe Hall had a profession now. Socially she was a society lesbian for whom these were party days. She and Una gave a fancy dress ball for Romaine at Guy Allan's Studio, their wigs and costumes made at Nathan's. Una went as Harlequin, John as an Indian chief. In *The Forge* she described such a ball:

> A tall oriental, naked to the waist, was followed by a harem of six veiled women … A youth dressed as a peacock gyrated, his magnificent tail furled and unfurled … An elderly lady in short skirt and yellow wig bowled a hoop in and out among the dancers … A man completely covered in silver paint danced gravely with a woman in crinolines … A couple of Grey Friars shouted disrespectful compliments to a Cleopatra whose breastplate had become displaced. Two women passed, dancing together. One of them wore the clothes of a Paris workman, corduroy trousers and jacket and soft peaked cap. Around her heavy handsome throat she had knotted a red bandanna … Then linking arms they wandered off in the direction of the garden.

American and Parisian lesbians knew the cues and joined the scene. Through Gabrielle Enthoven and Toupie, John and Una met Teddie Gerrard, Tallulah Bankhead and her lover Gwen Farrar. Teddie Gerrard wore backless dresses, had her black hair cut into a bob and liked women, drink and drugs. Noël Coward was her friend and she was in his revue *London Calling*. (Edith Sitwell was parodied in it as Hernia Whittlebot.) John and Una went to parties at Teddie Gerrard's flat in Sackville Street and at her weekend house, Orchard Cottage in the

Cotswolds. Una made a note in her diary of a night in January 1924 when Teddie and her lover, Etheline Cripps, took them to a Chinese restaurant 'and then we toured London till 12 seeking vainly for someone to devil'. On 7 February they all went to Violette Murat's party until four-thirty in the morning. Next day there was a tea dance at Augustus John's (Tallulah paid him £1,000 to paint her portrait) then a party at Gwen Farrar's until dawn. John and Una were special guests at Tallulah's first night of *The Green Hat* at the Comedy. They sent flowers to her backstage then went on with her to the Cave of Harmony in Charlotte Street in Soho.

Una tolerated this social whirl. It was not the image of John she wanted to promote. Una liked West End style, but she neither drank nor smoked. She had headaches if she went to bed late and she disapproved of demands on John's time. Una was the brake on excess. She promulgated a myth of austere respectability:

> the life that proudly and joyfully was mine: a life of watching, serving and subordinating everything in existence to the requirements of an overwhelming literary inspiration and industry, guarding and sustaining a physique that was never equal to John's relentless perseverance or to the strain she compelled it to bear.

Una exaggerated the pain. John's irascibility and bad temper were a problem, but there was nothing arduous about either of their lives. They were entirely indulgent. Both enjoyed great privilege and 'orgies' of shopping, travel and parties. They demanded high standards of service. Lyon the cook was out at a moment's notice 'for insolence and drinking our brandy'. They pandered to their ailments. Two doctors and a nurse, Miss Bruce, attended for a fortnight when John had a feverish cold. And they indulged their hobbies. They celebrated with champagne at the Eiffel Tower when Wotan won all the prizes at the Richmond Dachshund Show and was voted Champion. Una then mated him with Hexel and Pickles in the bathroom while John wrote *The Saturday Life*.

By Una's birthday in March 1924 *The Forge* had reprinted. John gave her another gold-backed brush for her dressing table. Next month the sale of the Sterling Street house was completed, their furniture went again into store and their jewels to the bank. They rented a flat at Kensington Palace Mansions, planned a holiday and searched for the perfect house.

At her Chelsea studio at 15 Cromwell Road, Romaine painted Una's portrait. Una had nine sittings and posed with two of the dachshunds. It was a portrait that belied her view of herself. Here was the master, not the servant. Romaine knew Una's power, the giving that was really control. Here was Una the Lady Troubridge, her face screwed to one side to keep her monocle in place. She was not to be messed with. Thin as a reed, there was the threat of bondage in the leather stock, the shirt bleached and starched by a servant, the mannish jacket, the chains and collars, restraining hand on the dog. She had a sleek cap of hair, pearls in her ears, a fob in her pocket and heartlessness in her eyes. One dog sat as instructed and stared submissively. The other stared elsewhere, no doubt at the prospect of John whose link was ever there.

Una hated the portrait. She told Toupie so and refused to believe the resemblance. Romaine had reflected her quintessential misanthropy. Una could not again be on friendly terms with her. Romaine exhibited the portrait at her shows at the Jean Charpentier Gallery in Paris and at the Wildenstein Galleries in New York, but not at the L'Alpine Club in London: 'Yes your portrait had very great success over there,' she wrote to Una of her American trip, '& was reproduced several times. It was not exhibited in London, I had the impression from Toupie that you did not like it & were worried about the resemblance. I'll send you some photos.' The portrait prompted Una to change not her character but her hairstyle – to a flicker of a wave and a quiff.

The Saturday Life took Radclyffe Hall nine months to write. The skills of many typists were taxed as they tried to comply with her needs: 'This involved never "tapping" while she spoke or while she was reflecting. For as she dictated she continued to polish and the typist had always to be prepared to "X" out at demand any word or sentence and continue her script with the substituted amendment.' None of them lasted. They were serially fired and complaints lodged with the agency that sent them. Only Una brought the necessary homage and application.

Radclyffe Hall dedicated the book to herself. *The Forge* she had dedicated to Una and *The Unlit Lamp* to Ladye. Subsequent books were to 'Our Three Selves', the homoousian genius of her art. In reality it was one self, her own. Dedicatees were, like Daisy the imaginary friend of her childhood, aspects of her own needs.

The Saturday Life featured reincarnation, Sabbatarianism and her oddball theories of recurring lives. Like most of her books it was burdened with discarded subplots and floating characters. Una called it the Sidonia book. Sidonia, incarnate on earth seven times, replays previous lives. Her problem, like her author's, is genius. 'That's why I'm morbid. Genius is always despondent. You none of you know how to treat a genius.' Aged three she shows 'abnormal aptitudes'. She draws, sculpts, writes poetry, plays the piano perfectly, all without lessons. She reads Swinburne, has residual memories of Attic dances under ilex trees and confounds her mother Lady Shore, an Egyptologist who cannot 'comprehend Sidonia as the outcome of so discreet a mating' as she had had with 'frail, small Sir Godfrey'.

Insinuating through the book, as in all Radclyffe Hall's work, were coded references to subversive sex. Lady Shore's best friend, Frances Reide, loves a log fire, uncle's portrait over the mantelpiece and a room that smells of beeswax, cigarette smoke and flowers. Sidonia wants to lure Frances from her mother:

> 'I ask you to kiss me and you won't!' she said furiously. 'Oh, you! You're all Mother's! Mother this, Mother that! God! I'm sick of it! Don't I count at all? ... Aren't I younger than Mother? Aren't I attractive? Don't I interest you enough? Frances' – she began to speak softly now – 'Frances look at me! Don't you love me? Frances, *won't* you be my friend? All, *all* my friend? I don't want to marry anyone, I tell you; I just want to work and have you, all of you. Frances, mother would never miss you. Listen, I'm not being beastly about mother, but please, please try to love me a little; I need you much more than she does.' She laid her hand caressingly on Frances' arm. 'Frances, why won't you love me?'
>
> Frances disengaged her arm very gently and left the studio.

It was a startling (if discarded) theme – the seduction of mother's lesbian partner. But Radclyffe Hall's writing is littered with such cameos of psychopathology. To manufacture a son (a problematic aspiration of Radclyffe Hall's), Sidonia marries David Morgan, a sexy lout with a family estate in Essex. He proposes in the zoo by the jackals' cage and they marry in church. 'It was all very neat, very British, very proper ... It was all very full of time-honoured words, man's words, that he printed for his own delectation and believed in for his own peace of mind ... It was really a great and desperate adventure dressed up in ridiculous clothes.'

It was also all very dissenting and dark, not comic and lighthearted as its publisher J. W. Arrowsmith supposed. Frances visits the newly-weds. 'Frances sat smiling the vacant smile of the great unwanted Third.' David calls her an unsexed, middle-aged virgin and fears she will grow hairs on her chin.

'Why haven't you married my dear?' he asks her.
    She thought: 'Supposing I tried to explain?' and began to laugh softly to herself.

The son John felt she should by rights have been and wanted herself to father is born on Christmas Day, a Saturday, and named Noel, a latter-day saviour with a lesbian mother.

While writing *The Saturday Life* Radclyffe Hall began another book, *The Cunningham Code*. It got nowhere and she abandoned it. Una called these aborted projects 'trolley books': 'to carry her from a fallow period to one of renewed production'. She took as a preamble to it a quote from Okofski:

The herd instinct common alike to animals and to primitive peoples, while strengthening the whole, must of necessity weaken the individual. What must be called, for want of a better term, the Family instinct, is but another and more specialised phase of the herd instinct, and as such must operate strongly against both mental and spiritual growth.

At heart Radclyffe Hall rejected the defining rules of society: family, parental authority, gender. She wove her fiction round her like a cocoon, a safe place where her fantasy self grew. *The Cunningham* fragment aired her preoccupations: a titled landowner in a baronial hall sires daughters though he wanted sons. The mother cannot love these daughters that disappoint her husband. One of the daughters feels like a boy trapped in a girl's body.

Four days after she finished *The Saturday Life* – on 29 May 1924 – Radclyffe Hall bought 37 Holland Street. It was a grand residence for a writer of standing. It was like a country house with large rooms and casement windows. As ever, there was much to be done to bring it to standard – parquet floors to be laid, gas fires installed.

John and Una planned to travel all summer while the builders worked. They left for Paris in June. John said she felt exhausted and drained. A varicose vein in her leg hurt. At the Hôtel Normande were two telegrams from Audrey Heath. Newman Flower of Cassell, much impressed by *The Unlit Lamp*, offered autumn publication, a £50 advance, fifteen per cent royalties on the first 3,000 copies, twenty per cent after that and the first option on her next two novels.

This was the great event of the year for John and Una. They had a joyful tea with Natalie Barney, hurried to London next day and booked in at the Grand Central Hotel. John signed Cassell's contract over lunch at the Berkeley with Audrey. She and Una then worked into the night and cut *The Unlit Lamp* to 108,000 words.

Back in Paris they again visited Natalie. Una read aloud from *The Forge* the passages based on Romaine – about beauty, riches and Bohemian ways. Romaine came in and according to Una 'made a hideous scene abusing *The Forge*, John, & Natalie like a fishwife!' She thought the writing trite and superficial and the portrait of herself ridiculous. She was vexed at their coolness over her portrait of Una and irritated by their impenetrable double act of aggrandizement.

John and Una moved on to Bagnoles-de-l'Orne in Normandy. For a month they 'took the waters', lazed on the hotel terrace and went to the casino. Audrey sent out proofs of *The Unlit Lamp*, Una corrected them in a day and sent them back by the evening post. In gratitude John bought her an ivory and gold bracelet. Una viewed it as a trophy of love.

'Great fuss made of John', Una wrote in her diary about the party given for them by their friends Vere Hutchinson and Budge Burroughes when they got back to London at the end of July. Violet Hunt was there, Leonard Rees, editor of the *Sunday Times*, Michael Arlen, best-selling author of *The Green Hat* and Margaret Irwin, author of *Still She Wished for Company*. John invited Leonard Rees to lunch at the Savoy. He then invited her to his party where she met E. V. Lucas the Chairman of Methuen, St John Adcock editor of the *Bookman*, the writer Rebecca West, the publisher John Murray, Alec Waugh literary critic of the *Sunday Times*. It was the way to get famous, the way to get known. 'Nine years', Una wrote in her diary on 1 August. She circled the date, went to mass and gave thanks.

The Unlit Lamp was published to good reviews. The *Daily Telegraph* called it 'a novel of uncommon power and fidelity to life', the *Observer* said it was 'strong and quiet – a very moving picture of a character refreshingly fine'. Romeike and Curtice sent five reviews 'all magnificent'. Ida Wylie praised it in the *Queen*. Cassell advertised it on the clock tower of St Pancras Station. John and Una drove to admire this, then went on to Harrods and The Times Bookshop to note with pleasure that all copies had been sold. Mr Francis of Cassell's publicity department had tea with them, stayed to dinner and got drunk. 'It was awful', Una wrote.

In October Una had 'electricity' treatment for her nerves, venereal disease or both and John resigned from the Society for Psychical Research. Being a famous author now took all her time. They took a week's break in the Grand Hotel, Folkestone – they always had room 455. They walked through the town looking in bookshops for *The Unlit Lamp*. In the evenings Una read aloud *The Broken Bow*. John began writing *The World*, a 'trolley book' about a dead cat, an asthmatic bank clerk and a German landlady. More happily perhaps, in the general election the Conservatives had a landslide victory and Mrs Leonard, in a now-rare sitting, predicted Twonnie would be *great*. Newman Flower who was a client of hers had told her so.

John and Una moved into the Holland Street house. Once again they created the illusion of a settled home. Taylor's Depository delivered the huge refectory tables, John bought a 'beautiful sideboard' from Narramores and a Steinway piano. It took a full day to shelve their 2,000 books and another to supervise the hanging of their pictures, their bewhiskered relatives, Sargent's portrait of Ladye, the Madonna and Child, the crucifixions, the pastoral landscapes.

Their maids wore starched aprons and caps; the chauffeur was in livery. Father Hague came to bless the house. He came to lunch and he stayed to tea. John and Una declared themselves enchanted with it all. It was convenient for Brompton Oratory, the parks, the shops. They shared a bedroom because the rooms were disparate sizes and they did not want to be on separate floors. 'John and I breakfasted in our bedroom', Una wrote every day until the year's end.

Andrea arrived from boarding school on Friday 19 December and was despatched next day to Ida Temple at Datchet with the housekeeper Miss MacLean. John and Una went to Highgate Cemetery to put a wreath on the door of Ladye's catacomb. They saw Tallulah in *Creaking Chair*, went on to the Cave of Harmony and down to Teddie Gerrard's cottage. They joined Andrea at Datchet late on Christmas Eve. 'John, I and Andrea to Midnight Mass, John's 10th with me' was Una's diary entry, the order of allegiance clear. Her Christmas present from John was the mirror of the gold dressing-table set. On New Year's Eve, back at Holland Street, Toupie came to dinner with her new lover, Fabienne

Lafargue De-Avilla, and Gabrielle Enthoven. They all danced together as the bells of midnight chimed. Vere Hutchinson and Budge Bur-roughes stayed home. Vere, who was thirty-three, had multiple sclerosis which was paralysing her body and unbalancing her mind.

16

Books about ourselves

'If we cannot write books about ourselves then I ask about whom may we write them?' Radclyffe Hall said in a lecture to the English Club on novel writing. The self about whom she wrote was drawn to the central grief of an unwanted child. Fear of abandonment loomed in her novels as in her life, whatever her fabrications of plot or grandeur of lifestyle. It gave a tension to her work which ameliorated its logical flaws and indulgence. She saw herself as rejected by her father, despised by her mother and answerable only to God.

She was also rich, theatrical and hugely ambitious. And Una was there to collude with her vanity. Una was a strategist, her objectives clear: Radclyffe Hall was the greatest living English novelist whose reputation must be served. Una's was not an inflectional love of moods and nuance. Pontifical, doctrinal, it was as absolute and rigid on day one as year twelve. She encouraged Radclyffe Hall's grandiose fantasies and gave her a safe place to weave her fiction. She allowed her to be a misfit, a man, a genius, martyr and messiah. The price of her indulgence was entrapment within the world they agreed. The trial was in living up to the fantasy. The danger was that life of some other sort might break in.

John knew the value of Una's devotion. Her next novel had, before its publisher protested, the unpropitious title *Food*. Its hero, Gian-Luca, marries a woman he does not love, but sees the benefit of her loving him: 'It is wiser and it leaves a man more free for his business.

When one loves one is all misery, all body and no brain. One becomes a fool, one says and does nothing but foolish things.'

John's business was to write books that changed the world. Publication of *The Unlit Lamp* and its good reviews was proof of her divine gift. Life at Holland Street reflected her importance. She controlled the household. She rang a handbell for service at table. She sacked the chauffeur, Budd, for driving Una too fast to the shops. She employed a secretary, Miss Clark. Miss Shackleton came to draw her, Mr Dywell called to cut her hair, Rebecca West and May Sinclair dined in April 1925. 'A very successful evening', Una said. When Alec Waugh came to supper with Leonard Rees, Una read *Kept*, his recent novel, aloud all afternoon so that John would appear informed.

Up in her study John now worked long hours.

If our literary instinct says 'Work all night' because by doing so your work will be better, if it tells you that, if you break for your lunch you are going to check a good bit of writing, if it tells you that by going out for a walk your physical condition may be improved but that your mind may well be distracted, then I think that you should sacrifice yourself to art. All art is a hard taskmaster at times, and takes very little account of the body.

She began *Food* on Tuesday 14 April 1925. It was long but she wrote it in six months. Its central allegory was of a surfeit of sausages and pasta and a starved soul. The idea came to her lunching with Una at the Pall Mall restaurant. Smart places inspired her with fantasies of deprivation. It was a way of subverting privilege. She could romanticize hardship knowing she was rich. She said she was going to write about a waiter so sickened by food he dies of starvation.

She took the road to Calvary theme, resonant with Christ's stations of the cross. Una bought a model of a lamb as an offering for the book's success. There was a kind of camp melodrama to their religiosity. The story was set in the Italian community in London's Soho. By way of research for authentic settings, they went to St Peter's Italian Church in Hatton Garden, to the best Italian restaurants and to a delicatessen called King Bomba in Old Compton Street. Una took notes on the stock: olives, split peas, Orvieto, tagliatelle, cheeses, coffees.

Una monitored the book's progress in her diary and took to staying in bed while John worked. Her entry for 22 April read: 'John had breakfast in bed and then sent me back there while she went to work. I staid in bed all day. Minna came in at tea time. Later I got up for dinner & John and I to first night Haymarket. V. amusing.'

And two days later: 'John and I breakfasted in our room & she to work after I had read her *Food* from the beginning. Minna lunched and staid till 4 oc. then John worked again till past midnight & then I read her work aloud to her.'

Food became the focus of both their days. There were fewer dog shows now, or visits to Mrs Leonard. Una interviewed men from Barker's when beetles appeared in Dickie the manservant's bedroom, she pasted reviews of *The Saturday Life* from the *Queen* and *Punch* into the scrapbooks, shopped at Harrods and Harvey Nichols, rested and saw the doctor, but nothing interested her other than living John's life. She rescinded any vestigial motherly tasks. Miss MacLean met Andrea from the station, took her to the dentist and despatched her to her father.

In a display of independence Una read and commented on manuscripts for Audrey Heath, translated *Le Grand Eunuque* by Charles Pettit and wrote arch autobiographical sketches, unrevealing pieces on pets, clothes and on never settling in any house. 'John wants me to do a book of them', she wrote in her diary. 'J worked till after 2.30 and so did I!' John wanted Una, it seemed, to fill her time so as herself to be spared the oppression of constant service, constant scrutiny.

There was less intimacy between them. John was protective of Una's health, insistent about standards of service to her in shops and restaurants, generous with presents, deferential to her views, mindful of her loyalty, but there was a sense of obligation about it all, a tightness of response. Gone were Una's diary entries 'We talked til late.' John now worked most nights. Una noted the long hours with implied recrimination.

The General Strike was an interruption. They saw it as perpetrated by Communists. By way of solidarity with the ruling class, they volunteered to drive casualty patients to Charing Cross Hospital. With Bradley, the current chauffeur, they ferried a boy with a crushed foot to and from Peckham. Like knitting socks for soldiers such gestures of citizenship passed with the day.

By Sunday 17 May Radclyffe Hall had written 115 pages of *Food*. She breakfasted in bed then went to mass while Una washed the dogs. Then Audrey called and for hours Una read it all aloud. The story that far was of Gian-Luca's forlorn childhood – absence of love, loneliness, compensatory desire. His mother dies giving birth to him, he does not know who his father is and his grandmother rejects him for causing her daughter's death. 'I have got myself,' he says. He grows up in his grandfather's store. There is an abundance of pickles, pasta and panetone, but not a book in sight. He joins the Free Library for 'he loved the sound of words'. He reads Tennyson and Wordsworth and at Hatchards bookshop buys the Italian poetry of someone called Ugo Doria, whose writing gives him an 'eerie feeling of familiarity'.

He works as a waiter at the Capo di Monte restaurant, reads Ugo Doria and falls for the Padrona, who has golden hair and blue eyes. She asks him to tea and he kisses the scar on her hand. He is sixteen.

> A boy's first love is a love apart, and never again may he hope to recapture the glory and the anguish of it. It is heavy with portent and fearful with beauty, terrible as an army with banners; yet withal so tender and selfless a thing as to brush the very hem of the garment of God. Only once in a life comes such loving as this, and now it had come to Gian-Luca.

Audrey 'loved it'. It made her weep. 'After tea we all went for a drive. John v. tired but v. happy,' Una wrote. A contract was drawn up with Cassell. Newman Flower insisted the title be changed. He said everyone would think *Food* was a cookbook. Una took over: 'Firmly rejecting John's frenzied suggestions, I ransacked the local Smith's for sources of inspiration and ended by finding what we required in Kipling's *Tomlinson*: "I'm all oer sib to Adam's breed that I should mock your pain." ' 'Sib' is archaic Scottish for 'related to'. Kipling was nowhere quoted in the book, so the title *Adam's Breed* though Newman Flower approved it, remained as mysterious as the dedication 'To Our Three Selves'.

John and Una's only travel that summer was with Gian-Luca. In June Bradley drove them to Lynton in Devon. They stayed in the Valley of the Rocks Hotel. John wrote her book in bed. Una designed the jacket for it and read aloud *Dracula* and *The Crossways of Sex*. They visited the Convent of the Poor Clares and made friends with the reverend mother. The weather was sunny and John bought a No. 2 Brownie box camera and photographed the sky and the coastline.

Andrea was sent to guide camp. Back in London in July Una's stony regard for her fifteen-year-old daughter grew stonier. Andrea had a boyfriend. Una summoned Dr Thomson. He 'confirmed her suspicions'. Una 'lectured' Andrea, despatched her to Datchet to stay with Ida Temple and then to the Troubridges with whom Una was not on speaking terms.

By September *Adam's Breed* was nearly finished. Audrey cried all the way home after another day of Una reading it to her. She said she could not bear to think how dull she would feel when it was finished. Una's mother, to whom it was also read hot from the page, called it a great book, 'finer and more interesting' than *The Unlit Lamp*.

It was an Old Testament saga of suicide. It was all about redemption and suffering and it troubled mothers less than tales of lesbian love. In the second part of the book, Gian-Luca becomes head waiter at the Doric restaurant. (John and Una toured the kitchens of the Berkeley Grill in their quest for authenticity.) A 'hard master', ambitious for riches, he 'carries within him the needs of an unloved child'. He meets Maddalena who wants him to find God. She is 'tall strong-limbed and full breasted ... her face was the face of a mother of men'. To please her, they marry in the Italian Catholic Church in Hatton Gardens. He does not desire her, but she gives him the home he craves: 'Home is a place in which we are wanted, in which there is someone to whom we matter more than anything else on earth.' He eats her pasta and tells her, as Radclyffe Hall might have told Una, 'I love you far more than when I married you sweetheart. It must be because you love me so much; all my life I have wanted someone to love me.'

Sex is a veiled problem and she does not have the children she wanted. Crisis comes when Gian-Luca's hero, Ugo Doria, books a table at the Doric. He arrives with a louche woman, is bragging, drunk and insecure. Gian-Luca sees 'a large, foolish, lovesick viveur of sixty'. Ugo Doria is of course Gian-Luca's father though neither knows it. There follows from Gian-Luca 'a tirade on the man who conceived him then abandoned him'. He rails at 'all the years of his lonely, outraged childhood, of his painful adolescence, his maturity of toil with its bitter will to succeed'.

Men seldom behave well towards women in Radclyffe Hall's books. Gian-Luca becomes crazy and unpleasant, hits his wife in the face when she serves him breakfast, gives his customers salmon when they ask for oysters and wants 'to grasp something that was infinitely stronger than he was'. He gives his money to a blind child beggar and wanders round Italy telling peasants to show mercy to their beasts. 'On they must stumble to calvary as Another had stumbled before them', he says of cattle led to the slaughterhouse, '... poor, lowly, uncomprehending disciples, following dumbly in the footsteps of God who had surely created all things for joy, yet had died for the blindness of the world.'

Back in London he tells Maddalena he is going away 'to find God in great solitude'. She packs his bag. He heads for the New Forest on foot and feels 'like a lover on the eve of ultimate fulfilment'. (Radclyffe Hall's father painted landscapes and rode horses in the New Forest.) He lives rough, birds eat out of his hands and he gets followed by a Roan pony. He asks the rabbits, 'Have *you* got a God?' After a year of it he finds God in his heart 'and in every poor struggling human heart that was capable of one kind impulse'. He dies of starvation blessing God as he does so and his body is laid out in a stable. 'The path of the world was the path of His sorrow and the sorrow of God was the hope of the world, for to suffer with God was to share in the joy of his ultimate triumph over sorrow.'

It was all very like the Bible. Given that these were years of literary innovation it was surprising that publishers liked it. James Joyce had published *Ulysses* in 1922, T. S. Eliot *The Waste Land*, Virginia Woolf was writing *To the Lighthouse* in 1925. H. D. and Edith Sitwell, Djuna Barnes and Gertrude Stein, were all breaking rules of content and form. Radclyffe Hall took no notice of their heresies. *Adam's Breed* was for readers resistant to stylistic innovation and modernism. It was all about redemption, suffering and Jesus Christ. The French did not take to it and in the States it sold less than four thousand copies.

There was hubris in the seeming humility of the story. Una compounded a deception. 'We followed Gian-Luca step by step to the New Forest,' she wrote, 'we trudged and waded in abominable weather.' It was not at all like that. Bradley, their liveried chauffeur, drove them there. They stayed at Balmer Lawn in the village of Brockenhurst and lunched at Winchester and the White Hart, Whitchurch. Radclyffe Hall wrote the chapters about Gian-Luca's demise in the Grand Hotel, Brighton. She and Una had breakfast in bed, sat in the sun, had stout and oysters for lunch at Chiesmans and potted meat for tea. It was all very well for her to extol starving to death in the woods when she was so well off. Her point of interest was herself and her interpretation of her life. She minded very much about cruelty to animals and hated the denial of their rights, but she indulged her pity. It was all very well in the morning to dictate lines like, 'In as much as your Christ had pity, so must every poor beast be Christian', then lunch on veal at the Berkeley Grill and in the afternoon buy a tigerskin coat for herself, a leopardskin one for Una and pearl earrings for them both. She gave money to beggars and to the Church but she was not egalitarian. Servants, waiters and tramps had their quarters. She viewed the aristocracy and Christian martyrs as the true elite. But she was also contradictory. She subverted what she had and believed, deconstructed her God and her politics, built up her houses in order to fracture them and in a way did the same with her relationships and work.

She finished *Adam's Breed* at the Grand Hotel at two in the morning on Sunday 8 November. Una prepared one manuscript for Cassell, another for the American publisher Doubleday. It was then parties and shopping, first nights and dog shows. 'We are hugely enjoying our well earned holiday', Una wrote. They had dinner with Toupie and Fabienne at the Kit Kat Club. The vet came and clipped the wings of Sappho the parrot, they bought a cockatoo from Gamages, went to a party at Violet Hunt's and to a matinée of *Where the Rainbow Ends*. John cried all the way home.

At Christmas they went as usual to Ida Temple at Datchet. Andrea travelled there by train with Dickie and the maid. John, Una and the dogs went by car. In London on New Year's Eve, John and Una 'intercepted' a letter to Andrea from her boyfriend. She was lectured 'for a long time'. Minna was told and the doctor was again called. Andrea was sent to her father for a fortnight, then given another lecture before being sent back to her current boarding school, St George's at Harpenden. James Garvin, Viola's second husband, tried to intervene on Andrea's behalf. 'Don't repress my little favourite Andrea too much', he wrote. 'She's full of sap and must follow nature. She will follow it more or less reasonably if emancipation comes by rather liberal degrees.' But Una's 'misery' about sex, her equating of it with infection, made her horrified at the prospect of her daughter's desires. No friend of Andrea's was ever invited to the house.

Ten days later, on 29 January 1926, Minna phoned early in the morning to say that Troubridge had died at a tea dance at Biarritz the previous day. Una made no pretence of sorrow. But she went into a scud of activity about money. She spent the morning on the phone to the Admiralty and in the afternoon saw the Accountant General there. Troubridge's total estate was £452 18s 11d. Her annual pension was to be £225 a year, Andrea's £25. 'To mother's', Una wrote in her diary that night. 'Viola very nice, Minna intolerable. John and I home to a quiet evening.'

Advised by John's solicitor, Theodore Goddard, Una appealed to the Admiralty for this pension to be increased. She presented herself as a penniless widow with a child to support. She checked on life insurance policies, put in a claim with the Officers' Families Fund, wrote to her stepson Tom Troubridge about Andrea's school fees and 'wrote her mind' to her mother who was 'more damnable than ever' when Una called at her house to retrieve her marriage certificate.

A requiem mass was held for Troubridge at Westminster Cathedral. Andrea had leave from school. Una braved the Troubridge congregation while John walked the dog. There was no hint of acceptance of her by them. 'She was waiting for me when I got home', Una wrote in her diary. Troubridge's obituary in *The Times* spoke of his distinguished prewar career and of the escape of the *Goeben*. 'His subsequent employment was not of a kind to afford him much opportunity of distinction. Personally he was well known and highly popular in many cities in Europe.'

As if to assert paternal authority John took Andrea to mass at Brompton Oratory then drove with her back to Harpenden. For Una, Troubridge's death added to the burden of what to do with his child, the unwelcome reminder of a former life, the parcel to be passed. 'She cld stay away 2nd part of hols', she wrote in her diary about Andrea's Easter break.

Una's appeal for an increased pension went before an Admiralty tribunal and was successful. 'Much rejoicing, hurrah', she wrote. John ordered her a new hat from Maud Moore's and they saw Noël Coward's *Hay Fever* for the second time and 'howled with laughter'. There was greater rejoicing when *Adam's Breed* was published in March. Una sent out more than 200 postcards by way of publicity. They drove to the bookshop Miller & Gill in the Charing Cross Road to see the window banner advertising it. Within a week Hatchards and The Times Bookshop were reordering. Within three weeks it was on its fourth reprint.

Mindful perhaps of the pearls and purple coat she had once been given, the passion she once inspired, Violet Hunt wrote to say that she was nominating it for the Femina Vie Heureuse Prize. Two Femina prizes were awarded annually, for an English and a French novel.

Newman Flower had expected more modest sales and was surprised by the book's popularity. Radclyffe Hall took courage from this success. She resolved now to speak out and put her name to a novel that told, she said, 'the truth about one of the greatest tragidees that exists in the scheme of nature'.

> I wished to offer my name and my literary reputation in support of the cause of the inverted. I knew that I was running the risk of injuring my career as a writer by rousing up a storm of antagonism; but I was prepared to face this possibility because, being myself a congenital invert, I understood the subject from the inside as well as from medical and psychological text books. I felt therefore that no one was better qualified to write the subject in fiction than an experienced novelist like myself who was actually one of the people about whom she was writing and was thus in a position to understand their spiritual, mental and physical reactions, their joys and their sorrows, and above all their unceasing battle against a frequently cruel and nearly always thoughtless and ignorant world.

She used the term congenital invert as if it was a category with specific attributes. It was true that the company she kept was lesbian (upper class, cultured, moneyed lesbians between the wars). She knew their dress codes, mores, love affairs and news. And Una had read aloud germane passages from works of contemporary sexology. But Radclyffe Hall embraced contentious theories with disconcerting ease. Her true courage was to speak out, to break silence, declare her sexual orientation, use pronouns truthfully and write 'she kissed her on the mouth'. Other lesbian writers shielded themselves behind allusion and *romans-à-clef*, where only the in-crowd knew the hes to be really shes.

In daily life Radclyffe Hall was an invert with standards to maintain and pleasures to procure. She fired the cook and employed a new one, Miss McDonnell. The secretary, Miss Clark, was replaced by Miss Ward, then Miss Ward by Miss Whibley. Bradley went and Una refused to be driven by his replacement Birdkin who she said was rude. His successor, Kayberry, crashed the car and was 'discharged'. John then hired a chauffeured Daimler from Harrods for £800 a year plus a shilling a mile, 'livery supplied'.

Again the house began to 'vamp' her. Sappho the parrot bit her and was despatched to the zoo. Una endured more injections and vaccines for her vaginal problems. Dr Curtis said 'there was no real means of getting her right except by an operation. 'Damn him to hell!!!' John wrote when his treatment hurt Una. She bought her peaches and sweets.

In the summer she left 'board and wages for six weeks' for Miss Mclean, McDonnell and Dickie and set off with Una for France, thermal baths, Paris bars and the casinos of the Riviera. In Paris they hired a car to take them shopping. They bought a dog called Tyke. They lunched at the Champs-Elysées Grill, then had tea with Colette and took her chocolates. At night with Natalie Barney and her current lover, Mimi Franchetti, they toured the lesbian clubs, the Select, the Regina, the Dingo. 'Home abut 2.30', Una wrote. At Natalie's Temple of Love they met her former lover the Duchess of Clermont Tonnerre and the Broadway actress Eva Le Gallienne, whose affair with Mercedes de Acosta had come to an end. They had dinner with Toupie and Fabienne and saw at the Théâtre Femina *La Prisonnière* by Edouard Bourdet, based on the love affair of Violet Trefusis and the Princesse de Polignac. 'Awful rot, but fun', Una said of it. They drove to the cemetery at Passy to put artificial violets on the grave of Renée Vivien, another of Natalie's erstwhile lovers. She wrote poems about 'nights of savage desire', drank alcohol and eau de cologne and died when she was thirty-one. In their twenties, she and Natalie had travelled to Lesbos together to revive 'the golden age of Sappho'.

At Bagnoles John and Una took the thermal baths, were massaged and manicured and had their hearts and blood pressure checked. Then they went on to the Riviera, to the casinos of Cannes and Nice and to the Grand Hotel, Monte Carlo.

Radclyffe Hall returned home a best-selling author. Mr Gentry, publicity manager at Cassell, said *Adam's Breed* was going so well no extra advertising was needed. G. K. Chesterton's latest novel had had to wait while they printed three thousand more. Radclyffe Hall talked to the Writers' Club about why she had written the book, to the Writers' Circle on the 'genesis and craftsmanship' of it and to the Bookman's Circle about 'true realism' in fiction. She was 'lionised' at a PEN Club dinner, a Women Writers lunch and a dinner at the Society of Authors, 'decorations worn'. She was caricatured by 'Tom Titt', 'Pax' and 'Matt' and photographed with bow tie, cape and monocle.

In November Violet Hunt phoned to say *Adam's Breed* had been shortlisted for the Femina Prize. Writing to her cousin Winifred, Jane Caruth's daughter, Radclyffe Hall said:

it is far and away the best thing I have ever written. I shall *not* give it you, you must buy it yourself in America for the good of the author.

Isn't it amusing that I should have become quite a well known writer? I sometimes cannot understand it myself. But there it is, it has certainly come to pass ... Lady Troubridge asks to be remembered to you.

She won the prize. Messages and letters of congratulation poured in. Photographers and interviewers called from the *Sphere*, the *Sketch* and *Mirror*. Photographs of Miss Radclyffe Hall and Colette were printed side by side. Mr Gentry told her the book was on display in every London bookshop. The prizegiving was held at the Institut Français. The novelist John Galsworthy presented the award. Writers and friends gave praise, including Sheila Kaye-Smith, Beatrice Harraden, May Sinclair.

At high mass John and Una gave thanks, then went to Ladye's grave and to seven churches. At Holland Street they then hosted a party for seventy. It went on until two-thirty in the morning. Ernest Thesiger, Helen Beauclerc, Lewis Casson, Sybil Thorndike and lots of famous people were there. 'Half the ladies present favoured masculine mode and half the latest Victorian effect', the papers said. J. Rosamund Johnson, Taylor Gordon and Florence Mills sang negro spirituals: 'Deep river, my home is over Jordan' and 'Oh what a shame I ain't nobody's baby'. Una called it all 'a huge success'. And even while enjoying this success Radclyffe Hall was halfway through her most important book which began as *Stephen* and became *The Well of Loneliness* and in which she knew she was laying her now glittering career on the line.

STEPHEN GORDON

17

Something of the acorn about her

The _Well of Loneliness_ is a cautionary saga about the fate of a 'congenital sexual invert'. Dubbed 'the Bible of lesbianism', in the telling there is no irony and few moments of fun. Radclyffe Hall described its hero, Stephen Gordon, as 'the finest type of the inverted woman'. She intended it to be a pioneer work and said it had a social duty, a threefold purpose:

> To encourage inverts to face up to a hostile world in their true colours, and this with dignity and courage. To spur all classes of inverts to make good through hard work, faithful and loyal attachments and sober and useful living. To bring normal men and women of good will to a fuller and more tolerant understanding of the inverted.

She wanted it read by schoolteachers, welfare workers, doctors, psychologists and parents so that they might 'cease tormenting and condemning their offspring and thus doing irreparable harm to the highly sensitized nervous system that is characteristic of inversion.' Here, she seemed to suggest, was a manual for the world on what not to do to these weird ones in their midst.

'You can't touch filth without getting filthy', her mother said to her when the book caused a stir. While Radclyffe Hall was writing it, she and her mother had a series of violent rows. Their only contact seemed to be when Mrs Visetti wanted money. In December 1926 in one of

151

her rages she fired the cook who, she said, drank, was a thief, and filthy dirty. There was a scene, she called the police and accused the cook of hitting her. All servants in her London house including the daily cleaner then left or were fired.

The Visettis went to the Metropole Hotel, Brighton for Christmas as guests of a friend. On 2 January 1927 Radclyffe Hall, working twelve hours a day on *Stephen*, as her *Well of Loneliness* was still then called, received a call from the hotel to come at once – her mother had pneumonia and her life was at risk. 'I arrived and saw the doctor, only to be told that her lungs were in no way affected. However, their hostess had to return to London the next day and mother could not remain behind at the Metropole which is quite *the* most expensive hotel in all England. What to do?'

Her mother could not return to a house without servants. She asked to go into a nursing home in Brighton. Radclyffe Hall insisted on one near Holland Street and hired an ambulance to get her there. She put *Stephen* aside and went through the Visettis' finances to see if they would be better off in a service flat.

'I can only say my God! I found chaos beyond my worst nightmares and debts everywhere.' The lease on their house had expired and under the terms of it they had a liability for repairs of £300. They owed rent and rates, had overdrafts at their banks and had spent their capital inherited from Grandmother Diehl. Mrs Visetti was entertaining extravagantly and 'spending God knows what on clothes, sometimes £60 to £70 at one go'. Alberto had retired in 1926. He had no income or savings and had not insured his life. He had given someone a piano as a wedding present which was not paid for and, he said, 'never would be'. 'In his old age he has come down on me his step-daughter is what it boils down to', Radclyffe Hall wrote to her cousin Winifred.

> Mother just sits back and either is, or pretends to be helpless when I urge any practical steps. Every suggestion I make she opposes in fury and her scenes and her tempers have completely worn me out so that I am unable to work and earn money. This I point out from time to time but I can make no impression on her. She only abuses me the more loudly. To nothing will she listen and frankly my mother acts as though she were deranged at times. She appears to literally hate me.
>
> Nothing softens her in spite of the fact that I have taken on my shoulders the whole burden of paying their rent, rates and taxes and all the expenses

of her illness (I have paid for all her illnesses for many years past, as well as meeting constant demands for sums of money) and have put all work aside to go into their affairs and am still hard at it. I have no idea when I shall be able to get on with my book & earn more money to augment an income which was OK before the war, but is now reduced owing to terrific taxation and trade depression.

Meanwhile I am devilled by my publishers and no wonder – I am so fearfully behind hand. Last evening I went to bed early because I was so worn out only to get a message to the effect that Albert was dangerously ill and mother *spitting blood*! Calling up their doctor I find that mother has a throat cough and that what she spat up was slightly streaked with blood from nose or throat and that Albert has a feverish bronchial cold and should be all right in a few days.

The whole business has shocked me beyond words. Albert is just frankly dishonest and as far as I can see always has been, making no provision and never attempting to pay his debts – my mother has developed into a worse fury than she used to be and that is saying a good deal I can assure you. Are they both mad? I dont know, I only know that their house has such a dreadful name that no decent servant will go near it and that this greatly shames me, who am living in the same neighbourhood and who am now very well known owing to my books. There are moments when I literally feel in despair ... My mother screamed at me so loudly in the nursing home that the doctor said that they would probably ask her to leave.

It was intolerable for Maria Visetti to have her daughter preaching to her about money. It rankled with her not to have benefited from her first husband's estate. She now had the prospect of rented rooms while her daughter lived like a lord in a palatial house. It made her hate her. The hatred was reciprocated. 'I have so often felt the bitterness of having no mother', Radclyffe Hall wrote. Her mother's tempers were, she said, a thousand times worse than in the past. She talked to Alfred Sachs about sending her to a 'nerve specialist'.

He assured me that in his opinion no nerve specialist could say more than that she is a woman of violent and uncontrolled temper and also extremely hysterical. He says that she is terribly *jealous of me*! Can you beat that? Moreover as I only seem to excite her every time she sees me, he advises my keeping away. The whole thing has made me rather ill myself.

Maria refused to look after Alberto while he was ill. She said to do so gave her vertigo. She refused to apply powder prescribed for sores on his body, and brought in two nurses at her daughter's expense. Radclyffe Hall decided to allocate her mother a monthly allowance on the understanding that 'all communication between us ceases and that she leaves me unmolested and in peace so that I can get on with my work.

What have I ever done to have such a mother, God knows! It's money they're both after – they always have been – well they will get my money but not me any more. I don't see why I should be expected to support my disgusting old Step Father, or why I should have to support Mother because she has run through her capital and does nothing but abuse me for all I have done already, but there it is!

... It has been a great drawback to me in every way that she ever married him, & now I have to pay for the privilege of having sustained that drawback ... Anyone to see & hear my mother in one of her rages would think that she was mad.

Against the background of such feuding she worked at her ground-breaking novel. She wrote into the small hours of the night at an American rolltop oak desk. She said her book was fictional over details of place and people and only autobiographical on the 'fundamental emotions that are characteristic of the inverted'. 'Then, I admit, I did draw upon myself, I drew very ruthlessly upon myself, hoping that by telling my readers the truth, *The Well of Loneliness* would carry conviction.'

She might have viewed bitterness towards her mother, anger at desertion by her father, disgust at Visetti as a stepfather, and dependency on the devotion of lovers, as emotions fundamental to herself, and explored such deep if troubled waters. She might have told of her loathing of her mother's instability, of fears of abandonment, of her need for control and sexual conquest. Instead, she took the nature not nurture line. If she was martyred, it was by God not Mother. Any physical resemblance to Maria Visetti or admission of her power was intolerable. Better to be a freak, misfit, changeling or man, than her daughter. God, the architect of all things, alone had parented Radclyffe Hall. He, 'in a thoughtless moment had created those pitiful thousands who must stand forever outside His blessing'.

Una read aloud about congenital sexual inverts, from *Studies in the Psychology of Sex* by Havelock Ellis, *A Manual of Sexual Science* by Magnus Hirschfield and *Psychopathia Sexualis* by Richard Krafft-Ebing. Radclyffe Hall took the bits that suited her, mixed them with Catholicism, spiritualism and her own ideas on endocrinology and came up with a theory of lesbian identity about as empirically reliable as the paternity of Jesus Christ or Mabel Batten's whereabouts on *ha!* sphere three.

She drew no conceptual distinction between belief and knowledge. Her huge archive on Mabel Batten's posthumous activities was evidence of her tenacity to maintain that what she wanted to be so, was so. Her theories stemmed from her need to control her world, her untutored mind, her attraction to the folklore theories of her time and her religious implacability. She claimed scientific objectivity but it was the world according to Radclyffe Hall.

Stephen Gordon, like her, was *the* congenital sexual invert, the *true* invert. Her attributes: small hips and breasts, broad shoulders, large feet, short hair, the look in her eye, 'the terrible nerves of the invert' were defining characteristics like the beak, plumage and mating habits of the crested grebe. Those who did not have these attributes belonged to a different genus.

← religious essentialism

Congenital inversion is not unnatural. These congenital inverts are born not made. They are put into the world by God's will alone – the God of infinite understanding, compassion and wisdom. Whether you like the fact or not it is one which must be accepted by all who value truth and justice...

Congenital inversion is caused by an actual deviation from the usual in the glandular secretions of the invert's body. Those glandular secretions influence the cells, & thus the whole human structure, physical, mental & spiritual. You can kill all the inverts but while they live you cannot make them other than inverted. They are and will always remain as God made them, and their sexual attractions will be therefore inverted as they were in the girl of whom I wrote – the unfortunate girl Stephen Gordon.

It was all rather resistant to scrutiny. At one moment God was thoughtless, the next He was infinitely wise. It was not clear what these secretions were doing or whether they were happening to less than 'true inverts' like Mabel Batten and Agnes Nicholls, whose bottoms and breasts were far from small. There was a curious hierarchy, a dangerous genetic model. 'Real' inverts were like Radclyffe Hall. Ersatz ones were like Una or Tallulah Bankhead.

Stephen Gordon is a third sex, an indeterminate sex, a 'man trapped in a woman's body', 'a blemished, unworthy, marred reproduction' of her father Sir Philip Gordon, who lives in Morton, a manor house in Malvern. His fixation on having a son, the way he calls her Stephen before she is born, teaches her to bat, hunt, drive and be a chap, is not presented as contributing to her dislocation over gender.

Stephen is born 'a narrow hipped, wide shouldered little tadpole of a baby'. Though destined to suffer, she is superior to the rest of the world. She is a martyr, not a victim. There was a distinction in Radclyffe Hall's view. Martyrs were on a theological par with the peerage. Victims were of a lower order and had no status or reward.

As a child, Stephen, 'bearing some unmerited burden', identifies with Nelson and Jesus Christ. 'She studied the picture of the Lord on His Cross and she felt that she understood Him.' She hates dresses, likes breeches, masochism and the housemaid. 'I'd like to be awfully hurt for you, the way Jesus was hurt for sinners', she says to her and wants housemaid's knee instead of her enduring it. The footman kisses the housemaid and Stephen is 'filled with a blind uncomprehending rage' and throws a broken flowerpot at him. Such kissing, she feels, should come from her.

She is tall, poised, purposeful, physically and mentally splendid, the fitness ideal of a later decade. She fences, lifts weights, wins horseriding trophies. 'There was a kind of large splendour about her ... grotesque and splendid, like some primitive thing conceived in a turbulent age of transition.' She speaks fluent French, appreciates 'all literary beauty', has impeccable artistic judgement, 'a great feeling for balance in sentences and words' and 'the intuition of those who stand mid way between the sexes, so ruthless, so poignant, so accurate, so deadly'.

Sir Philip hires a governess for her, Miss Puddleton, square shouldered and flat chested, who in her time has dallied with the ladies 'in accordance with the dictates of her nature'. Puddle, as Stephen calls her, knows Stephen has 'real red hot talent' and will be a great writer. 'Face yourself calmly and bravely, do the best with your burden,' she tells her charge.

'The invert's most deadly enemies are not infrequently his or her parents', Radclyffe Hall wrote in notes for an unpublished article about her book. Lady Anna loathes her daughter Stephen with a quintessential recoil. 'All your life I've felt a kind of physical repulsion, a desire not to touch or be touched by you', she tells her. Stephen is 'ill at ease and ungracious' at garden parties. She shakes hands too strongly and has nothing in common with other girls. She prefers men 'because of their blunt, open outlook', but they find her too clever, too like themselves: 'They were oak trees preferring the feminine ivy. It might cling rather close, it might finally strangle, it frequently did, and yet they preferred it, and this being so, they resented Stephen, suspecting something of the acorn about her.'

Stephen meets Martin Hallam, who owns farms in British Columbia. They are 'perfect companions'. He rides, hunts, fences and touches trees 'with gentle pitying fingers'. In Stephen's view they are like brothers, but he 'trembles before his own passion' for her. When he tells her he loves her 'over her colourless face there was spreading an expression of the deepest repulsion – terror and repulsion and something else too, a look as of outrage'. She feels that 'the loneliest place in this world is the no-man's land of sex' and that she has more in common with her horse, Raftery.

Why a man should desire a woman who finds him sexually repulsive is an unexplored theme. 'Is there anything strange about me Father that I should have felt as I did about Martin?' Stephen asks poor Sir Philip, who shuts himself in his study making marginal notes about her in *Psychopathia Sexualis* and *Sexual Anomalies and Perversities*. 'It had come. It fell on his heart like a blow.' He knows that his daughter is a Congenital Sexual Invert. 'His loins ached with pity for this fruit of his loins ... You have maimed my Stephen', he wants to say to God.

He and Lady Anna quarrel about the fruit of their loins. It would be a disaster if Stephen were to marry, he tells her. Anna is jealous of Stephen's closeness to him; 'she has taken you from me, my own child, the unspeakable cruelty of it', she says. Then Sir Philip gets killed by a falling tree. His dying words are: ' "Anna – it's Stephen – listen. It's Stephen – our child – she's, she's – it's Stephen – not like – " ... His head fell back rather sharply then lay very still upon Anna's bosom.'

He might have been going to say she's not like other girls, but mother knew that already.

18

She kissed her full on the lips

R adclyffe Hall had no abiding interest in the psychopathology of sex. Congenital inversion was not the stuff of daily life or popular fiction. She and Una were soon back to their normal reading matter – *Crazy Pavements*, *A Misjudged Monarch*, *Mother's Axe* – and to first nights in the West End: Noël Coward's 'awful play' *Sirocco Days* and *Thunder in the Air* at the Duke of York's.

She wanted authority of a clinical sort to get her book about the unfortunate Stephen Gordon past the censor and to hush cries of 'filth'. From Fox-Pitt, the Troubridges and her mother, she knew the force of homophobia. Her book was a protest against what she called 'the deadly campaign of silence':

> Not only has this constituted a grave danger to the inverts themselves who, in addition to all else have not hitherto dared to proclaim their existence, (a most undesirable state of affairs and one likely to render them morbid,) but this campaign of silence has been a grave danger to a hetero-sexual society, that has resolutely refused to face a problem which was and is above all things social.

As each chapter was typed, a 'special copy' was put aside marked 'for the attention of Dr Havelock Ellis'. She wrote and told him he was 'the greatest living authority on the tragical problem of sexual inversion' and asked him if he would write a preface. He said he always refused such requests but that he was deeply interested in the subject, 'having had many friends, both men and women, who were, as they sometimes say, "so" ', and he would like to read her book when it was finished. Radclyffe Hall persisted. A preface from him would give gravitas to her story. She called at his house uninvited and left a sycophantic letter. Her tenacity was rewarded. Havelock Ellis agreed that if the book appealed to him, he would 'express an opinion that might be used'.

By November 1927 Radclyffe Hall was on page 780 of *Stephen*. She was more ambitious for this than for any other of her books. Another literary award for *Adam's Breed* – the James Tait Black Prize – made her certain her new book would cause a stir. Una did a word count and came up with the title *The Well of Loneliness*. She read chunks of it aloud to Audrey and they all talked of how later chapters should develop.

Radclyffe Hall prepared for fame. Charles Buchel did a drawing of her, which she wanted used for publicity. She ordered new uniforms for the servants and two fur coats for Una – a Persian lamb and a mink. She had the house redecorated and recarpeted, bought leather chairs and more oak furniture. And she socialized with the lesbian *haut monde*, all of whom anticipated publication of her book. At dinner at Gabrielle Enthoven's she met Mercedes de Acosta, who was in love with Greta Garbo. Evelyn Irons, the Women's Page editor of the *Daily Mail*, who was in her twenties and lived in Chelsea with her partner Olive Rinder, interviewed her for a satirical article on 'How Other Women Run Their Homes'. 'If I spy specks of dust I have to control my itch to remove them, for I have the housewife's seeing eye', Radclyffe Hall was supposed to have said. Irons and Rinder, as Una called them, joined their set. Violet Hunt, who had so helped Radclyffe Hall win the Prix Femina, wrote, 'I want to see your new novel. I believe I shall like it better than *Adam's Breed*.' Toupie heard screeds of it read aloud.

Radclyffe Hall's assertion that *The Well of Loneliness* was fictional over details of place and people was not true. She did not invent in her novels. They were storehouses of her experiences and preoccupations. Her settings for the book were Malvern, the lesbian salons of Paris after the First World War, the Canary Islands where she went with Mabel Batten, the ambulance unit in occupied France as described by Toupie. Friends were in the narrative undisguised. The 'brilliant' playwright Jonathan Brockett, tall, sardonic, thin, was Noël Coward even to the bags under his eyes and 'feminine' white hands. The dilettantish writer, Valerie Seymour, with 'very blue, very lustrous eyes' and 'masses of thick fair hair', who rules the lesbian salon life of Paris, was Natalie Barney. 'Her love affairs would fill quite three volumes, even after they had been expurgated', Radclyffe Hall wrote. The swipe was pure Una about Natalie.

The Well of Loneliness had bits of pathological case history, religious parable, propaganda tract and Mills & Boon romance. From Havelock Ellis she took the idea of the 'congenital invert'. From the church she said God the Father created all things. To justify desire, she invoked sexology and the Lord. Her prose style was lofty, with words like betoken and hath. Stephen Gordon makes biblical utterances: 'How long O Lord, how long!' and 'I have the mark of Cain upon me.' But friends, everyday life and different constructions of lesbianism kept sneaking in to make the book more interesting: Natalie Barney's soirées, the suffragettes' revolt against patriarchy, Toupie and her ambulance unit.

Radclyffe Hall was too troubled a person to write an untroubled book, but she might have acknowledged the privilege, seductions, freedom and fun that graced her daily life. She indicted the 'ruthless pursuing millions, bent upon the destruction of her and her kind', but seemed to endorse the value system that saw marital, reproductive sex as best. Her model of 'the finest type of the inverted woman' was scary and doomed. Stephen Gordon was a transsexual, ill at ease with herself and her body, 'her strangely ardent yet sterile body ... she longed to maim it, for it made her feel cruel'.

Nothing overly sexy goes on in *The Well of Loneliness*. 'She kissed her full on the lips like a lover' is the subversive depth of the book. Lovers do spend the night in bed with each other, but they are 'in the grip of Creation, of Creation's terrific urge to create; the urge that will sometimes sweep forward blindly alike into fruitful and sterile channels'. (From time to time Radclyffe Hall said she wanted to father a child.)

When she is twenty-one, Stephen Gordon inherits a whack of money, like her author. She starts an affair with Angela Crossby, an American wife of the disaffected sort Radclyffe Hall liked to seduce. 'As their eyes met and held each other something vaguely disturbing stirred in Stephen.' Angela has a homophobic toad of a husband, Ralph, who, like Oliver Hoare, forbids his wife to see 'this freak'. 'That sort of thing wants putting down at birth', he says. Ralph gives Angela 'flaccid embraces', has a 'sly pornographic expression', is given to 'arrogant masculine bragging' and goes to bed in pink silk pyjamas. Stephen, by contrast, 'would sacrifice her life for the sake of this woman', gives her pearls, wears white crêpe-de-Chine pyjamas and drives a red 'long bodied sixty horse power Metallurgique'.

'Can you marry me?' Angela asks her. Marriage was an issue for Radclyffe Hall. She believed it should be an entitlement for lesbians. She described Una as her mate and said were she herself a man in the biological sense they would have married. But Una might not have wanted to marry such a man of a man, feeling as she did about sex. Nor, because of the Catholic Church, had she divorced Troubridge. In the religion they chose for the signposts it gave, homosexuality and adultery were sins.

It was all morally and semantically awkward. 'I cannot keep the fifth commandment', Radclyffe Hall wrote of her dishonourable parents. It was not the only commandment she could not keep. And yet, in her fiction and in her life, she kept pitting herself against manmade edicts, patriarchal values, in order to be martyred the more. In *The Well of Loneliness* Stephen writes a love letter to Angela, 'page after page ... What a letter!'

> You know how I love you, with my soul and my body; if it's wrong, grotesque, unholy – have pity ... I'm some awful mistake – God's mistake – I don't know if there are any more like me, I pray not, for their sakes, because it's pure hell.

Ralph shows the letter to Stephen's mother, Lady Anna, who banishes Stephen from Morton. 'I would rather see you dead at my feet', she says and calls her a scourge, vile, filthy, corrupt, against nature and against God. 'As a man loves a woman that was how I loved – protectively like my father', Stephen declaims. 'In my hour of great need you utterly failed me; you turned me away like some unclean thing ... If my father had lived he would have shown pity, whereas you showed me none.'

So much for mother; no vestigial maternal understanding, incapable of a hug for her daughter or a word of care. Work is Stephen's palliative. She is a great writer, a jeaneous, no less. Her novels of 'outstanding literary merit' have titles like *The Furrow*. She is 'true genius in chains, in the chains of the flesh'. Valerie Seymour finds her a house in Paris in the rue Jacob. In its grounds is a derelict temple, which Stephen renovates. (Radclyffe Hall filled her book with such allusions for the delectation of friends.)

In the 1914 war, instead of knitting socks in Malvern with Mabel Batten, Stephen, like Toupie Lowther, drives an ambulance in occupied France. She meets in her unit 'many a one who was even as herself', CSIs who have 'crept out of their holes' and 'found themselves' in the 'whirligig of war'. She gets her face lacerated by flying shrapnel, 'an honourable scar as a mark of her courage'. Like Toupie she is awarded the Croix de Guerre. She falls for Mary Llewellyn, who was orphaned as a child, is little, obedient, young and uneducated. 'She knew nothing of life, or of men and women and even less did she know of herself.' The head of the unit, Mrs Breakspeare, disapproves of the relationship and discourages it. She says 'it savours a little too much of the school-room'.

But Mary is besotted with Stephen. All her life she has been waiting for her. She wants to kiss her 'more than anything in the world'. Stephen warns her of the price she will pay:

> If you come to me, Mary, the world will abhor you, will persecute you, will call you unclean. Our love may be faithful even unto death and beyond – yet the world will call it unclean. We may harm no living creature by our love; we may grow more perfect in understanding and in charity because of our loving; but all this will not save you from the scourge of a world that will turn away its eyes from your noblest action, finding only corruption and vileness in you. You will see men and women defiling each other, laying the burden of their sins upon their children. You'll see unfaithfulness, lies and deceit among those whom the world views with approbation. You will find that many have grown hard of heart, have grown greedy, selfish, cruel and lustful; and then you will turn to me and will say: 'You and I are more worthy of respect than these people. Why does the world persecute us, Stephen?' And I shall answer; 'Because in this world there is only toleration for the so called normal!' And when you come to me for protection I shall say: 'I cannot protect you, Mary, the world has deprived me of my right to protect; I am utterly helpless, I can only love you.'

Mary is not put off. None of that matters at all. 'Can't you understand

that all that I am belongs to you, Stephen?' she says. Like Radclyffe
Hall and Mabel Batten, they go to Tenerife and Santa Cruz. They stay
in the same hotels and villas as they did. In Paris they set up home with
a dog called David in the house with the temple in the garden. Stephen
pays the bills and writes sensationally successful books. Mary does
wifely things like shopping, marvelling at Stephen's prose and lunching
with her at Pruniers.

'Being a woman', she wants ordinary things like friendly neighbours
and weekend visits to in-laws. Stephen has 'county instincts'. She is
law-abiding and wears berets and double-breasted suits. As a couple,
they are devoted and respectable. But they are ostracized. Lady Anna,
beastly as ever, will not let Mary near Morton. And Lady Massey who
was once a friend cancels an invitation for Stephen and Mary to spend
Christmas at Branscombe Court: 'Of course a woman in my position
with all eyes upon her has to be extra careful', she says.

Jonathan Brockett warns Stephen that Mary has become socially
isolated. Stephen takes her to Valerie Seymour's salon. They befriend
Pat whose ankles 'were too strong and too heavy for those of a female';
Jamie from the Highlands who is a 'trifle unhinged' and whose friend
Barbara gives her awful haircuts; Wanda, a struggling transsexual
Polish painter; Hortense, Comtesse de Kerguelen, 'a very great lady'
and Margaret Roland, Valerie Seymour's current partner, a poetess
with a voice 'like a boy's on the verge of breaking'.

Stephen and Mary dance together in clubs like Le Narcisse and
Alec's, 'to which flocked the battered remnants of men whom their
fellow men had at last stamped under'. Like Brockett these men have
soft white hands and 'the terrible eyes of the invert'. Stephen fears
Mary will herself become a battered remnant unless she has a husband,
children, and normal friends. She speaks of prejudiced people who are
'socially murdering' them. In an unlikely dénouement she pushes Mary
into the arms of her own old admirer Martin Hallam. To make Mary
feel betrayed and therefore able to leave, Stephen feigns spending the
night with Valerie Seymour.

Stephen then falls ever deeper into The Wells of Martyrdom. Her
purpose in life is to fight the cause of inverts. 'In their madness to
become articulate through her, they were tearing her to pieces':

They possessed her. Her barren womb became fruitful – it ached with the
fierce yet helpless children who would clamour in vain for their right to

salvation. They would turn first to God, and then to the world, and then to her. They would cry out accusing: 'We have asked for bread; will you give us a stone? Answer us: will you give us a stone? You, God, in Whom we, the outcast, believe; you, world, into which we are pitilessly born; you, Stephen, who have drained our cup to the dregs – we have asked for bread; will you give us a stone? ... Stephen, Stephen, speak with your God and ask Him why He has left us forsaken.'

And now there was only one voice, one demand; her own voice into which those millions had entered. A voice like the awful, deep rolling of thunder; a demand like the gathering together of great waters. A terrifying voice that made her ears throb, that made her brain throb, that shook her very entrails, until she must stagger and all but fall beneath this appalling burden of sound that strangled her in its will to be uttered.

'God,' she gasped, 'we believe; we have told You we believe ... We have not denied You, then rise up and defend us. Acknowledge us, oh God, before the whole world. Give us also the right to our existence!'*

THE END

---

* Richard von Krafft-Ebing in *Psychopathia Sexualis*, in the case study of 'S', quotes from her diary:

I relied on God, that one day my emancipation would come ... O God, Thou All-pitying, Almighty One! Thou seest my distress; Thou knowest how I suffer. Incline Thyself to me; extend Thy helping hand to me, deserted by all the world.

S was a Hungarian countess who 'knew how to imitate a scrotum with handkerchiefs or gloves stuffed in the trousers' and who to the chambermaids explained menstrual blood on her sheets as 'haemorrhoidal'.

THE TRIAL OF
RADCLYFFE HALL

19

Aspects of sexual inversion

ewman Flower at Cassell had first option on *The Well of Loneliness*. His hopes were high for a new novel by Radclyffe Hall after the success of *Adam's Breed*. A pious man, a devout Christian and a keen gardener, he had a precious manner and was the author of sentimental essays and poems. On 10 April 1928 Radclyffe Hall penned him a letter he must have sweated to receive. Were he to publish, she *'could not consent to one word being modified or changed'*. His was to be a disciple's role. He must 'stand behind this book to the last ditch,' she told him, 'go all out on it for the sakes of those for whom I have written'.

Having attained literary success I have put my pen at the service of some of the most persecuted and misunderstood people in the world. In a word I have written a long and very serious novel entirely upon the subject of sexual inversion ... So far as I know nothing of the kind has ever been attempted before in fiction.

It is doubtful whether Radclyffe Hall and Una, Natalie Barney, Romaine Brooks, Winnaretta Singer, Toupie Lowther, Colette, Evelyn Irons, Gabrielle Enthoven, Teddie Gerrard, Tallulah Bankhead and the rest, with their fine houses, stylish lovers, inherited incomes, sparkling careers and villas in the sun, were among the most persecuted and misunderstood people in the world. Nor did they need an apologist for their affairs, loves and sexual escapades.

Newman Flower replied to Audrey Heath within days. Radclyffe Hall was a great artist, he took his hat off to her, it was a fine book, but not one he could publish. It would harm his list. William Heinemann's director, Charles Evans, then said no. He viewed the book as propaganda, 'and inevitably the publishers of it will have to meet not only severe criticism but a chorus of fanatical abuse which although unjustifiable may nevertheless do them considerable damage. That consequence we are not prepared to face.' Martin Secker returned the typescript a week later. It was not a commercial proposition, he said, but he would happily give Radclyffe Hall a contract for whatever she wrote next.

Audrey Heath then offered the book to Jonathan Cape. Cape knew his fellow publishers had backed off because of its lesbian theme. He did not rate Radclyffe Hall's literary style, nor did he want 'to strike an attitude – portrait of a publisher doing something daring and heroic', but he respected her sincerity and sales figures and he liked innovative work. By 1927 his list included Ernest Hemingway, T. E. Lawrence, Sinclair Lewis, Edna St Vincent Millay and Mary Webb.

'I wrote the book from a deep sense of duty', Radclyffe Hall told him. 'I am proud indeed to have taken up my pen in defence of those who are utterly defenceless, who being from birth a people set apart in accordance with some hidden scheme of Nature, need all the help that society can give them.' Cape lunched with her, Una and Audrey on 8 May at the Berkeley. He outlined his plan to publish *The Well of Loneliness* in a sober manner that suggested a serious subject, of no interest to the prurient. The book would have a black binding and plain jacket and be priced at twenty-five shillings – about four times more than the average novel. He proposed a cautious print run of 1,250 copies to test public response. He offered Radclyffe Hall an advance of £500 against royalties and encouraged her to pursue a preface from Havelock Ellis.

A hitch about liability for legal costs in case of trouble gave her 'an agitated & worried evening and night'. It was then agreed that she and Cape would share any such liability. She signed the contract at his office at midday on Friday 11 May. She then drove with Una to Brixton to chivvy Havelock Ellis. He had only read part of the manuscript, but said he was confident the rest would please him equally. He would give a short appraisal for Cape to use.

John and Una went back to Holland Street to 'a peaceful and happy evening'. A nightingale sang in the garden opposite their house. They went to mass and visited Ladye's catacomb. John bought four hats for Una from Adèle's and was herself fitted for new suits at Weatherills. Ellis's 150-word appreciation, when it came, she thought 'perfect'. 'So far as I know,' he wrote of *The Well of Loneliness*,

> it is the first English novel which presents, in a completely faithful and uncompromising form, various aspects of sexual inversion as it exists among us today. The relation of certain people – who, while different from their fellow human beings, are sometimes of the highest character and the finest aptitudes – to the often hostile society in which they move, presents difficult and still unsolved problems. The poignant situations which thus arise are here set forth so vividly and yet with such complete absence of offence, that we must place Radclyffe Hall's book on a high level of distinction.

Ellis

John and Una went to *Turandot* at Covent Garden, which neither of them enjoyed. Poucette was sick in the car *en route* to the Windsor Dog Show where she came only third in her class. Men from Maples came to fit new carpets and curtains and a sunny room at the back of the house was fitted out as a sitting-room for Una who had shingles, thrush and an everlasting cold.

An American publisher for *The Well of Loneliness* proved hard to find. Doubleday, Houghton Mifflin and Harpers all turned it down. Then, at a literary party on 23 May, Radclyffe Hall talked to Blanche Knopf, wife and business partner of Alfred Knopf. She liked the avant-garde and had flirted with the idea of publishing Gertrude Stein. She evinced great interest. A copy of the manuscript was delivered to her at the Carlton Hotel that night. Six days later Radclyffe Hall dined alone with her. Una spent the evening with Minna. Blanche Knopf asked for an option on the book until the middle of June. She wanted to take legal advice in New York. Radclyffe Hall wanted unequivocal and immediate acceptance. She discussed strategy with Audrey, gave Mrs Knopf a grand dinner at the Savoy and tried to fathom her intentions at a session with Mrs Leonard.

Three weeks later Una wrote in her diary of a 'thousand alarms & excursions anent Knopf & book'. (Both Una and Radclyffe Hall favoured the Old English 'anent' instead of 'about' or 'in reference to'.) The contract Knopf offered had a clause that made Radclyffe Hall financially responsible for any action taken against the book under Manhattan law. Advised by Theodore Goddard, she instructed her American agent, Carl Brandt, to give Mrs Knopf a week to withdraw the offending clause. If she refused, he should offer the book to Harcourt Brace.

Proofs arrived from Cape and John and Una checked that not a word had been changed or deleted. They put their furs into store for the summer and Una ordered a divan and cushions for her new room. Cape intended to use Havelock Ellis's piece as a foreword, but wanted to change the phrase 'various aspects of sexual inversion', to 'one particular aspect of sexual life'. Sexual inversion, he felt, might offend sensitive minds.

Havelock Ellis agreed the change, but was uncomfortable at being dragooned into seeming so intimately to support this particular book. Radclyffe Hall was determined to blaze his endorsement. 'The thought of your appreciation of *The Well of Loneliness* sustains me perpetually', she wrote to him on 4 June. 'I say to myself, "What need you care what the fools of this world say, think or do, since one of the wise and great has set his seal on your work." '

She sent him handkerchiefs, regretted his reluctance to be her guest at supper and let him know that equal deference came for him from Una, 'the friend who has shared my home for thirteen years and who is prepared to stand shoulder to shoulder with me.' 'The mate of the invert must be strong unto death and not everyone can stay the course', she told him. (She was an invert, Una was an invert's mate.)

No such solidarity was accorded Blanche Knopf, whose equivocation tried John's nerves. 'My patience is completely at an end', she wrote to Brandt as the Knopf deadline drew near:

> It is not that I do not like Mrs Knopf personally, I do; but I am accustomed to dealing with men in business, to going perfectly straight for a point, and above all to sticking to essentials. I find it both difficult and tedious to deal with a woman and this I have several times told her quite frankly, asking her to settle all business details with my agents . . . it is better for women to keep out of business negotiations.

Perhaps neither she, Audrey or Una came into the disparaging category of women. Inverts and inverts' mates were men enough to stick to essentials and get to the point.

Blanche Knopf amended the contract and on 26 June Radclyffe Hall signed it at Audrey's office with Una as witness. She then went into action. No detail of publication was to be left unsupervised. Knopf were to typeset from Cape's proofs. She had ticked each page in red and if any word was altered or omitted she would 'consider it *a breach of contract*'. Blanche Knopf was on no account to use the publicity photograph Doubleday chose when promoting *Adam's Breed*. It made Radclyffe Hall look, she said, like 'a middle-age gent given to imbibing, or worse still a stout old lady masquerading'.

Proofs were corrected, copies collated, prelims prepared. At the end of June, Cape decided to bring forward publication to 24 July. Compton Mackenzie's novel *Extraordinary Women* was to be published by Martin Secker in September. It was a spoof on society lesbians, set on Capri during the 1914–18 war. In it he mocked the clothes, monocles, affairs and lives of Radclyffe Hall, Una, Romaine Brooks and Natalie Barney. He compared them to 'peculiar Aeolian fauna' and made them farcical in appearance and behaviour. They would, he said, make 'Freud blush, Adler blench, Jung lower his eyes and Dr Ernest Jones write his next book in Latin.'

His book was humorously malicious and designed to entrench prejudice, not dispel it. Cape and Radclyffe Hall saw it as competition and in the time-honoured publishing panic of which book the world will want, they aimed to get there first. Radclyffe Hall added £150 to Cape's £300 advertising budget and, in a metaphor as mixed as her depiction of gender, told him to use the money in 'the best and wisest way to defeat our rivals and steer *The Well of Loneliness* to success'.

She aspired to moral, financial and literary success. In the evenings Una read aloud Oscar Wilde's *Ballad of Reading Gaol*, his *De Profundis* and a biography of him by Frank Harris. Radclyffe Hall identified with Wilde's trials. If God willed she too would be spat at on Clapham Junction station, imprisoned, vilified, crucified. A generation after Wilde her cause was to rid lesbianism of the stigma of moral degradation. In her book she articulated a female homosexual identity. That, she knew, would incur the scrutiny of the law. 'Hitherto the subject has either been treated as pornography, or introduced as an episode, or veiled', she wrote. 'I have treated it as a fact of nature – a simple, though at present tragic fact.'

She prepared herself for fame or infamy. Nothing was left to the discretion of the publisher who might show concern for other books too. She and Una discussed every detail with Audrey over dinners at Boulestins and the Ritz. Large advertisements were booked in the *Yorkshire Post*, the *Spectator*, the *Sunday Times*, the *Observer*, the *Times Literary Supplement* and, for publication day, in seven daily papers.

Day after day it was eighty degrees in the shade. Day after day Una endured Alfred Sachs's interminable gynaecological treatments. Two of the dogs, Dickie and Baloo, lodged in kennels, got run over and, on 10 July, amid early morning preparations to exhibit Mitsie and Poucette at the Richmond Dog Show, Maria Visetti's solicitor phoned with the news that Alberto had died.

His death was an irrelevancy to Radclyffe Hall and led to no repair of the broken relationship with her mother. It took her a day to sort out funeral arrangements, see her solicitor, arrange the moving of Visetti's corpse from his house at Phillimore Terrace to the undertaker's. John was 'abominably received' by her mother, Una remarked in her diary. Visetti had died insolvent so John paid all burial costs and for his grave at Brookwood Cemetery. None of it deflected from the true crusade. She attended mass with vespers, benediction and the procession of Our Lady of Mount Carmel but her prayers were more for *The Well of Loneliness* than for her 'disgusting old stepfather's' journey to the damned.

Press copies were ready by 15 July. Cape hiked the print run to 5,200 copies, ordered paper for a 5,000 run-on, and now pitched the selling price at fifteen shillings. Radclyffe Hall rallied support. She sought allegiance to The Cause rather than disinterested appraisal for a piece of fiction. She was the vessel through which God's truth was poured. Criticism of *The Well of Loneliness* was sacrilege and silence cowardice. 'I know you will believe me,' she wrote to Una's brother-in-law James Garvin, who happened also to be editor of the *Observer*,

when I tell you that I wrote this book from a sense of duty, a sense of duty which I dared not disobey ... I have tried to bring the thing out into God's air and light – for the *Truth* must never be feared, since it is the truth ... It would be childish for me to pretend that I do not know how much your support in the *Observer* would contribute from the first appearance of my book on July 24th towards its success – above all towards its reception in the proper spirit, the spirit of desire for impartial justice and understanding towards an unhappy and very important section of the community.

Garvin's support was not forthcoming. The *Observer* was one of the few national papers not to review the book. Both Una's sister and mother disliked her relationship with Radclyffe Hall and the subject of lesbianism in general. They chose silence not justice and understanding. Their disassociation widened the gulf between them and Una.

More loyally, Ida Wylie was encouraged to give a glowing review for the *Sunday Times*. Vera Brittain was to review the book for *Time and Tide*, Arnold Bennett for the *Evening Standard*, Leonard Woolf for the *Nation*. Jonathan Cape phoned to say Havelock Ellis was annoyed to see his opinion piece used as an intrinsic preface when he had intended it as no more than a publicity puff. Radclyffe Hall and Una drove to Brixton to explain themselves but Ellis was out. They talked to Cape, lunched at the Ritz Grill, then drove again to Ellis, had tea with him 'and made all well', so Una said.

They had done all that they could and more to launch the book into life. They went again to mass to pray for it and to Mrs Leonard to see what Ladye knew. 'P of W of L', Una wrote in her diary on Friday 27 July. 'Dinner Here Everyone'. There were telegrams of congratulation, flowers, champagne. Andrea was packed off to guide camp. John and Una toured the bookshops. *Wells of Loneliness* were everywhere, row after row in W. H. Smith's window, in the Times Bookshop, in Trueloves and Harrods.

Next day, John had earache and the first of the reviews appeared. L. P. Hartley in the *Saturday Review* wrote of the book's force and sincerity, its powerful appeal, its passages of great beauty, but criticized its polemical stance. Ida Wylie in the *Sunday Times* wrote of Radclyffe Hall's courage, honesty and 'lively sense of characterisation'. Con O'Leary in *T. P.'s Weekly* said readers would agree with Havelock Ellis that 'poignant situations are set forth with a complete absence of offence'. Vera Brittain thought the book important, sincere, passionate, never offensive, but was confused as to whether Stephen Gordon's gender bend was because of nature or upbringing. Reviewers with sophisticated attitudes to homosexuality and exacting standards for literature were critical. Leonard Woolf in the *Nation* called the book a failure, lacking form, discursive, tendentious. Cyril Connolly in the *New Statesman* said it was 'long, tedious, absolutely humourless and a melodramatic description of a subject which has nothing melodramatic about it:

> *The Well of Loneliness* may be a brave book to have written, but let us hope it will pave the way for someone to write a better. Homosexuality is, after all, as rich in comedy as in tragedy, and it is time it was emancipated from the aura of distinguished damnation and religious martyrdom which surrounds its so fiercely aggressive apologists.

The subject matter was not a problem. The fears of publishers appeared misplaced. Reviews accrued over the next four weeks. Many were favourable, some were critical, all were unsensational. Una began a book of press cuttings. By 2 August Harrods and the Times Bookshop had sold all copies and reordered twice. Cape planned a third edition. John and Una were thrilled by what looked like clear success. They decided to leave London on 23 August for a long summer holiday. Una went to Cook's and booked travel tickets and hotel reservations. They planned to sail to Calais, take the Golden Arrow to Paris, go to Bagnoles for the thermal baths, then journey on to Italy and summer in the sun.

They had their hair cut at Harrods and took a course of treatment at Cyclax for their complexions. Andrea dined one evening, but they left her and went to the first night of *The Skull* at the Shaftesbury Theatre. The vet called to cut Lurulu's wings and claws. An acquaintance, Anne Elsner, a travel writer who admired *The Well of Loneliness* and who lived in a house called Journey's End in Rye, invited them to spend a weekend with her. John loved Rye. She was thrilled by the views of marshland and the sea, the distant lighthouse and the glimpse of France, the cobbled streets and Tudor architecture. At the Catholic church of St Anthony, the priest, Father Bonaventura, gave her a silver gilt medal of this saint and invited her to kiss a relic of the true cross. She resolved to buy a house in Rye after the summer holidays. She went home to London 'tired but happy'. In the *Evening Standard* Arnold Bennett wrote of her book's 'notable psychological and sociological significance' and called it 'honest, convincing and extremely courageous'.

On her forty-eighth birthday John went to high mass with Una and Andrea. In the evening Una read aloud Havelock Ellis's latest book, his seventh. It was called *Eonism and Other Supplementary Studies* and it was about transvestism. On Friday 17 August the *Daily Tele-graph* gave *The Well of Loneliness* the best of reviews and said it was 'truly remarkable', 'a work of art finely conceived and finely written'. More tours of the London bookshops gratified. *The Well* was in all the windows. Sales were fast. John went to the chiropodist and a Mrs Fowler came to collect Mitsie to keep her in kennels over the holiday.

John felt established as the 'bold pioneer', the first writer to 'smash the conspiracy of silence'. She was proud of the praise her book received. She did not know that Jonathan Cape had that morning received a note from James Douglas, editor of the *Sunday Express*, director of London Express Newspapers, member of the Garrick Club, author of *The Unpardonable Sin* and *The Man in the Pulpit*. Douglas informed Cape that he had written an editorial calling for *The Well of Loneliness* to be suppressed. It would appear in his paper that weekend.

20

Depraved practice

Jonathan Cape had not sent review copies of *The Well of Loneliness* either to the *Daily Express* or the *Sunday Express*. He wanted to avoid their editor's brand of lurid interest. But James Douglas read the book and knew he could drum up scandal of the sort that sold his newspapers. On Saturday 18 August *Express* hoardings advertised impending disclosure of 'the book that must be banned'. George Ellard, a sales clerk at Cape's offices at Bedford Square, said the phone did not stop ringing all day. Bookshops rushed to order more copies of *The Well*. Collectors and messengers queued outside the trade counter. 'They all wanted copies: ones, twos, sixes, tens, twenty-fives, fifties; and in the case of Bumpus, a hundred.'

Next morning, Sunday 19 August, at Holland Street, John and Una had the newspapers and breakfast brought to their bedroom by Cartwright the maid. Douglas's peroration spanned five columns of the *Sunday Express*. His inch-high banner headline was A BOOK THAT MUST BE SUPPRESSED. Publication of *The Well of Loneliness* was 'an intolerable outrage – the first outrage of the kind in the annals of English fiction'. This was a book that contaminated and corrupted literature. It was not fit to be sold by any bookseller or borrowed from any library. It was his duty as a critic to make it impossible for any other novelist to repeat this outrage.

Its theme is utterly inadmissible in the novel … I am well aware that sexual inversion and perversion are horrors which exist among us today. They flaunt themselves in public places with increasing effrontery and more insolently provocative bravado. The decadent apostles of the most hideous and most loathsome vices no longer conceal their degeneracy and their degradation.

They seem to imagine that there is no limit to the patience of the English people. They appear to revel in their defiance of public opinion. They do not shun publicity. On the contrary they seek it and they take a delight in their flamboyant notoriety. The consequence is that this pestilence is devastating the younger generation. It is wrecking young lives. It is defiling young souls.

It was, Douglas reasoned, perhaps a blessing or a curse in disguise that this novel had appeared. Its purpose was to make society face a disagreeable task which it had hitherto shirked, 'the task of cleaning itself from the leprosy of these lepers, and making the air clean and wholesome once more'.

The battle against this filth, he said, had been lost in France and Germany, but not in England,

and I do not believe that it will be lost. The English people are slow to rise in their wrath and strike down the armies of evil, but when they are aroused they show no mercy, and they give no quarter to those who exploit their tolerance and their indulgence.

It is no use to say that the novel possesses 'fine qualities' or that its author is an 'accomplished' artist. It is no defence to say that the author is sincere or that she is frank, or that there is delicacy in her art.

The answer is that the adroitness and cleverness of the book intensifies its moral danger. It is a seductive and insidious piece of special pleading designed to display perverted decadence as a martyrdom inflicted upon these outcasts by a cruel society. It flings a veil of sentiment over their depravity. It even suggests that their self-made debasement is unavoidable because they cannot save themselves.

This terrible doctrine may commend itself to certain schools of pseudo-scientific thought, but it cannot be reconciled with the Christian religion or with the Christian doctrine of free-will. Therefore, it must be fought to the bitter end by the Christian Churches. This is the radical difference between paganism and Christianity.

If Christianity does not destroy this doctrine, then this doctrine will destroy it, together with the civilisation it has built on the ruins of paganism. These moral derelicts are not cursed from their birth. Their downfall is caused by their own act and their own will. They are damned because they choose to be damned, not because they are doomed from the beginning.

We must protect our children against their specious fallacies and sophistries. Therefore, we must banish their propaganda from our bookshops and libraries. I would rather give a healthy boy or a healthy girl a phial of prussic acid than this novel. Poison kills the body, but moral poison kills the soul.

What, then, is to be done? The book must at once be withdrawn. I hope the author and the publishers will realise that they have made a grave mistake, and will without delay do all in their power to repair it. If they hesitate to do so, the book must be suppressed by the process of law … I appeal to the Home Secretary to set the law in motion. He should instruct the Director of Public Prosecutions to consider whether *The Well of Loneliness* is fit for circulation, and, if not, to take action to prevent its being further circulated.

Finally, let me warn our novelists and our men of letters that literature as well as morality is in peril. Fiction of this type is an injury to good literature. It makes the profession of literature fall into disrepute. Literature has not yet recovered from the harm done to it by the Oscar Wilde scandal. It should keep its house in order.

Radclyffe Hall's photograph was printed alongside this diatribe. There she was with short hair, bow tie, chappish clothes, hand in pocket, lighted cigarette, clearly lesbian, a decadent apostle of hideous and most loathsome vices, a moral derelict and a poisoner of souls.

Douglas's prose style seemed to parody her own. Each hectored, invoked the Lord and buried their argument beneath overblown prose. Both were ambitious, melodramatic, opinionated, upholders of the moral high ground, preachers of The Truth. Like Fox-Pitt with his 'grossly immoral woman' charge, Douglas was the outraged patriarch, the guardian of the nation's morals. In a single editorial he contrived to be offensive to homosexuals, lesbians, those with leprosy, the French, the Germans and all who were not Christians.

Jonathan Cape reacted in fear and haste. That same day, without talking to Radclyffe Hall or Audrey Heath, he sent a copy of *The Well of Loneliness* and a selection of its reviews to the Home Secretary. He invited him to pass the book, if he wished, to the Director of Public

'Always my mother. Violent and brainless. A fool but a
terribly crafty and cruel fool.' Maria Visetti, circa 1890

'I must have been a tiresome and disconcerting baby.' Marguerite in Philadelphia, circa 1883, with her mother, right, grandmother Sarah Otley Diehl, standing, and great-grandmother

'Would I have loved my father if I had known him?' Radclyffe Radclyffe-Hall, circa 1880 and Marguerite, aged five. Oil painting by Katinka Amyat, 1885

'My disgusting old stepfather.' Alberto Visetti, circa 1905, founding professor of the Royal College of Music, London

'I had no intention of allowing my mother to handle my estate.' Radclyffe Hall, circa 1910

'My true unfailing inspiration, my reason for all things'.
'Ladye', Mabel Batten, circa 1900

'I should not have been sidetracked
into marrying at all'.
Una Vincenzo Troubridge with her
daughter, Andrea, circa 1912

'Troubridge brought me no
spiritual development,
no evolution, no kindness.'
Admiral Sir Ernest Troubridge,
circa 1919

'Had I been a man I should have married Una.'
Una Troubridge, circa 1916

Prosecutions. He then wrote a reply for Douglas to print:

> If it is shown to us that the best interests of the public will be served by
> withdrawing the book from circulation we will be ready to do this and
> to accept the full consequences as publishers. We are not however pre-
> pared to withdraw it at the behest of the Editor of the *Sunday Express*.

Cape accused Douglas of giving widespread and unwanted publicity
to the book and of spoiling his own intentions of targeting 'the right
class of reader. Smut hounds and those with a taste for pornography
would now be seeking the book out.'

James Douglas was victorious. He printed Cape's letter on Monday
20 August in the *Daily Express*. His new headline was A BOOK TO BE
BANNED. THE HOME SECRETARY'S DUTY. He ranted about *The
Well of Loneliness* in another editorial. It condoned sexual perversity,
loosened 'the very sheet anchor of conduct and principle', made crime
and indecency a matter of individual judgement and inferred that 'there
were no such things as right and wrong in the universe. On these lines
murderers could be comfortably assured not merely of acquittal, but
of sympathy as the martyrs of their "psychological impulses". And
murderers only slay the body, while these perverts destroy the soul.'

Radclyffe Hall was incredulous when she read Cape's letter in the
Daily Express. 'This was the first that I knew of my publisher's intention', she revealed. 'His were the sins of imbecility coupled with
momentary panic.' Havelock Ellis was disbelieving too. 'I have not
anywhere met with approval of his action', he wrote to her that week.
'He *invited* the Home Secretary's opinion – which he might have known
beforehand!'

The Home Secretary, Sir William Joynson-Hicks, 'the Preposterous
Jix', was an evangelical moralist. He was President of the Zenana Bible
Mission and a fervent opponent of the Revised Prayer Book. Even the
Bishop of Durham called him a 'dour fanatic' who proceeded against
one cause after another with 'dervish like fervour'. Joynson-Hicks
instructed the police to patrol public parks 'for violations of public
decency', established the Street Offences Committee, chaired by his
wife, to crack down on prostitution, prosecuted dozens of nightclubs
and casinos for gambling and sexual offences, secured a judicial ruling
that made the Communist Party illegal and authorized a 200-strong
police raid on a small, unwitting Russian trade delegation.

He received Cape's letter and a copy of the book on the afternoon of Monday 20 August. His reply reached Cape by hand on Wednesday 22 August. 'One's mind reels', wrote Radclyffe Hall. 'In a few hours my book had been read & carefully considered! Over 500 pages – large format – 180,000 words.' But Joynson-Hicks had done more than consider the book. He had, in that short time, made sure that his colleagues who held high judicial office would manipulate the law to get it banned.

The Director of Public Prosecutions, Sir Archibald Bodkin, was away. Joynson-Hicks sent the book by messenger to Bodkin's deputy, Sir George Stephenson. He was at home in Newick in Surrey. Joynson-Hicks asked him whether, if Cape was prosecuted for obscene libel, a jury would convict. Sir George replied the same day:

> The book has been widely and favourably reviewed in the press. It is described as 'sincere, courageous, high minded and beautifully expressed.' The fact however remains that it is in effect a plea not only for the toleration but for the recognition of sexual perversion amongst women. With regard to the contention which might be made on behalf of the authoress that she did not intend to corrupt her readers, intent is immaterial, the question for the jury being 'whether the tendency of the matter charged as an obscenity is to deprave and corrupt those whose minds are open to such immoral influence and into whose hands a publication of this sort may fall'. (see Hicklin L. R. 3 QB 371)
>
> In my view this book would tend to corrupt the minds of young persons if it fell into their hands and its sale is undesirable. It is of course impossible for me to say more than that I think a jury *ought* to convict if proceedings are taken. Whether they would do so or not is another matter. My view however is that there would be a reasonable prospect of a conviction. Incidentally it would appear to be clear that the authoress is herself what is known as a homo-sexualist, or as she prefers to describe it an 'invert'.
>
> I may say that I have informally consulted the Chief Magistrate [Sir Chartres Biron] upon this matter; he has read the book and tells me that he would have no hesitation in granting process. I should add that before instituting any proceedings in this matter I should consider it my duty to take the directions of the Attorney General [Sir Thomas Inskip].
>
> I do not understand that I am asked to express my views upon the question of policy to prosecute. A prosecution would undeniably give the book a further advertisement and it may well be that the Secretary of

State would think it desirable to avail himself of the offer made in the letter of the publisher Messers Jonathan Cape to the Home Office to withdraw the book from circulation.

I return your files.

G.S.

Joynson-Hicks then had a 'long private conference with the Lord Chancellor. We came to the conclusion that the book is both obscene and indecent.' He drafted a letter to Cape, which Sir George Stephenson checked and sharpened. *The Well of Loneliness*, he wrote, was 'inherently obscene'; it dealt with and supported a depraved practice; its tendency was to corrupt; it was 'gravely detrimental to the public interest. I am advised, moreover, that the book can be suppressed by criminal proceedings. I prefer, however, to believe that in view of your letter you will accept my decision and withdraw the book, and this I now ask you to do.'

'If they decline, proceed at once', Joynson-Hicks wrote to Sir George. Cape appeared to comply with the Home Secretary's wishes. He feared the expense of the law and the effect of adverse publicity on his publishing house. His letter of capitulation was published in *The Times*:

Sir,

We have to-day received a request from the Home Secretary asking us to discontinue publication of Miss Radclyffe Hall's novel 'The Well of Loneliness'. We have already expressed our readiness to fall in with the wishes of the Home Office in this matter, and we have therefore stopped publication.

I have the honour to be your obedient servant,

Jonathan Cape

But Cape had also to fall in with the wishes of Radclyffe Hall, who was as determined as the Home Secretary. He contrived a devious strategy. Five thousand copies of the book were already in circulation, or available from shops and libraries. No order had been given to destroy these, no criminal proceedings were imminent. The scandal was creating a huge demand. The printer was about to run a third reprint. Cape cancelled this, but told the printer to make moulds of the type as quickly as possible and to deliver them to him. His plan was to ship these moulds to Paris and to get the book printed there.

John and Una were supposed to be up at five-thirty the following day to set off for Paris, Bagnoles and Italy. All was cancelled. They hurried to Mrs Leonard who failed to predict what would happen next. Mrs Smith, their current housekeeper, and Cartwright the maid left as planned for their holidays. 'All day at telephone, letters, wires etc.,' Una wrote in her diary.

21

Sapphism and censorship

The writer Arnold Bennett went to the Garrick Club on the day Joynson-Hicks told Cape to withdraw *The Well of Loneliness*. He saw James Douglas in the lounge talking to Sir Chartres Biron, Chief Magistrate of the Bow Street police court. 'I set violently on Jimmy at once about his attack on Radclyffe Hall's sapphic novel. Jimmy was very quiet and restrained but Biron defended Jimmy with *real* heat; so I went on attacking. I told Jimmy to come in and lunch with me. He did. He said there was an imp in me.'

Sir Chartres Biron had already been 'informally consulted' by the Deputy Director of Public Prosecutions on how to suppress the book. His real heat was to flare again two months later. He was the presiding magistrate when the book was tried as an obscene libel.

James Douglas voiced his bigotry to sell his newspapers. Chartres Biron, like Joynson-Hicks, used his judicial power to enforce his homophobic views. 'Unnatural practices between women,' Biron said, were 'of the most horrible and disgusting obscenity.' Inverts and perverts should be 'treated with condemnation by all decent people'. They were 'practitioners of unnatural vice, living in filthy sin'.

The Well of Loneliness posed problems for those it purported to defend. Lesbians might squirm at its theories and curl at its rhetoric, protest that its author's perceptions were not theirs, recoil at being claimed so categorically, or defined by its terms. But such embarrassment was a small price when set against the homophobia the book uncovered in the ruling class, the men of the establishment, the government that made the rules, the judiciary that enforced them, the press that disseminated them.

Radclyffe Hall was proved right in her suspicion that her book would provoke antagonism. Her courage was put to the test. 'I hate inaction', she wrote. 'I am by nature a fighter.' Havelock Ellis told her that unjust decisions 'light up the principle involved and stir enthusiasm'. Her book beamed like a searchlight into the dim lounges of clubs like the Garrick. It lit up the flawed men of power, gossiping with each other, plotting strategy, entrenching prejudice. It was not the state of literature that disturbed them. They did not care about literature. It was passion between women. They feared its acceptance if Radclyffe Hall was heard. They had their view of a woman's place and they intended to legislate against this affront to it. They had not forgotten Radclyffe Hall's challenge to Sir John Lane Fox-Pitt and Admiral Troubridge. The Home Secretary, the newspaper editor, the Chief Magistrate, the government of the day, closed ranks to silence her and to show that she was, after all, 'a grossly immoral woman'.

Radclyffe Hall was frustrated that it was Jonathan Cape not herself who stood accused by the Home Secretary. 'I,' she said, 'as nothing *more important than the Author*, I, mark you, could not take legal action.' Her book and her right to live as she did were under attack. There was an atmosphere of repression, of picking safe words and taking a stance. She was infected by it too. On 24 August, the *Daily Herald* printed a letter of protest from her 'on behalf of literature'. It was a pleading for freedom of speech, not a defence of lesbian rights.

> If seriously written psychological novels are to be subjected to arbitrary attack from the Home Office, which attacks result in their being withdrawn, what chance has our sane and well educated public of obtaining the best output from publisher and author?
>
> Must there never be any new pastures for the writer? Never any new aspects of social problems presented to the adult and open minded reader? Is the reader to be treated like a kind of mental dyspeptic whose literary food must be predigested by Government Office before consumption?
>
> Such action can only insult the public intelligence and discourage our authors from writing sincerely, especially our younger and less established authors some of whom may yet have new messages for us.

On behalf of English literature I must protest against such unwarrantable interference.

In literary circles the talk was of 'sapphism and censorship'. Virginia Woolf complained of the distraction in a letter of 30 August to Vita Sackville-West, with whom she was, in a way, in love:

> For many days I have been so disjected by society that writing has been only a dream – something another woman did once. What has caused this irruption I scarcely know – largely your friend Radclyffe Hall (she is now docked of her Miss owing to her proclivities) they banned her book and so Leonard and Morgan Forster began to get up a protest, and soon we were telephoning and interviewing and collecting signatures – not yours for *your* proclivities are too well known. In the midst of this, Morgan goes to see Radclyffe in her tower in Kensington, with her love: and Radclyffe scolds him like a fishwife, and says that she wont have any letter written about her book unless it mentions the fact that it is a work of artistic merit – even genius. And no one has read her book; or can read it: and now we have to explain this to all the great signed names – Arnold Bennett and so on. So our ardour in the cause of freedom of speech gradually cools, and instead of offering to reprint the masterpiece, we are already beginning to wish it unwritten.

Vita was in Potsdam on holiday with her two sons. To Harold Nicolson, her husband, she wrote that *The Well of Loneliness* was 'not in the least interesting apart from the candour with which it treats its subject. Of course I simply *itch* to try the same thing myself. You see if one may write about b.s.ness the field of fiction is immediately doubled.' (Harold Nicolson and Vita Sackville-West used their marriage as a cover and referred to their same-sex lovers as 'backstairs business'.) To Virginia she replied that she felt very violently about the ban, 'not on account of what you call my proclivities; not because I think it is a good book; but really on principle'. The preposterous Jix made her want to renounce her nationality, she said. 'But I don't want to become a German, even though I did go to a revue last night in which two ravishing young women sing a frankly Lesbian song.'
Radclyffe Hall scorned a protest that opposed the suppression of literature in principle but made no mention of 'either the merits or the decency' of *The Well of Loneliness*. Such an attitude would compromise her 'in the eyes of her public', she said. She could not tolerate the

Bloomsbury Group's intellectual superiority and equivocation. She felt they would disparage her book 'given sufficient scope'.

Which scope they had. In her diary, Virginia Woolf called *The Well of Loneliness* a 'meritorious dull book'. To Ottoline Morrell she wrote, 'The dulness of the book is such that any indecency may lurk there – one simply can't keep one's eyes on the page.' To her sister Vanessa Bell, she mocked her mother-in-law's interest in it. She said Radclyffe Hall 'screamed like a herring gull, mad with egotism and vanity' when E. M. Forster questioned its literary worth. *Orlando*, her own virtuoso novel, was to be published in 1928 to lasting praise. It won the Prix Femina that year. It was about and dedicated to Vita Sackville-West. The lesbian allusions in *Orlando*, its flights of gender, were too aerial and implicit, too clever and concealed, to interest the Home Secretary or the editor of the *Express*.

Radclyffe Hall felt patronized and paranoid. Here was support, but not the sort she wanted. She drew up her own letter of protest and with Una elicited the backing of doctors, booksellers, ministers of religion, social workers. The Bloomsbury petition dwindled to a short piece by Forster, a tepid defence of literary freedom, published in the *Nation* on 8 September, which he asked Virginia Woolf to sign too. It fumbled any mention of lesbianism; 'it enters personally into very few lives and is uninteresting or repellent to the majority', Forster wrote. To Leonard Woolf, he said he found 'Sapphism disgusting'.

Radclyffe Hall was the plodding amateur, not one of them, not of the elite. She lacked their intellect, style and wit. They did not seek to change minds as she did with her proselytizing, rather they reached out to like minds. They recoiled from her bluntness and felt compromised by supporting her. The use of the word 'proclivities', the closeting of their own sexual preferences, the guarded manner of their protest, spoke of their lack of candour and their vanity for the social show.

They had same-sex relationships but liked to demarcate between private indulgence and public discomfort. Vita was an aristocrat and a lesbian, therefore she should not sign a public letter for fear of jeopardizing her social position. Her novel about b.s.ness did not transpire, though both she and the love of her life, Violet Trefusis, believed they could outdo *The Well of Loneliness*. Vita's account of their affair lay locked away in a Gladstone bag and was not to be published until after their deaths.

The manuscript of E. M. Forster's novel *Maurice*, his admission of homosexuality, was hidden too until he died. A visit to Edward Carpenter in 1913 had inspired it. Carpenter, like Havelock Ellis, was another proponent of the idea of the 'intermediate sex'. His partner, George Merrill, fondled Forster's bottom 'gently and just above the buttock. I believe he touched most people's', Morgan wrote.

> The sensation was unusual and I still remember it, as I remember the position of a long vanished tooth . . . It seemed to go straight through the small of my back into my ideas, without involving my thoughts. If it really did this, it would have acted in strict accordance with Carpenter's yogified mysticism, and would prove that at that precise moment I had conceived.
>
> I then returned to Harrogate, where my mother was taking a cure and immediately began to write *Maurice*.

He was to shut his baby up in a cupboard for nearly sixty years.

On 1 September John and Una visited Noël Coward. He was in a London nursing home, having had his piles surgically excised. They found him writing the second act of *Bitter Sweet*. It was not his style to give public support to *The Well of Loneliness*, but he invited them to visit him and his mother the following weekend at his house, Goldenhurst Farm, Aldington, near Rye. It was a seventeenth-century farmhouse with oak beams, six acres of land, an orchard, ponds and views of the Romney marshes, the sea and the coast of France. John and Una lazed in the sun and had 'a delightful day'. They stayed at the Mermaid Inn in Rye and themselves hunted for a house away from the squalls of city life. They took a short lease on Anne Elsner's Tudor cottage, Journey's End, with its views of the River Rother, of timber ships with tall masts and of lighthouses and the sea. Lighted by oil lamps and heated by wood fires, it was, said Una, 'a heavenly haven of peace in which we pulled ourselves together for the next round'.

In London Radclyffe Hall offered the Holland Street house for sale. She took translation copies of *The Well* to Audrey Heath who within a week sold Dutch rights. She wooed Blanche Knopf with lunch at Kettners and dinner at the Savoy and urged her to keep her promise to publish in America. And Jonathan Cape pressed on with his subversive plan. His partner, Wren Howard, a stocky man with a military manner, blue eyes, red cheeks and a bristling moustache, flew to Paris on 6 September with the papier-mâché moulds of *The Well of Loneliness* in suitcases as hand baggage. It was the early days of air travel and scrutiny by Customs at airports was scant.

Howard delivered the moulds to John Holroyd-Reece, proprietor of the Pegasus Press at 37 rue Boulard. Holroyd-Reece had worked with Cape before and had met Radclyffe Hall at Datchet at Ida Temple's house. He had voiced interest in publishing *The Well of Loneliness* himself. European in outlook with a German father, Johann Riesz, and a Scottish mother, he was keen on taking risks and making money. He had a wife, a lover, a taste for lavish houses and expensive antiques. He instructed a London solicitor, Harold Rubinstein, a partner in the firm of Rubinstein, Nash & Co., 'a man of liberal and literary sensibilities', to act for him and Pegasus Press. He introduced Cape and Radclyffe Hall to Rubinstein who acted for them too.

Cape leased the rights of *The Well* to Pegasus and gave Holroyd-Reece a list of unfulfilled British orders and an overseas mailing list. Within three weeks pirate copies were printed and circulars sent to British booksellers offering the book at twenty-five shillings plus eleven pence postage. Here, the circular promised, was the original edition with not a comma changed. 'The book is concerned with the phenomenon of the masculine woman in all its implications. It deserves better than to be suppressed by government action following on a campaign by a single newspaper.' Orders were brisk. Holroyd-Reece appointed a London bookseller, Leopold Hill at 101 Great Russell Street, to act as his distributor. There was no formal ban on publication and initially no interference from the authorities.

Blanche Knopf, though, on 27 September 'ratted', as Una put it, on American publication. From New York she wrote that orders were coming not from the 'better type of booksellers' but from dealers in dirty books who expected something 'very salacious'.

Our decision not to publish it will, I am sure, come as a very great shock to you, but you must view the situation from our point of view. You are an English author, and you secured a reputable English publisher for this book. The English publisher, on request of a public authority, withdrew the book from circulation, and in this withdrawal you acquiesced. You made no attempt to compel him to carry out the terms of his agreement and thus bring the matter to the attention of the Courts, the only bodies competent to render a legally binding decision. We are thus faced with

the hopeless prospect of attempting to defend a book which has not been
defended in its author's own country.

She wanted to 'preserve' the signed contract as an option on the next
two books Radclyffe Hall might write. Radclyffe Hall scorned her. It
was not her nature to see 'the situation' from another's point of
view. Audrey Heath sent a cable to Carl Brandt: 'In view disgraceful
termination contract John absolutely refuses any compromise with
Knopf. Has already received alternative offers and has signed contract
with Cape.' Cape took over the American rights. Audrey sailed to the
States to try to find a new publisher.

In London Radclyffe Hall courted support and publicity. She gave
press interviews, wrote letters and with Una in one week went to first
nights of *The Song of the Sea*, *The Scarlet Pimpernel* and *Thunder on
the Left*. 'John mobbed for her autograph', Una said. Secretarial help
came in the form of a Miss Webber, who addressed envelopes all day.

'Now enter Mr James Douglas again', Radclyffe Hall wrote in her
unpublished account of the fate of her book. 'This time we get the
Daily Express breaking out into fresh invectives.' On 3 October a
journalist from the *Daily Sketch* phoned the Home Office saying he
had seen a circular issued by Pegasus about subscriptions for *The Well
of Loneliness*. He asked what action the government intended. 'Pending
consideration of the circular it was too early to make any statement',
was the Home Office reply. But Joynson-Hicks wasted no time. He
that day issued a warrant to the Postmaster-General 'and all others
whom it may concern'.

I hereby authorise and require you to detain, open and produce for
my inspection any postal packets which may be observed in course of
transmission through the post and which are addressed to the Pegasus
Press ...

Next day Douglas ran a story of how *The Well of Loneliness* was
pouring into Britain and all over the world. He demanded immediate
action from the Home Secretary. Joynson-Hicks issued another
warrant – to the Chairman of the Board of Customs Sir Francis Floud.
Floud was to prevent the book being imported. He instructed all the
ports. Copies found 'in goods or in passengers' baggage' must be seized.
At Dover a consignment of 250 copies addressed to Leopold Hill was
held. The *Express* aired Douglas's approval:

That is the kind of invigoratingly prompt and effective action that becomes a Government department. The book was suppressed for reasons of decency and taste. But other questions arise when an attempt is made to evade this suppression by delivering the offending novel through the post and from abroad. The matter then becomes one of deliberate affront to the constituted authority. As such it must be sharply resented and its perpetrators taught that they cannot thus trifle with Government.

A general election was imminent. Douglas was telling the Conservative government what it must do to get the support of readers of his newspapers.

Harold Rubinstein, for Pegasus Press, asked Joynson-Hicks on what authority he acted, 'so that our clients may take appropriate action to test the matter'. John Anderson from the Home Office replied: 'The matter is one for the Board of Customs and Excise, to whom any communication on the subject should be addressed.' The Board of Customs and Excise then replied to Rubinstein that it had a statutory obligation to detain literature that might be 'obscene and indecent'. Rubinstein asked them to hurry up and decide whether *The Well of Loneliness* was obscene and indecent. The Board replied that it was not a matter to be dealt with hastily and they 'were according it particularly careful consideration'.

In fact there was a problem. It was the duty of Customs to prevent the importing of indecent books under section 42 of the Customs Consolidation Act of 1876. By 9 October Sir Francis Floud and other members of his Board had read *The Well of Loneliness*. They did not think it obscene. Floud thought it a fine book. He called to see Sir John Anderson at the Home Office. Anderson told him that the Lord Chancellor and the Home Secretary intended proceedings under the Obscene Publications Act.

Floud wanted no part in it. He disliked the involvement forced upon him. He did not want to fob off Rubinstein, hold the consignment of books at Dover, or testify against the book in court. Nor did he want to flout 'the publicly expressed opinion of the Home Secretary'. He gave his view in a memorandum to the Chancellor of the Exchequer.

The subject is treated seriously and sincerely, with restraint in expression and with great literary skill and delicacy ... If the subject is one that can permissibly be treated at all in a novel, it is difficult to see how it could be treated with more restraint. If on the other hand the subject is to be regarded as inadmissible, it will be difficult to know where our censorship is to stop.

He asked for permission to release the books. The Chancellor deferred his decision until he had seen the Home Secretary.

Without Floud's support Joynson-Hicks had to put into place an alternative strategy of censorship. His colleagues came to his rescue: the Lord Chancellor Lord Hailsham, the Attorney-General Sir Thomas Inskip, the Director of Public Prosecutions Sir Archibald Bodkin, the Chief Magistrate Sir Chartres Biron.

On 11 October the Director of Public Prosecutions gave instructions to the Metropolitan Police. The Dover consignment when released was to be shadowed until delivered to Leopold Hill. A watch was to be kept on Hill's premises 'in case the parcel is removed to any other address'. Four copies of the book, ordered by Jonathan Cape and intercepted by the Post Office, were to be delivered at the same time as the Dover consignment. The police were to be waiting at both addresses with search warrants.

Joynson-Hicks had a further problem. He feared that if tried by jury *The Well of Loneliness* would not be banned. He knew the strength and eminence of those defending this book, how articulate they were, how wide their support of it and interest in it, how persistent the press coverage, how cogent and persuasive judicial defence might be. He intended to avoid such a trial and impose his prejudice. On 15 October, with the book still stuck at Dover, he warned of his intentions in a lecture to the London Diocesan Council of Youth. It was reported in *The Times* the next day:

> It may be possible in the near future I shall have to deal with immoral and disgusting books ... I am attacked on the one hand by all those people who put freedom of speech and thought and writing before everything else in the world, as if there were freedom in God's world to pollute the young generation growing up. There must be some limit to the freedom of what a man may write or speak in this great country of ours. That freedom in my view, must be determined by the question as to whether what is written or spoken makes one of the least of these little ones offend.

The following day a letter from the publisher Geoffrey Faber expressed disbelief:

He indicates the kind of censorship he will practise ... the whole of the content of English literature is to be restricted in future to such stuff as Sir William thinks it safe to put in the hands of a schoolgirl. Is it possible that a 20th century British Government can be contemplating such an incredible *betise*?

The answer was no. Hicks was not interested in literature or the minds of the young. He was not going to censor ill-written novels about murder, burglary, adultery, torture, war and cataclysm. It was sex between women that interested him. He thought it a pollutant and he was going to deal with it.

On 18 October, Rubinstein got a warning letter from a junior official at the Customs Board:

> Gentlemen
> I am instructed by the Commissioners of Customs and Excise to refer to your letter of the 10th instant and to inform you that instructions have been given to release the consignment of copies of *The Well of Loneliness* which were detained at Dover.
> I am however to add that the decision of the Commissioners to release the consignment is without prejudice to any action that may be taken by any other Department.
> I am Gentlemen
> Your Obedient Servant
> James Cook

The consignment, reduced to 247 copies, was delivered to Leopold Hill on 19 October. The four intercepted copies were waiting at Cape's office. Chief Inspector John Prothero of the Metropolitan Police Force and his men were at both places with search warrants. These had been issued under the Obscene Publications Act of 1857 by no other than Sir Chartres Biron, Chief Magistrate at Bow Street. The police took the books and circulars and proof of postage to customers. They tried to search Cape's private files until stopped by Rubinstein. They handed their spoils to Chartres Biron.

'The government was bent upon persecution', Radclyffe Hall wrote. 'Are we living in England? ... It seems to me that this shameless & benighted government of ours would gladly institute a rain of teror. They have tried by every means in their power to terrify me into cowed submission – but in this they have failed I do assure you.'

Summonses followed. Leopold Hill and Jonathan Cape were 'commanded to appear' at Bow Street Court on 9 November before Chartres Biron to 'show cause why the said obscene books so found and seized as aforesaid should not be destroyed'. Rubinstein had fifteen days to prepare what he thought would be their defence.

Radclyffe Hall galvanized support and worked at the statement she intended to make in court. It was clear to her that it was she who was on trial, the essence of her, her life, her sexuality and her book. Una typed this statement, honed it, read it out. They moved between the turmoil of London and the peacefulness of Rye, between walks with the dogs on Camber Sands and Romney Marsh and endless meetings with lawyers. They lunched at the Mermaid Hotel and took mass with Father Bonaventura in the small Catholic church. In the evenings Una read aloud *Orlando*.

22

A serious psychological subject

Rubinstein sent out 160 letters eliciting support for publication of *The Well of Loneliness*. He aimed to pack the Bow Street court with eminent professionals opposed to the destruction of the book, who would defend it persuasively. He compiled a mass of expert testimony to its virtues and gathered a glittering array of witnesses to give 'good cause' why the book should freely circulate. He believed that the numbers of the book's supporters, their status and expertise, would overwhelm any case for the prosecution.

He marshalled support from the literary, the erudite, the devout, the successful and respectable. Many of those he approached were anxious to avoid the witness box; 'they generally put it down to the weak heart of a father, or a cousin who is about to have twins', Virginia Woolf wrote. It was only Radclyffe Hall who wanted to stand in the dock, embarrass the world to its withers and declaim, 'I am an invert, read me.' The Archbishop of York foresaw 'practical difficulties' if he offered support. H. G. Wells had 'gone abroad'. Arthur Conan Doyle had 'left for South Africa'. John Galsworthy, President of the PEN Club, was too busy and did not think literary freedom was at risk. (Joynson-Hicks had personally asked him to testify against the book.) Bernard Shaw said he was himself too immoral to have credibility. Alec Waugh had not read it and hated legal proceedings. Harley Granville-Barker did not regard 'sexual perversion a fit subject for art'. Professor J. B. S. Haldane's 'scientific occupations did not permit him to take part in such controversies'. Geoffrey Faber, as head of a publishing company, could not defend particular books. James Agate declared himself ill and Eden Phillpotts declared himself a recluse.

Havelock Ellis would do no more than he had done already. 'I have *never* been in the witness box', he wrote to Radclyffe Hall. He said he 'lacked the essential qualities of a witness', that his book *Sexual Inversion* had been condemned as an obscene libel thirty years earlier, so he was 'tarred with the same brush'. 'The less said about me the better for you. In any case, for good or evil my testimony is already contained in the book itself. It is people of the highly conventional and respectable kind, and occupying a high position who will be really helpful.' Hugh Walpole agreed to stand, though he disliked airing the subject of homosexuality and thought Cape had undermined the defence by sending the book to the Home Secretary, then withdrawing it voluntarily.

Unequivocal support came from Robert Henry Cust, author and magistrate. He resigned from the executive committee of the London Morality Council because of its hostile attitude to *The Well of Loneliness*. Cheap bookstores, he said, were 'brimming with filth of the vilest kind', yet here was a 'heart-rending decent book'. 'Such a persecution of its authoress savours of medieval or even primitive barbarism.' Charles Ricketts, printer, thought it an admirable study of English rural and cosmopolitan life and would recommend it to any mother of daughters. Sheila Kaye-Smith called it sincere, moving, restrained. To judge literature by its possible effects on children or those of 'abnormal mentality', she said, would end in its total suppression, as no book could be guaranteed not to mislead the young or mad.

Many who offered support did so in defence of the principle of literary freedom rather than out of enthusiasm for Radclyffe Hall or her book. Leonard Woolf said that as literary editor of the *Nation* and proprietor of the Hogarth Press most books published in Britain passed through his hands. Taking the standards of modern books published every day and masterpieces continually republished in cheap editions, *The Well of Loneliness* was not indecent or likely to corrupt anyone. E. M. Forster said obscenity existed not in a subject but in its treatment and that 'Miss Hall's treatment is unexceptionable.' Radclyffe Hall did not like the word unexceptionable applied to her writing. Virginia Woolf, from whom any blandishment was laced with irony, said it treated a delicate subject with great decency and discretion. Storm

Jameson, until that year a manager for the London branch of Knopf, thought if it had not been for James Douglas's stunt, only the serious-minded would have bothered to read the book.

Rose Macaulay was rude about Radclyffe Hall's prose. She did not see how the book could corrupt anyone as its heroine had such a rotten time. Stephen Gordon, she said, was pointed at in the street, abused by her mother, snubbed by society and had to live in Paris to escape contumely. She seemed 'physically and mentally defective, an imputation which I am told is resented by addicts and which probably has a salutary effect on young or would be addicts'.

Naomi Mitchison thought the book long, very sincere, sentimental and distinctly depressing. Adolescents with homosexual tendencies would be discouraged. Normal men or women would see it as a call to be kind to their 'abnormal fellow beings'.

Laurence Housman called it 'an unexaggerated statement of the social sufferings and disabilities of an involuntary invert'. He recommended classification of these unfortunates be altered from the criminal to the medical and commended publication because it provoked discussion.

Joan Sutherland, author of *Beauty for Ashes* and *The Enchanted Country*, said she had a son and daughter, that *The Well of Loneliness* was a serious novel which could not harm them and that authors should be permitted freely to write what they desired to express.

Edward Garnett, whom Virginia Woolf described as a 'surly, shaggy, unkempt old monstrosity', had forty years' experience as a publisher's reader and literary adviser. He derided James Douglas's article in the *Sunday Express* as hysterical, uncritical and sensational. He had looked through all the twenty-four reviews of *The Well of Loneliness*. None had asked for the book to be withdrawn. Many praised its beauty, burning sincerity, high-mindedness, honesty. Some had thought it too long, sentimental and overcharged. None challenged it on the grounds of immorality.

Alfred Lyons, Cape's London salesman, said the only complaints he had received had been about the book's high price. Alfred Butes, manager and director of the Times Book Company and the Times Book Club, called himself 'an interpreter of the mind of a large reading public'. He thought the book admirable. If it was obscene, he would not have ordered copies. Library subscribers, he said, would not be dictated to as to what they ought or ought not read, but if he judged a book offensive he told the library superintendents not to put it on the open shelves. *The Well* was not in that category. It was in great demand after the success of *Adam's Breed*. Seven hundred copies were in circulation and he had not received a single objection from subscribers.

Those with medical qualifications gave their views to Rubinstein, however specious, with authority. James Norman, lecturer in mental diseases at the Westminster Hospital Medical School and author of *Mental Disorders*, said sexual inversion was a congenital disposition and *The Well of Loneliness* an interesting study of sexual inversion in the female. Dr Stella Churchill said the fate of the invert was a melancholy one and this book should act as a warning to young normal girls tempted to experiment with such relationships.

Norman Haire, who was to be Radclyffe Hall's star witness after Havelock Ellis bowed out, declared that homosexuality ran in families and a person could no more become it by reading books than he (if not she) could become syphilitic by reading about syphilis.

John Thomson Greig, Registrar of the University of Durham, thought society should be educated into accepting inverts. There were more of them than the world supposed and no psychologist worthy of the name confused inversion with induced or acquired homosexuality which was a form of sexual perversion.

Rabbi Joseph Frederick Stern, of the East London Synagogue in Stepney, had set out to read *The Well of Loneliness* 'like a prude on the prowl' looking for obscenities – which he could not find. He ended up feeling 'profound sympathy for tragic suffering'.

A. P. Herbert, author, barrister and father of 'three healthy girls and one healthy boy', read it on the recommendation of his wife. He thought postwar society was in an unnatural state with two million more women than men. 'This sort of thing was bound to arise from this state of affairs.' Not being a girl he could not say what effect the book would have on a girl's mind but if he found a healthy girl of twenty reading it he would say, Read on my child, but you'll be bored. If he found an unhealthy girl reading it he'd say, Read on, this will be a lesson to you.

Oliver Baldwin, author, journalist, politician and the homosexual son of the Prime Minister, said, 'Why England should suffer such an attack on the liberty of literature is beyond my comprehension unless we have returned to the days of "Here's something we don't understand let's suppress it," ' and Mrs Gladys Edge, author of *Spiritual Healing* and *Towards a Christian Commonwealth*, said all social workers knew of such cases of the tragedy of people born to such a condition.

Radclyffe Hall was grateful to her defendants but felt boxed in by their equivocation. Their testimony read like tolerance of a club to which others belonged. Their elicited comment seemed riddled with subtext and self-protection. Direct action might have been preferable: marching the streets, Romaine, Toupie and Una chained to the railings. Few of the supporters gathered by Rubinstein could break through the barrier of embarrassment, speak out and rid their words of awkwardness.

'Our thoughts centre upon Sapphism,' Virginia Woolf wrote to Quentin Bell on 1 November, 'we have to uphold the morality of that Well of all that's stagnant and lukewarm and neither one thing or the other; *The Well of Loneliness*.' Those due to appear in court met for a buffet supper at the studio of the architect Clough Williams-Ellis. Virginia Woolf left early. 'The company grew bolder and more outspoken as time went on,' Vita Sackville-West wrote to her, 'and the little waitress from Harrods sitting behind the buffet nearly exploded with excitement. There, I thought, is another young life gone wrong.'

At this supper, Leonard Woolf told Virginia she must not go into the witness box or she would 'cast a shadow over Bloomsbury' by saying what she and they thought of the book. Bernard Shaw 'made a long, paradoxical, witty and entirely destructive discourse', then announced that he was not going to turn up on the day. He was convinced the magistrate would take the line that the book's literary status was irrelevant and that the only issue would be whether he, the magistrate, regarded the book as obscene.

Up to the day of the trial, Radclyffe Hall plied Rubinstein with supplementary observations and considerations contingent to the case. As counsel, he engaged Norman Birkett for Cape, and J. B. Melville to represent Leopold Hill. Rubinstein advised Birkett that his client wanted to be cross-examined in court and gave him her prepared statement which she planned to read out. It was in the nature of a sermon and an appeal. She reiterated her now well-known high moral purpose: how it was her duty to tell the world the truth 'about this very grave social problem', how she was a practising Christian who had studied abnormal psychology, how she wanted to plead for those 'doomed to be abnormal'.

It is not too much to say that many lives are wrecked through the lack of proper understanding of inversion. For the sake of the future generation inverts should never be encouraged to marry.

I do not regret having written the book. All that has happened has only served to show me how badly my book was needed. I am proud to have written *The Well of Loneliness* and I would not alter so much as a comma.

... Inverts are certainly no better and no worse than normal people – only when they are good they deserve more praise because from their birth nearly every man's hand is against them. Hopeless outcasts are a social danger, and persecution is as harmful to the persecutors as to the persecuted.

According to Magnus Hirschfeld whose statistics are generally considered to be the most accurate fifteen person in every thousand are inverted and the question is of grave social importance.

Birkett knew the enemy. This was not a wily defence, given the prosecuting counsel. If Radclyffe Hall went into the witness box to pontificate about Christianity and 'the serious question of congenital inversion', she would compound their prejudice. He said the best interest of her book would not be served by her appearing. She became very agitated and wanted his reassurance that he would not give the impression that she was 'ashamed of her abnormality or that there is anything in such an abnormality to be ashamed of'. Nor did she want other writers to think her cowardly. 'Miss Hall maintains that her private life would compare very favourably with the private lives of ordinary respectable people', Rubinstein told him.

Radclyffe Hall was exercised too with the idea that Birkett might not fully grasp her distinction between inversion and perversion. Inversion was what her book was about, perversion was what she called a term of opprobrium. Birkett curled in his boots. He did not want to enlighten Chartres Biron on such conceptual niceties. He would have liked to imply that the book was about something quite other – irrigation perhaps, or geogony – and to focus on the absence of expletives in the text. But Radclyffe Hall was not going to compromise her cause or adapt to the theatre of this particular court. It was her trial and she wanted to speak out. 'We, neither you nor I,' she warned Birkett, 'must not *sell* the inverts in our defence – they trust me, and I trust you.'

Birkett reminded her that no one was to be 'accused' by the terms of the proceedings. What the defence had to do was 'show cause' why the book should not be destroyed. Given the homophobes to whom they were answerable, that was a hard task. Joynson-Hicks and Chartres Biron were men of like minds. So too was Sir Archibald Bodkin, Director of Public Prosecutions. The logistics of indictment were his. Joynson-Hicks had authorized him to be in court. Bodkin had represented Britain at Geneva in 1923 at the International Conference for the Suppression of Obscene Literature. He and Joynson-Hicks had been working as hard as Rubinstein. They had personally solicited testimony against the book from the Church, writers and doctors of medicine. Stanley Baldwin and Winston Churchill assured them of their support. The arm of government stretched wide.

23

I have read the book

Cartwright called John and Una at six in the morning on Friday, 9 November. John dressed in a leather coat with astrakhan collar and cuffs and a dark blue, wide-brimmed hat. Una wore mauve and lots of make-up. They picked up Harold Rubinstein from his office and drove to Bow Street Magistrates Court.

The court was packed. Sheila Kaye Smith said it was 'an assemblage which might have been called a galaxy, for almost every author of repute was there'. 'All London, they say, is agog with this', Virginia Woolf wrote. Policemen at the door turned visitors away from the public gallery when it became too full. There were about forty witnesses for the defence, 'eminent men & women of good will', Radclyffe Hall called them. 'We had doctors male & female, men of science, educationalists, clergy, journalists, prominent booksellers, & of course a great number of my fellow authors.'

E. M. Forster wrote of 'fidgeting' as to what figure he should cut in the witness box. Virginia Woolf described Radclyffe Hall as 'lemon yellow, tough, stringy, exacerbated' and called *The Well of Loneliness* 'the pale tepid vapid book which lay damp & slab all about the court'.

The door at the top of the court opened at ten-thirty and in came Sir Chartres Biron. The court rose, he bowed, then took his seat under the lion and the unicorn. He looked, said Virginia Woolf, 'something like a Harley St. specialist investigating a case. All black & white, tie pin, clean shaven, wax coloured & carved, in that light, like ivory.' He wrote with a quill pen, sipped from a glass of water and read out points of law from calf-bound books.

Biron had a different demeanour from when he was castigating the book some three months earlier in the lounge of the Garrick Club. Now in his judicial role, it was for him to determine impartially whether *The Well of Loneliness* was an obscene libel according to the law of the land. The relevant legislation was the Obscene Publications Act of 1857, which prohibited the sale of books, pictures and 'other articles' that 'depraved and corrupted' the morals of young people and shocked 'the common feelings of decency in any well regulated mind'. Under this act, D. H. Lawrence's novel *The Rainbow* in 1915 had been tried, condemned and ordered to be burned in the same court – also after one of James Douglas's outbursts.

The court must decide if depraved morals and shocked decency would follow from reading *The Well of Loneliness*. Would the book, Sir Chartres mused, if read by the weak-minded, incite them to vice? Would it 'deprave and corrupt those whose minds are open to such immoral influences and into whose hands a publication of this sort may fall'?

This was the test for obscenity as defined by Lord Chief Justice Cockburn in 1868 in what became known as 'the Hicklin Rule'. (He was judging an anti-papist pamphlet seized by the Crown. It was called *The Confessional Unmasked* and was by a man called Hicklin. Thereafter 'the Hicklin Rule' became the judicial yardstick of whether a publication was obscene.) Charles Dickens, in *Our Mutual Friend*, preferred the term 'Podsnappery':

> A certain institution in Mr Podsnap's mind which he called 'the young person' may be considered to have been embodied in Miss Podsnap, his daughter. It was an inconvenient and exacting institution, requiring everything in the universe to be filed down and fitted to it. The question about everything was, would it bring a blush to the cheek of the young person? And the inconvenience of the young person, was that according to Mr Podsnap, she seemed always liable to burst into blushes when there was no need at all.

It was perhaps difficult to grasp what test had been devised or applied to prove a correlation between reading *The Well of Loneliness* and the depravation and corruption of an impressionable mind. But it was clear that Sir Chartres knew filth when he read it. The 'substantial question before me,' he said, 'is does this book as a whole defend unnatural practices between women?'

> That is the question to which I must direct my mind. In considering this question it is necessary to speak somewhat plainly. These unnatural offences between women which are the subject of this book involve acts which between men would be a criminal offence, and involve acts of the most horrible, unnatural and disgusting obscenity. That is a fact which no one could deny.

The court was full of people who could and would, at least privately, deny that the acts between Stephen Gordon and her women friends were horrible, unnatural, disgusting or obscene. Nor was there a law which criminalized sex between women. A move to legislate had been defeated in 1921.

Radclyffe Hall called it 'the deadly campaign of silence' but at the Garrick they knew all about Radclyffe Hall and her depraved practices, her seduction of an admiral's wife, her blatant aping of manly ways.

Jonathan Cape and Leopold Hill had been 'summoned to shew cause' why *The Well of Loneliness* should not be destroyed. Their lawyers wanted witnesses to be cross-examined so that they might put their case as to why the book should be allowed to circulate freely. None of these witnesses was to be heard. Biron called only one witness. He was Chief Inspector Prothero for the Crown. Radclyffe Hall wrote:

> The policeman might get up & say that my book was obscene – & he did say so in carefully studied language. But not one of those eminent men & women might say that my book was *not* obscene. They were treated with the grosses discourtesy, were most offensively treated by Sir Chartres Biron, who rejected group after group with a sneer. These people had come from all over England – they were quiet, learned people of high character, but they sat in that court & heard themselves sneered at – I burnt with anger on their behalf, & I marvelled that a chief magistrate like Biron could descent to so grave a laps of courtesy in his own court, to me it seemed very shocking.

Chief Inspector Prothero, the Crown's mutual friend, described how on 19 October 1928 he did enter 101 Great Russell Street WC1 being premises in the occupation of Leopold B. Hill there to search for and seize all copies of an indecent and obscene book called *The Well of Loneliness*. Cross-examined by Birkett, he remembered what his masters had told him to say. Yes, he had read the book and yes, he thought its theme and treatment objectionable and obscene. It dealt with physical passion. He had experience of a great deal of obscene literature and this book dealt with the problems of an invert which was a subject which should only be treated in text books. 'The book is indecent; it deals with an indecent subject.' He did not agree with the opinions of the book expressed in the *Times Literary Supplement* or the *Sunday Times*.

Birkett asked Prothero if he would be influenced by the evidence of the distinguished specialists in the court. Biron intervened. 'I do not think the opinion of this witness is of very great importance', he said. It was a confusing intervention. Prothero was the only witness allowed. His opinion seemed important for that reason, and because it was the same opinion as that of Joynson-Hicks, Chartres Biron and the Director of Public Prosecutions.

Eustace Fulton had been employed by the Director of Public Prosecutions to represent the Crown. The Director sat beside him in court. Fulton then said the book dealt with an obscene theme and 'a person who chose an obscene theme could not but write an obscene book'. By the same reasoning he might have contended that a person who chose the theme of bigotry could not but write a bigoted book. What was true from his prosecution was that those who had prejudged the case could not but come to a foregone conclusion. The whole court process was a conceptual shambles, a philosophical fraud, silly and devoid of common sense. Biron invoked convolutions of logic that would have consigned swathes of literature and art to the King's furnace.

Norman Birkett arrived in court late. For the defence he contended that the word obscene had been misinterpreted and that the 1857 act never intended to 'touch a book of this character', that there was no public advantage to prosecuting it and to do so struck 'a great blow, not only against literature but against the public good'.

What he did not, or could not, outright address were the attitudes of Joynson-Hicks, Sir Archibald Bodkin, Sir Chartres Biron and James Douglas. He did not talk of their homophobia, their quangos of self-interest, their twisting of the judicial system, their repressive views of women. Nor did he or anyone conjecture that sexual relationships between women might be positive, enjoyable, permissible. There was moot acceptance that they might at best be said to be a misfortune or an abnormality. At worst, they were obscene.

Caught into posturing and mincing words, Birkett tried to reason with Biron. He suggested it would be folly to pretend that police officers were literary experts. The book had received 'a chorus of praise from those well-qualified to speak upon matters affecting literature in general'. 'I have here in Court distinguished people in every walk of life who desire to go into the witness box and testify that this book is not obscene and that it is a misuse of words for the prosecution to describe it as such.'

Sir Chartres Biron did not want to hear these witnesses. He said the evidence Birkett proposed was expert witness as to whether or not the book was 'a piece of literature'. 'That is not the point', he said. 'The book may be a very fine piece of literature and yet be obscene. Art and obscenity are not disassociated. This may be a work of art. I agree it has considerable merits, but that does not prevent it from being obscene and I shall therefore not admit this expert evidence.' Birkett protested. 'They have read the book, and have knowledge of the reading public and in their view this book is not obscene', he said.

Biron allowed him to call Desmond MacCarthy, editor of *Life and Letters*. In the witness box MacCarthy looked, said Virginia Woolf, 'too indifferent, too calm, too completely at his ease to be natural'. Birkett asked him whether having read the book he thought it obscene. Biron interrupted. Such evidence was inadmissible he said. It was only an expression of opinion. But it was the same question as had been put to Inspector Prothero. The difference was that Prothero gave the answer Biron wanted to hear. 'We could not be called as experts in obscenity, only in art', Virginia Woolf wrote.

'How can the opinion of a number of people be evidence?' Biron asked. 'The test is whether the book is likely to deprave or corrupt those into whose hands it is likely to fall.' Norman Birkett said that if Biron excluded expert evidence it would mean that the law could impose, through an individual magistrate, censorship of the whole field of literature so far as obscenity was concerned. 'I want,' said Birkett,

to call medical testimony, I want to call a minister of religion, critics, reviewers, authors, authoresses, publishers and people from the libraries in London. I want to give evidence from every conceivable walk of life which bears upon this test as to whether the book depraves the mind of the person who reads it.

'A more distinguished body of witnesses have never been called', he said.

He suggested there should be informed debate before books were burned. It was not a proposition Biron would pursue. The question that followed was who, if not any of those assembled in court, *was* in a position to say that a book was obscene and would deprave those who read it and what evidence was admissible to test such a charge. Biron had the answer. He was Mr Podsnap. He knew his daughter would blush if she read *The Well of Loneliness*.

'*I* am here to decide whether this book is obscene or not', he told Birkett. 'I may be a very competent or incompetent magistrate, but I am going to shoulder my responsibility.' No evidence was admissible except Chief Inspector Prothero's and no judgement was allowed but Biron's.

Birkett struggled on. Authors of distinction 'who have given their lives to this matter' could testify that the book would not 'tend to deprave or corrupt' anyone who read it. 'Oh no', said Sir Chartres. 'That could not be evidence under any circumstances.' 'Well I tender the evidence', said Birkett. He began to sound like a doomed salesman with his eminent witnesses. Booksellers, he said, would testify that *The Well of Loneliness* was not obscene. 'Booksellers are only tradesmen, they are not experts', said Sir Chartres with offensive irrelevancy as he had precluded the validity of expertise. 'I hope they are not present in court to hear that observation', said Birkett. He offered social workers, a magistrate, biologists. 'And I reject it all', said Sir Chartres. 'Well I tender it', said Birkett and asked for a higher court to determine the question of the admissibility of expert witnesses.

'Oh no', said Sir Chartres. The testimony of expert witnesses as to the book's literary or social value was irrelevant because it was opinion. 'I don't think people are entitled to express an opinion upon a matter which is the decision of the court', he said.

He *was* the court and therefore by some conceptual alchemy that transcended logic, his opinion transmuted into law. No matter that Arnold Bennett had confronted him in the lounge of the Garrick with James Douglas some three months previously and found both of them blustering about how the book must be banned. What Biron now pronounced was not opinion, prejudice, misogyny, homophobia, venom or crass stupidity. It was law.

Birkett floundered. He then tried to contend that Stephen Gordon's relationships with women, though romantic and sentimental, were 'purely of an intellectual character' and had nothing to do with sex. Sir Chartres called a halt. 'I have read the book', he said and adjourned the court for lunch.

Virginia Woolf had sat all morning absorbing the atmosphere of the court, the stuffy formality, the ruminations on what is obscenity, what is literature, when is evidence permissible, what is the difference between the subject and the treatment. In her diary she wrote that she was 'impressed by the reason of the law, its astuteness, its formality'. She was also mightily relieved that neither she nor anyone else had to go into the witness box. Outside the courtroom she talked to Una. They had last met at a tea party as children at Una's parents' house in Montpelier Square in Knightsbridge. Una's grandfather, Sir Henry Taylor, had been a friend of Virginia Woolf's great-aunt, Julia Margaret Cameron.

Una had hated the morning, the public humiliation, the airing of a subject which embarrassed her, the insult to John. John was 'flushed and tearful' and 'in a passion of indignation'. She went with Una, Birkett and Rubinstein to lunch at the Waldorf. It was a meal Birkett later described as the most miserable of his life. Radclyffe Hall said that her work had been 'shamed and degraded' and accused him of lying by his 'blatant denial' of sex in her book. 'I made it abundantly clear that unless Birkett got up and retracted his words I would get up before anyone could stop me and would tell the Magistrate the truth.'

It was no idle threat as Birkett knew. It was anathema to Radclyffe Hall to be so denied, so vilified and to have to keep quiet. 'In the eyes of the law I am non existent', she wrote to Havelock Ellis. This was her trial and it was of more than her book. It was of her right to be who she was. She wished for justice of a clear and open kind. She wanted to proclaim to the court that she stood by every word, was proud of it, had written it as a social duty, was herself a congenital sexual invert and a man in a woman's body. Denied a voice of her own and counsel of her own, she felt unrepresented by those appointed to help her.

Birkett when the court reconvened offered a stuttering capitulation. He was not, he told Chartres Biron, in a position further to contend that the book did not refer to physical relationships between women. It was the author's wish that he should correct this misapprehension. Sir Chartres Biron gloated. Norman Birkett then pleaded that the treatment of these relationships was in good taste and of high artistic and literary merit. He made a disconsolate distinction between inversion and perversion and knew that the game was lost.

J. B. Melville then gave defence on behalf of Leopold Hill the bookseller. He referred with apparent insouciance to Biron's open mind and offered to assist him in understanding the author's point of view. He said the theme itself should not be proscribed – 'the question is the treatment of the theme'. He went over incidents in the book in detail, bleaching them of sexual significance.

> The moral is it not, is this? These people who are born with this misfortune cannot expect happiness. To those at large it says there should be toleration and understanding for those who are God's creatures. I submit to you Sir that this book is written in a reverend spirit; that it is written in a manner which is not calculated to excite libidinous thoughts, but is an attempt to deal with a social question that exists...
>
> I know that you will act upon the principles upon which you in your judicial office must always act, and that is, that if you feel that this case is even doubtful it will not be resolved upon the side of the suppression of a work which is a thoughtful work, which has been said on all sides to be a fine literary work, which has, I am told and I believe, already taken up some two years of the life of a most distinguished writer.

Chartres Biron was not stung by such veiled rebuke and questioning of his integrity. At two-thirty he adjourned the court. He was going to read the book again in the light of the speeches of counsel. The court would reconvene in a week's time. 'It will be resumed then merely for me to give judgment', he said, so letting it be known that discussion, such as it was, was at an end.

John had neuralgia and was depressed. She and Una talked about the case until two in the morning with Audrey Heath and Holroyd-Reece. Next day Chesterton's estate agents surveyed the Holland Street house. A Mr Laskey bought it three days later. John and Una planned to be out by mid-January. All week John had meetings with Rubinstein, Audrey, Holroyd-Reece and Cape. Legal costs already ran into four figures. She saw Theodore Goddard about raising her fifty per cent share if, as seemed certain, the case went against them. Leonard Woolf offered to help by launching an appeal fund. Jonathan Cape sailed to America to try to save the book's life there. Holroyd-Reece returned to Paris to print more pirate copies.

On Friday 16 November John and Una lunched at the Savoy with Harold Rubinstein and Audrey, then went on to Bow Street where, said Una, 'Sir Chartres Biron lied solemnly for more than one hour and condemned *The Well of Loneliness* to be burnt as an obscene libel.' 'He made of my book a gross and filthy thing which could only bring shame to its author', Radclyffe Hall wrote.

> He degraded the work of more than two years to the leval of low paunography. I could scarcely believe my ears as I listened. I would rather be excused from repeating his words, they were too offensive & too unguarded. I say that he took an unworthy advantage of an adventageous position.

The court was again packed with all the same witnesses. *The Well of Loneliness*, Biron said, dealt solely with 'unnatural offences'.

> There is not a single word from beginning to end of this book which suggests that anyone with these horrible tendencies is in the least blameworthy or that they should in any way resist them. The characters in this book who indulge in these horrible vices are presented to us as attractive people and put forward for our admiration; and those who object to these vices are sneered at in the book as prejudiced, foolish and cruel.
>
> Not merely that, but there is a much more serious matter, the actual physical acts of these women indulging in unnatural vices are described in the most alluring terms; their result is described as giving these women extraordinary rest, contentment and pleasure; and not merely that, but it is actually put forward that it improves their mental balance and capacity.

It was all too much for poor Sir Chartres. Stephen Gordon's well of loneliness was not nasty enough. Had it been filled with prussic acid, immersion of its author in it, inch by inch, would have been too kind. Perhaps if Stephen Gordon had been covered in wens, pilloried by every citizen of Worcestershire, London and Paris and had erupted in sores after a single lesbian kiss, he might have allowed her life story to find its way on to Miss Podsnap's bookshelf.

As it was the book 'pleaded for the invert to be recognised and tolerated, and not treated with condemnation, which they are at present by all decent people'. He quoted episodes that showed that Radclyffe Hall condoned 'horrible practices' – he used the term eight times. He picked out the scene where Stephen Gordon tells her mother that she loves Angela Crossby; her jealousy when Angela spends a night with a man; her meeting with Mary Llewellyn in the war:

> *Biron*:   This takes place at the Front where, according to the writer of this book, a number of women of position and admirable character, who were engaged in driving ambulances in the course of the war, were addicted to this vice.

Goaded by an hour of his insults, Radclyffe Hall called out, 'I protest. I am that writer.'

> *Biron*:   I must ask people not to interrupt the Court.
> *Radclyffe Hall*:   I am the authoress of this book.
> *Biron*:   If you cannot behave yourself in Court I shall have to have you removed.
> *Radclyffe Hall*:   It is shameful.

Which indeed it was. He was telling her that her efforts at openness were obscene, that her book should be burned, that she should be condemned by all decent people, that no one should be allowed to defend her. She had sought martyrdom and she had got it. Sir Chartres Biron was her Pontius Pilate, mean-minded, dishonourable and powerful.

It had been punishing for her to sit and listen in silence to this defamation of her life and work. In a public lecture two months later she said she could not let this slur on Toupie Lowther and her army sisters pass. She had, she said, written of them with 'so much respect that it all but amounted to reverence'.

> I had written of them as I believed them to have been, pure living, courageous, self-sacrificing women facing death night and day in the service of the wounded. Yet that old man sought through his preposterous statement to bring shame, not only on me as an author but upon the women of the British Empire. My friends it was too much. I could not endure it so I got up and called him to order. He threatened to have me taken from the Court as though I were one of those habitual drunks with whom, no doubt, he is accustomed to dealing. But once again I called

him to order and I noticed that he did not repeat his insult to the splendid war workers.

Radclyffe Hall had said in her book that in the ambulance unit there was 'many a one who was even as Stephen'. For Sir Chartres Biron that translated into filthy disgusting vice-ridden perverted debauchees. Years later in a diary entry, Una referred to how John had in fact scorned Toupie's friends and the 'perpetual sexual carrying on between members of the same Army Unit' and how she 'gave Chartres Biron the lie so vehemently'. It was clear from their social meetings that Toupie was surrounded by lesbians from her army days. It was also clear from her war record that the ambulance unit she managed was efficient.

To Biron's thinking, a lesbian of good character was a contradiction in terms. He did not want to hear about their contribution to society. He did not care whether they were born like it, became like it, acted out of compulsion or choice, were promiscuous or monogamous, clever or stupid. They should all be eradicated, in his view. Referring to when Stephen Gordon's mother throws her from the house, he said it was 'not an unreasonable conclusion under the circumstances'. The stocks and gibbet might have been too kind. He found references to God in the book 'singularly inappropriate and disgusting'. He had no hesitation whatever in saying that *The Well of Loneliness* was an obscene libel, an offence to public decency and that it would corrupt those 'into whose hands it should fall'. He brought the proceedings to an abrupt close.

Biron: Now what do you say about the costs in this case, Mr Fulton?
Fulton: I submit that in a case of this sort the costs ought not to fall on the public.
Biron: Yes, I think that is only right.
Melville: Sir, I am sure that in all fairness you will allow me to repeat what I said on the last occasion, that the authoress, Miss Radclyffe Hall, was at all times most anxious to go into the box and give her view of the book.
Biron: That does not deal with the subject with which I was dealing. I was speaking about costs.
Melville: I thought you had dealt with the question of costs. I am sorry.

Fulton: Sir, I ask for 20 guineas costs on each Summons.

Biron: I think that is a reasonable order. I shall make the order for the destruction of the book with these costs.

24

Depress! Repress! Suppress!

'This is the End of It', the *Daily Express* declared. James Douglas praised the stand his paper had 'felt compelled to take on this insidious perversion of the English novel ... English literature is the gainer and nothing but the gainer.' Radclyffe Hall was tired, had headaches and was sick all one night. She and Una tried to find peace and ordinary life at Journey's End in Rye. They walked by the sea and in the shipyard, had tea at the Mermaid, went to mass and called the surveyor in because of the smell of the drains in the cobbled lane, Hucksteps Row, that led to their house. In the evenings Una read aloud *Elizabeth and Essex* and *The Shuttles of Eternity*.

Radclyffe Hall did not accept Leonard Woolf's offer of a public subscription to help with legal fees. She had assets. The sale of 37 Holland Street freed ready cash. 'Also, I am going to put down the motor', she told Havelock Ellis. She sold Sargent's portrait of Ladye. She offered it first to the Tate Gallery then to the Glasgow Museum of Art and she talked of 'going slow financially' until the storm was over.

The storm brought huge publicity and profit. Sales of her other books were brisk. In America Pascal Covici and Donald Friede planned to publish *The Well of Loneliness* in December as their first joint publishing venture. Pascal Covici was the publisher and friend of John Steinbeck. Donald Friede had been a vice-president of Liveright. They gave Radclyffe Hall an astonishing advance of ten thousand dollars, then sold the book at five dollars, not the usual two. Cape increased her royalties on the nine thousand copies already sold in Paris. Holroyd-Reece reprinted each month. Newspaper sellers with carts at the Gare du Nord sold the book to passengers on the Golden Arrow. In the rue de Castiglione dealers bought English first editions for six thousand francs and sold them for 'as high as anything you are silly enough to pay'. Sylvia Beach, who published James Joyce's *Ulysses* in 1922, had more orders at her bookshop Shakespeare and Company in rue de l'Odéon for *The Well of Loneliness* than she could meet.

In England newspapers filled with comment on the dangers of censorship and pleas for a change in the obscenity law. Silence about same-sex relationships splintered, though it did not break. There were whispers that they might exist. Hugh Walpole, in *Time and Tide* on 23 November, wrote of how between them James Douglas, Joynson-Hicks and Chartres Biron had 'caused certain subjects to be discussed, inquired into and pleasingly investigated as never before in the history of this our hypocritical country'. In the same issue, an editorial claimed that a world best-seller had been created and that now no reader was unaware of the subject of the book. A 'Modern Mother' wrote that she defied any young person to 'remain ignorant of certain facts which ordinarily would never have come to their notice'.

Other issues were glossed over. There was no discussion about institutionalized homophobia or the government's manipulation of the law. The fuss embarrassed women who might have liked to live openly lesbian lives. Janet Flanner commented that *The Well of Loneliness* was a rather innocent and confused book. In a more adult society it might have braved the way for books that gave other views, that reflected diversity.

Radclyffe Hall insisted on an appeal to a higher court. She fought on, so she said in her oratorical style, 'for the sake of the honour of literature, for the sake of all serious minded writers, for the sake of the freedom of the press which every writer holds sacred'.

The appeal against the Order made by Sir Chartres Biron was set for 14 December in the London Sessions Court. It was to be heard by Sir Robert Wallace KC 'and a very large bench of London justices'. They were to judge whether Biron's sentence should be upheld. Prior to the hearing, Rubinstein wrote to the Director of Public Prosecutions, Sir Archibald Bodkin, asking him to release copies of the book for these magistrates to read. Sir Archibald replied in problematic prose:

With reference to your request that I should supply copies of the above-named book to the Court of Quarter Sessions with a view to the Justices attending thereat in connection with the appeal should have an opportunity of reading the book before the appeal is heard, I beg to inform you that I have been in communication with the Clerk of the Peace, Sessions House, Newington, who, on the directions of the Chairman of the Court, informs me that it would not be appropriate nor practicable to act upon your suggestion. I therefore do not propose to adopt it.

The Chairman of the Court, Sir Robert Wallace, was seventy-eight. He had already made clear his horror of the book in the papers. 'His aged mind,' wrote Radclyffe Hall, 'evidently did not grasp that before being asked to pass judgement on a book the judges should one and all have read it.'

Sir Robert had been briefed by Sir Archibald as to how to proceed. And the Preposterous Jix was still there, positioning his men and stitching things up. The Attorney-General, Sir Thomas Inskip, was to act for the Crown. Sir Thomas's fee was much higher than for ordinary counsel. He was entitled, because of his high office, both to open the case and to close it. The Home Office pathologist, Sir William Willcox, was to appear in court. Two doctors and a bacteriologist were paid fees totalling 115 guineas for agreeing to testify for the Crown. The Bishop of Durham wrote in his diary: 'I received a letter from the new Archbishop of Canterbury conveying a suggestion from the Home Secretary that I should consent to give evidence in favour of prohibiting *The Well of Loneliness* as an obscene book.' He noted his own reply: 'I do not feel myself disposed, nor am I in the least competent to argue the case. Moreover, the whole subject is disgusting to me, and I have no desire to be mixed up with it, even in the modest degree your Grace suggests.'

Among writers solicited by the Home Secretary, Rudyard Kipling, a frequent guest at Whiteladies, Joynson-Hicks's home, agreed to testify. Stanley Baldwin was his cousin. Kipling's was the complex face of prejudice, as Hugh Walpole revealed:

I asked him at luncheon whether he approved of censorship (apropos of this tiresome, stupid *The Well of Loneliness*). No, he doesn't approve of the book. Too much of the abnormal in all of us to play about with it. Hates opening up reserves. All the same he'd had friends once and again he'd done more for than for any woman. Luckily Ma Kipling doesn't hear this.

The government, Radclyffe Hall said, was out for her blood. The defence knew that they would not be properly heard. The court was again packed with spectators. Marie Stopes, the advocate of birth control, was there. Her books were soon to be tried in the USA. Kipling showed up but left after Sir Thomas Inskip whispered to him that professional evidence would not be sought.

Twelve magistrates had been hired to condemn a book they were not allowed to read. The sole witness was again to be poor Inspector Prothero. The Attorney-General presided over this kangaroo court. He opened the case and closed it and pretended unanimity for the decision he and his friends imposed. He held *The Well of Loneliness* at arm's length, confided how loath he was to read aloud from it, bowed to the press and said, 'I shall have to go into a good deal of detail in these passages. I can only hope – and I am sure I may say this – that repulsive as it is to all of us the Press will show their accustomed restraint in reporting the many observations I may have to make.'

He had, he said, no idea whether the book had any literary qualities; his purpose was to show it was obscene. He chose his detail and gave his views. This book would suggest thoughts of a most impure immoral unclean and libidinous character to the minds of the young. It brought the name of God into corrupt passions. The practice in which its heroine Stephen Gordon indulged was referred to in a very well-known passage in the first chapter of the Epistle to the Romans and in a book of Juvenal. It glorified the vice of physical relations between women. It asked for toleration of the people who indulged this vice. It was

propaganda for the practice which has long been known as Lesbianism, a well-known vice, unnatural, destructive of the moral and physical fibre of the passive persons who indulge in it, who are the victims of others; this book is a plea for the active persons who practice this vice. . . . I submit that it is corrupting and obscene and its publication is a misdemeanour.

Sir Thomas passed two copies of the book to the twelve magistrates. The offending passages were marked with little bits of paper. 'He was very absurd and he over play acted,' Radclyffe Hall wrote: 'I thought him rather a stupid Counsel, but he managed to be extremely vindictive.

And yet as I listened to those parts of my book especially selected for its damnation, I was struck with the high moral tone of my writing & with my great decency and restraint.'

James Melville went through a ritual of defence. The previous evening he had sent telegrams to all his witnesses telling them their attendance would not be required. He knew the case was prejudged. He again pleaded for the freedom of literature, again urged the court to differentiate between the theme of a book and treatment of a theme. He might have saved his breath. While he was addressing the court, the Attorney-General Sir Thomas Inskip talked to colleagues and made a fuss about sending someone out for a railway timetable.

The jury retired at two twenty-five p.m. and returned at two-thirty p.m. Five minutes were all that were needed for Sir Robert Wallace to tell them what they must decide. 'The bewildered and sheepish expressions of Sir Robert's fellow magistrates provided a memorable spectacle', Rubinstein wrote. 'This was the only consolation afforded to our clients.'

Old Sir Robert delivered judgement. It was, he said, undesirable that there should be a constant repetition of the type of passages read to the court. The book was dangerous, corrupting, disgusting, obscene and prejudicial to the morals of the community. It was 'more subtle demoralising corrosive and corruptive than anything ever written'. It was enough to make anyone want to read it. He dismissed the appeal and the defence again incurred all costs.

Sir Archibald Bodkin was again in court. Joynson-Hicks had asked him for notes on the appeal proceedings. Here is some of what he wrote that day:

... The Court retired for about five minutes and the Chairman in delivering judgement dismissed the Appeal and said the decision of the Court was unanimous; that the book was regarded as a subtle and insinuating one and the more dangerous because of its literary character: that it was corrupting in its tendency, was a condonation of unnatural practices, was a disgusting and obscene book and prejudicial to the morals of the community. The order was therefore confirmed with costs and the Appeal dismissed.

I may mention that there were in attendance as witnesses on behalf of the informant Sir William Willcox [the Home Office pathologist], Dr Birley of 10 Upper Wimpole St, Dr Maurice Wright of 86 Brook St, Miss

Lillian Barker and Mr Rudyard Kipling. I desire to place on record the readily-proffered assistance rendered by all these persons and I have no doubt, although not a tenth in number of those proposed to be called on the other side, their evidence would undoubtedly have obliterated any impression which the so-called experts in literature etc., might have made upon the Court. I am writing to them individually to thank them. It may be that the Secretary of State would like to send a line personally to Mr Rudyard Kipling who, although far from well, attended at the Sessions House.

In view of the discreditable action, as I regard it, of Mr Jonathan Cape, it would appear undesirable to accept any undertaking in the future to withdraw objectionable books from circulation. I am afraid the unfortunate feature of the whole matter is that from the proceedings the appellant will have derived very considerable profits, but at least the standard of decent literature in this country has to some extent been maintained. The Attorney General especially referred to the position of the Secretary of State, not only in regard to the law of this country, but also its International obligations.

AHB

Thus the unedifying process of the law, the well-worn drama of the English establishment, the Old Boys, their intrigue, misogyny and blustering terror of sex. Sir Robert Wallace, Sir Thomas Inskip, Sir William Joynson-Hicks, Sir Archibald Bodkin, peers of the realm, oligarchs, guardians of the nation's morals, fools and bigots of their time, puffed with power, tainted with prejudice and sexual unease.

Their views and those of Radclyffe Hall polarized. She preached about congenital sexual inverts, truth, justice, and blind and ignorant persecution. They postured about filthy disgusting ungodly sin. Not much was said about women who loved each other, their partnerships and lives. There was no humour, generosity, enlightenment or ease. By this trial, the government stigmatized and criminalized a kind of love. Its idiocy echoed down the years, silencing writers, consigning people to concealment of their deepest feelings and to public scorn.

The case was lost. *The Well of Loneliness* was destroyed. Radclyffe Hall longed to get away from England. It had been punishing litigation, prolonged, personal and offensive. It was another rejection to compound with those of her formative years, another nail in the cross of martyrdom. She made heroic display and was more than hurt. She had headaches and trouble with her eyes and was exhausted. For Una it had all been part of the test of loving John, on a par with the Fox-Pitt 'grossly immoral woman' charge, the Troubridge calumny, Minna's disdain.

They arranged to leave the Holland Street house on 11 January. They sacked the servants, packed their possessions, took a lease on a flat at Kensington Palace Mansions and went Christmas shopping. John bought Una a gold watch, Una bought her a gold cigarette lighter. They had a sitting with Mrs Leonard, then went to Rye for Christmas. Andrea, Audrey and Patience Ross – also from the Heath agency – joined them there. All three went walking on Camber Sands on Christmas day and to John's annoyance were half an hour late for the turkey and plum pudding.

Radclyffe Hall became the butt of public jokes. She thought her phone tapped, her letters opened. She was particularly offended by *The Sink of Solitude*, a verse lampoon by 'several hands' in the tradition of Pope and Dryden. Published by Hermes Press it was dedicated to Compton Mackenzie's novel about lesbians, *Extraordinary Women*. Mackenzie was wistful at the Home Secretary's uninterest in his book. It only sold two thousand copies. He had planned to conduct his own defence. Raymond Mortimer, lover of Vita Sackville-West's husband Harold Nicolson, called it 'an expression of male pique and wounded vanity'.

The Sink of Solitude, twenty pages long, was in rhyming couplets:

> The way to make a modern novel sell is
> To have a preface done by Havelock Ellis . . .

It satirized all involved with *The Well of Loneliness* but in particular James Douglas with his bluster about killing girls with prussic acid rather than letting them read the book:

> Depress! Repress! Suppress! (Sunday Express)
> James Douglas knows what others merely guess –
> That woman-interest, sex and moral ire,
> Will set a million readers' veins on fire . . .
> Of rhetoric he need not burk a particle
> In this week's splurging moral-uplift article.
> JIMMY is menaced. He is far from placid.
> Ho Ho The Borgias! Who likes prussic acid?

Some women poison with a deadly look,
But RADCLYFFE poisoned JIMMY with a book!
The WELLS OF LONELINESS are far from pure
For poisoned wells JAMES DOUGLAS has a cure,
'Stop up the Well!' is JIMMY's urgent call
(Inset: A picture of MISS RADCLYFFE HALL).

A long preface by a Mr P. R. Stephenson was scathing about 'pathetic post-war lesbians with their mannish modes and poses', the 'sentimental scientificality of psychopaths like Havelock Ellis', the 'feebleness' of *The Well of Loneliness* as a moral argument, the 'uncritical criticisms' of James Douglas, the 'spinelessness' of Jonathan Cape.

The text was illustrated with cartoons by Beresford Egan in the style of Aubrey Beardsley. One of these showed Radclyffe Hall nailed to a cross, a naked woman with swinging breasts astride her thighs. Cupid on the cross cocks a snook at her. Joynson-Hicks slinks away, wiping his hand on his sleeves, the book in his pocket.

Radclyffe Hall thought the cartoon blasphemous. It caused her 'profound and painful spiritual reaction', Una said:

> throughout the remaining years of her life she could scarcely bear to speak of it, even to me. Once she did say: 'To think that I should have been used as a means of disrespect to Him ...', nor did her complete helplessness and innocence in the matter seem to afford her any consolation.

It was insult added to injury that her writing was suppressed but not the lampoons and satires that mocked her. She had wanted martyrdom. Here was her apotheosis. She thought of herself as on a par with the crucified Christ. 'I renounce my country for ever', she wrote to Audrey Heath. 'Nor will I ever lift a hand to help England in the future.'

Then came news from Donald Friede in New York. John S. Sumner, Secretary of the New York Society for the Suppression of Vice, had, with two detectives, raided the offices of Covici-Friede in West 45th Street and taken all copies of the sixth printing of *The Well of Loneliness*. The Society operated 'under Article 106 Sections 1140 to 1148 inclusive of the State's Criminal Code'. This legislated against Indecency: obscene lewd filthy disgusting books, magazines, plays or pictures, exposure of genitals, sale of contraceptive devices, disorderly houses, criminal surgeons, and men who lived on the earnings of prostitutes.

John S. Sumner had a bristly little moustache, a smooth sleek to his hair and pince-nez glasses. He had, he said, received twelve complaints about the book. He gained his warrant for the raid from Chief Magistrate McAdoo. Donald Friede was summoned 'In the Name of the People of the State of New York' to appear before McAdoo at the magistrates court at 314 West 54th Street on 22 January 1929 at 10 o'clock. 'Complaint having been made this day by John S. Sumner that you did commit the offense of violating Section 1141 of the Penal Law by selling an obscene book'.

Sumner then went on to Macy's book department and threatened them with prosecution if they did not stop selling the book. Which they did not. Until there was any adjudication of guilt the book stayed on sale all over the country with all the wild benefits of this publicity. Within a week sales reached 25,000 copies and by February 40,000.

Radclyffe Hall wanted to tell the world how she had been victimized. England and her party, the Conservative Party, had let her down. On 25 January 1929 she gave a lecture in Southend to Young Socialists. Rubinstein warned her to 'be very guarded' over what she said. 'Proceedings for contempt of Court might follow any definite suggestion that the case was pre-judged.'

'The torch is in your hands to lighten the darkness', Radclyffe Hall told her audience.

> Your Party is young, courageous, virile, it has just arrived at the glory of manhood. Who defended my book within a few hours of the dastardly attack in the *Sunday Express* – what paper leapt to my defence? the *Daily Herald* ... May you sweep the country clean at the next election and let some fresh air and sunshine into England. If we cannot have a country fit for heroes, if that is too vast an aspiration, at least let us have a country whose air is too pure for this present government to breathe.

She was, she felt, a hero. (Her flirtation with Socialism did not last.) She circulated a letter to writers saying she had proof of the government's control of her trial. She wanted to expose the conspiracy. But her story was cold. Arnold Bennett told her that 'no editor in London would now consider any item connected with the case as news'. Her trial was just another perversion of justice. She was humiliated, her book was suppressed and the papers were full of other things.

She and Una left for Paris on 4 February 1929 with Barber the maid and Gabriele the cockatoo. John Holroyd-Reece sent red roses to their hotel, the Osborne in rue St Roch. He was again reprinting *The Well of Loneliness*. Radclyffe Hall signed copies, lunched at Pruniers and was treated as a hero. 'Total strangers would come up to her in the street or in a restaurant and express their admiration of the book, their amazement and indignation at its persecution', Una wrote.

Natalie Barney gave a celebratory party in her Temple of Love. Her guests were invited for tea, cucumber sandwiches and a meeting with Miss Hall. Natalie wanted to give out copies of the book but Sylvia Beach told her she would have to wait for the next printing. All were sold as soon as they came into her shop.

It snowed, the Seine was frozen and John and Una's car skidded in the Bois de Boulogne. They skipped mass, stayed in the hotel and Una, for eight consecutive hours, read aloud *John Brown's Body*. They went to a party given by Gertrude Stein's friend the Duchesse de Clermont Tonnerre. John ate something there which gave her diarrhoea for which she was prescribed mulled wine. Una had her hair permed and bought camiknickers and hats in the Champs-Elysées. John bought diamond and sapphire cufflinks and a pinscher bitch she called Paris, which twice tried to bite Una. It was swapped for a bulldog that would not walk, then a griffon with distemper that died of convulsions. They had tea with Colette who talked of her house in St Tropez. It was in five acres of orchard and vineyard and a mile from the sea. She extolled the sea bathing, sunshine, seafood, nightingales and mimosa trees. Una pleaded with John to go south for a long holiday away from the battles of city life. John wanted to stay in Paris until the outcome of the New York trial.

25

The freedom of human beings

Pascal Covici and Donald Friede hired Morris Ernst as their defence lawyer. Ernst brought to the case fresh air, style and much-needed humour. He became famous in American censorship trials for his defence of *The Well of Loneliness*, *Ulysses* and *Forever Amber*, of magazine pieces about childbirth issues and pamphlets like Mary Ware Dennett's *The Sex Side of Life*. He wore bow ties and little round glasses, preferred biography to fiction and had left-wing liberal views. 'The causes that touch off my glands,' he wrote, 'do seem to me to have always the same central core: the freedom of human beings and human thought throughout the world.' It was a help to him that, unlike in England, the right to freedom of speech was enshrined in the Constitution of the United States.

'The only essential obscenity in life,' Ernst wrote, 'is stealth and cowardice and concealment.' He came from a modest background, paid his way through law school, married young – his wife was a teacher – and started a law firm with two college friends, Herb Wolff and Eddie Greenbaum. He spent summers on the island of Nantucket. He liked the 'gaiety and gab and peace and comfort' of the place. He kept a yacht there called *Truant*, made 'science notes' about flora and fauna, had his own lathe and made walnut tables, maple beds and pine bookcases.

The Society for the Suppression of Vice put its complaint to Judge Hyman Bushell on 21 February 1929. Ernst thought the judge would dismiss it. But Bushell took his cue from his English counterparts. Lesbianism was obscene. He declared himself worried, outraged, shocked and said the book idealized and extolled unnatural and depraved relationships.

> The book is well written and contains no unclean words, but on the other hand the whole theme of the story could hardly be more vile, unmoral and unsocial.
>
> I am convinced *The Well of Loneliness* tends to debauch public morals, that its subject matter is offensive to public decency and that it is calculated to deprave and corrupt minds open to its immoral influences and who might come in contact with it.

He upheld the complaint against Covici-Friede and referred the case to the Court of Special Sessions for trial. What he did not do was to manipulate the process of the law to ensure the outcome he desired.

The story was national news. No legislation could control the thousands of copies already sold or in the shops. Radclyffe Hall was in all the papers – her picture and her propensities. Here was the notorious creature who 'spilled filth into the minds of England's young'.

> She is Byronese in appearance and her friends call her John. Her jewels, large emeralds sunk in rings of platinum, are the only softening note in her mannish profile. Her short blond hair is combed straight back and her blue suit is Bond Street tailored. Her shirt is blue linen with a standing collar and the tie navy. She wears a monocle on a cord, a watch in her handkerchief pocket suspended on a leather fob from the lapel buttonhole. In the evening Miss Hall wears a moiré tuxedo with a black satin stock and a ruffled shirt front. Her hat is a large Montmartre.

She 'summoned her liveried car with a noble sweep and a deep voice' and lived with Una The Lady Troubridge. She needed no man, that much was clear.

Donald Friede, in France on business, had lunch and dinner with John and Una on 7 March. He told them of the runaway sales and that the book was a success whatever the decision of the court. While he was with them the publisher Gallimard rang wanting to do the French translation – the first novel by a woman in his imprint.

In New York on 8 April 1929 before Justices Solomon, Healy and McInerney, John Sumner singled out eighty-two pages of *The Well of*

Loneliness that caused him mortification – all about Stephen and Angela Crossby, Puddleton's past and Mary Llewellyn in the Ambulance Brigade. Ernst countered that if you looked for obscenity you could find it in a laudable book. 'Conscious censoriousness begets prejudice and renders fair appraisal impossible. Let the horrified Mr Sumner and his list of pages be cast aside. Let *The Well of Loneliness* be read with an open mind.'

Ernst had prepared a fifty-one-page brief. The basis of his defence was the constitutional right of liberty of speech. He played to the court, referred to the 'subject matter' and the 'tragic problem' and was careful not to mention congenital sexual inversion, lesbianism or kissing. He did not have Radclyffe Hall at his side to nudge him toward self-defeating candour.

The heroine of the book, he said, was flawed from birth emotionally and psychologically, 'doomed to a life of frustration', 'thwarted and bewildered because her instincts are not the instincts of others of her sex'. Hers was a tortured, desperate, barren life, a poignant tragedy that called for tolerance and understanding. Her story moved the reader to compassion and did not invite emulation. Who, he asked, was the book likely to hurt: the impressionable child, the moral weakling, the fatuous and vicious, the average intelligent adult?

Had Stephen Gordon been glamorous, a social wow and having a great time in bed, he would have needed to take a different tack. His purpose was to keep the book on sale, not to defend lesbian rights. The subject matter was, he said, about 'emotional maladjustment'. It was not new in contemporary literature. He reminded the judges of the 'well-known inability of Queen Elizabeth to adjust herself emotionally to men'. Any high-school girl in New York, he said, could go to a bookstore or circulating library and obtain copies of *Elizabeth and Essex* by Lytton Strachey, *Swann's Way* by Marcel Proust, *Death in Venice* by Thomas Mann, *The Intermediate Sex* by Edward Carpenter, or works by Voltaire, Whitman or Swinburne.

To suppress *The Well of Loneliness* because of its theme would, as a corollary, condone the suppression of hundreds of other works of literature and 'prevent the proper enlightenment of the public on an important social problem'. The Federal Public Health Service yearly distributed to adolescents and adults millions of pamphlets about masturbation, sexual intercourse and venereal disease. Times moved on, fashions changed, there was a time when literature urging the abolition of slavery was repressed, and a time when women in bathing suits on beaches were arrested.

He cited recent cases where printed matter 'calculated to appeal to lecherous instincts and to titillate the lewd and salacious' had been suppressed by the courts. There was *Broadway*, a pamphlet with pictures of naked women partly covered with lamp black which the reader was invited to rub off with a piece of damp bread. There was *Cupid's Yokes or the Binding Forces of Conjugal Life*. It had nothing to do with matrimony but 'abounded in disgusting and lustful details'. There was a dissertation on 'loathsome diseases of the degenerative organs', a broadsheet, *Lucifer the Light Bearer*, about 'unnatural intercourse', and various publications to do with coercive sexual acts and venereal complaints.

What, asked Ernst, had *The Well of Loneliness* in common with these publications? It was a 'sincere, serious, beautiful book, fearlessly published and disseminated'. In 500 pages there was not a filthy word or indecent scene.

> If Stephen were a man the book would be merely a rather over-sentimental bit of Victorian romanticism. There would be no element in it that could bring a blush of embarrassment even to the cheeks of the complainant. The sole objection is the theme itself. This presents the vital question in the case: Will the law condemn a book otherwise unobjectionable because of its theme?

The English magistrates had done just that. It was not a feasible rule. Who, Ernst asked, would determine the dangerous social consequences of one subject rather than another? Would the 'unorthodox emotional complications' of *The Well of Loneliness* cause more havoc than sadism in *Uncle Tom's Cabin*, abortion in *The American Tragedy*, incest in *Oedipus Tyrranos*, the adulteries of most contemporary fiction or the murder, robbery and assault of detective and crime novels?

Miss Radclyffe Hall was a prominent British writer with a place in literature. She had won two literary prizes. The courts suppressed pornography and punished 'purveyors of filth surreptitiously distributed'. They did not ban literary works by authors of literary acclaim. Her book had social significance, moral fervour, integrity of intention, distinguished style. She attempted to show a social problem, predicated by the assumption that such problems could only be solved by the interchange of ideas, not by throttling discussion.

He wooed the court, asked if it was now to renounce the enlightened policy of recent trials, 'brand this book as obscene and open the door henceforth to the wanton and undiscerning prosecution of legitimate literature'. He referred to two books recently cleared of the obscenity charge: *Madeleine, the Autobiography of a Prostitute* and *Mademoiselle de Maupin* by Théophile Gautier. The first, the 'life story of a strumpet', was badly written and without moral motive but not banned. Gautier had set out to shock with his salacious novel. Even so, the Court of Special Sessions acquitted the bookseller, who then got damages for malicious prosecution.

Both Gautier and Radclyffe Hall had respected reputations and high moral purpose. Gautier protested about prudery and moral bigotry, Radclyffe Hall about misunderstanding and intolerance. Morally, Radclyffe Hall occupied the higher ground. Much of Gautier's book was 'undoubtedly vulgar and indecent', *The Well of Loneliness* was 'free from salacious and objectionable allusions'. The tone of *Mademoiselle de Maupin* was 'light, bantering, pagan and frivolous'; it was anonymously published and had sexy pictures. *The Well of Loneliness* was 'characterized by seriousness, dignity and restraint', published by a reputable company and without 'sensuous word pictures' or illustrations. Ernst gave the judges a taste of Gautier's prose:

> She came up to me, sat down on my knees more quickly than lightning, passed her arms around my neck, crossed her hands behind my head and clung with her lips to mine in a furious embrace; I felt her half-naked and rebellious bosom bounding against my breast, and her twined fingers twitching in my hair. A shiver ran through my whole body, and my heart beat violently. Rosette did not release my mouth; her lips enveloped mine, her teeth struck against my teeth, our breath mingled. I drew back for an instant, and turned my head aside two or three times to avoid this kiss; but a resistless attraction made me again advance, and I returned it with nearly as much ardour as she had given it. I scarcely know how it would all have ended had not a loud barking been heard outside the door together with the sound of scratching feet...

No such passages spiced *The Well*. Nor, like a dirty postcard, could it be 'absorbed at a single glance' or like a sleazy pamphlet 'perused in a few minutes'. It was a voluminous work which required protracted reading, assiduous application. The seeker of obscenity would be thwarted after thirty pages. 'Readily corruptible persons' would be in for a hard time. 'No child, no moral defective, no impressionable seeker after prurient details would ever get far.'

It was in its sixth American edition, widely circulated, stocked by reputable stores like Brentano's and Macy's and was sold openly at five dollars, a price that precluded a cheap thrill. Dirty postcards went for a few cents. Children and 'moral weaklings' would not have five dollars. 'Vile postcards are vended by gutter peddlers. Booklets full of revolting details are sold in dives. Filthy motion pictures are filmed in secret and constitute back-door midnight entertainment.'

The Well of Loneliness, Morris Ernst declared, was nothing less than literature, defended by the great and good. A 'strenuous letter of protest' against its suppression had been signed by Sherwood Anderson, Theodore Dreiser, Scott Fitzgerald, Ernest Hemingway, Upton Sinclair and many more. It had received serious reviews. The *New York Herald Tribune* deemed it 'courageous and honest, more of a sermon than a story, a passionate plea for the world's understanding and sympathy, as much a novel of problem and purpose as *Uncle Tom's Cabin*, as sentimental and moralistic as the deepest dyed of Victorian novels.' The *Philadelphia Inquirer* called it 'remarkably fine literature'. The reviewer in the *Nation* said no subject of human interest and social significance should be *per se* undiscussable.

Ernst backed his arguments with the opinions of experts. Dr Logan Glendening thought the censor, not the author, had a pornographic imagination. Dr Joseph Collins said 'genuine homosexuality' was an endowment, not a vice or disease. Edna Ferber feared what would happen when the New York Vice Society discovered the Old Testament. Llewellyn Jones said prosecution was 'a silly piece of fanaticism', Herbert Asbury blamed the idiotic attitude of the British authorities, Rabbi Felix H. Levy said here was fine literary work without a single objectionable feature from the moral point of view.

The court adjourned, the judges went away for eleven days with copies of *The Well of Loneliness* and Ernst's brief. They reconvened on 19 April 1929 and gave their verdict:

> The book in question deals with a delicate social problem which in itself cannot be said to be in violation of the law unless it is written in such a manner as to make it obscene. This is a criminal prosecution and as judges

of the facts and the law we are not called upon nor is it within our province to recommend or advise against the reading of any book, nor is it within our province to pass an opinion as to the merits or demerits thereof, but only as to whether the same is in violation of the law. The people must establish that the defendants are guilty of violation of Section 1141 beyond a reasonable doubt. After a careful reading of the entire book, we conclude that the book in question is not in violation of the law.

Donald Friede sent a cable to the Hôtel Osborne with the good news. John and Una found it when they got back to their hotel from a cocktail party. Covici-Friede planned a celebratory edition. There was money to be made. 'The most controversial book of the century', he advertised. 'Suppressed in England and vindicated by an American court.'

Donald Friede asked Radclyffe Hall for a preface. She wanted to use extracts from 'letters received from my public'. Rubinstein warned of copyright problems and warned again of proceedings for contempt of court if she commented on the English legal process. She kept the piece neutral – effusive with thanks but that was all. Friede urged her to be more revealing. She refused. 'Tired as I am,' she wrote to him, 'I could not, even in supposition, face the merest possibility of being involved in any litigation concerned with any breach of the law ... I just can't and won't have any trouble myself so there it is.' Month after month of enduring the spite of the law, its bias, manipulation and expense, had taken its toll. In her novels she never again wrote about love between women. *So sad.*

Una noted in her diary the ever-spiralling sales – 72,000, 83,000, 100,000. Radclyffe Hall received a royalty cheque of $64,000 and an avalanche of letters. Morris Ernst winged in a bill to Pascal Covici. 'Long bitter experience has taught me that the time to send in bills is when clients are happiest', he wrote. He wanted to meet him to determine the final fee. 'As you will recall, I stated to you that our charges would take into consideration as an important factor, the result obtained.'

Radclyffe Hall had fame but not of the sort she wanted. It was tinged with notoriety and had a disreputable edge. She was disenfranchised, her country had branded her, she did not now know where to make her home. She was flattered to receive, in Paris on 9 April 1929, a letter from an American actress who thought *The Well of Loneliness* a 'great tragic story that would make a wonderful play'. Wilette Kershaw told Radclyffe Hall that she 'knew her' through her books and considered this a privilege. She would like to talk about a dramatization. 'I feel Steven strikes a big tragic note and think I could reach it.'

John and Una met her on 17 April. The meeting fitted in with worries over the content of the preface for Covici-Friede, tea with Dolly Wilde and Ezra Pound, Una having a permanent wave and the choosing of an 'unpardonably inbred' griffon called Tulip, which had six toes on each paw.

John told Wilette Kershaw she would not do the dramatization herself, nor could she suggest anyone. Four days later Una wrote in her secretarial capacity: Miss Hall was far too busy to meet again, she was preparing material for a special edition of *The Well of Loneliness* and working on a new book. Miss Kershaw should let Miss Hall know as soon as possible her 'definite plans anent dramatisation, theatre & financial basis, when, *subject to the dramatic rights being still available* she and her agent will gladly consider them'. Audrey Heath recommended Dorothea Fassett of the London Play Company in Piccadilly to act for Radclyffe Hall.

Wilette Kershaw drew up an agreement which licensed her to produce the play against an advance of £100. She would stage it in New York or Paris within eighteen months, show Radclyffe Hall the script and pay agreed royalties. On 7 May Radclyffe Hall signed this contract, though a page of it was missing. 'All my papers were mislaid and in disorder', Kershaw later said. The advance was paid to the London Play Company.

All seemed well. John welcomed all efforts to breathe life and good fortune into her book. She and Una shopped for their holiday. Una hired a car and a driver called Pierre from the Transports Automobiles. They left for the Riviera on Friday 17 May after an early breakfast at the Hôtel Osborne. They travelled with 'much luggage and impedimenta', Barber the maid and Tulip the six-toed dog.

THE MASTER OF THE
HOUSE

26

An awful shock

John and Una went south via Sens and Mâcon, Lyon, Orange, Avignon. They stopped when they felt like it, shopped for antiques in the markets, stayed in the best hotels and ate in the best restaurants. Pierre was told to drive at a snail's pace. Barber was given 'grave warnings' for fortifying herself with alcohol. When she put a left shoe tree in one of John's right shoes, Una threatened to pack her off back to England.

Colette had recommended Seaward Lodge, an English *pension* near St Tropez. John thought the rooms dark, the lunch poor and deplored the walk to the sea. By evening they were at the Golf Hotel, Beauvallon. 'Divine', Una said of their spacious rooms, the balconies that looked out over the private beach.

It was a perfect summer: clear sky, the blue Mediterranean, warm air from the wide open windows. John, Una said,

> grew as brown as a berry and her hair got bleached and her eyes were clear and very blue and her teeth very white in her tanned face ... All the lines of strain and anxiety seemed to disappear and her smile grew rakish and carefree again and I think I never knew her to be so well. I myself had grown positively stout: I turned the scales at nearly eight stone and was mahogany coloured all over ... Oh yes, it was indeed a holiday of holidays.

They swam naked, lunched on lobsters, drove to Colette's villa. The effort of a day was to buy a pair of sandals, go to the chemist, walk with Tulip on the golf course, or lie on their beds. 'All afternoon we rested by open windows and read *All Quiet on the Western Front*', Una wrote. Friends rented villas nearby – John and Jehanne Holroyd-Reece, Romaine and Natalie. John worked on her trolley book, *The World*, and made notes for her next novel, *The Carpenter's Son*. It was to be about the martyrdom of Christ, written, Una said, 'as an amends for that insult to her Lord and to her faith' made in Egan's caricature of her in *The Sink of Solitude*.

After two months, at the end of July 1929, they decided to go back to Paris then on to Bagnoles in Normandy for thermal baths and the attention of doctors. Barber was sacked for drinking and inefficiency and sent to England by train. And Pierre the chauffeur went the way of all servants. In Paris Una called at the Transport Automobiles, complained about him and his driving and said he should be sacked.

They lunched with Wilette Kershaw who told them that one of her three ex-husbands had dramatized *The Well of Loneliness*. He had added new characters and made it more cheerful. John thought her 'mad and blasphemous'. She and Una went to see her in a play advertised as 'banned', called *Maya*. *The Well of Loneliness* was said to be 'coming soon'. John found it all 'an awful shock'. She sent Wilette Kershaw a letter that was more patronizing than amusing:

Dear Miss Kershaw

I know you would wish me to be as perfectly honest & sincere with you as you have been with me.

Your performance last night, so essentially feminine and appealing, the very salient natural personal elements that went to enhance that appeal, only served to crystallise the doubts I have had from the first as to the advisability of your playing the part of Stephen Gordon.

I am not losing sight for a moment of the latitude afforded by fine acting. But when an actress allows herself to be lured by personal enthusiasm into undertaking a part that is essentially foreign to both her natural charm & her individual beauty of appearance, & can only achieve an impersonation by a negation of those things that have won her her public, she not only risks the right interpretation of the part, but she risks for herself losing all that public who want her to be that which they have grown to love & admire.

Dear Miss Kershaw, for both your sake & mine, you would be *mad* to cast yourself as Stephen Gordon.

Radclyffe Hall sent back the £100 advance, asked for the return by registered post of her copy of the contract, then left with Una for the Grand Hotel, Bagnoles, driven there by a 'mad, drunk & indecent chauffeur'.

Wilette Kershaw did not reply. Una kept phoning and eventually got through to 'a vague & irate friend'. Yes, the cheque had been received, Miss Kershaw would answer when she had a moment. Wilette Kershaw then wrote that she had no intention of abandoning the project and would keep her options open about who would play the part of Stephen Gordon.

Radclyffe Hall again became enmeshed in the process of the law. She sought consolation from it that it was never going to provide. She sent wires to Harold Rubinstein and Theodore Goddard and wrote a bitter letter to Dorothea Fassett. She made much of the fact that her copy of the contract had a missing page and was therefore in her view void. She said that if the contract was not cancelled within a fortnight she would hold the London Play Company responsible.

There was muddle and blame. Wilette Kershaw did not answer the high-handed letters showered at her. Dorothea Fassett passed the problem to Audrey Heath. Audrey wrote regretting the letters John had sent directly to Wilette Kershaw. These showed, she said, that John wanted to extricate herself from the contract because of a change of mind. Wilette Kershaw had not defaulted on the agreed terms. 'Probably we are in the right on a slender technical thread, but it is a very moot point as to whether a court of law would adjudicate on that and not on the general intention of the parties. Shall I get you a solicitor's opinion?'

Una sent an irate wire to Audrey. She was extremely distressed by her letter which seemed to be supporting Dorothea Fassett. John, she said, could not rush to London so soon after her thermal baths. Her veins were '*soft as pulp*' and it would '*asking for phlebitis*'. They would curtail their treatment and return to Paris. Audrey must meet them on Thursday 12 September as John's guest at the Hôtel Osborne. Meanwhile she was to make no concessions to Wilette Kershaw. 'We both think it very obvious that you are *not* (as you think) in touch with the *whole* situation.'

Distressed at the thought of failing them, Audrey took all the relevant paperwork to Paris and spent three days trying to revoke the contract. But Wilette Kershaw would neither accept repayment of her advance nor relinquish her rights. And as a further trial Theodore Goddard wrote that Mrs Visetti's solicitor had contacted him. She needed money for an operation.

Paris was hot and the ease of the holiday gone. John and Una could not reclaim their usual rooms at the Osborne. Those available were noisy. At dinner with Audrey, John nearly fainted. She reiterated her dislike of doing business with women and told her not to have further dealings with the London Play Company or to 'recommend her luckless authors to them any more'.

Audrey was never again quite in favour. Radclyffe Hall summoned Theodore Goddard. She met him at Boulogne and instructed him to sue the London Play Company and to injunct Wilette Kershaw. Goddard also thought the contract invalid because of the omitted page. 'There is no contract', he said. He drew up a High Court writ designed to stop Wilette Kershaw claiming she had the right to dramatize *The Well of Loneliness* or to go on declaring her intention to produce it in Paris, Berlin, New York or anywhere.

Radclyffe Hall signed this writ at the British Consulate in Paris on 18 October and it was served on Wilette Kershaw. She then worked long hours on *The Carpenter's Son*, her novel about the martyrdom of Christophe Bénédit. It contained much kneeling, clasping of crucifixes and agonized prayer. Una read it aloud, thought it inspired by God and called it an intensive study of the Passion of Christ.

The style was a mix of Provençale dialect and gospel sermon. Radclyffe Hall would wake in the night talking to Bénédit. She used words like 'perforce', 'bethought himself', 'nay' and 'thus' and 'many an one'. Aged four, Bénédit sees his cousin hit a snake with a stick. '"Stop, stop!" he screamed. "You are hurting my shoulders" ' – on which there then appears a long red weal – spelled wheal. He reads the gospels, has visions of suffering pack mules, goes into psychic catatonic trances and knows that a firm hand is binding him for inscrutable ends.

Andrea visited for a week. She was nineteen and had won a scholarship to read English at Oxford. Una met her at the Gare du Nord. They had not seen each other for nearly a year. Andrea did not know what to call Radclyffe Hall. John did not sound right. Una showed her the sights of Paris while John worked.

Wilette Kershaw did not back down. Her solicitor, Clarence Samuel Tomlinson of New Bond Street, established that Dorothea Fassett was prepared, if subpoenaed, to testify that the discrepancy in the contract was because a secretary had inadvertently omitted a page in the post. He provided evidence that Radclyffe Hall's real motivation in issuing a writ was that she did not think his client's acting suitable for the part. Wilette Kershaw reiterated on his advice that she proposed to produce the play in accordance with her contract of May 1929. And he added a bombshell:

> I have made enquiries and have ascertained that on the 16th November 1928 an Order was made at the Bow Street Police Court directing that all copies of the Plaintiff's book *The Well of Loneliness* (the same having been seized by the Police) should be destroyed upon the ground that they constituted an obscene publication. The memorandum of conviction is now produced.

Radclyffe Hall saw this as no more than a gratuitous insult to stir prejudice. But Goddard realized what should have occurred to him at the start: because of its suppression, *The Well of Loneliness* probably had no copyright. He took counsel from Sir Patrick Hastings who thought it highly doubtful that a copyright existed and advised against legal proceedings. Goddard asked for a 'Discontinuance' of the trial. Radclyffe Hall paid all costs incurred by Wilette Kershaw and herself.

She had sought to use a technicality of the law to overrule Wilette Kershaw in much the same way as Joynson-Hicks and Chartres Biron had overruled her. She lost. They had won. The obscenity ruling left her and her book unprotected. Her wishes did not count. Any charlatan could exploit her text.

She and Una returned to London. They stayed in the Grand Central Hotel and looked at houses and flats for sale in Kensington but liked none of them. John felt unwell. She had a rash, a racing pulse and giddy spells. Una gave her usual diagnosis of 'heart attack' and put her to bed. Dr Sachs diagnosed indigestion. Dr Curtis and Dr Scott Pinchen said 'her nerves were worn out' and she should rest. The savagery of the obscenity trial, the way she had been vilified, months of floating in Europe, Wilette Kershaw's disrespect, had left her brittle and depressed. Relationships with friends, with other writers, with Audrey, Cape and now her lawyers, all seemed spoiled.

Wanting peace she went to Rye. She stayed at the Mermaid Inn, hunted for a house to buy and chose one of the oldest in the town. Timber framed and in the high street, Una called it the Black Boy (the sobriquet attached to Charles II, who was swarthy and who was said to have stayed in it). It had once been part of a monastery. It had oak rafters, open grates and a priest's cell. John bought it for Una, the one person she trusted, in gratitude for all her years of devotion, love and unswerving support.

The builders moved in. While they worked she rented 8 Watchbell Street, a terraced house opposite Rye's small unfinished Catholic church of St Anthony of Padua. From the drawing-room she could see the nave of the church and votive candles. She poured money into this church. If the Black Boy was Una's, the church of St Anthony was hers. She paid for its roof, pews, paintings of the Stations of the Cross and a rood screen of Christ the King. A tribute to Ladye was engraved on a brass plaque set into the floor:

> Of your charity
> pray for the soul of Mabel Veronica Batten
> in memory of whom this rood was given.

She paid off all the outstanding debts of the church. It was as if she was buying her way to the right hand of God. Masses, benedictions, processions and venerations stemmed from her beneficence. The church's priest, Father Bonaventura, was indebted to her. Out of gratitude he gave her an oak chair for her new house.

As Radclyffe Hall worked at *The Carpenter's Son* she thought herself alone with God. At his communion Christophe Bénédit hallucinates a crucified man. He has searing pains in his hands when he tries to embrace a woman and his arms go rigidly cruciform. While writing, Radclyffe Hall felt itching and stabbing pains in her palms. Red stains appeared on them. A Dr Dowling X-rayed them which made them worse. She then wrote with her hands bandaged.

She 'felt like hell'. Una worried about the long hours she worked. 'At 12.30 I got up & went down to find as I suspected – fire out – bitter cold & she had made no effort to light the electric stove.' Una, neglected, chose decorations for the Black Boy – wood panelling, door fittings and fire guards – and did an adaptation of *Chéri* by Colette for the stage. Andrea visited. She missed the train. Una 'lectured her all afternoon and she left after tea'.

Radclyffe Hall wrote *The Carpenter's Son* to take refuge after the indictment of *The Well*. Maligned by Beresford Egan, the Conservative government, the *Daily Express*, her mother, called obscene and disgusting, humiliated and reviled, she responded by showing them all how high-minded she was. She, not they, was close to God. Una chose a new title, *The Master of the House*, from Mark chapter 13 verse 35: 'for ye know not when the master of the house cometh, at even, or at midnight, or at the cockcrowing, or in the morning...'

At the book's end Christophe Bénédit enlists in the war, is sent to Palestine, 'stares into the eyes of the Indestructible Compassion', exhorts the Infidels to lay down their arms in the name of Jesus Christ, gets crucified and tells God to abandon him: 'Lord if You are with me still do not stay ... do not suffer ... But the words sank down and were lost in a bottomless pit of physical anguish.'

September 1930 brought bottomless pits from Wilette Kershaw. *The Well of Loneliness* was staged in Paris at the Théâtre de la Potinière. Janet Flanner, who as Genêt wrote a fortnightly 'Letter from Paris' for the *New Yorker*, said the first night was something of a riot. The theatre filled with large ladies who would not sit where directed by the ushers. Wilette Kershaw's show was three acts containing eleven scenes of *tableaux vivants*. At the end she made a curtain speech

in which she begged humanity, 'already used to earthquakes and murderers', to try to put up with a minor calamity like the play's and the book's Lesbian protagonist, Stephen Gordon. However, she made up in costume what she lacked in psychology: dressing gown by Sulka, riding breeches by Hoare, boots by Bunting, crop by Briggs, briquet by Dunhill and British accent – as the program did not bother to state – by Broadway.

Holroyd-Reece called the production 'backboneless, sugary and unclean'. Posters advertised it as from the novel by Radclyffe Hall and gave quotes from Havelock Ellis and Bernard Shaw. Radclyffe Hall and Audrey published complaints in the press. Rubinstein's Paris agents served a lengthy 'protestation' on Wilette Kershaw, her solicitor and the theatre. The fuss was disproportionate. 'Miss Radclyffe Hall's press statement,' Janet Flanner wrote, 'that she knew nothing about the adaptation of her novel, and as soon as she did would go to law, made the public fear that her – well, loneliness was greater than had been supposed.'

Morris Ernst advised Rubinstein that any attempt to injunct a New York production would fail. The only course would be to 'use the censorship arm of the government' and invoke a criminal statute known as the Wales Law, levelled against obscene plays. It was, he said, an arm which long ago should have atrophied; it raised 'various spiritual objections' and he warned against calling 'more attention to the situation than the situation warrants'. It was a contradiction of principle, an hypocrisy and he did not want to get involved.

It was an irony that Radclyffe Hall emulated her opponents. Despite her rhetoric about free speech, she fought to censor what went against her interests. The *New York Times* reported the dispute, printed excerpts from Wilette Kershaw's contract and said she had sent Radclyffe Hall a 'substantial check' for royalties. Radclyffe Hall wanted to sue for libel. But after the large ladies departed, Kershaw played to empty houses, she and her production fizzled into oblivion, the dispute was only a codicil to a keener injustice.

John and Una moved to their Rye house, Father Bonaventura called to bless it and Maples called to fit the carpets, curtains and bedspreads. Miss McEwan was hired as a housemaid and Mabel Bourne as housekeeper. Una's *Chéri* opened at the Prince of Wales Theatre on 26 October 1930 with Gabrielle Enthoven in the lead. Edy Craig who lived at Smallhythe near Rye went to the first night. For good luck she took along a medal awarded to her mother Ellen Terry. It worked no magic. All the reviews were 'unspeakable'.

Dismissive of her own efforts, Una lived through John. Her failure was lost in preparations for Christmas: presents and tree trimmings bought in Hastings, a hamper for the Sisters of the Poor Clares at Lynton, mass at St Anthony's Church in Rye. For Christmas dinner at the Mermaid, John dressed as a French porter, Una wore velveteen. On 28 December Noël Coward and his lover Jeffery Amherst called for tea at the Black Boy. Coward 'adored' the house and there were 'howls of laughter' from them all. On New Year's Eve John and Una heard the bells of Rye at midnight and saw in their seventeenth new year together.

27

Just Rye

In Rye, as in Paris and London, Radclyffe Hall was drawn to the artistic lesbian and gay coterie that gathered there. Edy Craig, whom she had met at school, had inherited a sixteenth-century farmhouse, at Smallhythe near Tenterden, from her mother. She lived there with Christopher St John her partner of thirty years, and Tony (Claire) Atwood. Una called them Edy and the boys. Edy Craig staged monthly barn shows, with soliloquies and sandwiches, in her mother's memory. Christopher's real name was Christabel Marshall. A devout Catholic convert, like John and Una, the St John was out of affinity with St John the Baptist. Tony Atwood painted flowers, marsh scenes with sheep, and portraits of friends. She gave John and Una a relic of the true cross acquired by her ancestors from a pope. Una put it with candles and flowers in the shrine in her bedroom.

E. F. Benson, 'Dodo', the author of camp novels featuring Miss Mapp and Lucia, lived in Henry James's former home, Lamb House, down the high street from the Black Boy. He served John and Una awful lunches, regaled them with gossip and let them read the manuscripts of his novels. They savoured these for details of Rye. Una thought he had never been in love with anyone but was 'just fond of people'. His brother, Monsignor Hugh Benson, he told them, had been a Catholic convert and died leaving a box containing a 'discipline' – a scourge with small spikes clotted with blood.

Other friends were Francis Yeats-Brown, author of *The Bengal*

Lancer, the painter Paul Nash, who was the stepson of Una's great aunt and whose work she called 'chaotic compounds of disassociated fragments', Lady Maud Warrender, once mayor of Rye, who lived at Leasam with a singer Marcia van Dresser, Sheila Kaye-Smith, whose novels Noël Coward 'passionately admired' and who lived with her husband Penrose Fry in nearby Northiam at 'Little Doucegrove', a sprawling oast house.

Rye was accepting, English and eccentric. These friends wrote books, painted pictures, worshipped the Lord and pottered in their gardens. John and Una fitted in and vowed they would never leave. They were perceived as a respectable married couple. 'We desire order and fidelity and the privilege of a religious and legal bond', Una wrote. Horrified by an article in the *Twentieth Century* advocating sexual freedom, she burned the magazine before the servants saw it.

'Isn't Rye heavenly', E. F. Benson said. 'Long may the grass flourish between her holy cobbles.' Help was there for John and Una when Tulip haemorrhaged and died in May 1931. John wept all day, buried her in the garden and had a marble headstone made. Christopher St John said her heart ached in sympathy. She gave John and Una a key to the Smallhythe garden so that they might freely visit. E. F. Benson hoped there would be a future life for dogs. Mrs Leonard confirmed that Tulip had gone straight to Ladye. (A discarnate influence was helping her write her autobiography, *My Life in Two Worlds*.)

New friends replaced the old. Toupie Lowther fell from grace for claiming to be the inspiration for *The Well of Loneliness*. Gabrielle Enthoven was dropped for 'repudiating her own kind when opportune to do so'. She had urged discretion and camouflage from her new friend Wilma. 'She's a rat and we have no use for her,' Una wrote and blamed her for the failure of *Chéri*. John wanted to drop Audrey as her agent, but did not know who else to trust.

Radclyffe Hall's enthusiasm for socialism was brief. She despised Ramsay MacDonald, the Labour Prime Minister. In a broadcast to the nation he called for sacrifices. Income tax was at five shillings in the pound in 1931, the bank rate went to six per cent and Britain left the gold standard. Radclyffe Hall's investment income was halved. She worried about her gilt-edged securities, her failed shares in American Railroads and her mother who would not economize. To save money, she used coke mixed with anthracite in the boiler and to make money she bought another house, the Santa Maria in Rye, supervised

'One of the most successful kennels of Dachshunds in this country is that owned by Miss Radclyffe Hall and Una Lady Troubridge under the title of the Fitz-John Kennels.' *The Queen*, 23 August 1923

Miss Radclyffe Hall and Una Lady Troubridge at home
at 37 Holland Street, August 1927. Mabel Batten, painted by
John Singer Sargent, is on the wall behind them.

'BEST SELLERS. An affluence of authors at the Heinemann party.' Radclyffe Hall and Una, photographed for *Tatler*, 13 November 1935.

'It was not the countenance of a woman, but of a very handsome man.' Radclyffe
Hall, May 1934

'I had the impression from Toupie that you did not like it and were worried about the resemblance.' Una Lady Troubridge by Romaine Brooks, 1924

'Would it help at all if you tried to look upon me as a man who was already married when we met?' Radclyffe Hall, 1936

'No face seems beautiful to me but yours – your queer little ugley, alian Chink Face.' Evguenia Souline, circa 1934

'Fido (so good and chased as a rule) has developed a
ranting sex complex.' Circa 1939

its refurbishment, put stored furniture in it and rented it out.

Una described Rye as haunted by peace. She loved the rainbows over the marsh, the blossom, the primroses. The focus of her days was buying the marmalade and a book on pewter and reading aloud *The Ladies of Llangollen*, which had just been published. Radclyffe Hall was again the master. Children were not sure if she was a man. She worked long hours at her book about martyrdom. A ship's bell hung above her chair in the dining room and she rang it to summon the servants. A tailor from Brighton called to measure her for her smoking suits and breeches.

There were flowers in the vases, fires in the hearths and the oak furniture gleamed. But all was not right. John was a bundle of nerves. She felt exhausted and faint, had frequent colds and headaches and her eyes hurt. When her throat was sore, Una touched it with a relic of St Blaise, the patron saint of throats, which did not make it better. She was prescribed bromides, told to get fresh air, to rest and to cut down on cigarettes. Una ordered fourteen pipes and a long cigarette holder from Dunhill for her.

John's troubles seemed deep and Una could not allay them. The house stifled her. Chapter 39 of *The Master of the House* would not materialize. A blowfly buzzed in her room; the church bells pealed; the Salvation Army banged tambourines. She was disturbed by the chatter of the servants in the kitchen, the stoking of the stove, Una's wireless, sounds of music from the monastery. Trippers looked in at the window and parked their cars too close to the house. Una printed a card in large letters: 'Please do not park in front of my house. Una the Lady Troubridge.' John stuck it on windscreens.

Una asked herself whether any book in the world was worth what John was going through. She thought her nervous state was because Ladye was coadjutor, so John was in constant physical proximity with a ghost. Everything made her anxious. She found endless fault with Mr Breeds, the builder working on the Santa Maria. He sent 'a very insolent letter' saying he could waste no more time or trouble over the place. She worried about her mother. Audrey checked in the phone book that she was still at her address in Phillimore Terrace, Kensington.

As ever there were problems with the servants. Winifred Hales, the secretary, was railed at for leaving her key in the front door, then fired for wanting a holiday. 'Poor old Mary' the parlour maid, found talking to herself in the kitchen late one night, was dismissed in the morning.

Her replacement, Violet Evans, was three-quarters of an hour late coming down. She had been sick. Una diagnosed pregnancy. Violet was despatched and replaced by Bertha and by Quilter, a parlour man.

Una fussed about her own health, her periods and piles. A letter from Andrea in June 1931, saying she was in love with an actor and wanted to have his children, sparked a pathological response. 'I long to own some bit of immature childhood', Una wrote in her diary. 'I loathe the swelling breasts and calves, the incipient moustache of adolescence.' Now forty-five, dressed, like Radclyffe Hall, in mannish clothes, when she overdid the blue rinse on her cropped grey hair it turned a rich purple. Una commended the respectability of their long marriage. She and John grumbled about small matters, held hands and admired the marsh and the sunset.

Andrea was told to explain herself by return of post or Una would send Harold Rubinstein to investigate and would encourage Tom Troubridge to decrease her allowance. Andrea was nearly twenty-one. Una thought her unattractive and without talent. 'Lord how I wish she would marry and some man assume responsibility for her.'

> When I look back on my hopes when I was expecting her, on my immense care, spiritual and material, throughout her childhood, and upon the relentlessness with which she has grown up idle, deceitful, untruthful and quite without any moral pride or independence, grown up to avoid work and to sponge upon her father's relations, who she well knows hate and traduce her mother. It is not a cheering picture. However, I think I have done my best in the circumstances all along, and more than that no one can do.

Andrea had a thin twenty-first birthday. Summoned to Rye on 11 December, she arrived on the 11.17 train. John and Una waited for her in their library. Una scrutinized her. Her dark hair was waved and shoulder length, she wore lipstick and mascara, a little hat, imitation pearl earrings, a brown three-piece costume, a long coat with a fur collar, tight suede gloves, sheer silk stockings, high heeled court shoes, a fur muff with a zip fastening. She had, said Una, the 'pose of head and general movement of a rather weary vamp, the sidling, inviting walk of a professional whore, the indescribable look of sullen, brooding, determined sexuality rampant'.

She was living alone in a bedsitter in Shaftesbury Avenue, two doors away from the Palace Theatre where she had a part in a play. The young man she loved did not want to marry her, but they spent time together in each other's rooms. She had not been to confession or communion since Easter but went occasionally to church. Una interpreted her 'entire look, bearing, circumstances and attitude of mind' as 'indescribably disreputable'.

'Desperate with anxiety and disgust', she urged Andrea to move from Shaftesbury Avenue, not to entertain or visit men in a 'manner that must ruin her reputation' and to find reputable, well-paid work. 'Even better class theatrical managers would fight shy of any girl who suggested obvious immorality.' She called her 'a born degenerate' and reminded her of 'scandals at convent and college'.

Andrea left at three-thirty in the afternoon. 'As she left the house she wrapped her coat closely round her, so that her figure was clearly defined, placed her hands in her muff and glided down Rye High Street as though she were doing her beat at midnight on Piccadilly or, as she seems to prefer it, on Shaftesbury Avenue.'

The obscenity trial made Una more respectable. She extolled her own abstinence and fidelity. She saw herself as a good mother. Her daughter was born bad and she said she 'washed her hands of her'. To Andrea it might have seemed as if she had done that long ago. Una hired a private detective. She satisfied herself that Andrea was living in a brothel and that her landlady was 'an elderly foreign jewess'.

Radclyffe Hall finished *The Master of the House* in November. Una touched each manuscript copy with her relic of the true cross then cabled the news to Jonathan Cape, Audrey Heath and the Smallhythe crew. She and John went to mass and benediction to light candles and to pray for the book's success. Audrey came down to Rye, had the last eight chapters read to her and said it was by far the biggest book John had ever written. Cape was to publish it in America too. He had set up an imprint there in partnership with Robert Ballou.

At Christmas John and Una sent a hamper with turkey sausages, plum pudding and brandy butter to the nuns at Lynton. The Black Boy was decorated with shrines, a crèche, holly and mistletoe and 'the darlings' from Smallhythe came to stay. They walked on the marshes, went to midnight mass and exchanged presents – an etching of Smallhythe and an illuminated Benedictine prayer on goatskin.

When proofs of *The Master of the House* arrived, Una read them aloud for twelve consecutive hours. John paid for full-page advertisements in the *Publisher* and the *Bookseller*. She refused to have it mentioned that it was by the author of *The Well of Loneliness*. She went to London by Daimler for publication, stayed at the Grand Central Hotel and had publicity photographs taken by Howard Coster, in Essex Street. She was guest of honour at a Foyle's Literary lunch on 17 March. Seven hundred people came to hear her speak and she signed books for nearly an hour. The Smallhythe trio and many friends were there. Francis Yeats-Brown said she looked, as she lectured, like an ecumenical saint.

The book was published to bad reviews in the *Telegraph*, *The Times* and the *Times Literary Supplement*. The *Spectator* accused her of sentimentality and the *Saturday Review of Literature* called it a bad novel written to take cover after *The Well of Loneliness*. Much of the criticism was personal. Audrey sent red tulips and a card on which she wrote, 'they thought they were doing in Our Lord when they spat upon him'. Una's research on the Palestinian battle scenes in the book was criticized by *The Times*. She winged in a letter in her own defence.

There was some enthusiasm about the book's mystical religious fervour and praise in *Time and Tide* and the *Aberdeen Press*. A woman staying in a convent wrote that it was the most beautiful book she had ever read. Perhaps the worst indictment was that James Douglas commended it in print. Miss Lugsch, a fan from Chicago, sent hagiographical screeds and photographs of herself. Una termed her a 'raving nymphomaniac with delusions' and passed her missives to Rubinstein. The Literary Guild did not want to take copies, Gallimard did not want to translate it, it did not take off in the States. When it seemed that it would not go into a second impression, Una asked St Anthony to help. 'I cannot endure my beloved to be unhappy', she told him.

Radclyffe Hall, 'utterly cast down', talked of enemies, of people hating her, of not being recognized in literature. Sheila Kaye-Smith called at the Black Boy after mass but made no comment on her complimentary copy.

Then Cape's American company went bankrupt. The news sparked Radclyffe Hall's rage. She called him a dirty blackguard and a skunk. She told him he had ruined *The Well of Loneliness* in England and now *The Master of the House* in America. She said she would make his name stink for what he had done to her. He 'went the colour of weak lemonade' and murmured 'don't threaten me'.

John went home and went to bed. Snow blizzards shrouded Rye

and nine cases of smallpox were confirmed. She read books about chiromancy, necromancy and black magic and tried to read the future in her coffee grounds. When she dropped a log on her toe Dr Hartley called to take an X-ray. Life was not how she wanted it. The church did little to console her. Father Bonaventura had, she felt sure, gone mad. He made obscene remarks and bothered the nuns. She suspected him of stealing the money she gave to the church. The paintings of the stations of the cross for which she gave £225 only cost £160. He refused to heat the church and 'spoiled' mass for her by racing through it in twenty minutes. She did not want to have communion with him. He got Mabel Batten's name wrong and would give no date for when the church would be consecrated. Moreover, he omitted to feed the church dog, Rodney. John and Una instructed the vet to take the dog away and organized meetings to oust Bonaventura. As John saw it, he was an unsatisfactory servant who ought be sacked.

Worn out and thin, in June 1932 she and Una went to Bath to take a cure. They travelled with the dogs Mitsie and Jane, Gabriele the canary and Bertha the maid. Their rooms in the Empire Hotel looked out over the weir. They walked in the botanical gardens and in the evenings Una read aloud *The House by the Bay* and *Parsons Nine*. They had pine baths, diathermy and sunlight treatment.

They went on by train to Brighton and the Grand Hotel. Una saw Dr Conran because of her heavy periods. He prescribed iron injections and referred her to Dr Seymour, a gynaecologist. He advised a hysterectomy to remove fibroids. Una and John hurried to London to Alfred Sachs and a surgeon, Mr Prescott Hedley, who both confirmed the diagnosis and treatment. Sachs said had it not been for her 'married history' of venereal disease he would have recommended 'radium treatment'.

After much packing and praying she was admitted to a private hospital in Welbeck Street. Andrea visited, looking distressed. Una was touched by her concern. Minna, aged seventy-three but dressed like a girl, brought flowers. Una was taken to the operating theatre on 6 July 1932. She had her relic of Saint Celine sewn to her nightdress. Prescott Hedley took out her uterus, cervix and appendix. He left her ovaries and fallopian tubes. John, in a room at the Welbeck Palace Hotel opposite, had acute indigestion from worry.

28

Give us a kiss

It was births in the back rooms of the clinic, hysterectomies in the front. The contrast imprinted on John's mind. Una, centre stage, made all she could of her illness. Her focus was her own pulse, temperature and urinary habits. John's affairs faded into the shade. Two nurses attended day and night, friends sent flowers – three bunches from Audrey, three from Andrea, two from Ida Wylie, one from Sheila Kaye-Smith ('2 dead sweet peas and a withered rose') and countless of course from John, who 'went through days and nights of terror and anguish. What she had been in this illness no words even of her own living pen could describe. My whole soul rises up to bless her in a love which seems incredibly increased a thousandfold.'

John saw virtually no one but Una for three weeks. She regretted missing the Smallhythe show and feared she would never work again. She scrutinized Una's stitches, commiserated with her pain, knelt with Father Collingwood beside her bed and thanked God for sparing her from death. She took her bed jackets, peaches and lemon-yellow carnations and sat with her day after day. It was reminiscent of Ladye's demise.

After a month they left for a fortnight's convalescence in Brighton. They travelled by Daimler with Sister Richardson, whom Una called 'nanny'. At the Royal Crescent Hotel another nurse and a Dr Cummings were waiting to minister. Una got a vaginal abscess, infected gums, haemorrhoids then shingles.

John pushed her in a bathchair along the seafront and spent long hours sitting in deckchairs. She hated the constraints of invalidity and the Brighton crowds or, as Una called them, 'the subhuman, seething mass of weekend tripper Jews'. Herself menopausal, John was having hot flushes and not sleeping at night. She mourned the poor reception of her book, feared her talent had left her and worried about what to write next. Cape was now a blackguard, Jew, and unscrupulous villain. His autumn list trailed a book he was publishing by Chartres Biron.

It was a relief to return to Rye. Not that all was well there. Bertha swore at Mabel Bourne, was fired and out of the house by noon. Jane the spaniel was on heat. Una's mother came to lunch which she refused to eat because she had had a rock cake at the station. They took her to see Dodo's garden and the church. Bonaventura, unshaven, red and dishevelled, leered at her and kept saying 'put me among the girls'.

Minna told John that Andrea was hard up, had a cough and could not afford to see a doctor. She asked her to pay for her to see Montague Curtis. Una, furious with her mother for 'trying to make John responsible for a woman of 22 who had consistently rejected her wishes and advice', packed her off home in a crowded third-class compartment.

Theodore Goddard then wrote that Mrs Visetti was ill. She had gone to Monte Carlo for the summer. Standing on a chair in her hotel room to reach the top shelf of her wardrobe she had overbalanced, brought the wardrobe down on top of herself, and broken three ribs. She needed money for a nurse, daily visits from a doctor, hotel bills and incidental expenses.

John wrote that she could not and would not afford more than seven guineas a week. Mrs Visetti's doctor replied that she was depriving her mother of medical care and perhaps wished her to end her days in a charitable institution. John summoned Rubinstein, who came to Rye for the day. He told her to ignore her mother's upheavals and not to be drawn. Una hoped Mrs Visetti would die. 'John is genuinely broken-nerved where she is concerned and always has been', she wrote.

Such requests for money unnerved John whose income was halved. Her stockbroker told her the country was in for a difficult ten years. To save on chauffeur's fees, she bought a Harley Saloon 12 Deluxe. Dark brown and black with hide upholstery, she called it the Squirrel, or Squiggie, Una's nickname, took driving lessons and seemed to want a journey, an essential change of scene.

Friends changed partners or had affairs. Ida Wylie visited with Joe

Baker, an American with whom she was in love. Joe Baker was sixty, wore pince-nez, had gallstones and had left her partner of twenty-five years to live with Ida. Evelyn Irons had parted from Olive Rinder and was now with someone called Joy McSweeney. Christopher St John, who was in her late fifties and odd in manner and looks, was besotted with Vita Sackville-West. Friends were embarrassed and thought her unhinged. Ethel Smyth called Vita a rotter for leading Christopher on. At a Smallhythe barn show John talked to Vita, who sympathized over the banning of *The Well of Loneliness*.

Una deplored these infidelities and spoke of her own model partnership. But three months after her operation she seldom got up before noon, she laboured up the stairs and was absorbed in her digestive troubles, nausea and headaches. She ate runny boiled eggs, junkets and milk with Bovril in it and could do no chores. John had to walk the dogs and see to the stove.

John said the Church now held the only romance left in her life. She spent long hours in her study. She reworked short stories written when she lived in the White Cottage, Malvern with Ladye, added new ones and hoped they would be published as a single volume.

The lead story was 'Miss Ogilvy Finds Herself'. She had written it in 1926 'shortly before I definitely decided to write my serious study of congenital sexual inversion *The Well of Loneliness*'. In a preface that hit back at Chartres Biron, she said readers would find the nucleus of Stephen Gordon's girlhood and 'the noble and selfless work done by hundreds of sexually inverted women during the Great War'.

Miss Ogilvy has thin lips, an awkward body, flat bosom, thick legs and ankles and rocks back and forward on her feet when agitated. She only takes her hands out of her pockets to light cigarettes and drive her battered war ambulance in France. As a child she loathed 'sisters and dolls', liked the stable boy, catapults, 'lifting weights, swinging clubs and developing muscles' and insists her name is William. Her mother calls her 'a very odd creature'. Her relationship to men is 'unusual'. Three of them want to marry her – attracted to her strangeness. Her two sisters fail to find husbands, are neurotic and sexually frustrated and look on her as their brother. She provides for them on inherited money, they live in Surrey, she gardens and, at the age of fifty-five has no friends.

Then comes the Great War: ' "My God! If only I were a man!" she burst out, as she glared at Sarah and Fanny, "if only I had been born a man!" Something in her was feeling deeply defrauded.' While her sisters knit socks, Miss Ogilvy struggles with officials because she wants to go to the front-line trenches and 'be actually under fire'. She crops her hair and loves the uniform and her trench boots. She becomes a lieutenant and is 'competent, fearless, devoted and untiring'.

Back home she refuses to grow her hair and snaps all the time. Her sisters think it is shell-shock. And then one day she packs her kitbag and goes to a small island off the south coast of Devon owned by a hotelier, Mrs Nanceskivel. It is a time-warp journey to an erotic past. Mrs Nanceskivel shows her some old bones of a man shot in the Bronze Age. Miss Ogilvy has a moment of awakening and that night dreams she is covered in zigzag tattoos and body hair and is wearing a fur pelt round her loins. By her side is a virgin with brown skin, black eyes and short sturdy limbs. 'Miss Ogilvy marvelled because of her beauty', then takes her off to the cave where bracken is piled up for a bed. The girl

knew that the days of her innocence were over. And she thought of the anxious virgin soil that was rent and sown to bring forth fruit in season, and she gave a quick little gasp of fear:

'No ... no ...' she gasped. For divining his need, she was weak with the longing to be possessed, yet the terror of love lay heavy upon her. 'No ... no ...' she gasped. But he caught her wrist and she felt the strength of his rough, gnarled fingers, the great strength of the urge that leapt in his loins, and again she must give that quick gasp of fear, the while she clung close to him lest he should spare her.

Outside the cave throughout the night big winged birds swirl around and 'wild aurochs stamped as they bellowed their love songs'. In the morning fishermen find Miss Ogilvy sitting at the mouth of the cave, dead with her hands in her pockets.

Even within the tolerance world of whatever gets you through the night, it was a disconcerting tale. It was not every lesbian's dream of a sexy time, what with the bracken and the bellowing aurochs and Miss Ogilvy's startling change of appearance.

In Rye, as ever, Radclyffe Hall became embroiled in a trial. The essence of these trials was that she was right and the world was wrong. Through them she asserted her will. They were always a quest for control, for justice of a cosmic sort. If she lost she felt martyred and closer to God.

This time her quarrel was with the Church. She wanted Bonaventura replaced by 'a decently behaved parish priest' who would 'minister to our spiritual needs with sympathy, calm, and due order'. She prepared a formal complaint to be sent to the Bishop of Southwark. It detailed Bonaventura's rages, persecution mania and delusions about being in the secret service, his squalor and unseemly behaviour, failure to visit the poor, sick or dying, his indecent remarks, the women he had had (three of them Spanish), his confusion when giving holy communion, his swearing, raging and starving of Rodney the dog.

At St Anthony's Church, Bonaventura preached a sermon saying that those who spoke against him should be excommunicated. He then had a depressive episode, left Rye suddenly and went on leave to Malta. Radclyffe Hall wanted to ensure that he never came back. She got Harold Rubinstein to check that her complaint was not libellous and then sent it to the Bishop of Southwark with a request that the matter be reported to Rome.

She did not get the reply she desired. Father Thomas Grassman, Provincial of the Friars, would hold no enquiry in Bonaventura's absence. And Radclyffe Hall came up against another side of Rye that had no sympathy with the trials of genius, congenital sexual inversion or the fight for right. When she asked the Reverend Barnet to move his car from outside the Black Boy, he shouted and asked if she owned the whole street. There was a scene. An educated curate, she told him, does not start a brawl in the public high street with gentry from the parish. The police called to say she had been reported for non-payment of licences for her manservant and two dogs. A neighbour, Mrs Ross, was snide about her tailor-made clothes. Mr Cheyney defended Bonaventura. Radclyffe Hall cancelled his invitation to tea. Una called him a tradesman, rooted in his own class.

They suspected a conspiracy among the Rye Catholics. At a meeting Una reminded them that Radclyffe Hall was an eminent writer and she herself of a social position quite other than theirs. She let them know that they both acceded to acquaintance only because they were co-religionists, and she accused Mr Paterson and Mrs Sykes of slander and defamatory attacks. 'They would rather the rubric was mauled, the poor and sick neglected and the blessed sacrament in unsuitable hands than follow our lead. And then such people think *The Well of Loneliness* was not a necessary book to write!'

Molly Bullock called at the Black Boy and tried to conciliate. But

John and Una found they now had enemies. They could not see how insulated they had become, how sustained by fantasy, how arrogant they appeared. In their hermetic world strange codes applied. Una lived vicariously through an aggrandized version of Radclyffe Hall. But Radclyffe Hall now described herself as dry, as dry as bones, as not alive. She began to hate Rye. She talked of it as a place of dreary solitude and the Black Boy as a dark and airless prison. She said the house was infested with mice, she deplored the lack of garden, the noise, traffic dust and trippers.

She took a lease in February 1933 on 17 Talbot Mansions, a top-floor flat in St Martin's Lane in London. As always a new address gave the illusion of a fresh start. She had the flat rewired, the walls painted yellow, a marble bath installed. Father Arbuthnot blessed the place. Minna when she saw it said, 'How are the mighty fallen.'

John and Una divided their time between London and Rye. Mabel Bourne who had won their friendship travelled with them. Jane the spaniel was given to kennels because of her sharp bark and scrambling ways. From Chapmans in Tottenham Court Road they bought Harry, an Amazonian blue-fronted parrot. They renamed him Cynara. He cost £15 and said 'Hello Polly' in the shop. Back home he bit John, took food from her plate and strewed it round. He was returned. A hostile assistant said they had judged him too soon. Radclyffe Hall asked if he knew the name of the customer he was bullying, that she was a well-known author whose pets were frequently mentioned in the press.

Mr Chapman offered them Charlotte for £33. She nestled her head in their bosoms, loved grapes, barked like a dog, sang along with Una, belched, had a vulgar laugh and shouted bow-wow at mealtimes. Her vocabulary was wide: 'Give us a scratch', 'What about a scratch then?', 'Ta ta', 'Oh, dear', 'Hello father', 'Father's in love with his goose', and 'Give us a kiss.' They filed her nails, bought her two cages and taught her to say 'Goodnight'. Una took her for walks round Covent Garden secured on her hand with a cord and ring.

Soon Charlotte was saying, 'Mabel Bourne! Mabel Bourne *come on there*!' And soon John and Una were again in the swing. 'The cameras flashed for us', Una said. They were guests at Ernest Thesiger's cocktail party, they went to the first nights of C. B. Cochran's show, *Escape Me Never*, at the Apollo, to *When Ladies Meet* at the Lyric, and to see John Gielgud in *Richard of Bordeaux*. Radclyffe Hall sent a note: 'I salute your greatness', then went backstage to meet him. He invited them to supper. It was a long climb up to his attic flat where he lived with his friend John Perry.

John and Una went to the French bulldog club show at Tattersall. 'There is always something in us that wakes up at the sight of thorough-bred stock in the breeds that we love', Una wrote. Travelling home through the park, they were held up by an unloved breed, 'a demonstration of 60,000 anti-Hitler jews'.

Exposure to West End society now seemed mechanical. In her work, Radclyffe Hall had lost her way. Such fame as she had achieved turned to infamy with *The Well of Loneliness*. She gave a lecture to the English Club on 'Novel Writing' on 27 February 1933. 'The propaganda novel must be entirely fearless,' she told her audience of five hundred:

> If propaganda is to be the theme of a novel, then the novel should always be written for a cause in which the author has implicit belief, for a cause which he feels in his very soul has need of someone to rise up and defend it. Such an author will at least have something fine to live with; he will always know that he has given of his strength in order to fortify and help others. If he adds but one stone, however small, to the building of a better civilisation then that in itself is a glorious thing.

She was right. But it seemed she had no more stones to add. The spite of the law had broken her nerve. In Rye she searched for a different house. She hoped for one at Smallhythe. She found some acres for sale, called a water diviner, talked of bore holes. But Edy Craig got into a state and said no house could be built if visible from the farm. Which meant John could not build. Tony Atwood kept saying, 'We can't possibly have a house out here.'

Journey's End, the house John had rented in Hucksteps Row, came up for sale. She offered £750 for it, renamed it the Forecastle and loved its sunny secluded garden, the view of France on a clear day, the adjacent river. A German barque, *Elsa Kuhlke*, sailed by, swastika flying. John had no regret at leaving the Black Boy but it proved difficult to sell. At auction it failed to reach her reserve price of £1,800. She had spent £3,000 on it. Many properties were for sale in Rye.

She had the freedom of town and country living and a new house, but old preoccupations. The church of St Anthony of Padua was consecrated on 28 September 1933. John was 'in a towering rage'. No special invitation had been accorded to her, though she had bought the roof, the stations of the cross, the rood and all of it. The Bishop of Southwark sprinkled the walls with holy water. Seventy priests, students, and all the Rye Catholics attended. John and Una sat on camp stools. The Bishop spoke of Father Bonaventura's labours, the sacrifices he had made, the congregation's good fortune in having such a priest.

In November the Provincial came to Rye and took mass. From the pulpit he denounced those parishioners who had criticized Bonaventura. He told them to scrutinize their own lives to see whether their calumnies against the priest of God were born of malice. He spoke of libel, quoted Ecclesiastes and the gospels about backbiters and slanderers and compared Bonaventura to Christ who was given gifts of gold, then crucified.

Radclyffe Hall took the reservation card that marked her seat, tore it up, tossed the pieces on to the pew, stared the Provincial in the face, genuflected to the cross and left the church. She vowed never again to go in it while this order controlled it, and she threatened to secede. She sent back the oak chair Bonaventura gave her when she first moved to Rye.

She was beleaguered and locked in with Una. As they both hit out at the world, it seemed to recede. And Una hit out at her daughter. Andrea now wanted to marry a man called Toby Warren who had no clear profession. His mother, Lady Warren, who was divorced, had tea with Una and John and told them she 'expected the young people to make their way economically'. Andrea turned to Tom Troubridge, her half-brother, to help with her wedding. He offered his house for the reception, to 'give her away' and continue her allowance until her husband was better off. Una saw this as Andrea siding against her and offering her stepson 'another occasion for venting his spleen against me'.

Una vented her spleen too. The prospect of Andrea's wedding dredged up sexual disgust. The infection from Troubridge, the obscenity trial, her hysterectomy, her piety and high-handedness spilled into undermining her daughter. In August Andrea went on holiday with Toby Warren and Harry Wilcox – a former boyfriend of hers – and his current girlfriend Carol Goodner, 'a notorious whore' Una called her. None of them had any money. They stayed in a caravan in Dorking. 'I am disgusted with Andrea for making herself cheap and with Toby for having no respect for her reputation', Una wrote in her diary.

I can do nothing except ensure that Lady Warren also knows of this escapade and that I am not the confidante upon the assumption that I am less likely to disapprove. Toby is bringing his mother to luncheon next Saturday and I am not showing any discretion for anybody's sake. No man worth his salt would take his fiancée to stay in a caravan with a man, on whom she has long had a physical obsession, and his kept woman. I am now wondering if they *do* marry how long the marriage will last. I am afraid they have anticipated it in more respects than buying the car, the three dogs, and hiring the house. I did not notice any alacrity in respect of calling the date.

It was, Una recorded, an odious lunch. No doubt Andrea agreed. John kept quiet. She had no interest in Andrea, no intention of going near the Troubridges even if invited, which she was not. She offered no present, no involvement, no practical help.

Andrea sent a twenty-five-page letter to her mother. She would like her to be at her wedding but she asked her to retract her insults. She had heard said some pretty awful things about her and John, but wanted not to believe them. Una burned her letter and did not reply. She referred to her as the 'grim outcome of an old and diseased father and a young and diseased mother. It would have mattered less somehow if a really nice personality had been born of the union. This affair has been the last illusion and the last disillusion I shall endure on her behalf.'

Andrea wrote again. She did not want to arrange her wedding over her mother's head but she needed to make plans. Una replied with a copy to Tom Troubridge: she withdrew none of her criticisms, she would not be attending, not least because Andrea had made a disgraceful scene in her house.

Minna intervened for Andrea. Una told her that she too should not attend the wedding. Minna replied that it was a duty to be there. Una hung up on her whenever she phoned. 'She was my mother before she was Andrea's grandmother', she wrote. 'It is her duty to support me in a moral issue. She must of course as always for her own satisfaction, dress her inclinations in trappings of high moral colour.' Which was what Una for her own satisfaction always did.

Una 'retired from the whole affair'. At a first night of *Finished Abroad*, Andrea and Toby Warren were standing at the back of the stalls. Neither Una nor John greeted them. Una commented on how fat and plain her daughter's face was, and how 'slatternly and unwashed' the man she was going to marry.

Spite was provoked by her daughter's marriage, and a loathed reminder of past life. Andrea sent her a printed invitation. Her wedding would be on 15 November at St Mary's Church in Cadogan Gardens and afterwards at Tom Troubridge's house in Egerton Gardens. 'I shall merely ignore the communication', Una wrote. She instructed her bank to pay over £267 held in trust for Andrea and she sent a diamond ring given by Minna for her long ago.

> I shall not be present as she has deliberately made it impossible for me to be so. And John, who has kept a roof over her head since she was five, has not been invited. Sufficient reason were there no other to preclude my attendance. The reception will be given by Tom Troubridge, my stepson, who, for six years, ever since he learned that his father had infected me with a venereal disease, has never missed an opportunity of insulting me. Well, Andrea is 23, a grown woman, and I have done my utmost for her ever since her birth and now is the end. She will go her way and I will go mine. She becomes, if anyone's, her husband's responsibility and I do not expect to have any further contact with her.

Una was like steel. Life ricocheted off her. Old resentments found new targets. Bonaventura did not return to Rye, for which she gave thanks in Brompton Oratory to Sir Thomas More. Father Wendelin Braun was assigned to fill his place in January 1934. Radclyffe Hall went to see him about getting back her special pew. He was in his slippers by a blazing fire, taking snuff and eating sweets. He said he was glad if she and Una were resuming attendance at the church but that he had been instructed to refuse them reserved seats.

Radclyffe Hall told him that he was excluding the principal benefactor of the church. The matter would not rest. She would go to the Bishop, the Archbishop, the Pope. She would speak to the press, sue for defamation of character. Father Braun forwarded a letter from her to the Provincial, who did not reply.

John became ill. Preoccupied about who was sitting in her seat at church, she seemed defined by abandonment: no mother, no father, no gender, no book and now no pew at St Anthony's. The slightest obstacle made her cry. Her skin was grey, her eyes tired, she looked emaciated and her pulse raced. Dr Montague Curtis warned her that she would have a breakdown if she did not take care. She got a boil on her nose and Una feared this would lead to blood clots on the brain. Her volume of short stories was published by Heinemann to faint praise and no real interest. The American fan Miss Lugsch sent a bioscope of Chicago views that broke in the post. John put the package, unopened, into a bucket of water supposing it to be a bomb.

Una pleaded that they get away for the summer, that they have a complete rest. She reserved rooms in the Hôtel des Thermes in Bagnoles-de-l'Orne for 25 July. They would travel via Paris, have their thermal baths then go on to Sirmione in Italy, to the lake and mountains where their friend the novelist Naomi ('Micki') Jacob had a villa. Mabel Bourne was to care for the Forecastle while they were away. Charlotte was given to Lord Tavistock who had an aviary. John now found her intolerable. She shrieked and whistled, moulted everywhere and made a loud pinging sound when she ate.

SAME HEART

29

The intolerable load

They left London on 21 June 1934 with their paraphernalia of trunks, Mitsie the dog and Gabriele the canary. Paris was hot and airless. At the Sacré Coeur they lit candles by the memorial stone John had bought for Ladye and bought pious bibelots for the success of their cure – a faun drinking holy water, a sacred heart blessed by a priest.

They had a 'marvellous lunch' with Romaine who now had an apartment in rue Raynouard with views over the roofs of Paris. She arranged to join them in Sirmione. They saw Natalie and her current lover, a sales assistant at Schiaparelli. Natalie told John to write to d'Annunzio when she got to Lake Garda, send him a copy of *The Well of Loneliness* and he would meet her. They called on Colette in her eighth-floor apartment in rue Marignan, saw her bulldog Souci and met her *pécheur de perle*, Maurice Goudeket. Una thought him 'amiable if dull'. Colette wore St Tropez sandals, a blue sarong and her hair was dyed red. She was writing a novel, a film scenario and articles for magazines.

'And here we are at Bagnoles once more after five years', Una wrote on 26 June. They had their usual rooms on the fourth floor of the Hôtel des Thermes. French windows opened to a wide balcony and a view of a valley of pine woods. They began their regime of steam baths and doctors' checks. John's blood pressure was high and she was advised, yet again, to ease up on smoking.

Una got gastroenteritis and went to bed. She thought it was from drinking iced water in the Paris heat. John, at her wits' end, coped for a week 'bullying the dilatory hotel staff'. She then phoned the American Hospital in Paris and instructed them to send out a nurse. 'This they did and on the following day Evguenia Souline arrived.'

She came like a saviour. In her white uniform she seemed pale and calm, young and healthy, her English fractured, her manner shy. Una thought her 'a treasure and charming, unmistakeably of our own class, an extremely nice woman'. John was inordinately pleased with the help she gave, the errands she ran. And she was intrigued by her. She wanted to hear about her past.

A victim of the Russian Revolution Evguenia had no country, emotional ties or money. She was thirty and had had typhoid and tuberculosis. She hated nursing and dreamed of being a ballerina, an actress, a doctor. Her parents were dead. Her father had been a major-general in the Imperial Cossack army. She had seen people shot at random, deserters hung from trees and had herself been sentenced to death. She had lived with her family in tents on the Greek island of Lemnos and they had moved to Yugoslavia, America and then France.

'John was obviously ready to fall in love,' Evguenia wrote, 'she was waiting for her ideal. I was unprotected, a lonely pathetic figure, a refugee on whom she could bestow her reserve of deep affection and love, whom she could treat a little like a child. Yes, very much like a child, as the time went on it proved itself to be so.'

John went for walks with her. She gave her a signed copy of *The Master of the House*. 'I can see how you flushed to the eyes with pleasure that I wrote your name in it.' At dinner she insisted Evguenia be served first and given the best pieces of food. One morning, when John was late coming down for breakfast, Evguenia went to her room to check she was all right. ' "I have come on my own initiative," you said. I loved you for it Evguenia though I laughed because the words sounded so pompus.' In the car one day Evguenia said, ' "May I take off my cap please?" And all that you were then, or that I thought you were, seemed to me intensely appealing, and I felt the whole of me reaching out to you, crying out that I *must* and *would* protect you.'

Must and would were significant words for Radclyffe Hall, and the protection was to be of a sexual sort. She saw herself as Evguenia's saviour. She would defend her ferociously from the brutal world. She told Evguenia she thought her afraid of life and afraid of love. 'There was something definitely not quite ordinary and normal,' Evguenia wrote, 'all was not altogether right. She roused my instinct in some perturbing way. I decided that I must go as soon as I could so as not to be engulfed in this contradictory mass of feelings. The matter only grew worse when I said I had to go now that the patient was so much better.' But John insisted she stay though Una was recovered and the hospital charging 175 francs a day.

After two weeks John saw her off on the evening train. Evguenia went back to her Paris room in rue Francisque-Sarcey. She talked to her friend Lysa Nicolsky about her uneasy feelings. Next day there was a telephone call from John –

> ... that is how she wanted me to call her. I fought like anything within myself not to fall under her spell and repeated to myself over and over again: no, no, I do not wish to ... I must not let myself be carried away by this undetermined emotion. But John was obviously very determined. Her letters became at once very strong and emotional. She just would not hear of any reason on my part not to accept her affection, not to write to her or to see her.

Evguenia was bombarded with phone calls and letters. Una wanted to get John to Sirmione. They were to travel there via Paris, where they would spend two nights in the Hôtel Pont Royale. Paris for John now meant Evguenia. Her instructions to her were precise. Evguenia was not to worry about living in one small room – 'I am really a very humble person.' John did not want to meet any of her friends – 'You know by now I am shy of people.' She wanted to say things but not 'frightening' things – 'I always have a feeling that you are scared of me.' From Evguenia came a stiff note addressed to Miss Hall – 'never again can I be Miss Hall to you', John replied.

> Meet me at La Pérousse (you know Quai des Grands Augustins) at 12.30 and we will lunch there alone together, just you and I. After lunch we will go back to my hotel where I shall have a sitting room and there (if you are willing) we will spend the afternoon. We shall be quite alone ... Take care of yourself and know that I am counting on this meeting in Paris as I have counted on few things in my life.

John booked in at the Pont Royale on 24 July. Evguenia sent a note of welcome. 'Darling Yes I am here in Paris,' John replied, 'and it seems so strange that only a few weeks ago I did not know that Paris meant you. I want to come to you. It's red hell to be here and not to be able to see you until the day after tomorrow and then only for a few hours.'

Within days it was red hell to be with Una. 'John gave my ex-nurse lunch at La Perousse', she wrote in her diary on 26 July. 'I am sorry for the poor child who is lonely and not happy.' Soon she was lonely, not happy and sorry for herself. All afternoon John stayed closeted in an adjacent room. Evguenia, terrified, ate nothing at lunch. At some point she said, 'Do you want to kiss my mouth?'

And your darling lips were so firm and protective, so chaste and so competent to protect, so unwilling to give, so unwilling to respond. Why you kissed me like a sister or a child – or were you really experienced and not intending to do otherwise? Once, just once your lips gave way a little, a very little.

Darling lips and chaste kisses were a start. When they parted, Evguenia said, 'I can't believe that this is the last time I shall see you.' Even before leaving for Sirmione John's letters gushed out:

I am tormented because of you, and this torment is now only partly of the senses – but is now an even more enduring thing and more impossible to ease – my sweet, because it is a torment of tenderness, of yearning over you, of longing to help you – of longing to take you into my arms and comfort you innocently and most gently as I would comfort a little child, whispering to you all sorts of foolish words of love that has nothing to do with the body. And then I would want you to fall asleep with your head on my breast for a while, Soulina, and then I would want you to wake up again and feel glad because I was lying beside you, and because you were touching this flesh of mine that is so consumed by reason of your flesh, yet so subjugated and crushed by my pity, that the whole of me would gladly melt into tears, becoming as a cup of cold water for your drinking. And if this is wrong then there is no God, but only some cruel and hateful fiend who creates such an one as I am for the pleasure that he will gain from my ultimate destruction. But there is a God, make no mistake, and I have a rightful place in His creation, and if you are as I am you share that place, and our God is more merciful than the world, and since He made us, is understanding and He knows very well what the end will be, seeing what you & I cannot see, knowing why you & I have been forced to meet, and why this great trouble has come upon us.

Soulina I implore you to cling to this belief, because without faith our
souls will be undone at this time of all but unendurable suffering...

Something tells me that all this was meant to happen, that we *shall*
meet again, that our love will last, that our mutual desire the one for the
other is only the physical expression of a thing that is infinately more
enduring than our bodies. Surely Soulina, you must feel this too? Otherwise why did I let you go from me even as you came – I, who needed you
so and who could have made you incapable of resisting, could have made
you no longer want to resist? For you are not a woman of ice and this I
well know, my little virgin, and I agonized to take your virginity and to
bind you to me with the Chains of the flesh, because I had & have so vast
a need that my wretched body has become my torment – but through it
all my spirit cries out to you, Soulina, and it tells you that love is never a
sin, that the flesh may be weak but the spirit is strong – yesterday it was
my spirit that saved you. Must I always save you? I do not know. I cannot
see far beyond this pain.

John told Evguenia to lock up this and all such letters. She told her
that Lady Troubridge had been very wonderful, sent her love and
would write to her from Sirmione.

Lady Troubridge was not very wonderful for long. By the time they
arrived in Sirmione she was sweating in her sleep, thin as a grass blade
and praying for help to Our Lady of Victories. When John announced
she was going to see Soulina in Paris in October on their way back
to Rye she went haywire. She forbade it. She reminded her of her
hysterectomy, of every illness she had ever had, of Dr Fouts' warning
that she must avoid all emotion. She told her she had been married to
her for eighteen years, had stood by her through the obscenity trial,
given her all of her interest, all of her love, all of her life and now she
was going to die. 'After a scene which lasted all night, she suddenly
hurled herself onto the floor and looked as though she were going
demented. I think that it may very well be that her operation has made
her more excitable – women are like that after that operation.'

Una reminded her, until John felt she was going mad, of her obligation as the leader of inverts, of how she 'stood for fidelity in the case
of inverted unions', of how 'the eyes of the inverted all over the world
were on her', revering her, respecting her open and faithful relationship.

And when she says this I can find no answer, because she is only telling the truth. I have tried to help my poor kind by setting an example, especially of courage, and thousands have turned to me for help and found it, if I may believe their letters, and she says that I want to betray my inverts who look upon me almost as their leader. Oh, but what's the use of telling you any more of the hell I went through last night & this morning – I have a debt of honour to pay, I am under a terrific obligation, and can I shirk the intolerable load? It is less whether I can shirk my load than whether I have the strength to bear it.

'Nineteen years together', Una wrote in her diary on 1 August. Only twice had they spent a day apart or slept under separate roofs. She prayed to God, the Virgin Mary, St Anthony, Celine and Mabel Batten. She asked them to steady her health and nerves, put her mind at peace and sort this mess out. In church John whispered she would never leave her, they would remain together for ever and ever throughout eternity, Amen.

Una softened when John pleaded that without Evguenia she was too desolate to go on living, could neither eat nor sleep and would never write another book. Una permitted letters and a meeting in Paris provided John gave her 'word of honour not to be unfaithful in the fullest and ultimate meaning of the word'.

The holiday in Italy was not a success. John called it 'my terrible summer in Sermione'. They stayed at the Albergo Catullo near Micki Jacob's villa. Romaine joined them but found her room too primitive and left after a couple of days. Una got bitten by mosquitoes and stung on the ankle by a horsefly. John spent long hours locked in her room pouring out love letters to Evguenia or waiting in agitation for the post.

Distractions were fleeting. Una was delighted when the hotel proprietor gave her the framed photograph of the Duce that hung in the foyer. And she was thrilled when d'Annunzio agreed to see John, sent an armoured Alfa Romeo to collect her and gifts for them both of flowers, and bracelets with rubies and cabochon sapphires. He offered his villa in the garden of the Vittoriale for John to write her next book and said he would send his private plane to collect a first edition of *The Well of Loneliness*.

But John was no longer interested in her literary career. She could only have one obsession at a time and now it was Evguenia. She sent her forty-one letters in the six weeks she was in Sirmione. They were letters about herself, though God's will and destiny were categorically invoked. Love was to do with money, sex and coercion. It was locked in the time warp of Sunny Lawn. Long years with Una had not led to subtleties of expression. 'She would not give allowance for my own feelings', Evguenia was to write. 'John was very shy, but nevertheless it was she, her personality that dominated.'

On 31 July John arranged a bank transfer of £100 for Evguenia – a significant sum in 1934. In many letters she enclosed a hundred-franc or two-hundred-franc note. 'I want you to have everything on this earth that I can possibly afford to buy you', she told her. She promised coats with high collars, an apartment with a nice bathroom and a large sunny bedroom, holidays by the sea. 'I resented it at first but really who could resent it for long,' Evguenia said, 'when one is in dire need of everything, starting with a pair of pyjamas ... and she fretted that I was not eating well, had no money to buy shoes and dresses with. She could not bear the idea of my wanting anything. Besides I had to have something decent on when she would come back.' Evguenia protested that she felt uncomfortable about taking the money, had 'no right' to it, had done nothing to deserve it and could not repay it except with love and devotion.

Love and devotion suited John. And sex. John would 'make a woman of her' so Evguenia 'would know the meaning of passion'. She would protect her 'as if she were a baby'. She would like her to have her child. Evguenia, she said, was probably bisexual whereas she, John, was a 'congenital invert' who could never have sex with a man. What if, John asked, she were released from her promise to Una, would Evguenia then be her lover?

> I asked if you would give yourself to me. You say that you are not yet sure. Sweetheart were I in very truth your lover in the ultimate sense of the word – I might not always be very gentle. I might try to be so but I might not succeed, because the sex impulse is a violent impulse – I can't explain this to you very well because you know so little about it beloved. But this I tell you, were we lovers in deed you would not want me to be very gentle – not if you feel for me even the half of what I feel for you.

Evguenia was bombarded with such warnings of sexual intent. They invoked uncertain desire and terror. Apprehensive about their next tryst, her letters became stiff and formal. She was disturbed, attracted, interested, frightened silly. Once she wrote, 'I love you too much. When shall I see you?' In another letter she wrote that John was the biggest love in her life. More often she voiced worry that it was all somehow wrong.

She said she would prefer their love to be 'pure and vital' and 'only spiritual'. John asked if this was because some man had given her an emotional shock, 'even if this falling in love with me has been your first deep experience of love'. She told her to have the courage to accept her fate, view John as the Giver and the Master, do what she said and hold her head high.

John would be in Paris on Sunday 30 September on her way back to England. She would take Evguenia to lunch at twelve-fifteen on 1 October. They would then go back to Evguenia's apartment at rue Sarcey. 'You shall tremble in my arms which even you, *even you* must admit does not constitute either a rape or a "seduction".' Evguenia was to keep free all afternoons and evenings throughout John's ten-day stay. She was to say how much money she needed so as not to have to work for the hospital at this time. 'Money there is and money I will send if only you will tell me how much you need.'

Evguenia panicked. At the end of August she wrote that she might have to go to America two days after John arrived. A rich elderly patient, Mrs Baker, ill with all sorts of things, always asked particularly for her to nurse her when she travelled.

John responded with rage. She instructed Una to write to Evguenia. She arranged to go to Paris earlier. Mrs Baker 'appears to have more claim upon you than I have', she wrote. Evguenia was not to run about for Mrs Baker – doing her shopping, cashing her cheques, holding her hand. 'If you're anyone's slave you're going to be mine.' She warned her to keep to their schedule and to keep her diary entirely free for those days in Paris:

> Now listen Souline – do you know who I am? I am really a very well known author whose career is watched by a very large public, and as such I am naturally a busy woman ... I think it essential that I should remind you. You have fallen in love with Radclyffe Hall, not with Mary Jones or anyone like her, and Radclyffe Hall has a standard to uphold. I am so madly in love with you that you can force me to lower that standard by worrying me the way you have done, by making me utterly unfit to work by your own inability to stop being vague. Are you going to make

me lower my standard, or are you going to help on my work by giving me a minimum of peace and comfort? By giving me those ten days I ask for?

She could not concentrate on her new novel. Evguenia must do better. She would have to learn to love. 'I shall have to teach you.'

I haven't deserved this at your hands – to be pushed aside for someone else, to be treated as less than this other person when I have given you all I have to give of love, and you saying that you love me that I am the biggest love in your life. What in God's name does it mean, beloved?

In Paris on 23 September Una noted in her diary that John went out at eleven-thirty in the morning and returned just before midnight. In subsequent letters John made clear what went on. They spent the afternoon in Evguenia's room. She was in a state of terror. 'I found you a virgin and I made you a lover. I have made a new discovery through you. I find that to take an innocent woman is quite unlike anything else in life.' She called it 'perhaps the most perfect experience'. She wondered at Evguenia's 'ignorance of physical passion', told her the 'trouble' she showed was *entirely nerves* and that she did not 'get a normal reaction' because she was 'desperately nervous' – 'remember how you fought me, my darling!'

At supper Evguenia 'sat all crumpled up and in despair'. John fed her, 'as though you were a child and consoled you and reassured you as though you were a child ... I was your first lover. Through me you are now no longer a child. Wonderful yes but terrible also – terrible because so achingly sweet.' At midnight John went back to Una. She felt bad about leaving Evguenia but next day she was again in her room and for each of the ten days of her stay. 'Step by step – very quietly, I led you towards fulfillment. And this has made you doubly mine.' John told Evguenia the facts of life as she saw them. '*All* the facts of life I believe I have told you.' She omitted one or two things about how to get pleasure but would make those clear in time.

'Very often I would do something which was not what I wanted but I knew John liked me to do it and I usually gave in', was Evguenia's view of the exchange. It was an uneasy seduction. There was a touch of the Miss Ogilvies about it. It seemed to have echoes of the unwanted advances of Alberto Visetti, the misery of Marguerite as a child. It was enough to make the grand old men of England get out their gallows and gibbets.

'You woke me up,' John wrote to Evguenia, 'you little stray dog who had no collar, you little white Russian who had no home ... let me be your love, your home and your country. Beloved – please adopt my heart as your country.' This heart was feudal territory and desperate with need. 'Same Heart', John called Evguenia. 'You are not your own any more, you are mine.' The three selves had become four. Evguenia received quantities of cash, an emerald ring, clothes, a Kodak camera.

The promise to Una had not meant much. 'Inversion alas what things are done in thy name that would be perversion a hundred times over were they heterosexual', Una wrote in her diary. She was glad to get back to Rye. The garden was lovelier than she had remembered it, a mass of zinnias and dahlias. The house was welcoming and smelled of wood fires.

Distance and home did nothing to lessen John's obsession. 'You alone seem real – all the rest are dreams', she wrote to Evguenia. Round her neck she now wore a Russian cross, on her desk were two photos of Evguenia, in a locked box her letters. All her plans were to do with the logistics of their next meeting.

Evguenia had a nursing assignment in Zurich in October. She was to look after a Russian princess who had a new baby. She would then come to England in November, second class on the train, first class on the boat. John would meet her at Folkestone. They would stay three nights at the Grand Hotel then go alone to the Talbot Street flat in London. 'The hotel is so nice and we shall have peace,' John wrote to her, 'no servant, no telephone, no nothing but ourselves. Darling that does seem to me like Heaven.' Una was to stay in Rye. John wanted to show Evguenia the Forecastle, so they would join Una there just for a night: 'I do wish she'd lend it to us as I love it so much – but this she won't do I'm sure and neither would I in her place.'

John described herself as excited as a schoolboy. Una, she felt, was being remarkably compliant. Evguenia needed appropriate clothes, so she sent her money. She also needed a visa for the visit as she had no citizenship. Una wrote to the Home Office and was despatched to the Passport Office to give the necessary guarantees. 'As I have some standing as the widow of an admiral,' she wrote to Evguenia, 'I have stepped in and taken a hand.'

In London John sent the curtains in the Talbot Street flat to be cleaned, ordered wine, a new suit and shirts, found out what plays were on and slept with Evguenia's letters under her pillow. But for Evguenia the more the build-up of tension, the phone calls from Una about her visa and the exigency of the arrangements, the more she pulled back. Perhaps the Russian princess would need her to stay in Zurich, perhaps the baby would get ill. John lost her temper. She 'raved about the flat like someone demented'. 'Soulina I need you more than these lesser people', she wrote with her startling self-importance. The Russian princess was a drunkard, she pitied her husband and child.

John wooed Evguenia with money. She wanted to know how much she needed a week. 'It is natural and right that I should keep you. We have just got to talk finances when we meet.' She sent travel instructions for the umpteenth time and enclosed a £20 banknote. Una, she told her, was being 'a perfect brick', though who knows what Evguenia made of the cliché.

> She might have made it such red hot hell but instead she is doing her best to be friendly. She sees that the thing is too deep to be broken ... She has accepted the situation and really I think she has all but stopped fretting. She is ever so much happier now that she has made up her wise & clever mind to accept the inevitable.

For which seeming sagacity, John said she thanked the Lord on her knees.

30

A trois

John was waiting on the pier's edge at Folkestone. 'She would have come nearer were it at all possible', Evguenia said. Three glasses of champagne on an empty stomach in the Grand Hotel and John was drunk. 'I feel crazy sometimes remembering our days and nights at Folkestone', she later wrote. She declared herself madly in love, reborn, revitalized. This was like first love. 'No face seems beautiful to me but yours, no voice seems beautiful to me but yours. I am only half alive when we are apart.' She would do anything for Evguenia, her Royal Chinkie Pig, her Darling most Chink Faced Little Tartar. She wanted this love to last for ever and beyond: 'I feel an overwhelming desire to be with you day and night, both in moments of passion and in moments of rest that come after passion, and in moments of that simple companionship that we two are able to enjoy so much together.'

As for the wife back home in Rye: 'I am not and I have not been for years the least in love with Una. I feel a deep gratitude towards her, a deep respect and a very strong sense of duty.' But now she belonged to Chinkie Pig. 'Only you can make me feel alive. You are my rest, my joy and my ultimate justification.'

'We were both mad happy', Evguenia said of their early months together. Materially it was agreeable to be so treated, adored and indulged. Suddenly there was money for everything: clothes, first-class travel, taxis, any luxury she desired. There was even money for her friend Lysa when she became ill. But John wanted a lot in return. 'John was very impatient. If she wrote a letter she wanted the answer to her questions before the letter could even reach the addressee.' These questions were possessive, dictatorial, anxious. 'I must be all to you or nothing', she told her Chinkie Pig.

Alone in Rye Una prayed a great deal. She said the Angelus two or three times a day, and thought of Mabel Batten and the symmetry of their plight:

> All that I did to hurt her she has repaid in almost exactly similar circumstances. I was utterly selfish and cruel to her, partly it is true in ignorance but partly in the crude egotism of youth and personal desire. May being hurt at least teach me never again carelessly or deliberately to hurt anyone else. I would like to spare so far as is humanly possible even those who are not sparing me. But first and foremost I want the best, morally, spiritually and in all ways for my only beloved, and Ladye wants it too and for our Threeship. All other persons whatever their part in our existence and however much interest and affection they may evoke are outside and my John knows it as well as I do.
>
> Lord give me patience in tribulation and Thy grace truly to say Thy will be done on earth as it is in heaven. The things that I pray for good Lord give me the grace to labour for. Amen.

And labour she did, though resolutions of kindness disappeared into the ether. Una was a formidable foe. Her determination was absolute. She had clung too long to the host for her tendrils to be prised free.

John took Evguenia to Rye for a night on 15 November. They arrived early evening. Una had set the scene. 'I made the Forecastle put on all its war paint for Souline to see.' Log fires blazed, rooms were lit by candlelight, there were flowers in jugs and pewter vases. In the dining-room Una's shrine to Our Lady of Pity was lit by a tall red candle 'with red carnations in the chalice and yellow chrysanthemums before her'. None of it, Evguenia knew, was for her benefit. It was a warning to back off.

'A trois' became a much-used phrase, as familiar as Our Three Selves. A trois they had tea and dinner, lunch at the Mermaid and visited Smallhythe. Evguenia was their protégée, a Russian refugee in their care. In the evening John took her again to the Folkestone Hotel.

Evguenia went back to Paris on 17 November. They were to be apart six weeks. John poured out desolate letters. 'I feel as though the whole of me was bleeding, as though something vital had been torn away – and this wound will go on bleeding & bleeding until our next meeting, Soulina. Dearest – '

She kissed the bed Evguenia had slept in, gazed at her photograph and longed for letters. 'You have made me a stranger to what was once my life, for now I have no life apart from you who have become my life – you greatly adored little Chink-faced Russian.' At night she lay listening to the doleful sound of fog horns on the sea that separated them. She worried that Evguenia would drink spirits, or go out without galoshes. On a day when no letter came, she worried so much that Una phoned the American Hospital in Paris to check Evguenia was there.

This life that was now no life – life with Una – needed sorting out. Its determining rules had been violated. There were scenes which left them both shattered. There was a storm and Una felt as troubled as it. 'Very sad and unhopeful. Fruitlessly thinking of happier days.'

Evguenia was John's consolation for the trial of *The Well of Loneliness*, the failure of *The Master of the House*, the dead end of her feelings for Una. She said Evguenia had brought her back to life and because of her she could again work. But she needed Una to affirm this work. All that Una now did was with a view to ousting Evguenia. She used the novel John was writing, *Emblem Hurlstone*, as a weapon. She read it aloud and called it 'the futile frittering of a bogus book, an excuse for writing about Evguenia's mannerisms and characteristics, the man's reactions to them and his passion for her'. Set in Sirmione, it was about a man liberated by the death of his mother and his love for a younger woman. Una undermined it. She told John it lacked inspiration and urged her to abandon it.

Una pretended affection for Evguenia. She sent her linen handkerchiefs. Evguenia reciprocated with preserved fruit. John told Una, 'You are the wide river of my life. The others are tributaries.' She believed that somehow they could be a family of three. It was the kind of family she knew: warring, manipulative and incestuous. Its bonding was to do with possession, sex, money and control. Roles were questionable. None of them was sisterly. Una was a mother from hell, Evguenia a difficult daughter, John a dubious father. If *à trois* was husband, wife and mistress, Una wanted preferential rights. She was resentful when the doorbell rang and John said to her, 'Soulina there's someone at the door.' Evguenia complained of feeling like a stray dog, of not knowing where she belonged.

Evguenia now wore the ring John gave her. She was told to tell Mrs Baker it came from Una. John encouraged dependency and exerted control. Evguenia's rent and the concierge's wage were paid by banker's order, she had an allowance of £10 a month, she was to use Petrol Hahn on her hair – 'Honest darling, your hair is almost non-existant' – she was not to use red lipstick, wear grey or green or stay out late.

John's 'heart turned over' when Evguenia got a Christmas cheque from Mrs Baker. And she panicked that a Franco-Russian military pact might lead to her expulsion from France. She asked Rubinstein to get English naturalization for her. He said she would need five years' residence before it would be considered. He thought France would grant citizenship if she kept working at the American Hospital. With it, she could visit England for months at a time.

John could not now tolerate being alone with Una. Christmas at the Forecastle was a ritualistic affair: candles and plum pudding, a crib and angels on the tree. Una at her twentieth midnight mass with John prayed for a resolution of her difficulties. 'The way out is quite beyond my unaided guidance.' John prayed for citizenship for Chinkie Pig.

They both went to Paris in January 1935. John wanted to arrange Evguenia's French naturalization and find her a flat that would reflect her new status. 'Una wants to come with us,' she told her: 'She adores looking at flats & houses. I think that it will be kind of you if you let her come around with us – it will give her a lot of fun & pleasure.'

Evguenia met them at the Gare du Nord. They all stayed at the Hôtel Lutétia in boulevard Raspail. John gave her presents of satin trousers, stockings, pyjamas, a beret, scissors in a red leather case, an ivory hand mirror. They had supper *à trois* then Una went to bed with chest pains and breathlessness. 'I am perpetually anxious these days and with good cause. I live in a state of fear of what more will have to be met and suffered. This girl is being brought right into our lives, daily and hourly, so our old and treasured companionship, *à deux*, hardly seems to exist.'

She hoped that the more John saw of Evguenia the sooner she would tire of her. She scrutinized Evguenia to find fault: she was dull, childish with no looks, no brain, 'madly in love with John as is only natural'. She found John's 'doting infatuation' intolerable, the way her eyes followed Chinkie Pig about, the way she registered her every word and action: 'the devotion that for twenty years was all mine, overflowing for someone else, and a woman years my junior who has never been to John all that I have been. It hurts and hurts and is never for one waking moment out of my mind and heart.'

John promised not to leave Una alone all day and night. They would see friends together. But promises were glancing words. Natalie rang, wanting to see them. Una told her John was testing a secretary. She visited alone. Nadine Wang, Natalie's cook, chauffeur, secretary and lover was there. She had been a colonel in the Chinese army. Romaine was in America and Natalie planned to join her. Dolly Wilde called in, 'haggard and much aged by her career of dope'. John and Evguenia joined them all for supper. Evguenia was explained as a friend in need of help. *A trois* they went to a party of Natalie's, to the ballet *Spectre de la Rose*, to dinner at Antoine's with Sergei Lifar, to a Russian gala of Rimsky-Korsakov's music.

John spent mornings with Una. She fussed about her heart and how emaciated she looked, told her not to go out in the cold, and to eat soup. 'I don't want only to be of interest when I am ill', Una wrote. 'which I sometimes feel is the case.' She wished she had died in 1932 after her hysterectomy with the peaceful conviction that love was intact. John phoned her from Evguenia's flat and sent plants and flowers to the hotel. They were tokens of guilt. When with Una she longed for Chinkie Pig.

> Her mind never seems to leave the girl for a moment. It is Russia, the Russians, the Soviet, the old Russia, Russian music, Russian art, Soulina, her looks, her clothes, her voice, her opinions, her naturalisation, her past, her present, her future, all roads lead back to the same name and face. If we look in shop windows, what would suit her, if we go out anywhere, would she have liked it, and what a pity she was not asked. When she went today, I just frankly had my cry out.

Una heard a thud from the hotel wardrobe and thought it must be Ladye sympathizing. She then had her soup, corrected proofs and walked the Paris streets.

Una had always lived vicariously through John. Now she lived vicariously through John's relationship with Evguenia. At sessions with Mrs Leonard she had suffered the intensity of John's relationship with Mabel Batten. Now she suffered the intensity of her relationship with Evguenia. Alone together neither talked of anything else. Behind the humiliating of Una, itself a strange projection, was a test of strength, a battle for control. John had never spent a day or night alone. Her personality was precarious. She needed Una's validation for everything she did. Una had not served Mabel Batten, she had usurped her. She intended to do the same with Evguenia, however long it took.

John told Una that she would not leave her, that she wished to be with her yet not with her, that her own pleasure was marred by Una's unhappiness. Una told John that she loved her entirely, faithfully, exclusively, that in all the world nothing and nobody counted except for her. 'But how can I not suffer and be unhappy when after all these years of perfect union she imports a third and dotes upon her?'

Una was not going to leave or be left. She was not going to relinquish the money and lifestyle that were hers. She called herself the fixed star. However ghastly life had become, 'everything else shrivels away in comparison to fear of separation'. John said to her, 'the girl has me physically absolutely'. Una translated this as an attraction that would pass.

Often she accompanied John to Evguenia's door. 'It always seems all wrong, a sort of illusion when I walk or drive away leaving her with someone else and every time it makes me unhappy afresh.' She went to the British Consul to obtain an annual visa that permitted Evguenia to visit Britain as often as she wished for a month at a time. 'So there is another obstacle removed by me.' She walked back to the hotel with a constricted chest, 'as if there was a string round it'. She went with John to a solicitor Georges Hollander at 41 rue Condorcet to try to arrange Evguenia's French naturalization. She helped choose a black brindle bulldog called Boulinka as a present for her. It had distemper and was sick on Evguenia's bed.

What was planned as a stay of ten days in Paris extended to two months. John talked of residing in France, of going to the Riviera, of Evguenia getting work there. Una feared the financial and emotional dependency John was encouraging. She thought her demoralized by idleness. John disliked to be reminded of work or her literary career. She was no longer interested in Ladye, Mrs Leonard, or religion, except to ask St Anthony for help with Chinkie Pig's naturalization, and she never now read a book or wanted Una to read to her. 'Holy Mother of God, where will this thing end and where is it leading us?' Una wanted to know.

John told her, 'You're quite right, I really don't want to do anything in the world but play around with that girl.' Una marvelled that the greatest living English novelist, whose whole life had been dedicated to genius, beauty, loyalty and profundity, could be in thrall to 'a completely uninteresting, no worth little mediocrity, who even some-times goes so far as to criticise her and find fault with her in my presence'. Evguenia, she said, 'has no idea that she has been privileged to touch the hem of greatness'. She lacked 'even the dawning of an understanding of genius'. Evguenia had suggested John write a film script to make money. John said she found her refreshing. Which Evguenia was. It had proved a trial for Radclyffe Hall to try to live up to Una's projection of her. Perhaps it was like living a lie. Perhaps playing around with this girl made her feel more real.

The plans John made extended to winter and beyond. They were all built round Evguenia, her problems with visas and statelessness, the need to be with her. Una, who feared separation for even a day, was to tag along. She was to shuttle between England and Paris then go with them to the South of France for an indeterminate time. Before leaving Paris for London and Rye, John remarked that Evguenia's clothes were shabby. Una helped choose a model coat from the Samaritaine de Luxe and half a dozen hats to be sent to Evguenia's flat for her to try on.

3 I

How long O Lord, how long

Alone in London with Una at the end of March, John inveighed against the climate, traffic, theatres. She gave up the London flat to save on rent and servants' wages. 'O for the south and you, sunshine heat and you', she wrote to Evguenia. 'Don't you know that I am keeping myself free in order to be near you?' She saw her accountant and stockbroker and found she would pay no income tax if she stayed out of England nine months of the year. She arranged for the bank to increase Evguenia's allowance to 2,050 francs a month and told her not to let her Russian friends wangle the money out of her. In daily letters she fussed that Evguenia must eat two hot meals a day, keep her flat well heated, wear her fur coat, not sleep with her head near the window, travel on buses or go to cinemas, must 'beware of polotics and of all those fools who meddle in polotics' and 'remember she was a White Russian and hold her tongue'.

Evguenia must also hold her tongue about what she was up to with John. She now played table tennis with Natalie's lover Nadine Wang. 'Please, oh, please be jolly cautious what you say to her or before her. She is the person above all others who simply *must not* suspect our relationship. Via her and Natalie it would be all over Paris in 24 hours.'

'France and Russia can do no wrong', Una complained. John told her she wanted to be free of any ties that separated her from Evguenia.

In London the two of them shopped for their journey south *à trois*: trousers, panamas and shirts for John who had put on weight and could not get into last year's clothes, a brick-red dress for Evguenia, a white rabbit coat for Una.

Una was glad to go home to Rye if only for four weeks. Mabel Bourne had lit fires, the garden was full of daffodils, narcissi and primroses. Una dared to hope that what had been her life might be restored. She woke to birdsong and to sunshine on the pear blossom and the marsh. Together she and John gardened and went to mass. But one morning she caught her crying because she was missing Evguenia so much. John asked her if she would keep the house if she 'lost' her. Una supposed she meant by death. It would be her only possible refuge, she said. Her heart palpitated. Dr Curtis was called and prescribed bromides.

Disheartened by Una's criticism John gave up on *Emblem Hurlstone*. She began *The Sixth Beatitude* which featured Rye landscapes and their working-class neighbours in Hucksteps Row. There was no hint of Evguenia in it and Una thought it inspired. 'God has spoken and I feel we shall come to a safe port.' She read it aloud and praised the descriptions of marshland and river, the snow over Rye, the smallpox epidemic, the demolition of cottages.

Life fleetingly seemed back to normal. 'I scarcely dare to think it though, or set it down.' John bathed in Una's enthusiasm, called her 'the womb of my spiritual children' and said she owed her career to her. She warned Evguenia of the competition: 'I wonder how you would endure being with me when I am working at this terrific pressure? I am irritable – I can't eat my food, and sometimes I just fly out over nothing. I know this you see, but I simply can't help it. Una has had to endure it for years.' Evguenia offered to type the manuscript. Una kicked out. 'If she was to trespass on that ground also I might as well retire or offer my services to an orphanage.' She was the architect of John's career, her amanuensis, reader and muse.

Fear of abandonment haunted her. The trials of John's childhood became hers. *The Sixth Beatitude* was, she sensed, a valediction. John did not now want Rye if Evguenia was not there. They packed for France:

Lord how every fibre of me shrinks and winces about this fortnight ahead when I shall be left alone to think and think. And then after a bare month

it will begin again. And John petting and spoiling and pandering to moods
and holding her hand . . .

O please God bring me back with John some day to this darling cottage
with perfect and complete union between us two and Ladye and no
intruder or outsider between us.

Evguenia met them at the Gare du Nord. John had reserved rooms
for them all at the Hôtel Lutétia. She disappeared with Evguenia as
soon as they arrived. Una was left alone to think and think. John would
not leave her, but she did not want to be with her. She wanted her there
and yet not there and to approve of a relationship that excluded her.
Una's strategy was to watch, wait and erode. She accompanied them
whenever she was allowed. With nuance and glance she let Evguenia
know how intolerable she found her. She sniped at her while adulating
John.

All that John paid for she sought to control. She had loved Evguenia
in her uniform of service, her starched white coat and cap, evocative
of Nurse Knott. But she disliked her taste in civilian clothes. Now
Una was there, siding with John, undermining Evguenia's appearance,
letting her know by look, innuendo or with startling rudeness that her
preferred hat 'accentuated every defect of her face, its breadth and
flatness and the heavy square jaw'.

Evguenia had her adenoids out before the journey south. *A trois* they
selected her suite with bathroom and lavatory at the private clinic of
Dr Ruand. Una 'grieved thinking of the communal wc, only one on
each floor, for my 16 guinea room in Welbeck Street'. Una was Lady
and Wife: Evguenia should not have parity when it came to lavatories.

Evguenia lay in her private rooms with her nose bandaged. John sat
by her, plagued the doctors, bought her grapes, strawberries and a
gramophone, played their favourite song 'The Very Thought of You',
hired a night nurse. 'She hovered over me like a hen over her chickens
but too much so,' Evguenia wrote. Back at the Lutétia Una complained
endlessly of the violation of the perfection of their union, warned that
she, Una, was 'the perfect complement of John's being' and urged that
a brake be put on money spent.

Una and John went on ahead to the Riviera. Una carried Evguenia's
bulldog on to the train. The heat would not turn off in their compartment and the dog was not allowed in the restaurant car. At the
Golf Hotel, Beauvallon Una bartered for rooms: an interconnecting

suite with balconies, sea views and a private bathroom for herself and John, a small room with no balcony, no bathroom, for Evguenia.

With John Una sunbathed and put on weight. She made herself indispensable and marvelled at chapter eleven of *The Sixth Beatitude*. She also kept up corrosive comment about Evguenia, called the affair trivial and banal and said that soon John would be 'obligated to support the girl entirely in complete idleness'. She read her letters and hated John writing with a pen given by her. At night she lay contemplating 'an endless future of John talking, writing, telegraphing and obsessing about this girl'.

Evguenia did not want to leave Paris. She wrote of thoughts that came like black demons into her mind. She said she might have a nursing contract and that if she came she could only stay a month and would prefer to be in a *pension* and pay for herself. There were also problems over her work permit and identity card.

John would not brook opposition:

Pull yourself together Soulina ... *I am writing a Book*. I love you and I need you – I can't be happy here until you come. I'm the first artistic brain-worker that you have known intimately I think – and so probably you don't understand the tension in which we creative people live during the time of creation. But you've got to try to understand it, my darling. No more cold discontented letters, please ... Do you want to ruin a piece of fine work? ... *I do not want you to work before you join me* ... I gave plenty of money ... What's this rot about a pension and your only coming to me out here for a month and you paying for yourself – its the damnedest rot.

You mustn't play me up belovéd. You belong to me now and I mean to have you ... If I had you here I'd kill you with kisses ... Someone has got to be the Master, my child, and I am going to be that person. There is only one will and that is John's will.

If John was *the* lesbian role model, if the 'eyes of inverts worldwide were on her' and 'looked to her as their leader', they were in for a tricky time. To 'save John's aching hand', Una wrote telling Evguenia to go *at once* to the authorities about her travel permit, to get a doctor's certificate for the vacation and to telegraph her progress.

John met Evguenia on 14 June. They spent a night at the Hôtel Continental, St Raphael in rooms booked in Lady Troubridge's name.

Alone at Beauvallon Una went to the beach, put flowers and lavender water in Evguenia's room and 'marvelled at the infatuation my John can feel at this girl with a negroid face and eyes like currants'.

There was the sun, the sea, the full moon, starry skies and palpable hate. The strain on Evguenia told. Caught in their stifling familiarity, she could not stand Una's constant presence, her pulling of rank and putting her down, her sycophancy to John. She pointedly went out of earshot when Una read aloud John's work. One morning John asked Una to go with Evguenia to the hairdresser while she herself worked. 'The young girl shut me up very firmly when I began to explain to the assistant that the hair had been spoiled by permanent waving and must be treated carefully', Una wrote in her diary. Evguenia went off on her own to explore Cannes. John searched for her, 'berserk' with worry. At dinner John told her not to eat a green plum. Evguenia ignored her. John 'lost all control, leapt to her feet, slammed the table and shouted at her to leave the dining room'. Una said she would not have quarrels at mealtimes. John told her to shut up.

On the beach, while Una watched, John talked to Evguenia in undertones, disappeared with her into the bathing cabin on the pretext of fetching things, caressed her ankles or hands. They all bathed naked. Una noted high shoulders, a thick waist, knock knees, feet spoiled by shoes, thin hair of no colour. 'Beyond excellent teeth and a nice smile there is nothing at all.'

Each night John elaborately got ready in clean pyjamas then made some pretext about needing to go and put Petrol Hahn on Evguenia's hair. 'Oooh I *hate* this camouflage, these transparent devices which are so unworthy of us both. I said suddenly, Why call it that darling? You're going to sleep with her every night and I suppose it's natural or does you good, or seems to. You know it and I know it.'

John told Una she should take Evguenia into her life as she had done. Relationship for John was an aspect of self, three selves, four selves, one self. Una was an aspect of mirror image. What suited John must suit Una. That was the agreement of twenty years. John only saw things from her own point of view. She wanted to be alone with Evguenia. Una's discontent 'always spoils it a little'. At night, Una cried herself sick. She saw no way out of this snarl.

I am always coming across things that hurt, the door I must not open, the letter I must not read, the thing I must not say, the caresses that are

283

given elsewhere and not to me. *She* is the holiday the excitement and the pleasure and I am the tired old routine who offers nothing now. And John almost seems to expect me to dote on the girl as she does. The girl who fills my place in her arms. And God knows I wish her well, but He also knows how glad I should be if the girl were unharmed and John cured of this mania never to set eyes on her again.

Thus *à trois*. There were occasional social evenings with Colette, Maurice Goudeket and Jean Cocteau, or Natalie and Romaine at their pinewood villa Trait d'Union at St Tropez. There was a party with Mimi Franchetti who invited Una to 'have a little scandal', there was champagne on the Princesse de Broglie's yacht. But life's dimension for John, Una and Evguenia was a claustration of watchfulness, jealousy and offence. Una dreamed of being turned out by John at three in the morning and told to return to England alone without a sleeping berth.

All summer of 1935 they were closeted together floating through France and Italy from Grand Hotel to Grand Hotel. They moved from the Riviera to Sirmione. It was the same stinking air. This affair was in its second year. At the Albergo Catullo Una rebuked John for petting Evguenia at lunch. 'She is unconscious of how far this infatuation carries her.' John said she must have happiness and peace. She now shared a room with Evguenia. Una was beside herself and feared scandal.

Their friend Micki Jacob, author of *The Loaded Stick*, *No Easy Way*, *Honour's a Mistress* and *Leopards and Spots*, thought Una beautiful and spent a night in the garden under her window 'pining with love'. Of Evguenia she said, 'I simply loathe your young friend, she is a complete bitch.' Una thought her disloyal to John and sent a scathing letter via Anita the maid.

Evguenia missed friends of her own age and wanted to return to Paris. 'John looked upon me as a child. She wished me to be a child. And she would not let me go away from her even for an instant. She wanted me to be constantly with her, near her. She said everything tasted better, seemed brighter when I was there and yet at the same time she coerced me.'

Una wanted no independence. Evguenia cherished hers. She aspired to do something with her life, to study at the Sorbonne or start a business. She said that she loved John. She liked the style and plenty that now graced her life. But she could not tolerate being enclosed with

Una, the constant attention, John's obsessive caring, Una's loathing. Three months with them made her ill. Her lungs began bleeding and she had eczema.

Men were being conscripted in Italy. John bought black shirts for Una and Evguenia and they all wore Fascist ribbons in their lapels. Una called the Duce 'the only great leader in the world today'. In her view he had every right to invade Abyssinia, 'a barbarian, pagan country incapable of developing its own resources'. Italy, as she saw it, was small, and expansion essential to provide labour for its unemployed. She and John deplored opposition from Britain and the 'dunderhead' League of Nations. John called it 'Black Monday', 'The Day of Shame for England' when sanctions were imposed. She feared European war might separate her from Evguenia.

Micki Jacob did not share their enthusiasm for the Duce. She was Jewish, large, wore tweeds and clubbish ties and liked a drink. Una called her 'openly and indiscreetly disloyal to fascism'.

John hoped d'Annunzio would see her again. He sent gifts of onyx and topaz and a letter that began 'Darling little sister'. John walked with Evguenia in his gardens with waterfalls, sculptures and an open-air theatre, but she did not intrigue him enough and no further meeting took place. John Holroyd-Reece told her d'Annunzio had 'an obsessive fantasy about raping a virgin or any unwilling woman'.

Una longed for Rye.

> Why are we not living at the Forecastle in peace, she working and I helping her as I always have with reading aloud and keeping worry and disturbance from her and both of us enjoying our ordinary pleasures, reading books, going to the theatres, entertaining, caring for animals and doing our small charities. It was never dull or dreary God knows. We shared the same tastes, had the same friends, and the common interest of her work and career and of our aims to do what we could to help our own kind.

Una pondered their shared trials: Ladye's death, the Fox-Pitt attack, *The Well of Loneliness* prosecution. 'None of them once I knew John really loved me could really strike at the heart of me. But now the enemy has made its way into my innermost thoughts.' In a succession of hotel rooms she rowed about 'blemished fidelity' and 'those ethics which in *The Well* she tried to enunciate for others'. She rowed too

about money. 'Keeping a penniless young woman with a healthy appetite and luxurious tastes and a fierce disinclination to work is a large
order.'

'All my eggs dear Lord in that one basket', Una wrote. She resisted
and complied. Back in Paris she helped find a new flat for Evguenia –
in rue d'Armaillé near the Place de Gaulle on the fourth floor. It was
large and sunny with central heating. Una helped choose wallpapers
and furnishings, then lunched alone. Evguenia loved the flat but one
morning was forty minutes late returning to it. John and Una waited,
John in an anxious rage. 'You don't seem to realise Johnnie that I have
things to do', Evguenia said. John threw books about the room. This,
Una again hoped, was the beginning of the end.

In October she and John returned to Rye. 'Home to fires and candlelight.' John finished *The Sixth Beatitude*. It had taken her six disrupted
months to write and she called it her best book. Heinemann gave
£1,000 advance for it. Audrey offered it to Harcourt Brace in America.

Evguenia was to join them at Christmas. John found eight weeks'
separation intolerable, said she loved her more and more every day
and controlled her every move with letters, phone calls, wires. Boulinka
got diarrhoea. Evguenia had to get up to take him out in the night.
John urged her to chain him in the bathroom, return him to the vet.
Evguenia resisted. She liked the dog. John insisted. She said she had
kept dogs all her life. Boulinka would be happier in kennels, he could
not bond to one person. Evguenia suggested giving him to her friend
Lysa. John would not agree so Boulinka went back to the vet. Evguenia
was depressed at the loss. John thought her response 'too childish'.

Evguenia dreaded Christmas at Rye and 'Una's reactions'. John told
her to remember Una was Irish and too old to change. She warned the
walls of the house were thin and they would have to act 'like sister and
mother'. Evguenia wrote of wanting peace, and freedom from nerve
strain. 'Just now it seems if someone came and soothed me and took
me away far, so far that not one human foot has ever been there – I'd
say yes and follow', she wrote.

At first John thought Evguenia's depression came from drinking
spirits. She then panicked, phoned at half-hour intervals, feared she
was with a man, and turned nasty:

> You belong to me, and don't you forget it. You are mine, and no one elses
> in this world. If I left you for 20 years you'd have to starve. No one but

me has the right to touch you. I took your virginity, do you hear? I taught you all you know about love. You belong to me body & soul, and I claim you. And this is no passing mood on my part – its the stark, grim truth that I'm writing.

Much of the truth was stark and grim. Mrs Visetti was eighty, had pernicious anaemia and was in a London nursing home. Una bought a black suit – just in case. 'My poor old mother's death will not cause me grief', John told Evguenia. Mrs Visetti's doctor thought she would rally, return to the hotel where she lived, and 'drag on for an indefinate time'. John knew nothing of her mother's affairs. 'Me she so hates & has all along, that I dare not question her. I don't know who her solicitor is, or indeed if she has one ... She's so cruel – so terribly cruel Evguenia – no mercy on anyone in this world, and violent over nothing and filled with hatred.'

John arranged a mass for her mother at St Anthony's Church. Father Wendelin had taken over from Bonaventura. Una said he was fat and flabby with watery eyes. She and John had a session with Mrs Leonard, whose husband Freddie had died. Mrs Visetti, she told them, would not last long.

In the Births column of *The Times* Una saw she had a grandson, Nicholas Vincenzo Troubridge Warren. Not knowing Andrea's address, she sent a congratulatory telegram care of Tom Troubridge's wife. Andrea replied to it so Una visited her. She was in two sparse London rooms. Her husband earned £4 a week with an advertising firm. She did her own housework and sheets were drying over the bath. She made no mention of John, who waited in a taxi outside. For Una one visit was enough to satisfy her curiosity and compound her prejudice: 'The Warrens and the Troubridges will see that the child lacks nothing it really needs and I personally shall take no further interest in the menage.' She then drove with John to Dover. John wanted to inspect and reserve the best rooms at the Lord Warden Hotel for when Chinkie Pig arrived.

Evguenia was to stay a month. Una decorated the Forecastle with holly and mistletoe and filled a stocking for her with smelling salts and sugar mice. Evguenia gave Una two icons and a card: 'May every saint protect you and keep you well and happy.' Five Rye neighbours came for Christmas dinner – mock turtle soup, turkey and plum pudding. Una mused on how much Evguenia had that once was hers. 'All the glamour, emotion and romance that no longer is attached to me'.

On 27 December Audrey phoned to say Harcourt Brace would only offer $500 for *The Sixth Beatitude*. John became furious with Una for discussing the weakness of her career in America in front of Evguenia. 'She was grey and shaking with anger.' She said she would never forgive her and that all her affairs were to be taken out of her hands. She and Evguenia then went to the cinema. Una stayed at home, lying down.

On New Year's Eve the Rye bells tolled out the old year and pealed in the new. In the Forecastle John, Una and Evguenia each wrote a wish on a scrap of paper. They set fire to their wish with a candle flame, let the ash drop into a glass of champagne then drank it. It was, Evguenia told them, an old Russian custom.

32

His name was Father Martin but she called him Henry

John could not endure a day without Evguenia. Una could not endure a day without John. At the Tour d'Argent in Paris for Evguenia's birthday lunch on 9 January 1936, they had caviare, duck with pineapple, then pancakes. Una irritated John by not eating any of it. The bill was 300 francs. Back at Evguenia's flat, Judith Horn, an English friend of hers, 'common as dirt' in Una's view, called by. 'I say,' she said. 'Have you come into a fortune or is someone keeping you?'

That night they toured the clubs, the Monte Cristo, the Melody Bar, Le Monocle and drank cocktails and brandy until five in the morning. Una disparaged it all. She honed her invective. It was profligate pleasure, inferior cabaret with tarts and negresses, Evguenia was a Tartar Torturer, a stubborn little bitch, a coarse-minded brutal lying little gold-digger, a currant-eyed anthropoid, an incubus. Never, though, did Una elect to let her out of her sight. If John was going to hell, so was she.

'I have noticed,' Una wrote of Evguenia at the Hotel Vouillemont, rue Boissy d'Anglas, 'she more and more tries to avoid doing things *à trois* and seldom will come here like she used to do. She says she is shy of meeting me when they have been making love, and this, together with her announcing she will not dine with us in the evenings, leaves me with the alternative that John dines with her at her flat. John has promised that she will not allow such a situation to establish itself.'

At her flat Evguenia reiterated her grievances to John. She could not bear being a kept woman, an appendage to her and Una. She wanted to take a degree at the Sorbonne, do a secretarial job, start a chicken farm. She said John wanted a meek little subordinate to hang on her every word and 'lie down like a tart whenever she wanted her physically'. John cried to Una about such an insult. Una berated Evguenia, called her an ingrate, a primitive who grabbed everything costly then cut John to the core.

On occasion, at Una's insistence, she and John visited friends without Evguenia. Both were surprised by Gertrude Stein who arrived at Natalie's 'with an enchanting white poodle named Basket, a completely simple unaffected elderly Californian with delightful Red Indian eyes, a stout figure, dowdy clothes, a brick red face and melodious voice, an arresting intelligence, her manners perfect, her views kindly and clever, a charmer, and both John and I fell for her in one heap.'

With Natalie they went to tea with Gertrude Stein and Alice B. Toklas at their studio in rue de Fleurus, 'where they live in a bedlam of unframed canvasses by Picasso and others of his ilk'. John and Una failed to find a painting to like. They were offered bitter tea from Java which neither of them drank. 'And much pleasant talk went on beneath the Cubist dementia. Then John saw me home and went off to have it out with Evguenia' who was in bed, feverish and spitting blood. X-rays revealed a shadow on her lung. She was admitted to hospital with suspected tuberculosis. John was terrified she would die. Proofs arrived of *The Sixth Beatitude* but she took no notice of them. She vowed that if Evguenia's health required it, she would spend the rest of her life in some place like Sirmione and never go near England again.

She tried, while Evguenia was ill, to prevent her from having any visitors except herself and Una. Such strictures drove Evguenia wild. She called John a tyrant, threw poker chips and magazines across the bed, accused her of trying to keep her friends from her and threatened to discharge herself. John pleaded and cajoled:

For my poor sake be patient and good, for my poor sake put up with the boredom of having to be taken care of for a time, for my poor sake try to be a good patient. There is only one frame that I ask you to be in & that is the frame of my utter devotion. You can only take care of me in

Damn!

one way and that is by taking care of yourself because I am you – my Evguenia.

But Evguenia did not want to be John. Even less did she want to be married to Una. Dr Fuller, her doctor at the American Hospital, warned her to take care. He advised against her nursing or doing any strenuous work. He said the best thing for her, because of her history of tuberculosis, would be to spend the next three winters in a southern climate from October to May. John told him she would arrange this. Fuller told Evguenia it was an offer she should not refuse.

And so Evguenia was trapped. And Una too. They set off in March 1936 for Grasse, near Cannes and for the warmth of the South of France. Evguenia, wrapped in a fleecy Jaeger rug, travelled first class with John. Una went second class with the canary, the cockatoo and the dogs. Even before they arrived at the Park Palace Hotel, Evguenia wanted to return to Paris. 'And here we are,' wrote Una, 'in the back of beyond, John scanning her pass book with anxiety to see how it is standing the racket of all we are spending on this girl, *The Sixth Beatitude* left to launch itself.'

John's anxiety over Evguenia's illness billowed into neurosis. Una called it 'overprotective solicitude'. All John's thoughts revolved around whether Evguenia had gone out without a coat, sunshade or umbrella, had she opened or closed her window, had she rested and taken her temperature, was she wearing a vest. John was, Una said, a sick nurse and a slave, dancing attendance. She hired a succession of doctors: Bestier, Mineshoffer, Pouynayou. At night she took Nurinase to make her sleep. She did no work.

Tuberculosis or not, John wanted to go on having sex with Evguenia. Una was terrified of her becoming infected. She urged her to ask the doctors if kissing was safe. John was evasive with them. To her circuitous questions Pouynayou said that he would not let Evguenia kiss a small child. Una feared John would die. She felt upstaged. Illness was her province. She coughed up mucous streaked with blood. The doctor told her to take calcium and only have one cup of coffee a day.

Evguenia accused John of murdering her personality and of using money to bully her. She pleaded that she could not stay shut in a room all day with the windows closed. She said she was entirely redundant and asked only to do idiotic things. Una did everything of significance. Una ordered the cars and reserved the rooms. And at every opportunity she insulted and marginalized Evguenia. To strangers she referred to John as *mon amie* and never bracketed her with Evguenia as *mes amies*. If she, Evguenia, wrapped a parcel, Una redid it. When she darned one of John's socks, Una darned it again. It was all intolerable. She needed to work. John told her she must not and could not. Nursing was out because of her illness and 'thousands were clamouring for any other job available'.

Evguenia said that this triangle had caused her tuberculosis. She had never heard of a mistress being expected to put up with living with the wife. Una treated her like a dog, looked at her as if she was dirt whenever they were alone, snubbed her whenever she spoke and listened at the door when she was with John. When she dropped her napkin in the restaurant, Una picked it up with two fingers and an expression of repulsion. Love, she told John, meant doing what the other person wanted. And she wanted John and Una to go away and leave her, or at least let her go back to Paris on her own. She started packing. John locked her in her room.

John, always at a loss to understand another's point of view, talked of Evguenia's 'Una complex'. She suspected her of wanting to get to Paris because she had a man there. Una thought this unlikely 'because she was so unattractive and with the exception of an old professor and an anaemic Russian bookseller nobody could be in love with her'.

John warned Evguenia that unless she behaved she would put her in a sanatorium and if she tried to leave it her allowance would be cut. On a day in April when they set off together for a walk, John returned alone in a taxi 'white, grim and monosyllabic', then had her tea with her eyes fixed on the hotel entrance.

Una bided her time, watched, needled and blamed. She feared Evguenia was intent on ousting her and having a life *à deux* with John. 'With Ladye's help please God she will not succeed. But she goes on trying and making John feel she will never be satisfied in conditions which include me.' She kept up her lament about their smirched union and went with John to a sermon on the indissolubility of marriage. Evguenia got drunk on her own.

With Una, John alternated between resignation and rage. 'If you're thin because you think I'll leave you then get fat because I won't', she said. At other times she called her a curb and a bridle and said she would go away with Evguenia when and as often as she wished.

There were days of relative calm when they drove by Rolls-Royce to

Cannes and lunched on lobster, chicken, strawberries and white wine. They toured the Vosges and breathed the mountain air. But for them all it was three months of hell.

Back in Paris in June it was eighty-nine degrees in the shade. John and Una booked in at the Vouillemont, Evguenia went to her flat. She spoke of coming alive after being a prisoner at Grasse. John thought that only her caring for someone else could explain such unkindness. She planned to visit unexpectedly to see what she was up to.

Paris gossip columns made reference to the *trio lesbienne*. Albert de Flament in the *Revue de Paris* thought the young Russian always in the company of Radclyffe Hall and Lady Troubridge was the third person alluded to in the dedication 'To Our Three Selves' in *The Well of Loneliness*. 'Did I survive all the smears for this?' Una exclaimed. John feared Evguenia would leave her because of such publicity. Natalie and Dolly Wilde asked about the meaning of 'Our Three Selves'.

To placate Una, and for the sake of a public who did not notice, John lunched alone with her at Pruniers. Una did not eat and complained that John cared only about Evguenia's feelings, not hers. John told her again that she was in love with Evguenia without whom she had no life.

But Evguenia after two years of tension was less keen to have sex. On 22 June John called unannounced at her flat. Evguenia was alone but not pleased to see her. John's violence erupted. It equalled her mother's. She trashed the flat. She destroyed things she had given Evguenia, tore up photographs of herself, some of her letters, her own books. She broke the frames of pictures and etchings, cut up the crocodile bag she had given her for Christmas. In the desk she found only letters in Russian which she could not read. 'She appears to have wrecked the whole place with incredible strength and persistence', Una wrote in her diary. 'But I think she had had long and sore provocation.' Next day, Dr Fuller asked if they had had a peaceful time in Grasse.

There was summer to consider – where to go. John suggested St Odile, a religious retreat. As ever, Evguenia's lack of documents was a problem. John decided to adopt her to give her nationality. She wanted to be Evguenia's next of kin, her mother perhaps, or her father, or her husband. Una thought her parenting aspirations would be viewed with suspicion. She asked Dr Fuller if he knew of any 'respectable Englishwoman' who would adopt Evguenia for £300. He suggested one of his patients. Rubinstein quashed the plan. He told John adoption did not confer nationality in either America or England.

They set off again in July, this time in a hired car, with a trunk each, seven pieces of hand luggage, a dog, its basket and two birds. St Odile was full of tourists and dogs were not allowed. They moved to the Grand Hôtel de Bains du Holswald, 600 metres up in the Vosges. There were green meadows, canteen food, 'bourgoisie' and torrents of rain. They moved to the Grand Hôtel des Trois Epis, 700 metres above the valley of Munster. Una was fed up with it all.

In the two years since Bagnoles we have hardly been out of hotels. Paris, Beauvallon, Sirmione, Padova, Venice, Grasse, Cannes, Trois Epis, packing and unpacking in hotel bedrooms, fitting our possessions in inadequate accommodation, bargaining for prices and scanning large bills with anxious eyes, eating in uncongenial dining rooms, over-rich and unwholesome hotel food. A dreary perspective behind us and ahead of us for many months to come. A beloved home of our own which for all the good we get out of it is non-existent.

She was forty-nine, John fifty-five, Evguenia thirty-one. John would not return even for a few weeks to England until she felt sure that Evguenia was cured. She said she did not care if the Forecastle burned down. Una told her she was abrogating her genius and must stop living like a satellite in the orbit of 'this wretched girl'. Total sales, worldwide, of *The Sixth Beatitude* were only 6,249. Una deplored 'this strange and sudden incursion of the sex element from this Russian mediocrity' and pined for how she and John once lived. She read again *The Ladies of Llangollen* and evoked 'the great fight of *The Well* for themselves and all their kind'.

A letter was forwarded from a woman commissioned by Mrs Visetti to write a life of Alberto. She asked John to describe the influence of her stepfather on her career and to offer 'any suitable anecdotes'. Una told Rubinstein to reply that John forbade mention of her name in the book and to remind the woman that John's letters were controlled by copyright: 'We cannot allow her to be made ridiculous in connection with that dreadful, cretinous, lecherous old man, or any lies to be published concerning his fictitious influence.'

For a few days John and Evguenia went away alone to Ballon d'Alsace. They enjoyed each other's company, walked and took photographs of medieval buildings. But then John worried that Una would be fretting. She could not choose between them and she hurried back to Una. 'Had things been different my life might have been so contented, so peaceful', she told Evguenia, without focusing on what those things might be. 'I could not do much for her but be there', Evguenia said. 'She needed me like water, like air, it seems, and yet she would not give allowance for my own feelings when I was cooped up with them both. She knew that she was asking too much, I suppose, in the very deepest of her heart, but would not admit it to herself.'

Back in the hothouse of Una's hostility and Evguenia's discontent, John broke down. She cried when her morning coffee came without milk. She was pale and intermittently weak and exhausted. She walked like an invalid with trembling legs. Her eyes were inflamed and Una made a great display of bathing them. She spoke of life having defeated her and rounded on Una whose reproaches, jealousy and stranglehold she said made life hell.

Una fought back. She was, she said, totally cut off from normal life and had no one to talk to for advice. John would have to accept that she could not be calm and cheerful, that she would have to be superhuman not to mind. Twenty years' mutual fidelity had not prepared her to expect or endure all this. She dreamed she was a nun being stoned to death in Rye, suspected, wrongly, of having sex with the priest. His name was Father Martin but she called him Henry. He kissed her on the mouth which she felt to be wrong. 'We shall be apart in body but together in spirit', she told him, then was carried into the house of a woman who let her die there out of charity.

In September news came via Rubinstein that Mrs Visetti had a fractured hip, was in a Derby nursing home and needed money. She asked that none of her news be passed to her daughter. She just wanted her to pay her medical expenses.

John had become as adrift as her father, Radclyffe Radclyffe-Hall. She had no plans other than where to go for the sake of Evguenia's health and no strategy for resolving or ameliorating the emotional chaos she had created. Evguenia seemed robust, all infection gone. As ever, she longed for Paris but was now financially dependent on John. John wondered where they would all spend the winter. She thought of Merano in the Italian Alps. Una wrote to the Park Hotel about rooms. Evguenia did not want to go. 'What a woman she has fallen for,' Una wrote, 'hard as granite, shallow as a dish and without the elementary rudiments of gratitude or affection.'

In September they went to Paris to have medical check-ups with Dr

Fuller and to get a visa for Evguenia. They travelled via Freiburg, Colmar, Strasbourg. They went through Germany because Evguenia's mother had been German. Una was surprised not to see more swastikas or the Führer's picture. She thought him less in evidence than the Duce in Italy.

X-rays taken in Paris showed Evguenia's lungs were clear. Dr Fuller recommended that she take life easily and do no work. Of John he said there was nothing organically wrong with her, but she 'took Miss Evguenia too seriously'. He prescribed hormone injections for her, perhaps because of the menopause. Una resented the intimacy of Evguenia administering these.

John was 'delirious with joy' when Evguenia was granted an Italian visa valid for a year. She took her on a shopping spree for clothes for the snows and the Dolomites and had her measured for silk pyjamas. 'Oh yes but I love you deeply, deeply. You are rooted in my innermost being and I cannot tear you out if I would – were I to do so I should bleed to death – One heart – same heart – and no help for it, it seems.'

In October the three of them made their disconsolate way by train to Merano with ever more luggage and Gabriele d'Annunzio, the now-moribund canary. At Verona they had one of their terrible rows. Evguenia said her room was dark. John found her leaning out of her window in the rain. Evguenia would not shut the window or put on her coat and muffler. Una tried to drag her from it and close it. Evguenia pushed her away and told her to get out of her room. Una replied, 'It is not your room but John's and I shall go when she tells me to and not before. John is too tired and too ill to be tormented any more and I simply won't have it.'

They rowed for two hours. Una said Evguenia abused, baited and tormented John. Evguenia said she could not stand all the restrictions; she had to see her friends. She could not go on in this threesome, it was unbearable living with Una. If she had any living soul to go to she would have left long ago. John said, 'You have always known that I cannot leave Una. Do you want to give me up?' Evguenia said, 'On your conditions, yes.' John pleaded that she did not have sex with Una. Evguenia said she did not care whether she did or not. Una told her that she herself suggested John make this clear when Evguenia's illness 'debarred her from physical life'.

'She sneered and remarked, Debarred? I wasn't debarred. As though her illness had been in that respect a welcome respite. In fact she spared John no hurt, insult or humiliation.' Una thought it inconceivable that she would have to go on seeing Evguenia or speaking to her. 'At least I need not behave in future in any way as though I had any liking for her.'

In Merano Evguenia enrolled for a course in German and Italian at the Berlitz school. John feared she would catch germs from the other students and wanted her to have private lessons at the hotel in a room heated by a stove. There was a row about that, too.

Evguenia began spitting blood again. John had cystitis, an abscess under a tooth and a nervous spasm in her eyes. The lashes on her lower lids curled inwards and scratched against her eyeballs. The doctor pulled the lashes out but they grew again. She seemed to be having a complete breakdown. Una blamed that beast of a woman.

They went to mass for the Duce in the Duomo and joined the Fascist processions through the town. The Italian waiters in the hotel dining hall gave the three of them the Roman salute and preferential service. The hotel was 'teeming with jews', refugees, Una said, from the Führer's sweeping out of undesirables. At night Fascisti shouted catcalls and rang bells outside. 'Fascist anti-bolshevism is turning its attention to these communist jew elements', Una wrote in her diary. 'I'm inclined to think they may be right but we must have our rest at night.'

The English papers were full of the King's proposed abdication so that he could marry Mrs Simpson. Una saw a parallel with the intrusion of Evguenia. 'The king is captured, like my John, by a worthless woman with whom he is infatuated.'

'God bless the Duce', Una said and sent him a photograph of himself which she asked him to sign. John and she deplored the civil war in Spain. 'So long as this terrible anti-God bolshevism continues it must be met with and conquered by force' was the view they both held. For 120 lire Una bought a rifle for one of the ten-year-old moschettieri in Merano to learn to use. Her name was engraved on the barrel and it was given to a boy named Norberto Roeregger.

It may shock one's spirit to see children taught to use a rifle, but I have lived to see the alternative – children taught to forget God and never to know Him, to see priests slaughtered and nuns raped and infamous blasphemy rampant, and I have come to believe the world does not know how to use or accept pacifism and the armed crusade must of necessity come first.

Their Christmas tree that year was in Evguenia's hotel room, the customary crèche for Christ was in John and Una's. They went to mass in the unheated Duomo and sat in the front pew. John gave Una onyx and gold cufflinks in the shape of the fascio – a bundle of rods and an axe. To Evguenia she gave cultured pearls. Una gave Evguenia hand-made Tyrolean shoes. Evguenia gave Una an embroidered nightgown case. John said to Una, 'My darling Squiggie thank you for being on earth.' They watched the sun set behind the snow peaks and John talked of them all making a home in the Florentine hills.

OUR THREE SELVES

33

An empty fiction

Una wept with pride on the day in January 1937 when a soldier came to the hotel and delivered the signed photograph of the Duce. Mussolini had dedicated it to Lady Troubridge. John had it framed in Fascist colours and they drank the Duce's health in vermouth. A week later they both wept with sorrow when the canary Gabriele d'Annunzio died. John wrapped him in a lace handkerchief and Italian flag and buried him with a medal of Notre Dame de Lourdes in the garden of the Sisters of the Holy Cross in Merano.

At the town's celebrations to mark the eighteenth anniversary of the founding of the Fascist party, she and Una were given prominent seats. Their table was draped with the Italian flag. Una was thanked for the presentation of her rifle, the moschettieri fired blanks, drums rolled, there was much denouncing of the Bolshevik enemy and chanting of Duce Duce Duce. Una wrote in her diary: 'The teaching fascism gives these children is moral, honourable, courageous and self sacrificing, and the crucifix is there on the wall in the Casa Ballila and in the refectory a prayer to God in great letters.'

Una practised her Italian with a pro-regime nun called Sister Suoraghebarda. They lamented that Hitler lacked the Duce's religious conviction. John was appalled when the British government invited Haile Selasse, Emperor of Abyssinia, to the coronation of King George VI.

Despite her enthusiasm for the Pope and the Duce, John felt

uprooted. Tired of hotels, she wanted a home but only if Evguenia was
with her. Caring for her while she was ill had strengthened her affection
for her. 'I want her with the burden of her distress', she said to Una.
Una wanted 'to be two and not a crowd'. She longed to be at the
Forecastle but not with 'a disappointed and melancholy John' pining
for her Chinkie Pig. Una would not hear of Evguenia joining them in
Rye. She would sooner float anonymously round Europe living out of
suitcases. At least in England the legend she had promoted was intact.
Evguenia fantasized about studying medicine at Oxford or Cambridge.
Una, she said, 'knew very well how to persuade John not to let me
do it'.

Evguenia did not want to leave John in any permanent way. She
talked of an invisible thread that bound them together, a spiritual and
physical link, a definite union. 'No matter where I was I could always
come back to her.' But Una's sport was to deride her. She called her a
'glutinous embryonic creature', chronicled everything she ate, watched
'with horror' as she dipped her spoon into cream, mocked her efforts
at typing letters for John. Evguenia said she wished she had bottles and
bottles of vodka to drink.

The more goaded Evguenia was by Una, the more she tried to break
free from John. When she rejected John, John rejected Una. The more
habitual their contact, the more reflex their responses. John told Una
that she had clung too tight, that she should have stayed in Rye and
let her go to Paris every fortnight to be with Evguenia.

> I pointed out that such a programme would have reduced our home and
> union to an empty fiction and would have meant that we would have lost
> one another for if I was to be neither wife nor companion she knew it
> would mean returning home merely to work and await the next spree.
> Annie the maid could fill my place.

Una had not minded reducing Mabel Batten's home and union to an
empty fiction, then refabricating the story in a meretricious way. She
grieved to see John haggard and trapped but she would never relinquish
her, not for a day. She endured it when John accused her of spoiling
the relationship with Evguenia. She endured hearing her say she wished
she had let her have the Forecastle and money and left her. Una lost
John in all but the habit of partnership. Mabel Batten might have
cracked under the insult of such rejection, but not Una. She would

maintain her position as wife and companion. Her determination to win never faltered.

News of their mothers reached their hotel. Mrs Visetti was eighty-three and depressed by her financial difficulties and at living in a cheap London hotel. Her doctor wrote to John and offered to try to effect a reconciliation. Una replied, asked for more details and suggested Mrs Visetti move to a convent home.

From Andrea Una heard that her own mother had cancer of the rectum and had had a colostomy. Viola asked Una to pay half the medical expenses. 'I cannot and I will not', was Una's response. It was grisly, she said, that Minna was 'crazy to live at any price'. She had not seen her mother for four years, she told Viola. Minna had never done anything for her financially or in any other way. It was up to Viola to care for her now she was desperate. 'I am terribly sorry for mother but she is Viola's mother and not mine.'

John began a new book *The Shoemaker of Merano*. She smoked thirty-five cigarettes a night as she worked. Una became spiteful when, by the second chapter, the wife in it was Evguenia. But John's consolation, as Evguenia slipped from her control, was to bind her to her in fiction. She promised Evguenia that never again would the three of them live under the same roof. 'I think of what might have been but what is not. Could there have been friendship between you and Una?'

'If you want to live in Italy you may', John said to Una. In spring they all moved to Florence. They booked in at the Hotel Gran Bretagne. The rate of exchange was good and John was exempt from paying tax in England. The plan was to stay until it got too hot in summer. Evguenia would then go to Paris, and John and Una to Rye. Evguenia would join John for a holiday in England, then they would all return to Florence in October.

John found a flat for the autumn. It was in Lungarno Acciaiuoli, overlooking the Arno. It had French windows, parquet floors, timbered ceilings, a fine view, maids' rooms and a large bathroom. Evguenia made it clear that under no circumstances would she live in it too. John's chief wish was that Evguenia should winter with her in the warm. 'My chief wish,' Una wrote in June, 'is to get home as quickly as possible and have a rest from Evguenia and her surly nigger face.'

Paris, by contrast to Italy, was expensive. Natalie, Una thought, 'talked a lot of half-baked nonsense about the tyranny of fascism and of the Catholic church'. Evguenia renewed her work permit for nursing.

John felt threatened and feared such independence would separate them: 'Don't you think you have a right to rest on your oars? ... You have earned the security that has come to you. This is the way I see it my beloved. You owe me nothing but love, if you feel that you can still give it.'

It had become difficult for Evguenia to manage without John. Her quest for naturalization was more convoluted than ever. It now involved some back-door deal and the payment of 6,000 francs. To renew her Italian visa, to gain a visa for England, required payments and guarantees. Evguenia was uncertain about where to go or what to do. She was depressed at committing herself to September in Rye or winter in Italy. She wanted a holiday with her Russian friends. She wanted Paris and work, but not as a nurse. She wanted not to leave John but to see her without Una.

John found parting from her for eight weeks and returning to Rye unbearable. On the journey she spoke only of her. She sent a wire from the ship, stopped at Rye post office to send a telegram, then spent a day writing to her. 'This was our home coming after a year and a half', Una said. 'The cottage looks more lovely than ever,' John wrote to Evguenia, 'and were you here I could be in heaven, but heaven is not for such as me – at all events not on this earth.'

She was in limbo with Una:

Oh Evguenia, Evguenia – there are no words to express what I feel. I can only say to your half of our heart: 'Love me, cling to me, understand me. Understand my love, my desire to protect, my anxiety, my poor broken life.' No one on earth can know all this but you, since you are the reason for my joy and sorrow. Ten o'clock and no letter from you.

She dreamed of a future where Evguenia too lived in Rye in a house of her own. As ever, she shared this dream with Una. Una trod on it hard. She would not have John visiting Evguenia at all hours and 'scandal among our own class and the working people'. They had an 'angry discussion'. Una asked St Anthony to 'rescue John from the tentacles of this sterile and intolerable predicament'.

Una filled the house with sweet peas and roses, read aloud the 15,000 words John had written of *The Shoemaker of Merano* and tried to recapture past time. She hoped their resumed social life would oust the significance of Evguenia. They went to the Smallhythe barn show –

scenes from Shakespeare and a buffet supper. Edith Evans was Mistress Page and Sybil Thorndike King John. A small fire broke out backstage and there was an adder somewhere under the seats. John found concentration difficult. The 'Smallhythe lot' seemed older. Edy Craig was in a wheelchair. Vita Sackville-West looked 'stout and crimson'. Christopher St John had recovered from her passion for her. Ethel Smyth seemed frail and very deaf. Tony Atwood was excited because the Tate Gallery had bought one of her pictures.

Una invited Olive Chaplin and her new lover, Lucy Gower, to dinner at the Forecastle. Olive was now fifty. Lucy was twenty-seven, called herself Lucian, wore a man's lounge suit and 'looked like hell in it because she was fat'. Una gave them cocktails, iced consommé, roast duckling, apple sauce, peas, new potatoes, cherries with syrup, brandy and cream, 1924 Châteauneuf du Pape and then liqueurs. Olive got out her Tarot cards. She said John's future lay over the water and that Una was not happy.

Andrea visited for a day. She had no work and her marriage had failed. Her husband drank and had lost money in property deals. Una continually called Andrea, Evguenia, which disconcerted John: 'She seemed incapable of doing otherwise. Every few minutes it was Evguenia this and Evguenia that until at last I said: "My dear your child's name is, or used to be *Andrea*!"'

Andrea went with Una to visit Minna. She was living in Slough in the 'dreadful little villa with hideous furniture' of her aunt by marriage, Audrey Nash. The pictures on the walls were by her aunt's two stepsons, Paul and John Nash. Minna Una described as

> a grim horror that must be seen to be believed, her bedclothes and nightclothes soaked with stains of unmistakeable origin and odour. She refuses to wear the proper pads saying they make her look stout. Her drawn and raddled face plastered with paint. Her girlishly curled hair, her allusions to things a decent old woman should have forgotten, her preoccupation with things of vanity and the body. The will to live at every cost. It is no affair of mine.

Going home in the car, Una asked John, 'Do you think I could get like Minna?'

John felt disconnected from it all. She thought only of Evguenia. 'I cannot go anywhere or do anything without it seeming to have some bearing on you.' The beauty of the moon over the marsh and on the sea that separated her, hurt her. 'Everything I see I refer to you in my mind – wanting to share it with you.' She tried to be less possessive. She was pleased when Evguenia went walking in the Alps with Lysa, but she was jealous too. She feared that by some chance Evguenia might re-meet a young man she once had loved. When the papers gave news of a train crash in France with forty dead, John felt physically sick.

With Una she now had less than half a life. Loyalty meant no more than not leaving her. Una became a mass of insignificant symptoms of illness. John viewed her with pity and anxiety and called her a burden. Her life was letters to and from Evguenia, Evguenia's visit in September, their reunion in Florence in the autumn.

And Evguenia, it seemed, was missing her and wanting to be with her. John referred to her dear, tender and consoling letters. Evguenia told her how she was more calm and normal because of separation from Una, of how she missed John's weatherbeaten face and the comfort of her love. 'If only Johnnie would appear on the path', she wrote when she went walking in St Malo with Lysa. She asked what John wanted for her birthday on 12 August. 'There is nothing you can give me,' John replied, 'except a baby Chink made by me. When we come together again in the Autumn then you shall give me my birthday present – clasped in my arms my beloved.'

John was 'beside herself with joy' when on 25 August Humbert Wolfe at the Home Office granted Evguenia an annual visa that allowed her to stay in England for six weeks at a time. She had taken him to lunch at the Berkeley. Even her anti-Semitism faltered. 'Never again will I speak against the Jews for Humbert is a Jew.' It seemed like an omen of freedom. Evguenia was to come on 28 September 'to your John's own country England!' They would spend a night at the Lord Warden Hotel in Dover, then go to Brighton for a week together. John spoke of it as their honeymoon and bought a silk dressing-gown for herself in anticipation. 'Thank you good & kind saints Anthony and Expedite for answering John's prayers. Oh I bless you and cherish you my own little stray white Russian who has found a place in my heart.'

But the saints had a different agenda. On 26 August John slipped on the doorstep at the Forecastle. She fell with her right ankle under her. She was in great pain. Una and Annie the maid got her upstairs to bed. Una could not get hold of the doctor. He did not arrive until midnight.

He said there was no broken bone and advised cold compresses. John's main thought was to spare Evguenia anxiety. She wrote reassuring letters. 'Nothing matters but your love and your darling sympathy.' X-rays taken six days later revealed multiple fractures. She was taken by stretcher and ambulance to the London Clinic. A Dr Taylor tried to reset the bones under anaesthetic. John became very ill. She vomited for six hours.

Andrea phoned the news to Evguenia, who wanted to come and take care of John. John wanted very much to see her. 'If only the door would open and you would come through it. Separation in illness is past all bearing.' She feared Evguenia might leave her if she became a mass of ailments. Una did not leave her for a second. She seemed to consume her now she was hurt. She kept saying, 'I suppose if Evguenia had been here she would have known we ought to have had an x-ray at once.' Her fussing irritated John. 'She finds fault with me at every turn', Una wrote in her diary. 'It has been a hard day and an unhappy one.'

Evguenia came a week earlier than planned. Una met her at Victoria Station and set about making her life intolerable. Evguenia wanted to take presents for John to the clinic. Una said there was no time to get them from her luggage. To eclipse Evguenia's flowers, she filled John's room with pale pink rosebuds. She dashed out for the fondants Evguenia forgot. She made a great display of replacing the engraved platinum wedding ring John had given her in 1915 and which had split. She asked John to put the new ring on her finger. 'When I have left you, God have you in his special care and bless the ring I have put on your finger', John said.

Evguenia found reasons not to sit with them all day. She chose to eat at her hotel, saying she liked the food. Una told John this was proof that Evguenia was uncaring, selfish and self-centred. John burst out about the atmosphere Una created. She wept with grief at the prospect of losing Evguenia. 'My every thought is with you,' she wrote to her. 'Oh don't feel jealous of Una – don't.' She walked in the corridor of the clinic but was exhausted after it, her pulse too high.

In Rye Una had the cobblestones in the lane by their house paved and smooth carpet laid in the house. Evguenia proved an indispensable nurse. She helped John manoeuvre the stairs and cheered her. 'I can't lean on a flea like Una', John said. 'I seem to get on John's nerves', Una wrote. 'It is difficult to believe that she cares for me at all or that I have any reason in her life.'

Insult provoked Una. She again belittled John's new book, told her it was as worthless as *Emblem Hurlstone* and that Ladye would flood her with the real book when the time was right. John cried at such discouragement. By damning her writing and her love of Evguenia, it was as if Una was draining her of life.

Because of visa restrictions, Evguenia went ahead to Paris on 24 October. John and Una followed with a Nurse Bright. There were gales on the Channel and the Golden Arrow was delayed. Mary the dog got bitten by an Alsatian. At the Gare du Nord, Una and the nurse could not get John and her wheelchair off the train. John had lost strength in her undamaged leg and seemed in a state of collapse. A porter said they would all end up in a siding.

In Paris Dr Fuller said John was nervously exhausted and Una in a hysterical state. They could not get four adjacent sleeping berths on the train for Italy until 10 November. John worried that the weather was too cold for Evguenia. In Florence they all booked in at the Hotel Gran Bretagne. Evguenia kept to her room, studied after breakfast and went to bed at eight-thirty in the evenings. Una beat on her door and told her she was neglecting John. Evguenia felt she wanted to scream.

She found a flat for herself in the via dei Benci. It was on two floors of the Palazzo dei Fossi and had several small rooms and a blaze of sun. John began walking with difficulty and with the aid of two sticks. She had no enthusiasm for moving with Una to their flat at 18 Lungarno Acciaiuoli. Una was energetic at furnishing it. John's only interest was in Evguenia's place. She could not bring herself to speak to Una and recoiled if Una touched her. 'She denigrates and ignores me and tells Evguenia how wonderfully she gives medicine or plumps a pillow.' John implored Una to be nicer to Evguenia. 'Whatever she is she is as she is and good or bad I need her.'

They all had stuffed turkey for Christmas and their usual prayers. On New Year's Eve Evguenia took offence at Una's insults and flounced out back to her flat. John asked Una to phone and persuade her to return. When Una complied, she thanked her for being so generous.

34

Never mind Una

John's inability to choose between Una and Evguenia seemed like manipulation. She was omnipotent but dependent as a child. She bought two bullfinches, one for Una, one for Evguenia. She called them Caterina and Bambino and put them in a cage. When they started pecking each other to death she separated them.

For a while in Florence it seemed as if compromise was achieved. Evguenia studied Italian, art and typing, liked her flat and invited students back to it. Una sniped. 'Of course this "study" is all balderdash and will lead to nothing ever.' But it was from a distance and Evguenia was spared her perpetual presence. And John no longer insisted that she share her every waking hour.

Una had a perfect apartment in her favourite city. She decorated it as a showcase of status. If not quite a home with John it was a triumphalist snook at Evguenia. John assured her she would never leave her but she asked her nastily if she intended wearing sandals until she was seventy, and when she wanted her shoulders massaged told her to get Maria to do it. Una thought of all John did so eagerly for Evguenia, even frictioning her hair to make it grow.

John divided her time between them. But keeping them separate was not what she wanted. She could not abide by it. This was her family and she thought it ought be united. She cried when Evguenia had a cold and refused to come to Lungarno Acciaiuoli to be looked after. She wanted her to work as her secretary, 'that way you would have earned your £300 a year and I would have been spared hearing that you want your own money. You are mistaken if you think that Una would have opposed your working as my secretary. Only of course you would have had to let her help you a bit to get into the work and this I suppose you would not have liked.'

The American publisher Covici-Friede invited John to write her autobiography. At first Una encouraged this to divert her from *The Shoemaker of Merano*. She typed twenty pages of *Forebears and Infancy*, but then went off this idea too. She feared revelations about women whom John had loved and wanted none of it aired. She told her to 'write the thing privately for eventual publication after we are all gone'. John protested that the Merano book contained her best style and writing and she wanted to dedicate it to Evguenia. Una objected with corrosive persistence: it was not a true idea, it lacked inspiration, John would make no progress while Evguenia was in her life.

> Every task except writing to Evguenia is a burden. She does not answer letters to the public. She does nothing about her translations or reprints. All her ideas vanish into thin air. All is dead sea fruit. God only knows when the phoenix of her talent will rise again from the ashes of the ruin. Art is a jealous goddess and does not admit of a divided allegiance.

Una and Art went hand in hand. She described herself as fostering John's talent 'with night and day care and solicitude'. It was only elements of this talent she would foster. All that opposed her she would in time destroy. She undermined *The Shoemaker of Merano* and called it too personal. It was life, she said, of a worthless sort, not art. But all of Radclyffe Hall's writing was autobiographical. She seldom invented. *The Shoemaker of Merano* explored the hold of one person over another. It was without religious zealotry and on a par with *The Unlit Lamp*.

Una could not deny or destroy John's letters to Evguenia. Into them went the voice of desire that the government forbade, her complex fractured personality, her obsessive love, her intolerance of the will of others and, after many destructive years, her slow disillusion with how the world was.

John packed her suitcase each week and went to stay with Evguenia. It was no solution. The problem was about commitment and trust. And Una pursued her. She complained that she was compromised in the eyes of their Florentine friends and her cousins, the Tealdis. She went to mass at the Santa Trinità and prayed for John's release from purgatory and her restoration to genius and honour. She phoned to let John know she had bruised her leg after falling over a tramline in the via dei Fossi. Life, she said, was now made up of lies and subterfuge 'and I a lover of truth compelled to be a master dissembler'.

February was the ninth anniversary of the concordat between the Vatican and the Fascist party. At 18 Lungarno Acciaiuoli they hung out the papal flag. John and Una went to a Wagner concert at the Communale. They heard the music Hitler listened to while composing his speeches: the *Meistersinger* prelude, the *Parsifal* prelude, *Das Rhein-gold*.

In Florence there was elaborate road mending, decoration of the streets and preparations for a visit of the Duce and Hitler. The Commune fixed flag irons to John and Una's windows. Una loved the beflagged streets, the swastikas, the black banners with the gold fasces, the heraldic devices on stathes tipped with gold spears and axe heads.

Their neighbour, Signor Lumbroso, was put in prison for three years. He had circulated an anonymous pamphlet protesting against Hitler's visit and plan to annexe the Tyrol. 'Horrified recipients rushed off with it to the Questora', Una said. It was traced to Lumbroso's typewriter. Una called him a fool or a knave and commended the Duce's planned legislation against Jews: 'they have been found to be at the back of all the centres of anti-fascism. The truth is that as citizens of any country they are impossible and cannot be trusted.'

John went with Evguenia to the station to see Hitler's train pass through. With Una from the windows of their apartment she watched the cordons of soldiers and blackshirts, the military processions, the police on motor cycles and then, standing in a slow-moving car, the Duce and Hitler, the Duce 'with the kindest most beautiful smile on his face'. She and Una yelled Duce Duce until they could yell no more.

In England Anthony Eden resigned from the Cabinet and was succeeded by Lord Halifax. Europe seemed in turmoil and on the edge of war. John too was in turmoil. She lost all confidence. She pleased neither Evguenia, Una nor herself. Her eyes tormented her and she walked with a limp. She had lower back pain and looked ill. She was tense when the phone rang and slept only with drugs.

Neither work nor love now anchored her. She believed she had sinned as when she was with Ladye and that the purgatory she felt herself to be in was payment due. 'I would like to sleep for a very long time,' she told Evguenia, '& then wake up near Ladye who was always so patient, so kind & so wise.'

In April Evguenia called in a state to see John, asked Una to leave them alone, then read out a letter from the French authorities. She was no longer eligible for French citizenship because she had left France within three years of making her application. John's protection, her ignorance of French domiciliary law, her insistence that Evguenia live in a warm climate, had all conspired to spoil her chances. Miserable and contrite, John prayed in seven churches and to her relic of the true cross.

Evguenia went back to Paris in June, angry at what she saw as the destructive consequences of John's control. She took and failed the entrance exam for the Sorbonne, then resumed nursing at the American Hospital so as not to lose her work permit. Though her pay was only thirty francs a day plus lunch, she stayed at the Hôtel Vouillemont in rue Boissy d'Anglas, wore pearls and designer suits and subsidised her Russian émigré friends.

John hated Florence without her. The flat which had seemed so perfect to Una was now too hot for John. The noise of an ice-making machine in a nearby restaurant stopped her working or sleeping. She was infected with restlessness. As in the previous year, she proposed that she and Una spend the summer in Rye. Evguenia would come for a holiday, then they would all winter in Florence. Evguenia could have her separate flat and do a course at the university.

For herself and Una she found a new flat at 8 via dei Bardi. It had marble floors, amazing views, an immense study and loggia. She took a lease on it from October on and wrote to Evguenia that she would adore it. It was so much the flat for a writer, she said, and wished they could live in it together. It was cheap because its owners, the Mortaras, were Jewish and hounded out of Italy.

Evguenia replied that she would not return to Italy in the winter and that never again would she live in the same town as Una. She intended to resit the entrance exam to the Sorbonne in November. She wanted her own home and a life for herself. Their relationship would have been different had John been free but she was not. John had this splendid flat with Una. The situation was impossible and she could not cope with Una's hatred. John implored and cajoled:

Can we never get away from Una and think only of ourselves? Even if
she did hate you, which I absolutely deny, can't my adoration for you
make up for any hatred in the world? What does it matter so long as we
two love each other? Oh, I know that it would be happier for you if my
circumstances were different – if I were free; I know this and I sympathise
with all you feel: but am I to be sacraficed to my circumstances? No my
honey-sweet, you cannot, you will not do this thing. Why can't we be at
peace – Oh, give peace to your poor John who loves you. I can't eat, or
sleep, let alone work, for my heart is never certain or at rest. Would it
help at all if you tried to look upon me as a man who was already married
when we met? Had I been a man I should have married Una and then
met you and loved and loved you and forced you to love me back – as I
have done. The result would have been that I could not have divorced a
faithful Una even had I wished to. She on her part would never have
divorced me, she is a Catholic & would not divorce Troubridge. So our
situation would have been much the same as now, only with more scandle.
There are many people living à trois here in this very town, I find, but
they generally all manage to keep on terms. That is all you need do, just
be on terms with Una. She matters so little to you really, you know – I do
feel you give her undue importance . . .

There were conundrums, lies and leaps of logic. Una imputed
Evguenia with cunning tactics. She thought her stance a ploy to get
John for herself. Una knew that the problem of their triangle was now
irresolvable. The point of its resolution had passed. Now, no side of it
worked without the other. Una feared that if Evguenia left, John would
be so desolate and their own relationship so intolerable she would have
to let John go. John, when Evguenia withdrew, found it impossible to
be alone with Una. She vented anger and disappointment on her. She
told her she intended spending six months of the year with Evguenia.

Then my nerve went after these four weary years and I cried and stormed
as I never thought or meant to do and could not get my control, while
John raged that she would go away with Evguenia whenever she felt
inclined. That she was going to Paris, would live there, that Evguenia
should not be asked to live where she did not like.

Thus the well of woefulness. And the games people play.
    The Forecastle seemed dead and the garden empty of flowers. Annie
the maid was dour and there were moths in the carpet and in the rugs

of the car. John did not want even to unpack. Her consolation was that Evguenia had agreed to join her for a fortnight's holiday. She was to take her to Malvern, the place where she liked to declare love to her women, where she had lived with Dolly Clarke, then Mabel Batten and where with Una she had 'broken faith' with Mabel Batten in 1915.

Contrite that she had caused Evguenia to lose her chance of French nationality, she battled with the Home Office on her behalf. She told them Evguenia would never depend on the state because she guaranteed her in every way. She saw Harold Rubinstein and changed her will to make ample provision for her after her own death. Una professed to be glad. 'I should not like any eventuality to leave the matter in my hands and so compel contacts I should rather avoid.'

John willed half her capital to Una and Evguenia. Dividends from the other half were to serve covenants for Mrs Visetti and the medical needs of them all. After the death of her beneficiaries that half of the capital was to go to the Sisters of the Poor Clares in Lynton.

At Smallhythe Edy Craig asked where Evguenia was. John said she was coming over on 15 August and that she was going away alone with her for a fortnight. She said Malvern was 'too high' for Una. Edy replied that it was not high at all. She wanted to know if John planned to leave Una. Olive Chaplin wondered how John would manage without her. 'It was all to me inexpressibly humiliating, painful and degrading', Una wrote.

John humiliated Una as she had humiliated Mabel Batten twenty-three years previously. It was hard to believe there was not some level of intended punishment, some score to settle, some test of acceptance or equation of revenge. When she left to meet Evguenia, Una spoke of writing to her while she was away. John said, 'You aren't going to pursue me with letters are you?' Such notes as John then sent were instructions to a secretary. Una was to return John's revised will to Rubinstein, check with the Home Office about Evguenia's visa, check with Cook's about Evguenia's ticket to France. Alone at Rye Una found philosophical consolation. She interpreted events to suit herself and she apportioned blame:

I shrink under the consciousness that to outsiders we are just one of so many couples where the male dashes off to fresh fields and the female remains at home, enduring because she must, and trying to hide her hurts. And yet what is known, and will be assumed, is not the truth either, for

no one will ever realise that in John fidelity and faithfulness go hand in
hand. The physical never mattered to me anyway after the first misery
and in any case was so small a part of our mutual devotion that it could
be ruled out. Her spirit, through all the storms and suffering and angers,
and through all Evguenia's unceasing efforts to detach it, has been faithful
to mine and this must be my consolation.

It was a stark admission. And it was just not true that Evguenia had
pursued John. John's efforts at detachment were on her own account.
    On John and Evguenia's return they all went to the Home Office.
'Lord what a jam, jews, jews, jews waiting to know how and where to
find refuge', Una wrote. John convinced a Mr Perks that Evguenia was
her ward and a major beneficiary of her will. An unconditional visa
was granted that gave her resident alien status. John was euphoric. 'I
have no words to express my gratitude to God', she said. But over tea
Evguenia lamented how she had wanted a French passport and French
nationality. She said she would have been all right if left to manage her
own affairs. Una said, 'Well you didn't seem to have managed very
well when we met you.' A row followed.
    Evguenia went back to France with Europe on the verge of war. The
Duce expelled all Jews from Italy. John and Una listened on the wireless
to Hitler at Nuremberg. 'This stupendous and terrible pageant', Una
called it. They heard again the overture to Wagner's *Meistersinger*, the
shouts of 'Heil, Heil, Heil'. 'He is an hysteric,' John wrote to Evguenia,
'I think an epileptic, a patriot in the extreme sense of the word and a
fanatic.'
    Chamberlain went to Munich to appease Hitler; 'God bless
Chamberlain', Una said. There was mobilization on land and sea. Gas
masks were distributed in Rye. John lost pounds in weight worrying
about Evguenia. She appealed to her to come to Rye at once. Roosevelt
appealed to Mussolini and Hitler to settle disagreements by discussion.
And then on 29 September Chamberlain, Mussolini and Hitler signed
the Munich Agreement. War seemed to have been averted.
    John and Una left for Florence within days. Evguenia met them in
Paris. She had filled their rooms at the Vouillemont with flowers. She
seemed resigned to working as a nurse as the price of independence.
John had a small growth on her lip which a Dr Ries excised. She
smoked eighty cigarettes a day but no biopsy was taken.
    In Florence bells pealed and the air was like champagne. John and

Una marvelled at the cheapness of everything and the elegance of their flat in via dei Bardi. They bought furniture for what seemed like no money: a fourteen-foot sofa in blue damask, a twelve-foot Renaissance refectory table, a Venetian carved and painted bookcase. They acquired a poodle called Fido, which had pustules between its toes and which hated their other dog, Mary. They displayed their photographs of Mussolini, d'Annunzio, themselves, Ladye and Evguenia, the ivory statues of St Anthony and the usual votive offerings. But John, when unpacking, found that a textbook on flowers of the Dolomites had been left in Rye. She blamed Una. She became grey, incoherent and gasping with rage. She threw things round the flat, gripped Una by the shoulders and threatened to throw her into the street.

Evguenia wrote reiterating what she had tried so many times to say. She would not be coming to Florence for the winter. John had her book to write. They would only quarrel and accuse each other. Evguenia truly wanted to change their relationship. John went into black misery. She cried for two days. Her eyes were bloodshot, the lids puffed out. She wanted to go to Paris. She sent a wire asking Evguenia at least to write, at least to let her know where she was. Una with 'sheer hatred' rang Evguenia. Evguenia then wrote that if John wished she would come for a few days, as Una suggested, but what purpose would it serve?

She came from 13 to 20 November. John booked her a room at the Gran Bretagne. On an evening together there Evguenia told truths that it hurt John to hear. She was more normal than John thought and she did not want to have sex with her any more. She felt uncomfortable at being in a same-sex relationship and wanted if possible to marry a man. She hoped they would stay friends, go on seeing each other and writing letters but she was adamant about not being in the same town with Una for more than brief periods. John should accept that she herself was not free.

John went to Una in despair. Only involvement with a man could explain such rejection. Evguenia must be having an affair with a Russian soldier. She wanted to kill him. She herself was not going to live without sex, she would get it where she could and did not care who with. Una told her she was fifty-eight and should exert self-control or she would make life hell for herself. They got to bed at two in the morning.

Una was worn out. She could not bear to witness John's suffering and abasement, 'the pain of her caring so intensely for another, the ever recurrent doubt how can her affection for me be anything but a habit and a sense of duty. Would she really care deeply if it were I whom she must lose? Life is no easy road to travel these days.'

John said she wanted to spend Christmas at the bottom of the Arno. There was to be no tree, no presents, no festivities of any sort. The lavatory overflowed, Mary was given away for yelping and incontinence and Pearl Buck won the Nobel Prize for Literature. Then Evgucnia wrote that because John sounded so depressed and was 'pig pining' so badly, she would come out at Christmas, take her holiday and stay into the New Year. Una felt panic and despair. 'In the weeks to come I shall owe any hours alone with John to Evguenia's wish to be away from her or with others.'

John resurrected. She wired money to Evguenia, bought presents for her, filled the place with decorations and food: smoked salmon, anchovies, artichokes, turkey, mince pies, plum pudding, cake, marrons glacés, oranges, tangerines, bananas, grapes. 'I do not think that even Evguenia will manage to consume it all', Una wrote. 'John urges me to get more and more.'

Evguenia was to arrive on Christmas Eve. At ten thirty in the morning she phoned from Torrino to say that snow in the mountains had delayed the train and she would not get to Florence until five thirty. Una had a heavy cold. She and John went to the station to check out this information. They were told no train would arrive until six forty-five. John would not believe this and insisted they go back to the station at five-thirty. She sat in a warm anteroom drinking rum grogs while Una 'paced up and down the platform in the blast'. A train arrived at six, but Evguenia was not on it.

They returned home to find she had rung from Pisa to say she would reach Florence at eight. They went again to the station. The train arrived at eight-thirty. Evguenia was wearing a fur coat and a hat that Una described as 'a brown saucer crowned by two felt asses ears. She was not at all tired after 26 hours' travel. She was laden with smuggled caviare, black bread, cigarettes and cucumbers. John was tenderly pleased that even as "only a friend" she had wanted to come to her.'

35

The rain pours down, the icy wind howls

The holiday was not a success. Una described their life as like the classical view of hell: Sisyphus eternally pushing a rock up a hill, the Naiads pouring water into bottomless vessels, Tantalus reaching for elusive food. She made no mention of Cerberus, the monstrous dog, guarding the entrance to the lower world. Evguenia remarked that Una always echoed John's views. Una told her to shut up. 'The fat was in the fire. Torrents of abuse and accusations poured forth. She spat venom in John's face. She ranted like a streetwalker.' Una told Evguenia if she went on tormenting John she would write to Dr Fuller and queer her pitch at the American Hospital. On New Year's Eve she counted the alcoholic drinks Evguenia had.

John got laryngitis and lay on a daybed in her study. Una and Evguenia ate together at a table by her open door. In a curious scene, Evguenia whispered about Una in the third person: 'Una won't do it just because I suggested it. It's enough for me to say anything for Una to contradict it. Una's mean mean mean.'

Evguenia, desperate to get back to Paris, said the visit had been a mistake. As she left she said, 'Johnnie would you like me to stay?' John replied, 'Yes of course, but only if you really want to.' Evguenia ranted again. Of course she did not want to stay, she wanted to go, to be free, free. Una made her life hell. She read her letters, pried into her financial affairs. As Evguenia slammed the front door Una wished her a comfortable journey. John puzzled about the outburst and thought it because of Evguenia's limited command of English.

Una wanted a break. John went with her to Viareggio and Lucca. Driven there by Tito their chauffeur they travelled with Fido the poodle, three birds and Maria the maid. John was thin, coughed a lot, had infected gums and ingrowing eyelashes. At the Hotel Astor their lavatory smelled and the radiators were lukewarm. John ate no food, sat looking into space and talked and talked of Evguenia. 'You have held in your white hands the body and mind and soul of me', she wrote to her. 'You have been my desire, you have been all my thoughts, you have been in every prayer that I have prayed, for you I have bombarded the gates of heaven.'

On the day they went to Lucca she was in despair. 'The church was cold but not such as to explain her deadly coldness.' She thought only of the time when she had been there with Evguenia. It was intolerable to return there with Una. They lunched at the same hotel. 'Something very intimate has gone from my life – how can I explain? It is childish perhaps but many very little things have gone together with the one great, big thing. I feel bereaved.'

Evguenia reminded John that from the first she had wanted 'just to be friends'. She was herself lonely and felt anxious if she did not get a letter from John every day. But even if it meant foregoing her allowance she could not live à trois again. Una brought out the worst in her and she only felt normal in Paris. She moved to a *pension* in rue d'Armaille in the seventeenth arrondissement. Dr Fuller said she was well and could winter where she chose.

John retracted the threat to make Evguenia's allowance dependent on her wintering in Florence. She told her she wanted her to be secure, gave her stocks, shares, a War Loan and topped up her deposit account with 4,400 francs. She said she had made ample provision in her will and Evguenia would inherit a substantial income 'unless you do something entirely outrageous which you will not, will you my darling?' With Una, John would not commit herself to living anywhere unless Evguenia came too. She talked of a villa in Fiesole, a flat in Paris, a house in England though not in Rye.

She urged Evguenia to get a British visa in case of war. 'In war we aught to have the same country.' More immediately she urged her to visit Florence for Easter. Evguenia agreed but only if she came with her friend Lysa.

Pope Pius XI died and was succeeded by Eugenio Pacelli. John and

Una thought him an accomplished statesman, a good fascist and on excellent terms with the Duce. They went to mass for his coronation and outside their windows flew the Fascist flag and the Union Jack on staves with studs and spearheads.

Army recruits poured past their windows. 'Italy is calling up class after class in an alarming way.' John commended Hitler for 'keeping order' in Czechoslovakia and Chamberlain for taking the news calmly. Little nations, she wrote to Evguenia, were an 'awful menace and as such cannot be allowed an existance'. Fascists, like pedigree griffons and upper-class congenital sexual inverts, were genetically superior. 'Jews', she wrote:

> Yes, I am beginning to be really afraid of them, not of the one or two really dear Jewish friends that I have in England, no, but of Jews as a whole. I believe they hate us and want to bring about a European war and then a world revolution in order to destroy us utterly ... And what of Jew-ridden France, England & Russia? There will soon be no room for us Christians.

She and Una subscribed to an English-language lending library. It was run by Lillian Baird-Douglas who thought people should be free to read what they chose, not just Fascist propaganda. She stocked literature banned by the regime. Una told her she should not keep books like *Inside Europe* on her shelves. Lillian said she did not understand how Radclyffe Hall could have written *The Well of Loneliness* and suffered its destruction and yet make propaganda for Fascism.

Una withdrew their subscription, returned their library books via a friend, Maria Carolina, then lodged a formal complaint with the authorities about Lillian circulating *Inside Europe*. 'We are clear of any complicity if there is any trouble', she said. She then helped foster a rumour that Lillian was a drug addict and an alcoholic.

John thought Hitler only wanted justice. 'I don't feel I care what he takes', she wrote to Evguenia after he invaded Bohemia and Moravia. 'I am too tired to react to anything.' Una said the one hope for Europe lay with the Duce 'who is both a genius and a good man'.

In April Italy invaded Albania. Five thousand German troops passed through Florence for an unknown destination. Evguenia and Lysa arrived and John met their evening train. They all went to Fiesole and

Siena. John wanted time alone with Evguenia. She booked a hotel room for a night at Montecatini, just for the two of them, and arranged a car. Evguenia saw it as an intended seduction. She thought the trip a bad idea and warned they would quarrel.

John cancelled the room and the car, sat on the town wall at Volterra and cried. Lysa asked Una why John did not let Evguenia go. Evguenia, she said, had no other romantic involvement, but felt she had become like a drug to John. She loved her but wanted to be free to live life for herself. When Evguenia left for Paris she sent John a card, 'Why quarrel when the sun is shining and the sky is blue? I am still of the same opinion, but I love you.'

John had headaches and a pain that ran down her left arm. Dr Lapiccirella diagnosed high blood pressure, an underactive thyroid and 'toxic poisoning of the aorta caused by nicotine'. X-rays revealed scars from childhood tuberculosis. He advised no cigarettes and a warm climate for winter. John became 'skinless with nerves' as she tried to stop smoking. Una blamed all her maladies on 'that slug of a female who battens on her and cannot even write without bullying or distressing her. If she did not exist all other troubles could be overcome.'

Evguenia asked Una's cousin, Sandra Tealdi, to speak to Lapiccirella and let her know what was wrong with John. Sandra wrote to her in Paris:

> He told me to tell you that John is very ill with nerves and that she is in constant need of care. And would you believe it, Una phoned me the next day and Lapiccirella had told her that I had telephoned in order to know the news of John. I felt the blood freeze in my veins, but thank goodness he hadn't spoken to you and Una interpreted it as just a kind thing on my part. I beg you never to disclose a thing.

Una's tyrannical hold on John was common knowledge. John's only escape was her obsession with Evguenia. It invaded her like a cancer. Her health broke down and her life spiralled out of control. As did Europe. There were rumours of German attacks on Corfu, Malta, Gibraltar, Egypt, Kenya. It was said that Hitler planned to invade Poland on his birthday. On 28 April John and Una listened on the wireless to a two-and-a-half-hour speech by him. He had broken agreements with Britain and Poland. He wanted control of Danzig and a German corridor through Poland. Una went to the British Consul to find out whether Fido could go with them if they had to leave Italy in a hurry. John made Tito their chauffeur get a Swiss visa.

Evguenia returned the lottery ticket Una sent her as an Easter present. 'I refuse in advance to participate in it', she said. She wondered about starting a craft shop. 'As I am getting older there is nothing else for me to do but to have something of my own.'

John planned to go to Rye and sell the Forecastle. In four years she had spent little time there. It had proved to be, Una said, 'the melancholy little house we built to be so gay in'. Andrea wrote that her son Nicholas was in an isolation hospital with diphtheria and had had two mastoid operations. Viola asked Una at least to write to Minna who was so very ill.

John did not now read the newspapers. 'What's the good? Anyhow I am sick of it all.' Her letters to Evguenia became unconfident and stripped of hope. 'The sense of failiour is heavy upon me all too often these days.' She felt lost and thought perhaps her broken health might lead to a path that must be followed.

Giving up smoking was another bereavement. She took sedatives, chewed gum and craved nicotine. To take a cure she went to the Grotta Guisti, Monsummano, in Pistoia. She sat on a bench in a cave full of steam emanations then lay sweating on a bed and was massaged. She felt as if she was suffocating, came out in a virulent itching rash and had one of her spectacular temper losses when the nurse failed to give the cook her special menu.

She and Una left for Rye via Paris at the end of July. Evguenia agreed to go with them to England for a month 'unless something unforeseen happens'. 'The flat is in dust sheets,' John wrote to her, 'and looks sad as do all homes about to be left for even a short time.' They would meet at the Vouillemont for 'our long talk about the future'. 'Oh Piggie my heart is so terribly heavy sometimes when I think of you and all that might have been. NO – NO – I have not written that, please don't take it up angerally when you answer this letter.'

Evguenia looked fit. She was wearing a Burberry suit that cost her 1,750 francs, her hair was dyed red and she had bought a Topolino car. John would not travel in it and left a performance of *Cyrano* at the Comédie Française in panic at the thought of Evguenia in a crash. During their 'long talk' Evguenia told her she was going to study at the Sorbonne. She would see John often she loved her and did not want to lose her, but she had a sense of community in Paris with her

Russian friends. She and Lysa planned to rent a little country cottage at Rambouillet for the weekends.

Una sensed Evguenia was strong and her resolution real. Such confidence infuriated her. Evguenia's freedom did not give her the victory she sought. It made her own life untenable. It pushed her toward a truth she would never accept: John was not, and had not been for many years if ever, 'the least bit in love' with her. She seemed to find life alone with her intolerable and not worth living. Una fought on, excelling with insults:

> I suspect Evguenia has native blood. The negroid nose and lips, the queer little eyes when asleep, she looks amazingly African. And of course her character. The lying and deceiving, the superficiality and unreliability and the indolence, all suggestive of the half or quarter breed. It may be some quite distant strain but I strongly suspect it is there.

Evguenia feared John was seriously ill and asked to see Dr Fuller with her. At the end of the session she tried to speak to him without Una. Una would not allow it, 'I cannot get over the impudence of her trying to prevent my speaking to him and saying John was her patient when she had left her to live or die.'

In Rye John put the Forecastle on the market for £1,750 and accepted the first offer, which was for £1,500. She and Una had a session with Mrs Leonard who assured them there would be no war. Troubridge appeared, eighteen inches above Feda's head, and offered Una sympathy and help. She clasped his hand in friendship. Evguenia spent most of her time with the Smallhythe trio, working in the garden. They liked her and found her obliging.

Andrea came to Rye. After five years of marriage she was going to divorce Toby Warren. She said he took no interest in their son and that sleeping with a drunk was repulsive. She wanted to break free while young enough to marry again. She had left the Catholic Church as she would not take comfort from its rituals when she could not observe its teachings.

At lunch in the Mermaid Evguenia tried to tell Una that John ought not drink spirits because of her blood pressure. Una said, 'I can't listen now Evguenia, I'm busy.' Back at the Forecastle she pursued the remark:

> I knocked on Evguenia's door and receiving no answer pushed it ajar and said, 'Could I come in?' to which she replied, merely, 'Yes', and I went in

saying very quietly, 'Now you are alone Evguenia, will you tell me what it was you wished to say about John?' Immediately she was launched. 'Oh no. I'm not going to tell you anything now.' I replied, 'O yes. You must tell me anything you know about John's health. After what you have suggested you can't refuse.' There followed a perfect torrent of shrill vituperation. No sense to it at all. John drank too much, cocktails, spirits, wine, her blood pressure was high and her liver upset and I cared nothing what happened to her so long as I could oppose her, Evguenia. She mimicked me. 'Oh I hear you. Darling have a glass of wine. Darling have a cocktail. Darling have another helping.' John ate too much also, and more incoherent fury. Terrified that John should hear, and be dragged into a scene, I made for the door, saying we could not possibly have such an upheaval while she was ill. Whereupon the fury flung herself between me and the door, took me by the shoulders saying, between clenched teeth, 'Oh no, you don't leave the room,' and threw me away from the door so that I nearly fell over. I recovered my balance and said with what dignity I could muster, 'Evguenia, this is outrageous you cannot lay hands on me, and keep me from leaving a room in my own house. Let me pass please.' In which she, bearing down threateningly upon me, raged, 'Oh, can't I! I ought to strike you! strike you! but now I've got you here, and you're going to hear all I've got to say to you, and I would have you remember that I'm your guest, and it's your duty to be civil to me.' To which I replied, 'I'm your hostess and I intend to leave this room,' and going up to her I said, 'Let me pass,' and put my hand on her shoulder to push her aside. Again she seized me, and flung me away, wrenching my shoulder as she did so. Then I outwitted her, I leaned from the window and called, quietly, to Annie below, 'Will you come up to the spare room as I have something I want to say to you?' Annie came, and Madam was actually refusing to let her in, or me out, when John, who had heard me call Annie, suspected there was something wrong, and arrived on the scene and released me, only to be met by a fresh flood of abuse from Evguenia, who went downstairs and stood in the dining hall, shouting her fury and vituperation of me, with Annie an amazed witness.

On 1 September Hitler invaded Poland. Two days later Chamberlain announced that Great Britain was at war with Germany. After the announcement, 'God Save The King' was played on the wireless and the air-raid sirens sounded in Rye. John, Una and Evguenia put their gas masks round their necks and moved their luggage to the George

Hotel. Dodo Benson, who was the Mayor of Rye, came by wearing some kind of anti-gas outfit and a tin helmet. He did not know if it was a real air raid. The town was full of evacuated children. John collapsed with heart pains.

On the church door was a poster, If Your Knees Knock, Kneel on Them. On 7 September men from Taylor's Depository moved the furniture from the Forecastle. While they were doing so the prospective purchaser withdrew his offer. The following day Paris was evacuated because of the threat of German invasion. Application to leave England had to be made to the Home Office and took a month or six weeks to consider. A permit to land or travel in France had also to be obtained. The Treasury ruled that only cash and at a limit of £25 per person could be taken out of Britain. Travel was chaotic and the prospect of reaching a destination uncertain.

'But for Mr Eden, the Third International and the Jews it would never have occurred', Una said of the war. Evguenia was desperate to get to Paris. They all went to the French Consulate to see if a landing permit would be issued to her. There was a queue halfway across Bedford Square. Una flourished her title and got to the front of it. Permits for John and Una would take several weeks to obtain but Evguenia's application would have to be referred to France and there was no saying how long this would take or what the outcome would be.

John collapsed in tears. She had a terror of Evguenia going to Paris, of not knowing if she was safe, injured or dead. She feared Fido might be killed in an air raid or neglected. Una was on a high. Evguenia's misery was her victory and Evguenia's misery was intense. Una accused her of making John ill by threatening to return to Paris and said it was 'sheer murder'. She addressed all her remarks to John and managed not to speak a word to Evguenia for three days. She now referred to her as Florrie, 'alias Florence Nightingale because she don't want to nurse and Flora McCossak, Bitch of the Steppes'. It had slipped her mind, in this Strindbergian nightmare, that Florrie was the name of John's sister, who died three weeks after John was born. 'Florrie is in a chronic rage that a world war has dared to interfere with her plans for a life of indolent futility with John's money and her car in Paris.'

John was like a faded wraith. Thin and weak on her legs, she took barbiturates three times a day which affected her coordination and thinking. Her speech was slurred and she kept falling asleep. The entire row of her eyelashes had turned in on the eyeball and her face twitched in a nervous spasm.

They all loaded up a hired car with as much luggage as would go on it and set off for Lynton in Devon. Petrol was rationed. John had been going to Lynton since 1919 and she thought it would be safe from attack. There was a Catholic church there and the convent of the Poor Clares of the Reform of St Colette, the eventual legatees of half her capital.

They took four rooms at the Cottage Hotel. John needed help to dress and to wash, so she had a bell in her room which she rang for service from Evguenia or Una. She knitted scarves for soldiers and seemed out of it. Una guarded her like a spider.

Evguenia's plight was terrible. A prisoner of circumstance, she was now captured by all that she had tried so hard to resist. This war was worse for her than the Russian Revolution. Her fate was the more cruel in that freedom had seemed to be achievable. Now she was caught between John's demands and Una's vitriol. Her horror at the prospect of being incarcerated with them was intense. She developed a rash all over her face and body which Una said was from eating sweets.

Evguenia had alien status. She could not move even to a different county without police permission and agreement from John who was her guarantor. John refused to contemplate separation because of risks of air raids or German invasion. She worried even if Evguenia went out for a walk. She tried to prevent her, saying she would 'attract undue interest or attention'.

When Evguenia received letters, John wanted to know who they were from. She wanted to be nursed by Evguenia and asked her to massage her shoulders. Una then said Evguenia's 'ignorant interference had done definite harm'. John sprained her left ankle, asked Evguenia to bandage it, then let Una redo it. She was in pain and asked Evguenia to sleep in the same room with her. Evguenia agreed to do so for a night. Una then wanted to sleep in Evguenia's bed. She claimed the mattress was harder than her own. John gave her permission. Evguenia shouted at her, ' "You fool, you blind fool," glared at us both, her face which is now a mass of spots, urticaria, plus sweets and temper, positively swelled and bloated with fury, her eyes like jet beads and rushed out of the room banging all doors within range. I really do not know what I am to do.'

Una knew exactly what to do. More of the same and then more of the same. All her symptoms of malaise disappeared. For the first time in years she was enjoying life. Evguenia's desperation compensated for the loss of Florence, the Forecastle, Smallhythe. 'Florrie is surly, morose, spotty and melancholy and gives us, thank God, not much of her society', she wrote.

Evguenia stayed in her room for hours and ate alone. She heard Mrs Baker had died. Had she kept that connection she would probably have been a beneficiary of her will. John's bank informed her that because of currency restrictions she was unlikely to be able to pay Evguenia an allowance were she to go to France. Evguenia 'cried herself into swollen frightfulness and hints at suicide', Una wrote. John told Evguenia she could not bear to think of her exposed to danger or illness and thrown on her own financial resources. She asked her to go with them to Italy if the war allowed. Evguenia said she would not do so for any reason. Una saw this as proof of her lack of love: 'The rain pours down, the icy wind howls and I see all chances of keeping our home in commission vanishing down Florrie's moloch maw. She is infinitely the strongest of us three, since John is handicapped by affection and I by scruples, while she knows not the meaning of either.'

Evguenia sought the help of a Dr Anderman. She went to him and cried. He tried counselling John and Una. He told Una not to fuss over John all the time or ask her every minute if she was comfortable or in pain. He advised John to get out of doors and said Evguenia's rash was nervous and that she needed to get away. 'My suspicions are confirmed,' Una said, 'that she has posed as the nerve shattered victim of an elderly hypochondriacal malade imaginaire and her hysterical accomplice to whom she is the indispensable bond slave.'

Anderman she dismissed as 'that Cossack Jew'.

36

At the Wayside

Una refused Evguenia any domestic task then criticized her for not doing anything to help. When John caught a cold Una dosed her with anti-phlogiston, cough mixture, Sanatogen, malted milk and cocoa, took her temperature four times a day and would not leave her 'because of the risk of Florrie making her ill in my absence'.

John then had gastric trouble for which she was given morphine. Dr Anderman thought she might have an ulcer and advised a stomach X-ray. He told Mrs Pidgeon, the proprietor of the hotel, that with 'thoroughly nervous patients' it was worth spending money on reassurance. Evguenia was thoroughly nervous too. She was admitted to hospital in Barnstaple. Una described her as a 'horrible spectacle with blotched skin. The bill for Evguenia is £15. All for nettle rash caused by temper.' She wrote malicious couplets about her:

> I may despise the tender heart and bite the hand that
> feeds.
> But I never despise the cheque book that supplies my
> daily needs.

'God curse you', Evguenia said to her.

A succession of doctors advised Evguenia to move away from John and Una. She moved to Exeter, got a job in a psychiatric hospital nursing German prisoners and stayed at the Osborne Hotel. Una described the hospital as full of drugged lunatics scowling in armchairs. Evguenia, she said, 'languidly served meals to Nazi spies and Jew Bolshies' and was not nursing anyone. John called it a 'fearful asylum place among the loonies' and insisted Evguenia leave. Which she did, but not to go back to Lynton. She returned her nursing badge, and enrolled to study art and French literature at Exeter University.

As late as March 1940 they were all hopeful that it would still be possible to leave England. John Holroyd-Reece, who was in France, thought he could arrange visas and the London Passport Office extended all their exit permits. John hoped the Bank of England would relax the rules about allowing money to be taken out of the country. But Hitler invaded Denmark and Norway, Mussolini joined forces with him and Italy became enemy territory. John and Una said Mussolini had been baited by the British government and the British press. They worried about their possessions in the via dei Bardi and about Fido in quarantine in Paris.

It was a bitter English winter. Snow swirled. 'Our hours are spent indoors behind tightly shut windows', Una wrote. She wore two vests, a woollen body belt, a flannel shirt, long-sleeved sweater, jodhpurs, a leather waistcoat and a lined tweed riding coat. At night she slept with two hot water bottles, three blankets, an eiderdown and rug.

She and John moved with their gas masks, the canary and John's mandolins to the Imperial Hotel, Lynton, run by Mr and Mrs Chivers. John had a large bedroom and a sitting-room with views of the sea and the moors. She bought an antique desk in Barnstaple and hoped to start writing again. She was immensely relieved that Evguenia was safe and in the same county and that she could provide for her. Here, she felt, after all their vicissitudes, was proof of God's care and guidance.

Suppose you had gone out of England at the beginning of the war – where should we be now? I ask you – I could not have got money to you & I would not be permitted to draw enough money (had I joined you) for all of us to live on – a nice state of affairs. Well, my Pig here you are in my dear country and for that I do thank God, and perhaps one day it may also be your country, who knows? . . .

P.S. Darling, if as you tell me, you only stayed when war broke out because you had promised me not to go in the event of war – then thank you. By so doing you have saved me fearful anxiety.

Evguenia was lonely in Exeter. Her skin complaint did not clear up. She spoke of John being all she had, and admitted to crying when they parted. She promised to go to Lynton if John became ill or 'SOS'd' for her. They wrote to each other every day. John felt that at last she was protecting her. She sent her £25 a month and more for heating. As ever, she was pathologically fearful about her safety. She told her to check out people's political views before having anything to do with them because the university was 'simply bursting with Reds', and she sent her a police list of towns 'prohibited to alians'. 'Now please no Russian Blues over these forbidden areas', she said. It was significant of God, she thought, that Lynton and Exeter were not on the list.

Dr Anderman told John to avoid worry and to lead a calm life. She worked at the Merano book, finished a first draft and with Una rode ponies, Harmony and Titbits, on the moors. Evguenia visited at weekends and stayed with a Mrs Widden. She socialized in a way that John and Una did not. 'Florrie plays badminton with the local bourgeoisie who are just her calibre', was Una's way of putting it.

In the summer of 1940 Hitler's blitz on Britain began. Italy formally declared war on Britain, and Paris was occupied by the Gestapo. Churchill broadcast to the nation and said Britain would fight until victory was assured. There were air raids and nightly blackouts. A German bomber plane was brought down four miles from Lynton. On an evening when Una saw a chink of light through a neighbour's blind, she rapped so hard on the window she broke the glass and cut her wrist.

Exeter became a prohibited area for Evguenia. She moved again to Lynton and stayed with Mrs Widden. She felt trapped. John feared she would be captured if Hitler invaded.

John and Una became dissatisfied with the Imperial Hotel. The Devonshire cream was sour. Mr and Mrs Chivers tired of their complaints and asked them to leave. They moved to a house called the Wayside, owned by Jack and Molly Hancock. All their possessions were sent from Rye but there was nowhere to put everything and their rooms looked like those of people who have come down in the world. Lord Tavistock's aviary got bombed, so they reclaimed Charlotte, the maligned grey parrot. They acquired a Pekinese from Barnstaple and

Fido arrived from Paris, very fat, but 'crazy with joy'.

Only John persisted with the fantasy that these new quarters would turn into a home for what she perceived as her family. 'As Evguenia has for years refused to make a family life with us she must now continue to make one of her own', was Una's view. She did all she could to exclude her then criticized her for staying away. She objected to the way she played with Jane, John's spaniel. The dog looked out for Evguenia, who took her for walks. Una said she could not be trusted to keep the dog away from a neighbour's Labrador so Evguenia was stopped from taking the dog out. She hated the way it stayed shut in the bedroom, whining. Una saw her concern as a pose, a way of undermining John: 'The implication is that John is cruel, confines Jane unduly, under or over feeds her, is too fussy over her, neglects her, is at fault because of her determination never to let her off the lead where there are dangerous traps, or traffic.'

Una fed John's anxiety so as to make John provoke Evguenia. She became very good at it. Evguenia made a friend, Doris Woolley. Together they went to art classes and the cinema. Doris Woolley had lived in Cornwall and knew Dod Procter and the Newlyn group of painters. Una implied that Evguenia was having an affair with her. John watched and questioned Evguenia who lost her temper. Una then accused Evguenia of making John ill.

On a day in September when Evguenia went to Lynmouth with Doris Woolley, John told her to get a taxi home. Evguenia did not want to. John began weeping at the prospect of her being killed or arrested. Una told Evguenia she would get a taxi. 'Are you a nurse or a fool?' she said. Evguenia said she had to move to a different town. Una called Anderman. He sat for an hour with John and the following day took her for a drive. He tried to persuade her that it would be for the best if Evguenia left Lynton.

Few options were open to Evguenia. She had lost her friends, possessions and the city where she felt at home. Her status in England was fragile. There were only certain districts in which she was allowed. She was entirely dependent on John who retained her papers and was officially responsible for her. And John, never emotionally rational, was now 'mercurial to an inconceivable degree'. She said she wanted to die and would welcome a bomb on the house. She had written nothing since she stopped smoking in May 1939 and felt that she would never write again. Tired and wretched, she spent much time in bed or sitting by the window knitting blankets in blue and green.

Una knew the root of her malaise: 'This woman has fastened herself on to us, sucking every ounce of gain she can, sabotaging John's health and spirit. This woman is callously killing my John.'

John would not let Evguenia go and Una made it hell if she stayed or tried to leave. She found out what Evguenia wanted then made sure she did not get it. She referred to her as a swollen sheep tick, a mass of blubber, a white slug, an insignificant amoeba, a bloated Tartar polypus. She urged John to cut her allowance to £200 as a means of keeping her in line and to write to Harold Rubinstein about changing her will.

When Evguenia said she was going, John got 'cardiac pain'. Una went to the police. The Chief Inspector told her Evguenia could not move unless John appointed a deputy guarantor, with police consent, to act for her. This guarantor *must* live in the same town or village as Evguenia and accept financial and all other responsibility for her. 'So there goes another thread from Florrie's garment of emotional blackmail. She must do *exactly* as John appoints.'

Evguenia 'launched a broadside' against Una. Her jealousy, she said, was intolerable. She wrote to the Home Office and was granted leave to apply for national work. But she needed a reference from John. Una told her 'it was our duty to inform the Home Office that Evguenia had twice been in a sanatorium. No government or concern would want to risk an outbreak of tb.'

Dr Anderman was again called. He said Evguenia was fit to work anywhere.

> We demurred pointing out that she had broken down formerly and that John was therefore worried at her having applied to the Home Office and giving her as a reference. He was most insulting, implying that John might wish to speak ill of her in order to prevent her obtaining national work away from Lynton. When John told him he had no business to make such implications he left the house.

Una took John to the police station. The police reiterated that no application for residence from Evguenia would be entertained without John's permission.

In June 1941 Germany invaded Russia. Una hoped they would mutually exterminate each other. At mass she felt inspired by the 'unearthly beauty' of the nuns singing 'like angels'. Confession, though, seemed a waste of time with Father Parkin 'yawning with boredom over her trivial sins' and telling her to say the Apostles' Creed once more. Adept at working the black market, she got vegetables, chicken, sugar, chocolate, boiled sweets. 'After all,' she said, 'we may as well have them as leave them to the Jews at the Valley of the Rocks Hotel, who fall like locusts on any supplies, ready to outbid any gentile.'

When Churchill announced the alliance of Britain with the Soviet Union, John and she resolved that at the war's end they would leave England, never to return. 'Henceforward we, a Christian people, are the allies of the openly professed Godless Russians.'

Una refused to speak to Evguenia or be civil to her in public. She seemed now to control John who became alarmingly limp about any effort. All John looked forward to in the day was to go down to Evguenia's lodgings for an hour. At the end of July, Evguenia told her she had obtained a police permit of absence for a fortnight and was going to Oxford with a friend for a holiday. John became faint and lightheaded. A Dr Nightingale told her she had an anxiety neurosis. John asked if he would pass her for life insurance and he replied that he would not. Una put it all down to 'the USSR Destroyer Florrie'. She thought it 'simply inconceivable' that Evguenia could go away knowing John's condition and her own 'pallor and emaciation', how single-handed she had to list the laundry, groom and exercise the dogs, clean the birds, mince the meat, prepare the bread sauce.

Charlotte the parrot developed a monotonous and persistent whistle. She kept it up for hours on end. Una covered her cage to shut her up, so Charlotte spent most of her time under a blanket in the dark.

John feared Evguenia had gone for good. She went to her lodgings to see if she had taken her belongings. She had not. On her mantelpiece was a letter. Evguenia had asked Mrs Widden to give it to John on her sixty-first birthday on 12 August. It thanked her for her goodness and generosity and expressed the hope that one day she would understand Evguenia better.

Evguenia returned to Lynton on the last day of her two-week police permit of absence. John called to see her. Evguenia told her she hoped to do an engineering training in Gloucestershire, organized by the government who gave placements after it. John hurried back to Una:

I advised John and for once she took my advice and put her foot down flat sending by Mrs Hancock a note to the effect that it was only fair to make it quite clear that if Florrie persisted in attempting any unsuitable schemes such as that proposed her allowance would not be reduced but would cease all together there and then.

Evguenia then asked John if she wanted in writing to disclaim any financial responsibility toward her. John assured her that she did not. But Una wanted just that. She sensed she was winning this protracted battle. Income tax was ten shillings in the pound. John's wealth was not what it was. Sex and money were John's expressions of power. If Evguenia had neither, the relationship might break.

John's eyes got worse, with ingrowing lashes and a kind of crusty conjunctivitis. In August 1941 she went to Bath to see a Dr Tizzard. He chainsmoked, was a seceded Catholic and dabbled in spiritualism and psychic things. 'We think he is unquestionably inverted,' Una said. He intended somehow to cut away the skin round John's lashes. He was going to do one eye at a time under local anaesthetic with a week in between.

John and Una took a twin-bedded room at his Church Street Medical and Surgical Home. They also had a room at the Francis Hotel for Pippin the canary who had gone bald and Jane the Spaniel. Una filled the nursing-home room with flowers. She seemed in her element, 'our two narrow beds awaiting us'. She had her own platinum needle for injections 'in place of the communal fishhook' and supplies of calves' foot jelly and Brands Essence.

Evguenia, she told John, could not possibly visit. There was not a room for her in the whole of Bath, and any tears or movement of John's facial muscles might lead to scarring. Evguenia wrote every day, often twice a day. 'If you want me of course I will come', she said. John dictated to Una daily letters for Evguenia. Una amended these as she felt fit. 'I write daily to the brute giving her reports and details to which of course she is completely indifferent if she troubles to read them.'

Tizzard operated on 25 August and said the eye must stay tightly bandaged for five days. John vomited, her eye haemorrhaged, she was in pain and the bandage kept getting soaked in blood. Una antagonized the staff. She phoned Tizzard while he was in the operating theatre. When the nurse tried to sit John up, Una said,

I am sorry Miss Goodrich, I have spoken to Mr Tizzard on the phone, and he says the patient is not to be moved until he comes. She looked as though she would kill me and said, very violently, Lady Troubridge I must speak to you, come outside this room at once. With a word of reassurance to my poor John I followed her, and she flew at me, and said I was presuming on her authority and she would not have it. I replied, quietly, that I was very sorry if I had transgressed against etiquette but that in each emergency the haemorrhage, the vomiting, moving the patient, I had had no alternative. The first two occasions she was unobtainable and no one else would consent to call up the surgeon. The third time Mr Tizzard had given definite orders. Then she demanded that I should use the visitors' telephone and not the dialling one and I replied that I had only been told two days ago of its existence or I should never have spent threepence each on twopenny local calls. Fearing that she would vent her spleen on John or turn me out I apologised profusely for having been in the right.

When she said she did not know why Tizzard was making all this fuss about this operation, I replied, 'I think Mr Tizzard realises what it would mean to his career if one of the best known writers in England left this house with her eyes damaged by his surgery. I am bound to say that she had no reply.

John's eye was a mess. Given a mirror she was incredulous and felt she had been disfigured for life. The scar was inflamed, the lid sagged and did not close when she slept. The lashes started growing in again, the eye still twitched and she still had conjunctivitis. Nor as time passed did it heal. She was not going to let Tizzard touch her other eye. She was prescribed hypnotics, bromides and barbiturates. Una applied an ointment called Pancovaine with a glass rod.

Back at the Wayside Evguenia left cakes and chrysanthemums for John's return. She called every day to be as helpful as was allowed She was working in an army canteen and had made friends with a Mr Benn, 'a very distinguished man of letters', she called him. He told her positive things about 'communism and the new re-born Russia'.

I was happy to hear someone so certain about the outcome of the war because the Russians would push the Germans back. My political views were non-existent but if anyone said something silly about Russia it was always galling for me to hear. I suppose one never forgets the country where one was born.

John was adamant that she must not see Mr Benn. The police, she said, were watching him for subversive Bolshevik activities and Evguenia had now done for herself socially in Lynton. Evguenia reminded her that 'we Bolshevists are now the allies of England.' She was needled by condescension to her refugee status, the jibing about Russians being a primitive race. At the Wayside she said only fools failed to understand what the Soviet Union was trying to do. John said, 'May I ask if you are calling me a fool?' Evguenia said, 'No it's that woman there who is a fool.' John said, 'You must not speak of Una like that.' Una said she would summon Dr Nightingale if Evguenia did not leave. Evguenia said she was welcome to do so, she was going to Oxford on 18 November, she had rented a room in a house where there was no telephone, she intended doing a course in interior design or perhaps shorthand and typing and she would go without her allowance if it came to it.

John wept which made her eyes 'like raw meat'. Una gave her barbiturates and prompted her to send a letter to Evguenia chastizing her for her friendship with Mr Benn, her provocation about Oxford, her 'deliberately and with full medical knowledge doing her utmost to make a scene' and cutting her next month's allowance by £5.

> Then follows endless and unceasing discussion of Evguenia. What will she do, or not do. Can she be prevented. Should she be prevented. Is she being misunderstood. Why can't she be contented. Couldn't she work here. And so on, and so on, until exhausted and drained once more by this insignificant amoeba, the writer of *The Master of the House*, *The Well of Loneliness*, *Adam's Breed*, and I, a woman of no mean intelligence and some character stagger to bed, though not to sleep.

Next day John lost all control with Una. It was her fault if anything happened to Evguenia. She, John, would never get over it. She ordered her from the room and sent Ivy the maid with a note for Evguenia asking her to call. She begged Evguenia to change her plans. If she did, she would increase her allowance to £300 again. Evguenia said the chief constable assured her she could return to Lynton when she wanted. She would come for holidays and hoped John would visit her in Oxford.

The day before she left she had lunch at the Wayside. At John's request there was soup, roast lamb, redcurrant jelly, sprouts and roast potatoes, baked apples with apple jelly, Swiss pastries and coffee. 'She sat there fat, bloated and slit eyed', Una said.

In December 1941 John went to London to see Lord Dawson and Dr Williamson Noble about her eyes and general health. She and Una booked in at the Rembrandt Hotel, Knightsbridge, opposite Brompton Oratory. Dawson told her there were two components to her illness, one organic, the other depressive. Her gums were infected and her lungs in a bad way from all those years of smoking. Noble advised against further operations on her eyes. He said entropium was a difficult condition to treat, that the spasm in her eye was incurable and that it was better to endure pulling out lashes than to have another drooping lid. John had given him a copy of *The Well of Loneliness* which he was reading.

John told Una she wanted to see Evguenia in London. There was a flare-up. 'I simply prayed and implored and also protested', Una wrote in her diary. 'She capitulated. She said she must be fair to me and she gave me her promise. The Mongol idiot is to come for a day and then is to be told to remain away.'

On the day of Evguenia's visit John waited eagerly for her from early morning. At lunch Una took off her spectacles 'so as to avoid seeing her horrid face'.

37

John's Calvary

John was very ill in the Rembrandt Hotel. A chest infection developed into pneumonia and pleurisy. She became irrational, spoke of malevolence all around her and asked constantly if there was post from Evguenia. Una got out her relic of the true cross, made the sign of the cross over her, then put the relic on the mantelpiece behind a lit candle. She gave her Bengers with brandy and told her Evguenia was 'a primitive undeveloped creature, incapable of any true impulses or affection'.

Una's grip tightened like a vice. She forbade Evguenia to visit. She told her to write cheering letters every day, send affectionate telegrams and not to mention anything worrying or refer to symptoms of her own. Una's signature was now on the cheque for Evguenia's monthly allowance. 'I am acting on John's authority at the Bank.' She read Evguenia's letters aloud to John with her own intonation and omissions. 'The bitch doesn't even write every day and when she does the letters have about as much feeling in them as flat soda water. Even in this dire stress she does not seem to try even to ape humanity.' Evguenia turned up at the hotel unannounced. Una told her to stand inside the door of John's room. When she tried to approach the bed, she was 'removed'.

Una kept guard night and day. She sat beside John, holding 'her dear tired hand'. She made professional nursing impossible. The night nurse said, 'I don't see why Lady Troubridge should be in here at all.' The day nurse quit. John cried when she heard she was leaving. When her replacement wanted time off, Una would not allow it. She took the woman into her own room so that John could not hear.

> I told her that the patient was not so well on account of her having upset her. I told her quietly that she must not raise her voice as the patient would hear her and she need not trouble about an evening off as I had already arranged for a new nurse. She flew into a rage and stormed. Then I went straight to the telephone and obtained a new nurse from the Cowards agency ... I called the nurse from her room to mine told her to pack her case, bring me her account, and to go at once.

Una went out only to get food, which John did not want. She waited outside Harrods in the mornings for the food hall to open. At the meat counter she grabbed one leg of a poussin while another woman grabbed the other. 'And I triumphed and bore it off.' She won the contest for sea kale and was ninth in the queue at the toffee counter. The new nurse thought it would be better if *she* arranged Miss Hall's food. Una told her Miss Hall would starve if left to her efforts.

Una wrote daily notes to Evguenia, ostensibly on John's behalf, about expectoration, purée potatoes, John's nerves and how she, Una, had to keep her *very quiet*. The main problem, Una told Evguenia, was John's bowels. 'She is terribly flatulent' with 'an absolutely unmanageable irregularity of her bowels'. Glycerine suppositories, hot ginger drinks, olive oil and turpentine enemas did not work and English doctors were hopeless.

For six weeks John saw no one but Una. She was desperate to see Evguenia. 'I am almost too depressed to live', she wrote of herself when well enough to do so.

> These are grim days for the whole world and my own troubles pour heavy upon me – there is so little to look forward to, or so it seems to me. I am patient, or try to be, but so many dreary weeks in this damned hotel bedroom – all too awful ... But Piggie Hall is coming on Friday & perhaps will cheer me up – yes, yes, it *will* cheer me up – it will go out to buy Pig-pants & so on. No more now dearest.
> Your John

Father Munster came to give her communion and she asked him for an interpretation of the text 'Make Ye Friends to Yourselves of the Mammon of Unrighteousness', but received no satisfactory reply.

Evguenia sent boiled sweets, urged her to attempt a little more each day and arranged to spend holidays with her. She told her she was finding shorthand difficult but had made friends in Oxford.

Una described herself as 'simply stuttering with anxiety' at the prospect of her visit. John cheered up because of it. Evguenia slopped over her with a lot of soft soap, Una said. When she left, John became depressed again. She pined for past time and asked Evguenia to pray for her. 'Don't you remember how you & I went to the Easter mass in the Russian church in Florence? That seems a very long time ago and to think about it makes me want to cry a few tears which are strictly forbidden me as you know.'

She kept harking back to her mother's neglect of her in childhood. She told Una she was still in love with Evguenia and wanted her to come to Lynton. 'Oh how weary I am of these four walls,' she wrote, '& how I do long for a breath of fresh country air with Royal Chinkie Pig very pompous & self-important taking me for a walk! Can't you see it with its crown over one ear & its hoofs polished?'

When John was well enough to return to Lynton, Evguenia arranged to take her holiday, go down in advance, prepare things at the Wayside and to be there to meet her. *En route* she stayed for three nights at the Rembrandt. While there she and John had a row. As Una put it: 'the dreadful creature stood at the foot of John's bed, fat and pasty and bloated, her eyes glinting like boot buttons a sneering smile on her blubber lips while she bullied my miserable John.'

The substance was that John again began insisting that Evguenia live in the same county, if not the same town. Evguenia again said she could not and would not. She had to be free to go where there was available work. At Una's instigation John then had a letter delivered to her: if she insisted on living in a different county her allowance would be cut to £100 a year, and this amount would be dependent on her letting John know her address at all times.

Evguenia replied that she would keep herself. John panicked. Una then wrote a letter that began 'Evguenia' and was signed 'Una V. Troubridge':

I think it only right to repeat what I have already told you. Lord Dawson warned me that John had been in a very low state when she fell ill, that she had been 'very, *very* ill', that her convalescence could only be a very lengthy one. He is sending her to Lynton to recuperate & if in such

circumstances you decide to go away without keeping her informed of
your address (& this at a time when air raids are frequent) and if the
strain breaks her down & she dies it will be your doing & on yr. conscience
all yr life.

Evguenia replied that she would always let John know her address.
But she did not go to Lynton. She took a job with the Red Cross in
Basingstoke, 160 miles away. John longed for her. She asked her to
wear an Identity disc inscribed with Radclyffe Hall and the Wayside
address. And she asked to be given as next of kin. 'Always do this my
little, little Piggie because that is what I am to you ... You can bandage
my soars a little if you will definately promise always to give me as
your: Next of Kin. Promise this darling, because you do know, don't
you, *that I am your next of kin.*'

It was cold at the Wayside. Una slept in the same bed with John and
counted the number of times a minute she breathed in and out. She
pulled out her ingrowing eyelashes with the aid of a magnifying glass
and a mirror fixed on her forehead. John could not eat the milky
puddings, ox tongue, calf's head and sheep's head brawn she proffered.
She began smoking again, said she had lost her hold on life and could
not clearly recollect past events. She broke her other ankle and had her
leg in plaster of Paris up to the knee. For long hours she sat in dull
depression, knitting a patchwork blanket or staring into space. On a
day when she could not find a business paper she threw things out of
cupboards in a desperate way.

Una had a nightmare in which John was a man in a gloomy bedroom.
A creature covered in bandages came in and threatened them both. She
woke to find Jane had diarrhoea and wanted urgently to get out of the
house.

None of Evguenia's jobs lasted. After nursing at Basingstoke she
moved to Evesham in the West Midlands working for the BBC World
Service on French and German broadcasts. She visited Lynton to tell
John about it and urged her to be pleased. She would get £300 a year
plus bonuses. But John fretted until two in the morning. Una overheard
her telling Evguenia that after the war she wanted them all to go to
Florence with a view to settling there. But when Una said she longed
for Italy, John would not commit herself unless Evguenia would come
too.

John felt like a prisoner and looked forward to nothing. She worried about enemy planes over the Midlands and was fearful that Evguenia might go out without a raincoat or rubber boots. She got paler, thinner and weaker and seemed like an empty shell. Her eyes were sunk in her head and she was cold even in a warm room. 'And all because that dough faced idiotic moron makes her indifference brutally obvious and because she has taken a job which makes it impossible for them to meet more than once or twice yearly.'

On days when the postman brought no letter, John closed off with depression. Una felt overwhelmed that after nine years, with John sixty-two and herself fifty-five, 'this dreadful alien woman' still ruled their lives.

Evguenia lost the BBC job after a few months. She had found it arduous, could not hear clearly through earphones and her English was not good enough. John was relieved. She increased her allowance to £300 a year again with no conditions. But she asked her to avoid cities and in particular London because of fogs, air raids and her lungs.

For herself, her only travel was to London to see doctors and dentists. She had more teeth out, more X-rays. Una took her to a service for the sick in Horseferry Road Church, held simultaneously with one in Lourdes. John sat near the altar with the ailing and moribund. In the afternoon they bought a cockatoo called Victoria from Harrods. It was winged but had not lost the instinct for flight and it kept toppling over. It was soon described as a vulture and given to the vet at Taunton.

As Christmas 1942 approached John's thoughts were of Evguenia's visit. A driver was to meet her train at Barnstaple on 15 December. Una was sent out on missions to acquire turkey, plum pudding and black market delicacies. But then Evguenia suddenly got a job with the Foreign Office. 'I have had very many disappointments in my life but never one quite so bitter as when I got that telegram', John wrote to her. 'I saw myself as one returned by the skin of my teeth from the grave and no RCP here to welcome me back.'

Evguenia was not allowed to divulge the nature of her work, or where she was living. Letters from her arrived opened by the censor. Letters to her were addressed to a box number at Western Central District Post Office, London. 'What has happened seems like a mad kind of blackout', John wrote. She watched for the postman, phoned a mutual friend Marjorie Hatten for news and worried that Evguenia might be sent overseas.

On Christmas Day Evguenia asked Mrs Widden to deliver white

chrysanthemums and a pot of white heather to John. 'I am touched to the heart', John said. Father Parsons, the new priest, came to lunch and ate the Christmas fare and drank the Australian burgundy.

In January 1943 the weather was cold, with snow and icy rain. Una foraged for food. She plodded to the shops and the market for sheep's heads, liver, kidneys, tripe and tongues, rabbits, ox tails and cows' heels. She bought black market cream and chickens and gammon rashers and Golden Syrup from the nuns. John wanted none of it. She was extraordinarily tired, had no appetite, kept running a temperature and had both constipation and diarrhoea. Dr Manners was repeatedly called. He told John not to leave her room.

Evguenia saved days of leave so that she could visit at the end of February. She reserved her room at Mrs Widden's. John wanted her to have all meals at the Wayside. Una complained that she had no ration book and she was not going to allow her John's butter and sugar. John wanted to give her their chocolate.

While John stayed in the warm Una went alone in a north wind to meet Evguenia. She waited for three buses. Evguenia was not on them. She had gone straight to Mrs Widden.

> There a veritable spectacle awaited me. Her hair permed into a dry frizz, sticking out wildly behind one ear, behind a slouch hat imitating that of the Canadian army. The hair, moreover, is now dyed a golden auburn and when the hat was later removed was seen to have become so thin that it is combed over an almost bare scalp. She now makes up her lips in the *derrière de poule* style. The eighteen-guinea coat is a dyed cat. She has grown very much fatter.

Delighted to see her, John stopped being an invalid. They went shopping and had coffee with women from the badminton club. Excluded, Una sat by the fire and remembered the 'dreadful and desolate days' when John and Evguenia were together in Paris and she was alone.

> The memory of when John's one thought was to find all her relaxation and pleasure away from me. I still feel a sick little sadness when, as soon as this heartless and worthless woman comes over the horizon, I feel that John wants to know me safe and well but *not there*. That when I am there her pleasure is spoiled. It is just the feeling that while to me she is all sufficing and my sun rises and sets only on her, to her there is still

attraction in this worthless creature. She still thrills to the slightest most patronising expression of affection or interest and sits gazing lovingly at her really repellant face.

Evguenia read John's manuscript of *The Shoemaker of Merano*. She asked for a signed photograph of her and wanted to know when they could meet in London. She feared John had cancer. She had tried on a previous visit to talk to Dr Nightingale but was made to feel she was meddling. 'I sealed my mouth ever since', she said. Dr Anderman, sacked by Una for his frankness, was no longer consulted.

John cried when Evguenia left. Una busied herself getting a boiling fowl, a dozen eggs, pork chops and clotted cream, but John could not stand the sight of any of it. She felt sick and had 'agonizing haemorrhoids'. Nightingale advised a barium X-ray of her gut. Una summoned a Dr Harper from Barnstaple who diagnosed a severe chill, which Una thought she had got from going to early mass in an unheated church.

Nights became a misery of pain. John was alternately dosed with kaolin and laxatives. Una got no sleep. She hired Nurse Baldwin, a policeman's wife, who called her My Lady. Evguenia wrote letters of anxiety and affection which John read again and again. She asked Una to write really nice replies but Una wrote nothing.

On 9 April 1943 John for eight hours had excruciating pain. Nightingale, late in the day, made an 'agonizingly painful' rectal examination. He said there was an almost total obstruction which might be haemorrhoids and 'might be something more serious'. He wanted her to go to Barnstaple hospital. Una insisted on London. But none of the hospitals would let her have a bed too and she would not be separated.

With John's money she could buy what she wanted. She booked a suite at the Ritz, five guineas a day for two bedrooms, sitting room, bathroom and wc. A Daimler ambulance was to take them there on 11 April. Nightingale said to Nurse Baldwin, 'I don't envy you the journey tomorrow.' Late at night he pushed painkillers through the letterbox of the Wayside. Una found them at four in the morning.

The landlord Jack Hancock helped get John into the ambulance. The journey to London took seven hours. At the Ritz Dr Armando Child said a colostomy was inevitable. He returned with a surgeon Cecil Joll. He told John he would operate next day at a private nursing home in Hadley Wood run by Lady Carnarvon. He said it might be a temporary colostomy but he could not say more until he had opened her up.

Evguenia went to the Ritz that night. In the morning Father Geddes from the church at Farm Street anointed John. In the afternoon Una, Nurse Baldwin and Evguenia took her to the Hadley Wood nursing home. Joll operated at nine in the evening after his hospital work was done. It took him thirty-five minutes to do a colostomy. The anaesthetist was a Mr McGill. Joll then told Una the cancer was widespread and inoperable. He said if John pulled through, she would for a time feel better than for a long while.

Had John died on Lady Carnarvon's operating table, Evguenia would have been a rich woman. By the terms of John's will, probated in 1938, she had, as she told Evguenia in many letters, made 'ample provision' for her. She had left her 'a substantial income'. But John lived another six months. Una did not write regularly in her diary during those months. What happened in them was clear from later entries and from copies Evguenia kept of her letters to Una.

John was seven weeks in the Hadley Wood nursing home. The place had 'gone to pieces', it lacked even rudimentary management, nursing was non-existent and John was the only and last patient. It suited Una, who had total control. John was in great pain. She had a second operation, 'a terrible dilating operation' Una called it. Una never left her. She slept on two armchairs by her bed. Her vigilance was unflagging:

> When you began to retch I would run to fill up the glasses with bicarbonate and water, while you waited in patient misery for the agonizing spasms to begin and continue till they exhausted you.
>
> I harried and urged you to get up, to lie on your side in bed, to move, to eat. I said your muscles would never get strength while you lay on your back, always, like a crusader on a tombstone. And you were hurt and angry ... How I wish that Joll had told me honestly that your case was utterly hopeless and that I could let you do as you wish.

Joll had told them both that she had inoperable cancer, a clear appraisal. It would have helped had someone insisted on efficient nursing care.

How far Una harried and urged John about Evguenia, played on her anxieties of how she could not be trusted with money, would squander it on rash projects then be left vulnerable and ill, is not recorded. But her past and what followed indicted her.

Lady Carnavon sold her run-down nursing home. John was moved to a 'ghastly' place in Primrose Hill, then to the London Clinic and then at the beginning of August to a flat Una found in Dolphin Square, 502 Hood House.

John's demise was protracted and terrible. She was given Omnopon, an opium preparation, and Diamorphine – heroin. Her body, Una said, was wasted, shrunken and disfigured. She 'scarcely knew day from night in the interminable cycle of hours of pain and sickness'. She unceasingly voiced her desire to die and thanked God when each day and each night was over. She told Una she was only sticking this illness for her sake. It was as if she needed her permission to die. Una had become her trial. She was always there and gave John no chance to see Evguenia alone.

Armando Child told Una that she would break down if she kept this twenty-four-hour vigil. He also, more accurately, told her she was as strong as an ox. At the end of September he said John was dying and would go any day or more likely any night.

On 28 September Una summoned Harold Rubinstein to the Dolphin Square flat. John revoked her previous will which gave Evguenia a substantial income and made another. It was very short:

> I appoint Margot Elena Gertrude Troubridge (known as Una Vincenzo Troubridge) to be Sole Executrix of this my Will and I Devise and Bequeath to her all my property and estate both real and personal absolutely trusting her to make such provision for our friend Eugenie Souline as in her absolute discretion she may consider right knowing my wishes for the welfare of the said Eugenie Souline.

It was witnessed by Armando Child and Nurse Sailes, who was Nurse Baldwin's sister. Radclyffe Hall's signature of endorsement sloped backwards as it used to when she was a child and she had hyphenated her name. Una was ecstatic.

> I saw your eyes as they looked at me after you had made your will and said, 'I've left you everything', the clear, blue happiness and as it were triumph in them. I think you realised how it crowned me and set me for ever before everyone, alone and apart as the one you had chosen, loved, proved and trusted, without rival or reserve.

Such was Una's projection. It was her own eyes that were clear, happy and triumphant if not blue. She was delivered of a wonderful weapon of revenge. She had described their triangle with Evguenia as like a classical image of purgatory. To the company of Sisyphus eternally pushing a rock up a hill and Tantalus reaching for unreachable fruit, could now be added Una, for ever taunting Evguenia with money promised but not to be acquired.

Next day Una wrote in her diary: 'My John is dying. She is going where I shall not see her or touch her hand or hear her beloved voice again until God allows me to join her.'

The truth of why John changed her will in Una's favour within days of dying is not told in Una's diary. The new will was a document of befuddled faith, drugged exhaustion, or extraordinary change of heart. It gave a lie to the nine corrosive years of their triangle, the letters John had written to Evguenia, her obsession with her, her possession of her, her promises to her. It drew a line under the scenes John had had with Una about her, the depth of hatred Una felt for Evguenia, her pathological resentment of her, the stream of poison and vitriol that she poured out about her day after day, for nine long years.

Evguenia wrote of how two days before John died she and Una stood either side of her deathbed. John united their hands over her and said, 'You must be friends and live happily. I have provided for you both to live in comfort if not in luxury, but you Evguenia, must ask Una's advice.' Evguenia protested that she was a grown-up woman of forty. 'John smiled and patted my hand. I did not say anything any more as she was very, very weak that day. It was only a couple of days before she died.'

John was sixty-three. She knew she was dying. She had with Una a 'last talk' in which she said, 'You'll be good to that Russian I know.' No doubt Una said, Trust me. In this talk Una obtained John's permission to destroy the manuscript of *The Shoemaker of Merano*. She pleaded that it was about John's love for Evguenia, destructive of their legend and too autobiographical to be art. But John had called this book the best of her work. Una gave a reciprocal promise that she would destroy her own diaries because of the criticism they contained of Evguenia.

Una described John's dying days as a time of joy and fulfilment. This, she said, was John's Calvary. Suffering was her penance, an opportunity 'to wipe out a thousandfold every moment of pain you ever caused me'. For nine years John had been beyond her control. Inoperable carcinoma of the bowel made her pliant. Her weakness gave Una scope for the breathtaking reconstruction of reality at which she excelled. 'There was never an hour when I would not in my passion of love and pity and adoration have kissed the poor wounds that tortured and humiliated you even as those saints kissed the pitiful & wonderful wounds of Christ.'

Una was exhilarated, 'for ever certain that nothing and no one, except by my own act, could ever come between us or mar our unity'. Never, in life, had Una achieved such certainty of possession. Now she could control John and turn her into pure legend. In these dying days, in an opium haze, only Una had ever, could ever, would ever belong to John. 'Today she said suddenly to me, "I want you, you, you. I want only you in all the world." '

They several times received Holy Communion together, with Una kneeling by John's bed. Notes dictated to Evguenia and signed Your John did not signify:

> She looked up at me saying, I put Your John, but of course I'm not her John, I'm entirely yours. Only it wouldn't be kind to change it and might arouse a feeling of jealousy, if you don't mind my doing it.
>
> Needless to say I reassured her, touched to my soul that she should regard such trivial things as possibly hurting my feelings.

Since 1934 John had written 576 letters to Evguenia, her Piggie Hall. They were all signed Your John. Same Heart, she called her. If they were all duplicitous Evguenia had been gravely cheated. But now, at the end, if John could not be sure to whom she belonged, Una would be sure for her. Absolute possession was in her grasp. 'Never in all our twenty-eight years together has she given me such perfect assurance that of everyone on this earth I only am necessary to her. I alone have her entire love and devotion.'

Radclyffe Hall went into a coma on 6 October. Evguenia visited in the evening and stayed half an hour. 'John does not want her or anyone but me', Una wrote. 'My voice was the only one that reached her brain.' Micki Jacob called but Una refused to let her see John. 'I said that she had no right to prevent me.' Una replied that she had every right.

Dead and laid out, John looked, Una thought, like a medieval ivory carving of a saint, or like an airman or a soldier who had died of wounds. 'Ivory clear and pale, the exquisite line of the jaw, the pure

aquiline of the nose with its delicate wing nostrils, the beautiful mod-
elling of eyelids and brow. Not a trace of femininity; no one in their
senses could have suspected that anything but a young man had died.'

God, supposedly, was in His senses. What reason could He find to
refuse admission to the pleasure ground of paradise to this man, this
husband, this war hero even, devoted to his wife for close on thirty
years, who had confessed and repented the transgression of infidelity.

'You were all mine when you went', Una wrote of John. As was all
the money – £118,000 excluding book royalties. Una slept the night
beside the corpse 'resting together in prone submission to the will of
God, confident that nothing can ever divide us now'.

My John, My Johnnie

38

Mine for ever

Una adapted well to John's death and the inheritance of all her money. There were obituaries in *The Times* and the *Telegraph*. She arranged low mass at Westminster Cathedral and then a requiem mass at the Church of the Immaculate Conception in Farm Street. About a hundred people attended, though few of the friends of former years. John's coffin was placed next to Ladye's in the vault at Highgate Cemetery. This did not imply their easy reunion. Una installed a marble slab inscribed with lines from Elizabeth Barrett Browning's sonnet 'How do I love thee?'

> AND, IF GOD CHOOSE,
> I SHALL BUT LOVE THEE BETTER AFTER DEATH. UNA.

She said if God came to her with the offer, You may have her back if you want to, she knew she 'would have the strength to say, *No, No, No*, Lord. You keep her happy and safe for me'. The last decade with John had been extraordinarily punishing. All her love had been for Evguenia. With her dead and Evguenia so punished, Una was set free.

She worked to regild the legend of their perfect love. 'I feel I must leave an unequivocal record of our life and love, just as the Ladies of Llangollen did, to cheer and encourage those who come after us.' John's poor inverts, she felt, needed their role model of good relationship.

Una called herself the 'guardian of the lamp of John's genius and our enduring love'. The first thing she did in this dual role was to burn *The Shoemaker of Merano* manuscript. 'Such a decision rested exclusively with the writer herself and I had no alternative to that of honourably carrying out her wishes … I gave her my promise, and after her death I lost no time in carrying out that promise.'

It was a heinous act. Worse than the consigning of *The Well of Loneliness* to the king's furnace by Joynson-Hicks and his friends. They only delayed publication for twenty-one years. Una prevented it for all time. She left a fragment of the manuscript – about thirty pages. 'There is nothing there to give away anything personal & it is one of the loveliest things you ever wrote.' It was enough to show the compelling tone of the writing, the fatal attraction of the main characters Ottfried and Ursule. Una also burned all Evguenia's letters to John. She omitted to burn her own diaries, though when John was dying she had promised her she would do so. She could destroy John's work but not her own. She had a great conceit about her diaries and enjoyed rereading and annotating them. They were, in her view, on a par with Pepys and she wanted their publication. Here she thought was 'a fine record of a deep, loyal and lasting inverted love, and how triumphantly that love weathered all adversity'. And here, she said, chronicled as nowhere else, was the truth about John and Evguenia.

> My diary shows how entirely you subordinated your own desires to her needs, how when she became ill you became lovingly and eagerly her celibate nurse, night and day, how, in spite of my misery and jealousy I helped and supported you throughout. And how, in spite of your overwhelming infatuation for her, your deep and devoted love for me remained and survived it all … Darling, that record of mine *must* survive.

And survive it did. After Radclyffe Hall's death Una called her diary entries 'Letters to John'. She addressed her in a tone of complicity as if certain of endorsement of all she said and did. John was now as Una thought she ought be. John, it now transpired, had thought Evguenia so dull she never knew what to talk about to her, but she was 'fond of the poor mutt'. In her final illness 'everything went completely into focus'. She and Una understood each other entirely. They decided to share the burden of Evguenia and 'were perfectly happy over it'.

Only Evguenia might contradict this version of events and Evguenia had no money or clout. Catholicism helped Una reshape the world.

John had never been more all right than she was now: 'You are with Him in Paradise. You are young, well, free and active. You can use your creative genius to its full extent and to the glory of God. It blossoms without obstacle. You are not lonely, you have me in your life.' Una wished that they had had a 'beloved and loving child of our own' – a son, to whom eventually to leave all their treasures. She was not too forlorn about it. 'It won't matter when we are together', she wrote.

As for John's absolute trust in Una's absolute discretion over provision for their mutual friend Evguenia, that was no problem. Una knew just what John wanted: to give Evguenia minimal funds with a great deal of goading and humiliation. She said she knew John's wishes because she had discussed them with her 'exhaustively' before her death. She told Evguenia she had no legal obligation to give her anything. Before John's body had left the embalmers, Garstin's of Baker Street, for Westminster Cathedral, Una could not resist telling Evguenia the terms of the will. Evguenia told her it was John's money, not hers, and it was always John's intention that she, Evguenia, should have a share of it. Una's sentiments to Evguenia were: 'Cards on the table, Evguenia & no more pretence: you never after a first physical flare loved John. Even her terrible suffering never moved you. You were and are infuriated that you did not make a bigger financial haul from her will.'

Evguenia lost her job with the Foreign Office the day after John died. She had taken too many days off while John was ill. She told Una she hoped to get a flat in London. Una made it clear no funds were available for such projects. She said she intended to continue to pay Evguenia's medical expenses and the basic allowance John had given her: £100 a year plus £24 for fuel if she was working, £250 a year if she was unemployed. Evguenia protested that John had given her a basic £324 a year when she was out of a job.

She went to see John Holroyd-Reece. She showed him John's letters that said she was well provided for and would have a substantial income. She told him of the ten years of their life together, of John's demands and expectations and the promises of inheritance she had made. She said it was intolerable to be dependent on Una for her allowance. She could not bear the prospect of deferring endlessly to her. It was not fair that Una should have so much and she so little or that Una should benefit if she, Evguenia, worked. She could not believe

John would have changed her will in this way when so near death, unless Una had urged her to do so.

She had gone to the wrong man. Holroyd-Reece managed Una's money and benefited financially from her. He was still the Pegasus publisher of *The Well of Loneliness*, a lucrative long-term venture. He warned Una that Evguenia could say a lot about her relationship with Radclyffe Hall. He advised her only to make payments erratically to emphasize their voluntary nature. He asked her if it would be worth her while to give Evguenia £5,000 to buy her off to prevent publicity. Una withheld all payments while matters were sorted out: 'after all my precious, all your dispositions were made in the belief not only that she was not as bad as she seemed, but that your illness had shocked her into penitence and reform, which I knew within a few hours of your death was not (how far from it!) the case.' John had wanted Evguenia to have an emerald ring of hers. Holroyd-Reece delayed giving her this in case she sold it to finance legal action.

Evguenia saw a solicitor, a Mr Judge. She tried to contest the will on the grounds that Radclyffe Hall changed it in the last week of her life, when she was not rational, and because of undue pressure and influence exercised by Una. 'It's all horrible & incredibly vile my darling', Una wrote to Dear John. She feared 'yet another court case with implications', like the Fox-Pitt trial and the two *Well of Loneliness* trials. 'I don't mind a hoot for myself, what can it do to me, for if the world boycotted me I could hardly be more alone in it than I am, but I want universal respect and veneration for you, my beloved in heaven.'

She also wanted all John's money for herself on earth. She turned to Harold Rubinstein for help. He passed the case over to his partner and brother Stanley. Perhaps he felt he had witnessed too much. He had drawn up the original will in 1938. He knew how protective John was of Evguenia, her concern that she should always be provided for, her desire to adopt her, her anxiety for her naturalization. He must have known that morally Evguenia had a case. But Una, not Evguenia, was his client. He advised her to prepare a statement giving her version of why John changed her will.

Una drew up a curious document which implied more than it answered. Radclyffe Hall, Una wrote, had for nine years and three months done everything, despite 'grave provocation', to benefit Evguenia Souline 'morally and materially'. But her 'steadfast loyalty' was to Una to whom during her final illness she had said, 'It's entirely for your

sake I'm sticking this, darling; I'm not sticking it for Evguenia of whom
I'm intensely fond, but who is on the very outskirts of my existence ...
I want you, you, you, ... I want only you in all the world.'

Some thirty years later, long after the principal players in the drama
were dead, Una's literary executor, Horatio Lovat Dickson, asked
Harold Rubinstein about the earlier will. Rubinstein replied:

> Your letter enquiring about John's earlier Will could have embarrassed
> me if I had not been able to tell you that none of the files relating to these
> matters are now extant, and that my memory is exceedingly tricky ... It
> would be unethical for a solicitor to disclose contents of documents
> prepared for a client, dead or alive.

What Radclyffe Hall had meant or wanted quickly became irrelevant.
What signified was the document she signed in her sloping regressive
hand seven days before she died.

Evguenia's attempts to challenge the will on the grounds of 'undue
influence' came to nothing. Una, she was told, could give her as little
or as much as she liked. Evguenia would have been hard put to find a
lawyer to help her with a palimony suit. *The Well of Loneliness* was
still banned as obscene because of its lesbian theme. In 1940 and 1941
convictions had been obtained against booksellers who stocked it. To
be lesbian was to be obscene according to the government and the
judiciary. Joynson-Hicks and his repressive regime left women like
Evguenia stigmatized and unprotected by the law.

Her position was invidious. She was not litigious, she had no money
and she was stateless. She did not want to harm Radclyffe Hall's
reputation or for that matter her own. Reticent about having had a
lesbian relationship, she thought it in some sense wrong. Dr Armando
Child informed Evguenia's solicitor that in his opinion Radclyffe Hall
was rational when she changed her will. Armando Child and Una were
on good terms. She paid his bills, bought him dinner, gave him an
emerald tie pin of John's. He gave her a letter for the priest asking that
for health reasons she be allowed breakfast before early morning mass.

Stanley Rubinstein advised Una not to write to Evguenia, entertain
her, give her presents or have anything to do with her. 'I would only be
misunderstood and I should expose myself to its being said either that
I feared her or that I was "fond of her" & I have no doubt of what he
meant by that latter implication!'

Through Rubinstein Una arranged a seven-year covenant to pay Evguenia £100 a year. This, Evguenia was told, might be renewed but only if Una wished to do so or felt she could afford it. At Christmas, also via Rubinstein, Una sent her £1 and a 'little non committal note' on a card of Millais' *Christ in the Carpenter's Shop*. For John's sake, she said she 'must try to help the poor demented creature'.

Una rejoiced in the revised terms of her relationship with John. With her death 'the focus changed completely'. In life she had controlled her career, now she planned to control her legend. Evguenia of course had the bombshell of her letters. She owned them but copyright over publication rested with Una. Una intended to use money as a lever 'to make Evguenia remain quiet and behave herself'.

Una, in posthumous possession, adopted the appearance of the woman through whom she had for so long lived. She wore John's clothes. She had her jodhpurs and cavalry cord breeches altered to fit. 'I wear your poplin shirts and ties, your stockings, your shoes, your Jaeger dressing gown, your cardigans, your berets.' For everyday she wore John's grey tweeds, for best her blue tweeds altered by Aquascutum, her blue poplin shirt, her blue Ugolini tie, her cufflinks, her emerald and diamond tie pin, her key chain. Like John she developed a callous on her finger from wielding a pen. Like her she kept everything exceedingly tidy. In bed she covered herself with the patchwork blankets John had knitted and sewn.

At Communion the priest put either two wafers or one very thick one on Una's tongue. She took it as 'a sign of grace'. 'It was the story of the two palms over again.' Visiting Highgate Cemetery, she noticed with approval that the floor of the catacomb was clean, the altar crucifix and candlesticks dusted, the ceiling blue. But a bunch of immortelles had been laid on the altar at the foot of the crucifix and a holly wreath left there with 'an absurd card'. Una threw it all out and told the porter that no one was to have the key to the vault and no offerings but hers were to be allowed. Her marriage was inviolable now.

Nor were flowers to be laid any more on anniversaries of Mabel Batten's death. Ladye's grave was, Una thought, 'merely a necessary repository and had nothing emotionally to do with either of us'. If in life John's affections had been equivocal in death she belonged to Una:

nothing ever for a moment succeeded in dividing us from one another,
nothing ever was able to come between us even in the flesh and how much

more so is that true now that there is only my negligible flesh in the way
and how gloriously more so when as the angels we shall be free of all
flesh & know ourselves into one for ever.

Fusion through love and sex might have eluded Una but she would
achieve it through death. Death was her element. Life's temptations
and griefs were beyond Radclyffe Hall's reach. 'Thank God you are
safe, safe, safe,' Una wrote of her, 'nothing can hurt you, neither
rumbling doodlebugs, nor unseen & unheard terrors from the strato-
sphere, you cannot be killed or much worse maimed or blinded, so I
can't fear for you, and you, now knowing *all* of God's will & purpose
can't fear or grieve for me.'

It was the ultimate release from responsibility. The words of William
Penn held resonance for her: 'They that love beyond the world cannot be separated by it. Death cannot kill what never dies.' Una had
great recompense – worldly wealth and the sanctuary of heaven.
Off she went to lunch at Pruniers with Andrea – oysters and scram-
bled eggs, but the oysters were tasteless so she complained to the
manager.

Maria Visetti, who was ninety-one, heard of the death of her daughter
when a resident at the Viennese Hotel in Hove, where she now resided,
asked her if she had seen the *Telegraph*. 'She showed me the Deaths
and wondered if it was a relation of mine, of course when I saw
"author" I knew. I told the woman I did not think so.' Una had not
told her that John was ill. 'How she dared to show me such disrespect
I cannot think', Mrs Visetti wrote to her niece, Jane Caruth. In an
obituary she saw that Marguerite had suffered for six months with
cancer. 'It has upset me more than I like to think. The Troubridge
woman told me nothing and to the last ignored me.'

Mrs Visetti's anxieties then focused on money. She was appalled that
Una was the sole executor of the will and she herself not named in it.
Decades of bitterness over her divorce settlement and at what she saw
as her daughter's profit at her expense spilled out:

all these years she has been using money which really belonged to me.
This was her last chance to give it back. Marguerite had such power and
from a money point of view treated me so badly. All along the line I was
cheated. It was all wrong. She had not an ounce of my blood in her. She
was Radclyffe through and through, morally and mentally.

Through her solicitor, Mr Woodbridge, Mrs Visetti, like Evguenia, challenged the will. Her doctor, Dr Horsford, phoned Armando Child. He too asked if Radclyffe Hall was *compos mentis* that week before she died. Armando Child again said that in his view she was.

Mrs Visetti then tried 'the human touch'. In December 1944 she wrote to Una regretting negotiations had 'got into the hands of lawyers who only see facts'. She said Marguerite had always promised her £300 a year. Una considered the letter blackmail. She told Rubinstein 'to keep her in order for me'. At Una's instruction John Holroyd-Reece drew up a covenant which Rubinstein sent to Mrs Visetti's lawyer. It granted her £200 a year on condition she gave no interviews about her daughter, said nothing detrimental, provided no publicity and surrendered to Una all biographical material connected with her, all childhood photographs and the portrait by Katinka Amyat of Marguerite aged five with blonde curls.

'If I comply with all this, I may get a hundred or two a year out of £118,500 all left to the Troubridge woman', Mrs Visetti wrote to Jane Caruth.

> When you realize the £2000 a year I gave up to ensure her inheritance, thousands of capital *legally belongs to me*. The Troubridge woman seemed to control Marguerite. What can I do? accept all insults, all unfair pressure and bow my head in gratitude to this woman who has allowed all this evil to be done to me? Pity me and pray that I may be given control not to act in any way aggressively and so lose the assistance to live. My grief, my rage, are both telling on my nerves. I am not well.

For two months Mrs Visetti delayed signing this covenant. Una therefore delayed paying her any money at all. Una assured Dear John that she was doing her utmost to act fairly and justly but she was *not* going to pander to extortion and threats. Mrs Visetti's prevarications, she complained, cost her an extra £36 in tax.

Una intended to write a hagiographical memoir of Radclyffe Hall. Its aim was to eulogize and sanctify both their lives. She did not want Evguenia or Maria Visetti telling the world they had been swindled and deceived. If they made any public utterance, financial penalties would follow.

Una had a psychopath's skill to convince herself of the truth of her lies. She called her book *The Life and Death of Radclyffe Hall*. Death was the lever of her control. Her book was to be *'sincere and truthful'* a record of 'lasting & fulfilling devotion', of perfect lesbian love that nothing could blemish. The world was to learn how Radclyffe Hall's genius had found expression in her literary masterpieces, her 'fight for the persecuted of her own kind' and of course her love for Una.

It took Una a month to write – from 19 February to 18 March 1945. She could not then remember a word she had written. It was, she maintained, the most surprising experience of her whole life. She supposed this was because a higher power was guiding her hand. The way round her problems of vanity, falsification and omission was to abnegate all responsibility. She claimed that Radclyffe Hall authored it and that she was only the amanuensis, the guided hand. *'Truly your mantle descended upon me! ... quite suddenly I suppose you began to write it and it fell into its place. Not an account that would satisfy Evguenia's illusions about herself for that is impossible.'* Radclyffe Hall, Una said in a foreword, 'always dwelt of choice in the palace of truth where I dwelt with her, and I have decided, so far as in me lies, to tell the truth, the whole truth and nothing but the truth.'

She used the courtroom oath and let slip a telling pun. She wrote of Radclyffe Hall's unhappy, bullied childhood, her mother's 'lunatic rages' and brutality and of how despite 'such cruelly uncongenial soil' she grew up to have a profound personality and be a great artist. Enduring love of Una was the guiding light of her life. Evguenia tried to intrude into their love and blemish their lives. Radclyffe Hall yielded against her better judgement to conciliate her. She showed 'marvellous patience and charity' and through all the stress and anguish never stopped loving Una with 'indestructible devotion'.

Una read again John's

> darling little notes of love & missing me when you were away with Evguenia for only a few days. How desperately hard you tried, even under the stress of an intense attraction & infatuation not to hurt me, to spare me all you could, how *faithful* you really were to me even in the first flare of your surface infidelity; how your generous, pitiful, loyal nature kept you so good, so deeply devoted & loving all through.

'Evguenia', she said, 'will never in this world be able to wash out the fact that you treated her well, and she treated you badly and she may think herself fortunate that she and the record are in my merciful hands.'

Una was well pleased with her book. She called it a monument and thought it conveyed Radclyffe Hall's creative genius, simplicity, humility, piety, courage and passion. She trusted she had not appeared 'spiteful or unjust' to Evguenia. (She described her as 'violent and uncontrolled as a savage ... a bucking bronco, headstrong, wild and inconsistent, with alternating moods of incoherent rage, of abysmal gloom and crazy optimism'). She figured that Evguenia had 'got all the advantages of the situation' and continued to do so, so must 'take the implications and be courageous about it'.

Una wanted her memoir published so that 'honour be done to John'. She showed the manuscript to Horatio Lovat Dickson, a director with the publishing house of Macmillan, and to Harold Rubinstein. Lovat Dickson thought it 'beautifully written' but not documented or substantial enough. 'I think such solemn documented biographies are seldom readable and seldom read', Una said. Lovat Dickson asked a reader at Macmillan to give an appraisal.

The reader damned the book. Lovat Dickson showed the report to Una. It made her tremble and feel sick. It called her work sketchy and no more than notes for a book. It said there was not enough about the trial of The Well of Loneliness, Radclyffe Hall's lesbianism or Evguenia and the sexual triangle. Most cutting of all, it said Una's eulogizing accorded Radclyffe Hall an unjustified literary eminence.

Harold Rubinstein, whom Una called 'the most Christian of Jews', wrote a 'paean of praise' after reading the manuscript but said that it libelled Evguenia. Una would either have to omit all references to her or contrive to get her consent. He advised her to put the manuscript aside while Evguenia was alive. Una wondered whether to withhold Evguenia's allowance unless she agreed to publication.

Lovat Dickson told her that the right biographer would be found. He suggested A. L. Rowse. Una bought a volume of his poems wanting 'to judge of his mind by the quality of his verse'. The idea was not pursued. She asked Lovat Dickson to write it himself and offered to give him all her papers. He said he was too busy to consider it for some years. Una accepted this as Radclyffe Hall's and Saint Thomas's will.

In February 1945 Mrs Visetti had a stroke. She was ninety-four. Dr Horsford asked Una for £14 for a radio for her as she was bedridden, and for £50 to pay his fees. 'The answer of course is in the negative. It is only yet another dodge by the wily old devil to get extra money.'

The following month Una heard from Harold Rubinstein that the wily old devil was dying. Dr Horsford again asked if Una would give financial help to cover nursing and chemist's bills:

> I certainly don't give Mrs Horsford or her offensive husband or anyone a vague permission to spend my money (yours) as they may choose. If they let me know definitely of something she needs I will consider it. If I send money vaguely it will probably be spent on some foolishness & I ain't doing it. I know they have something in hand and £16 goes to her bank in ten days time anyway.

Mrs Visetti died three weeks later on 14 April. 'I have done for your mother exactly what you did yourself,' Una wrote in a Letter to John, 'and left her in the circumstances she chose and preferred and that is that.' Mrs Visetti was, Una said, 'crudely and terribly unworthy of having given birth to Radclyffe Hall'. She supposed that mother and daughter would not meet again because not even God in His infinite mercy would put them on the same plane.

The notice of death in *The Times* described Mrs Visetti only as Alberto's widow and made no mention of Radclyffe Hall. She was to be buried at Brookwood Cemetery in the same grave as Alberto. Una was now the freeholder of the grave. She supposed they would have to apply to her to open it. Permission would not be forthcoming until she received the portrait of Radclyffe Hall by Katinka Amyat.

The portrait was sent to her. Una asked Tony Atwood at Smallhythe to paint out the blonde curls so that it looked like 'a little boy's face'. It was one more lie. Thus doctored, she intended to include the picture in *The Life and Death of Radclyffe Hall* when the time came for publication. (The illustrations she chose for her book were only of herself and John. There was none of Mabel Batten or Evguenia. All those of John made her look like a man.)

Mrs Visetti's solicitors then sent a letter asking Una to pay what was owing on her estate for funeral expenses and doctors' fees – nearly £300 – or to return the Amyat portrait. Una thumbed her nose. Mrs Visetti's debts were nothing to do with her. Surrender of the portrait was a condition of the covenant she had made when granting her an income.

Una let slip in her diary that John had wanted Evguenia to have an annuity 'on a larger scale than I intend'. For a while Evguenia worked as a translator with Reuters. Una wanted to know her salary and all expenses. When Evguenia lost the job Una saw it as a ruse to wheedle money. Evguenia, she said, was determined not to take and keep a routine job with decent hours. She pointed out to her how hard Andrea worked and told her it cost a great deal in tax to give her any allowance. Through a solicitor Evguenia forwarded bills from doctors and dentists. Una accused her of crooked accounting. 'I will not have her getting away with deliberate dishonesty in addition to her chronic moral dishonesty.' She also accused her of keeping £25 John had loaned her in case of emergencies. She called on her without warning, found her living in one 'very very dilapidated room' and thought it significant that there were no photographs of John in sight.

Evguenia was desolate when at the war's end she was refused a resident's visa for Paris. All her furniture was in store there and she could not afford to pay to get it to England. Her 'nest egg' of savings – some thousands of pounds – had been taken by the Gestapo. In her Letters to John, Una wrote, 'That is a result of her putting it in a bank there on her own instead of telling you all about it and letting you bank it safely.'

Evguenia grew tired of the hoops she had to jump through to get a pittance wage from Una, the way Una cavilled at everything she did, her vitriol and accusations. She wrote to her that none of it was worth the trouble. She got a job as a nurse with the United States Army in Germany. Before she left London, she met Una and had a showdown. She asked for a month's allowance in advance to help with moving country. Una refused. Evguenia accused her of cheating, of not keeping to the spirit of John's will and of exerting influence over John when she was dying.

'I hung on to my temper like grim death,' Una wrote, 'resisting an almost irresistible impulse to tell her to get out. I told her that it was entirely on my own initiative that I paid her any allowance, that I had no legal obligation of any kind, that she must reflect on this and not make me feel that it was impossible for me to go on helping her.'

Evguenia left without giving Una an address. The £100 a year covenant was paid into her bank. Una asked the Information Bureau at Selfridges what a foreign nurse employed by the United States Army would earn. She was relieved that she had gone and hoped she had seen the last of her. She found that the best way to deal with her was not to think of her at all. She longed for Italy, cried when the Duce was murdered and turned off the news so as not to hear eyewitness accounts of conditions at Buchenwald concentration camp.

And then in July 1946 Evguenia sent her a letter saying she was married. Vladimir Makaroff, her husband, was a Russian emigré, a former cavalry officer. She had met him in Paris where he worked for the Russian Red Cross. 'It was all settled in a moment', she said. She had been in France once in September 1945 for two days and then for four days in June 1946. He was thin, not tall, and about fifty-five. He had lived for twenty years in Czechoslovakia but moved to France during the war.

Evguenia had not realized that she needed written authority from the United States Army to marry and so she had been court-martialled. She was going to bring Vladimir to England where at least 'thanks to Johnnie' she had resident alien status. Her husband hoped to find work but it would not be easy because he spoke no English at all.

'God knows what she has picked up', was Una's reaction. She supposed he was a 'worthless dud'. But the main thing was that Evguenia was his responsibility now. Una resolved to stop paying her the £24 a year fuel allowance, any medical bills or insurances. 'This marriage closes the account except for the £100 a year as a purely grace offering', she wrote. John, she reasoned, would have withheld even that given Evguenia's behaviour since her death.

If it was martyrdom Radclyffe Hall sought, she had it now. Her work had been destroyed, her lover whom she had so wanted to protect was punished and the apostle in whom she had placed her absolute trust had betrayed her for thirty pieces of silver and more.

39

He is my occupation

At the war's end Una's thoughts turned to Italy '& a Christian climate, not this land of swamps and rain and wind and ice'. She figured that every self-respecting bird got out of England for most of the year and so, therefore, would she. People, for which as a species she had never felt warmth, all were fatally flawed. She thought them base and did not court their affection:

> I can't remember a time when every kind of thing wasn't said of me. I ill-treated my step-children, I behaved disgracefully to my husband, and of course, since the publication of *The Well* I have been notorious & always shall be & no doubt when Evguenia came on the scene they all screamed with delight & hoped that it meant shipwreck for me & you and everyone, only it didn't!

She wanted Italy 'where no one talked at all'. After Radclyffe Hall's death she lodged for a time with John Holroyd-Reece in his house off Chancery Lane. But she suspected him of being after her money and his house got bombed, so she went to stay with Etheline Cripps, who had been Teddie Gerrard's lover in those far-off twenties days. Then for some months she was a guest with the Smallhythe trio in Rye. None of it was right. John Holroyd-Reece was 'brutally unfaithful' to his dying wife Jehanne. Etheline's brother Roy was intolerable and offensive. When Mrs Urquhart came to lunch wearing fashionable clothes

Roy said of her that she was a *real* woman, 'not a damned half and half'. Una, in flannel shirt, John's breeches, collar and tie, went to her room saying 'Damn and blast your soul to hell'. Your brother, she told Etheline, is an insolent swine.

Viola she called a spiteful bore, 'a hard woman and no kin to us in any way'. Viola asked if Andrea knew she would never inherit Radclyffe Hall's money and was this punishment for some misdemeanour. Una thought it no business of hers.

Visiting Minna, Una perceived her as 'a ghastly wreck, partially toothless, terribly emaciated, her speech almost unintelligible, dressed in a short sleeved low necked nightgown that increases the horror ... As usual she begged to know if I loved her and of course I took her in my arms and assured her I did.'

Audrey Heath was now a 'poor little ailing mouse' who meandered in her speech, had walked into a lamppost in the blackout and was taken to hospital unconscious. Olive Rinder had 'sparse, grey hair, yellowed by repeated curling' and 'washed-out, frightened eyes'. Cara Harris, Mabel Batten's daughter, wrote saying she had been very ill and asking for photographs of her mother. 'I will not let her have anything of Ladye's', was Una's response. 'She looked madder than ever with her dyed yellow hair when I saw her recently ... I can't risk resuming relations with her.'

Toupie Lowther invited Una to stay. Toupie, Una said, was drunk, lonely and dying of tuberculosis. At night she railed at God from her bedroom window for taking her wife Fabienne Lafargue De-Avilla from her. Fabienne was 'tough, promiscuous, cruel' and living with her 'amant de coeur', Liza, in a nearby cottage owned by Toupie. They were waiting for Toupie to die, so as to scoop her inheritance, Una wrote in Letters to John. 'They *want* me, lonely and without your protection and with the money you left me.' She was not going near. Toupie died on 30 December 1944. Fabienne then married and Liza 'made a terrible fuss'. Una expressed 'less than no sympathy' for them all.

Before leaving England for what she knew would be for good, Una tried in June 1946 to get published a 'Collected Memorial Edition' of the works of Radclyffe Hall. She hoped it would include *The Well of Loneliness*. The book had sold steadily in America and other countries for eighteen years without confounding the institution of marriage or depraving the young.

Peter Davies, director of the Windmill Press, thought the post war Labour administration might oppose the suppression of literature and lift the ban. Una wrote to the Home Secretary James Chuter Ede. Davies wrote to a friend, Sir Oscar Dowson, who was legal adviser to the Home Office. Davies asked what would happen if, as requested by Lady Troubridge, he published the book. Unknown to Una, he added a postscript, typical of the awkwardness the book provoked in publishers: 'I am not really anxious to do *The Well of Loneliness* and am rather relieved than otherwise by any lack of enthusiasm I may encounter in official circles.'

Sir Oscar passed this letter to the Home Secretary. Chuter Ede sought advice. He wanted to know 'the desirability or otherwise' of publishing *The Well of Loneliness*, the technical and legal issues this raised, how and by whom a prosecution could be instituted, whether by the Director of Public Prosecutions, the police, or a 'common informer' and what his own powers in the matter were. He wondered if more harm than good might be done by continuing to suppress the book though he had, he said, 'the impression that the perversion which it is supposed to celebrate is more widespread than is commonly thought'.

His advisor was a senior civil servant, Mr F. H. Logan, in the Dangerous Drugs Branch. Banned books and banned substances perhaps came into the same category. ('I would rather give a healthy boy or a healthy girl a phial of prussic acid than this novel', James Douglas had written. 'Poison kills the body, but moral poison kills the soul.')

Mr Logan's advice to the Secretary of State was unequivocal:

From the Home Office point of view it would be most undesirable to have the question reopened. The 1928 proceedings provide a fixed point in regard to one aspect of sexual morality in a field where it is peculiarly difficult to establish any satisfactory standards. If it were to be thought that the authorities are now inclined to take a more lenient view of *The Well of Loneliness*, it might well lead other and less scrupulous writers than Miss Radclyffe Hall to make use of the same theme with results that could scarcely fail to be embarrassing to all concerned with the administration of this branch of the law.

It seems to be very desirable therefore that Lady Troubridge should be discouraged from including *The Well of Loneliness* in the proposed edition of Miss Radclyffe Hall's works.

And discouraged she was. Chuter Ede wrote to her that any publisher reprinting *The Well of Loneliness* would 'do so at the risk of proceedings'. The views of a supposedly reforming, egalitarian government were enforced. Lesbianism was obscene. It was a widespread perversion. To write about it was embarrassing. Silence was required.

Una returned to Florence on 16 November 1946. Initially she found herself disorientated and diffident. 'Oh it *is* painful my sweet & sad, sad, *sad* to be alone here', she wrote in a Letter to John. But she was excited too and knew she would 'soon slip into it all'. She was in robust health and had enough acquaintances for life to be social in an undemanding way: May Massola, Maria Corsini, Fonfi Piccone. Romaine invited her to her Villa Gaia high up in Fiesole with views over Florence. She fed her on roast pheasant, baked apples and cream and 'nasty sweet white wine'. Sandra Tealdi told her about the 'black lire' which gave her £2 for every £1 she cashed. 'It is of course pleasant', Una told the ghost of John. Funds were 'prosperous'. Stanley Rubinstein cheered her by telling her she would pay practically no income tax or surtax for the next ten years. Her pension from Troubridge increased. She bought stocks with surplus investment income. 'Minna's money when it comes will be in Trustee stocks.' Six months' royalties on American sales of *The Well of Loneliness* in 1946 totalled £353 for 5,300 copies – three and a half times Evguenia's annual allowance.

Una was appalled by the war damage to Florence, the bombed bridges, the destroyed houses of the Borgo San Jacopo and by photographs in *Life* magazine of the Duce, dead and hung upside down by 'the Communists'. But the shops were full of produce. She was amazed at the variety of food compared to England: chicken, guinea fowl, fresh vegetables, cakes made with real cream, marrons glacés. She found a flat opposite San Jacopo sopr'Arno with 'the church shining in the moonlight opposite'. A daily communicant at the churches of San Spirito or San Felice, she disliked not being first 'in case the priest's fingers are wet from other lips'.

She retrieved the belongings she and John had abandoned in 1939: linen, furniture, silver, pictures and clothes. There were seals of sequestration on the rooms where it all was stored. For an entire morning she destroyed more of John's papers. Dressed in John's silk coat and diamond and onyx cufflinks she indulged again her passion for opera. She went to *Lohengrin*, *The Pearl Fishers* and *La Bohème*.

Minna, her mother, died in January 1947. Una did not return for the funeral. Nor would she let Andrea's second husband, Brigadier Turnbull, act as co-trustee of the estate as Harold Rubinstein suggested. 'If only she didn't give everything before marriage', Una said of Andrea and thought both she and this new husband drank too much.

The sight of Evguenia's handwriting on an envelope always gave her a thud of anxiety. She dreaded she might come to Florence: 'I simply can't face up to her coming here and either telling our friends that you promised to leave her money in equal shares with me & then didn't do it, or that I am not carrying out your wishes & all the rest of her poor crazy imaginings. From Jack and Marjorie Hancock at the Wayside, she heard that Evguenia had taken her husband to Lynton. They had stayed with Mrs Widden and slept in separate rooms. Una gathered that he was 'a queer looking man, like a navvy.' She called him 'just a boneless Slav, who would never make a prosperous way for her or himself'.

Vladimir found a factory job 'packing food parcels'. Evguenia hoped when his English improved he would get something better. In 1948 she worked as a newsreader with the BBC World Service. It had always been her desire to have a home of her own. She had resented being an appendage of John's life with Una. She leased a house in north London at 33 Lynton Road, Kilburn and let out rooms in the hope of realizing a rental income. But her boarders were Russian refugees and students with no money. The house needed extensive repairs; the bathroom ceiling was falling down and the front path needed laying. She asked Una for £60. 'I am not rising to the bait. She has her salary, her husband is in a job, she has boarders and she has my allowance. I leave her to it for the present. Luckily I am keeping her allowance on the lower scale. I have sent her £15. I am not a perpetual running fountain of cash. The next costly request will have to be refused *in toto*.' Evguenia could not maintain the house and after two years sold the lease for no more than she paid for it.

In January 1949 Una moved to a smart flat at Palazzo Guicciardini. She put Radclyffe Hall's name on the front door as well as her own. She bought antiques, had the floors polished and bells installed in all the rooms to summon her maid, Primetta. She adorned the walls with devotional paintings and was adamant that a Madonna and Child she had acquired was by Botticelli. It and Buchel's portrait of John were floodlit. She filled the rooms with jonquils, freesias and pink blossom in marble vases, and gave her visitors fine wines and lobster for lunch, the table laid with Sienese linen, wrought-iron candleholders and gleaming silver. Primetta wore a uniform and served at table.

In her vast salone, lying on damask cushions on the sofa and wearing John's Jaeger dressing gown, Una listened to *Parsifal* on her 'mammoth' radio. 'How Wagner *does* iron one out flat', she said. She heard *Manon Lescaut* and *Otello* broadcast live from La Scala and played opera records and Paul Robeson singing *The Blind Ploughman*. 'I am deeply grateful to the survival of my love of opera which gives me now the only emotional pleasure I know.' She slept well and put on weight with Primetta's home-made pasta. She enjoyed home cooking after 'years of too much restaurant seasoning' and developed a taste for whisky, fine wines and cocktails. Her hair was now cut as short as John's. 'Once a fortnight now is my rule.' A barber called, but she insisted he use her scissors, clippers, brush and comb.

She went often to the cinema and translated *Don Camillo* for Gollancz, and Colette's *Maison de Claudine*. Young gay men, Newell and Merf and Dick and Marshall, befriended her. Together they went to operas and concerts with Una dressed in John's black pinstripe suit and black bow tie. They called to listen to the music channel on her special radio, went to antique auctions with her and gave lavish dinners of sole with spinach, stuffed pigeon and angel cake soaked in rum.

Evguenia did not reconcile herself to the discrepancy between John's promises and the way Una treated her. In letters to her, year after year, she returned to the injustice. After John's death she found it hard to do better than get by. Because of her marriage she did not achieve naturalization, or hold a British passport, or merit a state pension. In April 1950 she asked Una to invest £3,000 to provide her with a pensionable income when she was sixty. 'I beg of you to help me in the name of this Holy Year, in the name of all that is sacred to you, in the name of your friendship with John, who seemed to be so fond of me when she was alive.'

Una sent her £5, told her she was not yet fifty, had a husband and a job and that she, Una, was doing exactly what John had considered adequate. If she could afford it she would go on sending her £100 a year for the next seven years, but this was simply out of generosity. 'She can't be trusted,' Una wrote in a Letter to John. 'If she were certain of a guarantee for the future she is free of the only curb possible upon her venomous tongue and there is no limit to what she is capable of saying or doing ... so long as she is uncertain of my payments or ultimate intentions, there is *some* measure of wholesome restraint.' Una worried about Evguenia's simmering resentment and what she might say publicly about promises made. She wondered whether to tell her that if she found her 'failing in loyalty' to Radclyffe Hall, no further money would be forthcoming.

On 29 July 1950 Evguenia, in a detailed and passionate letter, reminded Una that John on her deathbed had said she wished 'us *both* to be *comfortably* off if not living in luxury'. She accused Una of disregarding both John's inordinate attachment to her and her promise to provide for her after her death. 'How often she used to say to me: "Evguenia, you can put your Piggie hands in your pig-pockets and whistle, your future is well taken care of." '

John had insisted that she could not live without her and had told her again and again she was sure they were related. She, Evguenia, had for nine years struggled to make a life for herself but John 'made me take part in your life, even while I was trying to get away in order to work & to be independent'. And now life with her husband was far from harmonious. They got on each other's nerves in one small room with no privacy or comforts. She had to provide for him. He could only find menial work because his English was so bad. He had worked in Walls's Sausage factory and then on night shifts packing Peak Frean's Biscuits. It was not like being with John, who had spoiled her immensely. John, she said, were she alive, would come to her rescue. She asked Una to help her buy a house.

'My dear Evguenia', Una replied:

> I shall not attempt to deal with the entirely fictitious and imaginary deathbed scene which you have evolved, or with your enumeration of promises that John never made. You have doubtless brooded over this matter until you can no longer distinguish the false from the true. But as regards your renewed request that I should enable you with use of my capital to buy a house and launch a boarding establishment...

John, she said, would not had she lived have continued helping Evguenia. Evguenia's atrocious behaviour and ingratitude would have precluded such help. But she, Una, would probably go on giving her £100 a year and Evguenia should count herself lucky.

Evguenia remained resentful at how different life would have been had she received her inheritance. She repeatedly tried to winkle out of Una some of what she felt was due. The prospect of Una's derision and high moral tone did not deter her. In 1951 she asked her to help pay off an overdraft of £475 she had incurred to buy a house at 35 Russell Road W14. To deflect trouble, Una wrote to Evguenia's bank manager and paid £300 of the debt. She told him she had no legal obligation to Mrs Makaroff and that this payment did not mean she should be regarded as a guarantor. She wrote one of her cutting letters to Evguenia telling her not to apply to her for payments of debts that were not her concern.

Evguenia's affairs and even thoughts of Radclyffe Hall were now of distant interest to Una. She had become absorbed in the life of an opera singer, Nicola Rossi-Lemeni. 'To hear him is one of the greatest pleasures I can have.' His, she said, was 'the greatest voice of the age, greater than Chaliapin'.

She met his wife Vittoria Serafin on Sunday 25 March 1951 at a cocktail party she had gone to with her gay men friends. It was given by an American music agent, Rock Ferris. Una had arranged to go to Milan at Easter to hear *Parsifal* at La Scala and Vittoria and Rossi-Lemeni would be there too. Vittoria said she would take Una to her husband's rehearsals of *Lucrezia Borgia*. 'It looks as if I should make my way a bit into the *coulisses* of La Scala,' Una wrote in Letters to John, '& meet some of the singers, which will be as interesting as anything can be to me nowadays.'

She stayed in the same hotel as the Rossi-Lemenis, the Regina, and sent them a note inviting them to dinner at Giovannino's restaurant. She went to his rehearsals, he gave her two of his records, they lunched together and he asked her to help with the translation into Italian of *Emperor Jones* in which he was to play the lead in Rome the following January. Una was flattered. 'I am having a small but real part in a production of great interest.'

She stayed on in Milan weeks longer than she had intended, worked at the translation and helped choose his press photographs. At the first night of his *Lucrezia Borgia*, she shared a box with Vittoria and had supper with them both after the performance. She acquired all his records, read his poems and went to seven operas at La Scala but paid for only two. By the time she returned to Florence, it was agreed she would help with his next production too.

Bit by bit she immersed into his world. At Bologna she heard him singing Mefistofele and stayed at the Baglioni Hotel with him and Vittoria. She dealt with his fan mail, helped him with publicity and followed him to opera houses in Ravenna, Rome, Milan, Genova, London. She heard him sing Don Giovanni, Boris Godunov, Bloch's Macbeth. She wrote of his peerless art and said she listened to him singing 'with her very soul skinned'.

She became his *confidante* over his emotional problems with his Russian mother Xenia Makedon and with Vittoria, whom he was to divorce. 'It is a blessed thing that he wants and depends on me', Una wrote in Letters to John. 'He loves me more than his mother.' She called him Nika and was part mother and part flirt. She viewed herself as the stable influence in his life. 'Nika could not do without me, would never be able to do without me.' She gave him John's cufflinks of cabochon sapphires, went to cowboy films with him, went to rehearsals, told him he was always right. He gave her a gold and coral charm of a hand. He became her point of fixation and worship. She sat with him until he slept, spoiled him, slavishly served him, rubbed his feet and massaged his head and back with an electric vibrator:

> When we were alone in the two big armchairs he suddenly thrust his feet into my lap & when I smiled and rubbed them and kissed one of them, he did a lovely thing. He showed me his heart with both hands & threw it to me three times then said, 'Ma tu sai che lo faccio solo per scherzo [but you know I am only joking].'

Like opera, like the ceremonies of the church, her devotions were performance, ritual and display. Una was in service again on terms singular to herself.

In March 1952 Evguenia lost her job at the BBC. She asked Una to increase her allowance to £250 a year. What about income from boarders, Una wanted to know. She declined the request and wrote a letter of reproof at Evguenia's less than grateful response to her Christmas present of £5.

Una liked to buy Nika costumes for his operatic roles: silk shirts for Boris Godunov, a crown that she said looked as if it was from Cartiers, an orb, a cloth of gold with mock sapphires, emeralds, diamonds and pearls. 'He looks so beautiful in it all. There is no doubt that Nika transfigures on the stage as Nijinsky did and becomes from a fine-looking young man inclined to be fat, something so beautiful that one is spellbound.'

In 1956 he married Virginia Zeani. She was Cleopatra and he the title role in Handel's *Julius Caesar* at La Scala. Una absorbed into their family and was godmother to their child. 'Nika asked me what I did with my life when he was away and I told him generally – of reading & seeing Florentine friends – but he does realise that *he* is my occupation and I can feel is glad of it.'

'She lived my life,' Rossi-Lemeni said of her. Only Evguenia intruded on this transference of devotion. In October 1956 a letter came from her saying she had cancer. A colostomy had been performed. She could not hope fully to recover. She would welcome financial help from Una for medical and living expenses.

'There is the usual appeal to sentiment', Una wrote in what she still called Letters to John. 'Of course she may die "and go straight to dear Johnnie". After nine years of abominable cruelty she left you even when you were in extremis and came to me directly after your death to see what she could get.' Una said she would 'detest' going to England about this matter. She wrote to Armando Child and asked him to obtain a full medical report from Evguenia's surgeon and doctor. She wanted to know her health prospects, what state assistance she could get and what her husband earned.

> Her decision that she will be an invalid or a semi invalid for the rest of her life requires investigation, as she would be the last to inform me of any total recovery. If, as I hope and suspect, a very small tumour has been removed with assistance of a temporary colostomy she may recover entirely and never look back. I pray God and Our Lady it may be so for my sake as well as hers.

Armando Child wrote back that Evguenia's colostomy was permanent and that she could not be expected to work. Una gave her what she called 'the unemployment allowance' of £250 a year. This was £74 a year less than John's basic allowance of twenty years previously.

On 9 January 1957 Una wrote to Stanley Rubinstein. She asked him to ascertain Evguenia's state benefit entitlements. Ten days later she loaned Nicola Rossi-Lemeni three million lire (£1,800) for the down payment on an apartment in Rome in the Piazza di Novella. Una took an adjacent apartment for she now did not countenance life apart from him. Nika would pay her back as he could afford to, or as she wanted him to. 'After all, the money lies idle anyway', she wrote in her Letter to John. She made a codicil to her will leaving her effects to him though not her capital (that was to go to the Sisters of the Poor Clares in Lynton). She left her burial arrangements to him and was 'pleased that he wants me near him after death'. Ladye, John, Our Three Selves and the Highgate catacomb were all forgotten now.

In the summer Evguenia became ill again. She was seen, she wrote to Una, by 'a young and bumptious internee' who told her there was nothing wrong with her. She then went to a private physician and asked Una to pay his bill. Una wrote one of her startling letters of refusal. Evguenia replied to it on 8 July:

> Please forgive me for having 'sprung' on you as you say in your letter these additional expenses but I was always under the impression that John wanted me to turn to you if I were in distress especially if I were ill. Had she been alive she would have done everything to alleviate my pain. Please forgive me and forget I have asked for help. I shall pay my physician somehow.

Una might persist with her Letters to John. Evguenia had kept every one of her Letters from John. Wronged by Una one time too many, she now wanted these published. They were her side of the story. Though mortally ill she began to type them out. To do so made her 'terribly sad'. It was, she said, 'a torment, a gruesome task, to relive those past years again'.

On 6 September 1957 Una received a letter from a lawyer representing Vladimir Makaroff. He understood Radclyffe Hall had made provision for Evguenia in her will. Evguenia was now critically ill and required medical treatment, convalescence and nursing care. Una saw the letter as attempted blackmail. She passed it to Stanley Rubinstein and stopped all correspondence and all contact with her. 'I am willing to make her presents of money but *not* to recognise any obligation', she wrote to John. 'She *must* have recourse to National Health which I feel she is determined not to do. Also one doctor said she was being hysterical and we know she can be.'

A month later another letter came from Stanley Rubinstein. Makaroff had called to see him with a copy of Radclyffe Hall's will and some of the letters Evguenia was now typing for posterity. He told Rubinstein that Evguenia was very sick, needed care and believed Una had not observed the spirit of Radclyffe Hall's will. The letters spoke most clearly of Radclyffe Hall's 'wishes for the welfare of the said Evguenie Souline'. They made promises of inheritance and declarations of love. One of those he showed Rubinstein was written when John was in Sirmione and Evguenia in Paris in 1934. It was the start of the nine years:

> I think that being deeply in love is the greatest pain & the greatest joy. I have no real life at all except the life I am living through you, and now all that I see I seem to see through you – its difficult to put this into words, I can only say that you're everywhere, that apart from you nothing has any meaning.

'My poor sweet,' Una wrote to the memory of John, 'you sure did *tomber mal* when you conceived an affection for that woman. The only hold I have on her conduct is the ability to reduce or cancel the allowance if she gives trouble.' Rubinstein again repeated that Una had no legal obligation to Evguenia under the terms of John's will. Una paid the £20 a month, maintained her silence, kept her distance, put the matter from her mind and left all dealings to him.

On 25 July 1958 she received a note from Armando Child. He enclosed a cutting from *The Times*. Evguenia had died on 16 July. She is beyond suffering now, Child said. She had died aged fifty-three of carcinoma of the rectum with secondary deposits in her spine and abdomen. Her funeral had been on 21 July with Russian orthodox rites. Her will was a meticulous document of small bequests to her many friends. She was buried in Mill Hill Cemetery. 'I do not feel that I can blame myself where she was concerned', Una wrote. 'For nearly fifteen years I have given her the same as John allowed her. Ever since her illness she has had full "unemployed" allowance even though I sometimes felt it might be interpreted as yielding to threats of scandal.'

By the same post came Una's visa for America. Nika was to sing the role of Archbishop Thomas Becket in Ildebrando Pizzetti's *Murder in the Cathedral* at Carnegie Hall, New York in August. Una was to go with him for a six-week trip. There were itineraries to be checked, aeroplane reservations to be made, rooms to be booked at the Hotel Meurice on 58th Street, interviews, press photographs and recording sessions to be arranged. That afternoon she booked two seats with Pan American then went to the sale-rooms with Nika. They bought blue and gold Bohemian glass, a walnut bookcase, a mahogany couch carved with rams' heads. Una then walked a while in the cool breeze of the Roman evening and took a taxi home.

'I cannot pretend that I feel any sorrow at her death', she wrote that night of Evguenia.

> She has always been disastrous in both our lives. I imagine the husband did not notify me as he hoped to get a couple of extra instalments of the allowance. I have of course written today to stop its payment.
>
> Her death of course clears the way for publication of my book. Strange that having treated you so cruelly throughout your last illness she should herself die in exactly the same manner! Perhaps it was her purgatory?

Or perhaps Una had forgotten what she wrote of herself fifteen years previously after Radclyffe Hall died: 'It would not even be strange to me if *my* flesh took on the stigmata of your suffering and I went to my death by the same road. I should be afraid perhaps but *glad*.' But Evguenia's purgatory, John's Calvary and Una's possession were trials of the past. Una was cast in a different part and served another master now.

BOOKS AND NOTES

Published works by Radclyffe Hall

POETRY

1894 *Reverie and other poems* (untitled and privately printed)
1906 *Twixt Earth and Stars* (Bumpus)
1908 *A Sheaf of Verses* (Bumpus)
1910 *Poems of the Past & Present* (Chapman Hall)
1913 *Songs of Three Counties* (Chapman Hall)
1915 *The Forgotten Island* (Chapman Hall)
1948 *Rhymes and Rhythms. Rime e Ritmi* (Orsa maggiore, Milan)

FICTION

1924 *The Unlit Lamp* (Cassell)
1924 *The Forge* (Arrowsmith)
1925 *A Saturday Life* (Arrowsmith)
1926 *Adam's Breed* (Cassell)
1928 *The Well of Loneliness* (Cape)
1932 *The Master of the House* (Cape)
1934 *Miss Ogilvy Finds Herself* (Heinemann)
1936 *The Sixth Beatitude* (Heinemann)

Unpublished works by Radclyffe Hall (in Texas)

Michael West
Forebears and Infancy
Novel Writing
Why I Write
Lecture notes on the trial of 'The Well of Loneliness'
Miracle of St Ethelflaeda
The Faith of Father Dearing
Woman in a Crêpe Bonnet
The World (fragment)
The Career of Mark Anthony Brakes
The Cunningham Code
Like Cures Like
The Scarecrow
Emblem Hurlstone
The Shoemaker of Merano (fragment. mss destroyed by UVT)

BOOKS

Bagnold, Enid, *Diary Without Dates* (London 1978)

Baker, Michael, *Our Three Selves: A Life of Radclyffe Hall* (Hamish Hamilton 1985)

Barney, Natalie Clifford, *Adventures of the Mind* (New York University Press 1992)

Beach, Sylvia, *Shakespeare & Company* (Faber and Faber 1956)

Belford, Barbara, *Violet: the Irrepressible Violet Hunt* (Simon & Schuster 1990)

Bell, Anne Olivier and McNeillie, Andrew, eds, *The Diary of Virginia Woolf* (Hogarth Press 1977–84)

Blunt, Wilfrid Scawen, *Poetical Works* (London 1914)

——, *My Diaries* (London 1919)

Boyer, Paul S., *Purity in Print: the Vice-Society movement and book censorship in America* (Saunders 1968)

Brittain, Vera, *Radclyffe Hall: A Case of Obscenity?* (Femina Books 1968)

Carpenter, Edward, *The Intermediate Sex* (Allen & Unwin 1908)

Castle, Terry, *Noël Coward and Radclyffe Hall: Kindred Spirits* (Columbia University Press 1996)

Cline, Sally, *Radclyffe Hall: A Woman Called John* (John Murray 1997)

Collis, Rose, *Portraits to the Wall: historic lesbian lives unveiled* (Cassell 1974)

Cook, Walter, *Reflections on 'Raymond'* (London 1917)

Cossart, Michael de, *The Food of Love: Princesse Edmond de Polignac and her salon* (Hamish Hamilton 1978)

Coward, Noël, *Present Indicative* (William Heinemann 1937)

Craig, Alec, *Banned Books of England* (London 1962)

Dickson, Lovat, *Radclyffe Hall at the Well of Loneliness: A Sapphic Chronicle* (Collins 1975)

Douglas, James, *The Unpardonable Sin* (London 1907)

Ellis, Havelock, *Psychology of Sex* (London 1909)

Ernst, Morris L. and Seagle, William, *To the Pure: obscenity and the censor* (New York 1929)

Faderman, Lillian, *Surpassing the Love of Men: Romantic Friendship & Love Between Women from the Renaissance to the Present* (Junction Books 1982)

Field, Andrew, *The Formidable Miss Barnes* (Secker & Warburg 1983)

Fitch, Noel Riley, *Sylvia Beach and the Lost Generation: a history of literary Paris in the twenties and thirties* (Souvenir Press 1984)

Flanner, Janet (Genêt), *Paris Was Yesterday 1925–1939* (Angus & Robertson 1973)

Ford, Ford Madox, *Memories and Impressions* (Harper & Row 1911)

Forster, E. M., *Maurice* (Edward Arnold 1971)

Franks, Claudia Stillman, *Beyond 'The Well of Loneliness': the fiction of Radclyffe Hall* (Avebury 1982)

Friede, Donald, *The Court of Special Sessions: 'The Well of Loneliness'* (New York 1929)

Frye, Jennie Cooper, *A Study in Censorship: Radclyffe Hall's 'The Well of Loneliness'* (mss)

Gallup, Donald, *Pigeons on the Granite: memories of a Yale librarian* (Yale University Library 1988)

Glasgow, Joanne, *Your John* (New York University Press 1997)

Glendinning, Victoria, *Vita* (Weidenfeld & Nicolson 1983)

Grosskurth, Phyllis, *Havelock Ellis* (Knopf 1980)

Hanscombe, Gillian and Smyers, Virginia L., *Writing for their Lives: The Modernist Women 1910–40* (The Women's Press 1987)

Henson, Herbert Hensley, *Retrospect of an Unimportant Life* (Oxford University Press, 1944)

Hirschfeld, Magnus (ed. Norman Haire), *Sexual Anomalies and Perversions* (Encyclopaedic Press 1952)

Hookham, Paul, *'Raymond', a Rejoinder* (London 1917)

Hunt, Violet, *The Flurried Years* (Hurst & Blackett 1926)

Jacob, Naomi, *Me and the Mediterranean* (Hutchinson 1945)

——, *Me – Yesterday and To-day* (Hutchinson 1957)

——, *Me and the Swans* (Kimber 1983)

Jeffreys, Sheila, *The Spinster and Her Enemies: feminism and sexuality 1880–1930* (Pandora 1985)

Kaye-Smith, Sheila, *All the Books of My Life* (Cassell 1956)

Kermode, Frank, *Puzzles and Epiphanies* (Routledge & Kegan Paul 1962)

Krafft-Ebing, Richard von, *Psychopathia Sexualis* (Pioneer Publications 1953)

Lee, Hermione, *Virginia Woolf* (Chatto & Windus 1996)

Lees-Milne, James, *Caves of Ice* (Chatto & Windus 1983)

Leonard, Gladys Osborne, *My Life in Two Worlds* (London 1931)

Liou, Liang-Ya, *The Sexual Politics of Oscar Wilde, Radclyffe Hall, D. H. Lawrence and Virginia Woolf* (University of Texas, PhD dissertation, 1993)

Lodge, Oliver, *Raymond* (London 1916)

Longford, Elizabeth, *The Life of Wilfrid Scawen Blunt* (Weidenfeld & Nicolson 1979)

Lottman, Herbert, *Colette* (Secker & Warburg 1991)

Mannin, Ethel, *Young in the Twenties* (Hutchinson 1971)

McLaughlin, Redmond, *The Escape of the Goeben: Prelude to Gallipoli* (Seeley Service 1974)

Nicolson, Nigel, ed., *Vita and Harold* (Weidenfeld & Nicolson 1992)

Nicolson, Nigel and Trautmann, Joanne, eds, *The Letters of Virginia Woolf* (Hogarth Press 1975–80)

Ormrod, Richard, *Una Troubridge: The Friend of Radclyffe Hall* (Cape 1984)

Salvo, Louise de and Leaska, Mitchell, *The Letters of Vita Sackville-West to Virginia Woolf* (Hutchinson 1984)

Secrest, Meryle, *Between Me and Life: a biography of Romaine Brooks* (Macdonald & Jane's 1976)

Souhami, Diana, *Gertrude and Alice* (Pandora 1991)

Stephenson, P. R. (intr.), *The Sink of Solitude: a verse lampoon by several hands* (Hermes Press 1928)

Troubridge, Laura, *Exit Marriage* (London 1929)

——, *Life Amongst the Troubridges* (John Murray 1966)

Troubridge, Una Lady, *The Life and Death of Radclyffe Hall* (Hammond Hammond 1961)

Weeks, Jeffrey, *Coming Out: Homosexual Politics in Britain from the Nineteenth Century to the Present* (Quartet 1977)

——, *Sex, Politics and Society: The regulation of sexuality since 1800* (Longman 1981)

Weiss, Andrea, *Paris was a Woman: portraits from the Left Bank* (Pandora 1995)

Wickes, George, *The Amazon of Letters: the life and loves of Natalie Barney* (W. H. Allen 1977)

Wilson, Edmund, *The Twenties: from notebooks and diaries of the period* (Farrar, Straus & Giroux 1975)

NOTES

ABBREVIATIONS

Berg:	Berg Collection, New York Public Library
CL:	Cara Lancaster
Cornell:	Cornell University Library
ES:	Evguenia Souline
Ottawa:	The Lovat Dickson bequest. National Archives of Canada, Ottawa
PRO:	Public Records Office, London
RH:	Radclyffe Hall
SPR:	Society for Psychical Research, London
Texas:	Harry Ransom Humanities Research Center, University of Texas
UVT:	Una Vincenzo Troubridge

Una Troubridge's diaries at the time of writing are in three places:

Those from 1913–1931 are in Ottawa (available on microfilm).

Those from 1931–1943 called Daybooks are in Texas.

Those from 1943–1963 called Letters to John are in London but will go to Texas.

Radclyffe Hall's 576 letters to Evguenia Soulina are in Texas (available on microfilm). Many are included in *Your John*, edited by Joanne Glasgow (New York University Press 1997).

Radclyffe Hall's notes on sittings with Gladys Leonard are owned by the Society for Psychical Research and are at the Cambridge University Library.

Mabel Batten's diaries and letters are owned by Cara Lancaster, London.

Government papers relating to the trial of *The Well of Loneliness* in England are in the Public Record Office, London.

Joan Slater in London has an archive of papers relating to Radclyffe Hall.

Private matters

xi	*Even if they add*	author to Departmental Record Officer, The Home Office, 11 December 1998
	in the interests of national security	Home Office Record Management Services to author, 9 February 1998

MARGUERITE

1 The Fifth Commandment

4	*Always my mother*	*Forebears and Infancy*, mss (Texas)
	I pity those	ibid
	A night of	ibid, second draft
6	*They quarrelled*	ibid
7	*My mother had me*	ibid
8	*Without her*	ibid
	an altogether	*Michael West*, mss (Texas)

2 Sing, little silent birdie, sing

11	*It was delicious*	*Michael West*, mss (Texas)
12	*A foolish indefinite*	ibid
13	*She knew that*	ibid
15	*a touch of the 'grand manner'*	Agnes Nicholls Harty, *Mr Albert Visetti* (The Royal College of Music Magazine, vol. 24, no. 3)
	She felt as she	*Michael West*

16	*It was a place to dream*	ibid
	Here then the great	ibid
17	*lest we have*	UVT Letters to John, 30 June 1945
	A faded, shiny	ibid
18	*Sing, little silent*	'The Birth of Spring', from *Poems dedicated to Sir Arthur Sullivan*, by Marguerite, 'Toddles', January 1894
	They did not like	*Michael West*
19	*She knew she was different*	*The Well of Loneliness* (Cape 1928)

3 Come in kid

21	*passionate declarations*	*Michael West*, mss (Texas)
22	*These lessons*	ibid
	And when I did	ibid
	Her music and	ibid
23	*I bobbed like a cork*	ibid
	They were even inclined	ibid
24	*I only feel that I have missed*	*Forebears and Infancy*, mss (Texas)
	There were some things	ibid
25	*pleased, revolted*	*Michael West*, third draft
	I used to watch	ibid

4 The pearl necklace she gave me

28	*the Lord had not*	UVT, *The Life and Death of Radclyffe Hall* (Hammond Hammond 1961)
	Man is vile	Violet Hunt, Diary July 1907 (Cornell)
	Perhaps even now	RH to Violet Hunt, undated, 1907 (Cornell)
29	*She loved me so hotly*	Violet Hunt diary, May 1907 (Cornell)
	I had never seen	*Michael West*, mss (Texas)
	I wondered angrily	ibid
30	*I was tongue tied*	ibid
	Those were carefree	*Forebears and Infancy*, second draft, mss (Texas)
31	*A gondola*	*Twixt Earth and Stars* (Bumpus 1906)
	If you were a Rose	ibid
33	*I was so embarrassingly*	Radclyffe Hall, 'I must have been a tiresome and disconcerting baby', mss (Texas)
	He has found	Mabel Veronica Batten to Cara Harris, August 1906 (CL)

5 Sporks, poggers and poons

35	*I was as wax*	*Michael West*, third draft, mss (Texas)
36	*she accepted homage*	*The Life and Death of RH*
	I do hope that you do not	George Batten to Mabel Veronica Batten, undated 1875 (CL)
37	*He has a perfect mania*	Lady Strachey to Mabel Batten, November 1875 (Strachey papers, India Office Library, London)
38	*Batten is the only*	quoted in Philip Magnus, *King Edward VII* (John Murray 1964)
	I warned him	Wilfrid Scawen Blunt Collection (Fitzwilliam Museum, Cambridge)
40	*Very soon it was born*	*Forebears and Infancy*, mss (Texas)
41	*She used to come and sit*	Violet Hunt diary, August 1907 (Cornell)
	the seeds were sown	*Forebears and Infancy*

JOHN

6 John and Ladye

47	*Never sends a line*	Mabel Batten to Cara Harris, 17 February 1911 (CL)
	I find Jonathan	ibid, 7 February 1911
51	*They seem very happy*	ibid
	How I wish	ibid, 14 February 1911
52	*Sir, Have the Suffragettes*	RH to the *Pall Mall Gazette*, 4 March 1912

7 If I can fix something for Ladye

54	*Johnnie is pink*	MVB to Cara Harris, 8 December 1912 (CL)
	They say he suffers	ibid
56	*Every appointment*	RH to Cara Harris, undated, June 1916 (CL)
57	*Johnnie almost feels*	MVB to Cara Harris, 19 September 1913 (CL)
59	*It leaves Rome far*	RH to Cara Harris, 19 April 1914 (CL)
	Travelling grows	ibid
60	*Once, when I suggested*	ibid, 10 June 1916
	What manner of men	*Malvern Gazette*, 11 September 1914
	Recruiting is	MVB to Cara Harris, 13 September 1914 (CL)

8 Roads with no signposts

63	*compelling, devouring*	*Out of the Night*, mss (Texas)
65	*All eyes are fixed*	*The Modern Miss Thompson*, mss (Texas)
	They always came back	'I must have been a tiresome and disconcerting baby' (Texas)
	But he seemed	*Forebears and Infancy*, mss (Texas)
67	*For very good reasons*	*The Life and Death of RH*
69	*I came to believe*	UVT Letters to John, March 1944
70	*He had no right*	UVT Daybook, 8 February 1931 (Texas)
	The physical never mattered	UVT Letters to John, March 1944
	Having chosen	UVT *Clothes*, unpublished essay (Texas)
	Troubridge brought me	UVT Letters to John, March 1944
	Gradually and infallibly	UVT Daybook, 5 November 1931 (Texas)
71	*It is horribly*	Crichton-Miller to UVT, 23 November 1913 (Ottawa)
73	*He said to me, 'I am a naval officer'*	UVT 'A Thumbnail Sketch of the Rt Hon. Sir Winston Churchill & Admiral Sir Ernest Troubridge, Royal Navy in 1914', unpublished essay (Ottawa)

9 Chenille caterpillars

74	*Una here to breakfast*	MVB Diary, 22 January 1916 (CL)
	All I knew or cared	*The Life and Death of RH*
75	*There are three*	Crichton-Miller to UVT, 21 September 1915 (Ottawa)
76	*I can shut my eyes*	UVT Daybook, 23 August 1938 (Texas)
78	*Felt chilled*	MVB Diary, 26 February 1916 (CL)
80	*I don't understand*	RH to Cara Harris, June 1916 (CL)
	I have tried	ibid
	Her grief	*The Life and Death of RH*

TWONNIE

10 The eternal triangle

85 *I have a great*	RH to Cara Harris, June 1916 (CL)
It was lonely	*The Life and Death of RH*
86 *She is so very*	RH to Cara Harris, June 1916 (CL)
87 *I should think*	Oliver Lodge, *Raymond or Life and Death with Examples of the Evidence for Survival of Memory and Affection After Death* (Methuen 1916)
Great happenings	ibid
The King and Queen	ibid
88 *made from emanations*	ibid
The idle apprentice	*The Life and Death of RH*
89 *I understood then*	Gladys Osborne Leonard, *My Life in Two Worlds* (Cassell 1931)
90 *heaps and heaps*	RH Notes on Leonard sittings, October 1916 (SPR)
92 *Tell my Ladye*	ibid, 3 October 1916
94 *I often wonder*	UVT Diary, July 1917 (Ottawa)

11 A very grave slander

97 *So very interesting*	UVT Diary, 11 January 1917 (Ottawa)
as an educated woman	*The Life and Death of RH*
99 *Their offence to me*	UVT Daybook, 31 March 1931 (Texas)
100 *Mrs Salter now*	RH to Sir Oliver Lodge, 2 July 1918 (SPR)
102 *He could not take the child*	RH Notes on Leonard sittings, 26 March 1919 (SPR)
I think it so damnably	UVT Diary, 17 November 1919 (Ottawa)
103 *It is my misfortune*	Hugh Crichton-Miller to UVT, 15 January 1920 (Ottawa)

12 A grossly immoral woman

105 *Miss Radclyffe Hall*	*The Times*, 19 November 1920
106 *Miss Radclyffe Hall*	ibid
Admiral Troubridge	ibid
107 *as horrible an*	ibid
109 *You say that*	ibid
What did you pay	ibid
112 *I feel I can*	UVT Diary, December 1920 (Ottawa)

RADCLYFFE HALL

13 Octopi

115	*Miss Hall had*	Winifred Hales to Monica Still
	Why in the name	UVT, *Beds*, mss (Ottawa)
116	*Writing, it was like*	*The Well of Loneliness*
	unmarried daughters	*The Unlit Lamp* (Cassell 1924)
117	*They wither away*	undated notes (Texas)
	I'm not a woman	*The Unlit Lamp*
	plenty of work	*The Life and Death of RH*
118	*I wonder why it is*	*The Memoirs of Ethel Smyth*, introduction by Ronald Crichton (Viking 1987)
119	*Olaf went over*	UVT Diary, February 1920 (Ottawa)
	'The Fitz-John Dachshunds'	*The Queen*, 23 August 1923
120	*The minute my house*	RH 'How Other Women Run Their Houses', *Daily Mail*, 11 May 1927
122	*All between members*	UVT Letters to John, 24 February 1946
	One always feels	RH to ES, 6 September 1934 (Texas)

14 Octopi and chains

124	*My plans depend*	Romaine Brooks to RH, 11 September 1921 (Ottawa)
	We had both	*The Life and Death of RH*
	We could lunch	Romaine Brooks to RH, 23 December 1921 (Ottawa)
125	*Paris ones*	Sylvia Beach, *Shakespeare and Company* (Faber and Faber 1960)
127	*One of the women*	RH *The Forge* (J. W. Arrowsmith 1924)
128	*Long hours*	*The Life and Death of RH*

15 How to treat a genius

129	*It is pleasant*	RH 'First-Nighters', *Sketch*, February 1924
130	*a bedlam afternoon*	UVT Diary, 12 June 1923 (Ottawa)
131	*the life that proudly*	*The Life and Death of RH*
132	*Yes your portrait*	Romaine Brooks to UVT, undated (Ottawa)
	This involved	*The Life and Death of RH*
133	*I ask you to kiss*	RH *A Saturday Life* (J. W. Arrowsmith 1925)

16 Books about ourselves

138 *If we cannot*	RH *Novel Writing*, The Taylorian Institute Oxford, 27 February 1933
It is wiser	RH *Adam's Breed* (Cassell & Co. 1926)
139 *If our literary*	*Novel Writing*
141 *A boy's first love*	*Adam's Breed*
Firmly rejecting	*The Life and Death of RH*
143 *We followed*	ibid
144 *Don't repress my*	James L. Garvin to UVT, 22 December 1926 (Ottawa)
145 *His subsequent*	*The Times*, 30 January 1926
146 *I wished to offer*	RH letter to Gorham Munson 2 June 1934 (Texas)
148 *it is far*	RH to Winifred Macy, 22 January and 13 June 1926 (Texas)

STEPHEN GORDON

17 Something of the acorn about her

151 *To encourage inverts*	RH, letter to Gorham Munson (Texas)
152 *I arrived*	RH to Winifred Macy, 23 January 1927 (Texas)
I can only say	ibid, 15 February 1927
153 *He assured me*	ibid
154 *What have*	ibid
155 *Congenital inversion*	RH handwritten notes for a lecture on the trial of *The Well of Loneliness*, given 25 January 1929 to Southend Young Socialists
156 *The invert's most*	RH 'The Well of Loneliness'. Draft of unpublished article, undated, 1931 or 1932, retrieved from the wastepaper basket by Winifred Hales (Monica Still)

18 She kissed her full on the lips

158 *the deadly campaign*	RH 'The Well of Loneliness', unpublished article
159 *having had many*	Havelock Ellis to RH, 21 April 1928 (Texas)

The Trial of Radclyffe Hall

19 Aspects of sexual inversion

167	*could not consent*	RH to Newman Flower 10 April 1928 (Ottawa)
168	*and inevitably*	Charles Evans to Audrey Heath, 27 April 1928 (Ottawa)
	portrait of a publisher	quoted in Michael S. Howard, *Jonathan Cape* (Jonathan Cape 1971)
	I wrote the book	RH to Jonathan Cape, 17 April 1928 (Ottawa)
170	*The thought of your*	RH to Havelock Ellis, 4 June 1928 (Texas)
	the friend who has	ibid
	The mate of the	ibid, 2 December 1928
	My patience is	RH to Carl Brandt, 21 June 1928 (Ottawa)
171	*the best and wisest*	RH to Jonathan Cape, 29 June 1928 (Ottawa)
	Hitherto the subject	ibid, 17 April 1928
172	*I know you will*	RH to James Garvin, 15 July 1928 (Texas)
173	*lively sense*	*Sunday Times*, 5 August 1928
174	*failure, lacking form*	*The Nation*, 4 August 1928
	long, tedious	*New Statesman*, 25 August 1928
	notable psychological	*Evening Standard*, 9 August 1928

20 Depraved practice

176	*They all wanted*	Michael S. Howard, *Jonathan Cape*
179	*This was the first*	RH to Havelock Ellis, 25 April 1929 (Texas)
	His were the sins	RH to Harold Rubinstein, 25 April 1929 (Ottawa)
	I have not anywhere	Havelock Ellis to RH, 28 August 1929 (Texas)
	dour fanatic	Herbert Hensley Henson, *Retrospect of an Unimportant Life* (Oxford University Press 1944). Quoted in Jennie Cooper Frye, *A Study in Censorship: Radclyffe Hall's 'The Well of Loneliness'*, mss
180	*One's mind reels*	RH handwritten notes for lecture on the trial
	The book has been	memorandum from Sir George Stephenson to Sir William Joynson-Hicks, 20 August 1928 (PRO)
181	*long private conference*	memorandum from Sir William Joynson-Hicks to Sir George Stephenson, 21 August 1928 (PRO)

182 *All day at telephone*   UVT Diary, 23 August 1928 (Ottawa)

21 Sapphism and censorship

183 *I set violently*   *The Journal of Arnold Bennett*, 24 August 1928 (London 1933)

     Unnatural practices   transcript of *The Director of Public Prosecutions v. Jonathan Cape and Leopold Hill*, Bow Street Police Court, 16 November 1928 (Ottawa)

184 *I hate inaction*   RH handwritten notes for lecture on the trial

     light up the principle   Havelock Ellis to RH, 3 November 1928 (Texas)

     I, as nothing   RH handwritten notes for lecture on the trial

185 *For many days*   Virginia Woolf to Vita Sackville-West, 28 August 1928 (Berg). See: *A Change of Perspective: The Letters of Virginia Woolf*, vol. III, ed. Nigel Nicolson (Hogarth Press 1977)

     not in the least   Vita Sackville-West to Harold Nicolson, 31 August 1928 (Berg)

186 *meritorious dull*   *The Diary of Virginia Woolf* vol. III, ed. Anne Olivier Bell (Hogarth Press 1980). 31 August 1928

     The dulness   Virginia Woolf to Lady Ottoline Morrell, early November 1928, *A Change of Perspective*

     screamed like a   Virginia Woolf to Vanessa Bell, 2 September 1928, ibid

     Sapphism disgusting   *The Diary of Virginia Woolf*, 31 August 1928

187 *gently and just*   Endnote to E. M. Forster *Maurice*, begun 1913, finished 1914, dedicated to a Happier Year, first published 1971

     A heavenly haven   *The Life and Death of RH*

188 *better type*   Blanche Knopf to RH, 27 September 1928 (Ottawa)

189 *John mobbed*   UVT Diary, 3 October 1928 (Ottawa)

     Pending consideration   Notes on the suppression of *The Well of Loneliness* (PRO)

     I hereby authorise   Joynson-Hicks to Postmaster General, 3 October 1928 (PRO)

190 *so that our clients*	Harold Rubinstein to Custom House, London, 10 October 1928 (Ottawa)
were according it	Harold Rubinstein, 'Scotland Yard and *The Well of Loneliness*' (Ottawa)
The subject is treated	memorandum from Sir Francis Floud to the Chancellor of the Excheqeur, 9 October 1928 (PRO)
192 *The government was bent*	RH handwritten notes for lecture on trial

22 A serious psychological subject

194 *They generally*	Virginia Woolf to Quentin Bell, 1 November 1928. *A Change of Perspective*
195 *I have never*	Havelock Ellis to RH, 20 October 1928 (Ottawa)
brimming with	Harold Rubinstein, 'Scotland Yard and *The Well of Loneliness*' (Ottawa)
198 *The company grew bolder*	Vita Sackville-West to Virginia Woolf, 3 November 1928 (Berg)
made a long	ibid
199 *we, neither you*	RH supplementary notes for Counsel (Texas)

23 I have read the book

201 *an assemblage which might*	Sheila Kaye-Smith, *All the Books of My Life* (Harper 1956)
All London	Virginia Woolf to Quentin Bell, 1 November 1928. *A Change of Perspective*
eminent men	RH handwritten notes for lecture on the trial
fidgeting	E. M. Forster, *Abinger Harvest* (Harcourt 1936)
lemon yellow	*The Diary of Virginia Woolf*, 10 November 1928
the pale tepid	ibid
something like	ibid
202 *deprave and corrupt those*	transcript of *The Director of Public Prosecutions v. Jonathan Cape and Leopold Hill*, Bow Street Police Court, 9 November 1928 (Ottawa)
'Podsnappery'	see: Jenny Cooper Frye, *A Study in Censorship*
203 *substantial question*	ibid
deadly campaign	RH draft of letter for the press, 1931

The policeman might	RH handwritten notes for lecture on the trial
205 *too indifferent*	*The Diary of Virginia Woolf,* 10 November 1928
We could not	ibid
207 *impressed by*	ibid
shamed and degraded	RH to the novelist Gerard Hopkins, 14 November 1928 (Berg)
In the eyes	RH to Havelock Ellis, 2 December 1928 (Texas)
209 *He made of my book*	RH handwritten notes for lecture on the trial
210 *so much respect*	ibid
211 *perpetual sexual*	UVT Letters to John, 24 February 1946

24 Depress! Repress! Suppress!

213 *This is the End*	*Daily Express,* 17 November 1928
Also, I am	RH to Havelock Ellis, 2 December 1928 (Texas)
214 *as high as*	Janet Flanner (Genêt), *Paris was Yesterday* (Angus & Robertson 1973)
for the sake	RH handwritten lecture notes on the trial
215 *With reference*	A. H. Bodkin, Director of Public Prosecution Department to Rubinstein, 27 November 1928 (Ottawa)
His aged mind	RH handwritten lecture notes on the trial
I received	*Retrospect of an Unimportant Life*
I asked him	Charles Carrington *Rudyard Kipling: His Life and Work* (London 1955)
216 *I shall have to*	transcript of *The Director of Public Prosecutions v. Rubinstein and Leopold Hill,* Bow Street Police Court, 16 November 1928 (Ottawa)
propaganda for vice	ibid
He was very absurd	RH handwritten lecture notes on the trial
217 *The bewildered*	Harold Rubinstein 'Scotland Yard and *The Well of Loneliness*' (Ottawa)
The Court retired	memorandum from Sir Archibald Bodkin to Sir William Joynson-Hicks, 14 December 1928 (PRO)
219 *The way to make a*	*The Sink of Solitude* (Hermes Press 1928)
220 *profound and painful*	*The Life and Death of RH*

	I renounce	RH to Audrey Heath, 7 April 1929
221	*be very guarded*	Harold Rubinstein to RH 9 January 1929 (Ottawa)
	no editor	Arnold Bennett to RH, 17 December 1928
222	*Total strangers*	*The Life and Death of RH*

25 The freedom of human beings

223	*The causes*	Morris Leopold Ernst *So Far So Good* (Harper 1948)
	The only essential	ibid
224	*The book is well*	*Saturday Review of Literature*, 4 May 1929 (Texas)
	She is Byronese	*New York Telegram Magazine*, December 1928
225	*Conscious censoriousness*	Morris Ernst's brief for the defence (Texas)
226	*If Stephen were a man*	ibid
228	*The book in question*	'*Well of Loneliness* Cleared in Court' *New York Times*, 20 April 1929
229	*Tired as I am*	RH to Donald Friede, 4 May 1929 (Texas)
	Long bitter experience	Morris Ernst to Covici-Friede, 20 April 1929 (Texas)
	a great tragic story	Wilette Kershaw to RH, 9 April 1929 (Texas)
230	*unpardonably*	UVT Diary, 17 April 1929 (Ottawa)
	definite plans	UVT to Wilette Kershaw, 21 April 1929 (Texas)

THE MASTER OF THE HOUSE

26 An awful shock

233	*grave warnings*	*The Life and Death of RH*
	grew as brown	ibid
234	*All afternoon*	UVT Diary, 21 July 1929 (Ottawa)
	as an amends	*The Life and Death of RH*
	mad and blasphemous	UVT Diary, 8 August 1929 (Ottawa)
	I know you would wish	RH to Wilette Kershaw, 9 August 1929 (Texas)
235	*Probably we are right*	Audrey Heath to RH, 6 September 1929 (Texas)

	soft as pulp	UVT to Audrey Heath, 7 September 1929 (Texas)
	We both think	ibid
236	*recommend her*	RH to Audrey Heath, 4 October 1929 (Texas)
	'Stop, stop!' he screamed	Radclyffe Hall, *The Master of the House* (Jonathan Cape 1932)
237	*I have made enquiries*	Affidavit from C. S. Tomlinson, 25 October 1929 (Texas)
238	*At 12.30*	UVT Daybook, 7 January 1931 (Texas)
	lectured her	UVT Diary, 13 January 1930 (Ottawa)
239	*in which she begged*	*Paris was Yesterday*
	backboneless	J. Holroyd-Reece to RH and UVT, 2 September 1930 (Texas)
	that she knew	*Paris was Yesterday*
240	*use the censorship*	Morris Ernst to Harold Rubinstein, 30 September 1930 (Texas)
	howls of laughter	UVT Diary, 28 December 1930 (Ottawa)

27 Just Rye

241	*just fond*	UVT Daybook, 26 February 1931 (Texas)
242	*Isn't Rye heavenly*	ibid, 16 April 1931
	a future life for dogs	ibid, 27 May 1931
244	*I long to own*	ibid, June 1931
	When I look back	ibid, 1 November 1931
	pose of head	ibid, 11 December 1931
245	*Even better class*	ibid
	As she left	ibid
246	*they thought they*	UVT Daybook, 1 March 1932
	went the colour	ibid, April 1932

28 Give us a kiss

248	*What she has been*	UVT Daybook, 6 July 1932 (Texas)
249	*the subhuman, seething*	ibid, August 1932
	put me among the girls	ibid, 2 October 1932
	trying to make	ibid
	John is genuinely	ibid, 14 March 1933
250	*shortly before I*	preface to *Miss Ogilvy Finds Herself* (Heinemann 1934)
	'My God!'	*Miss Ogilvy Finds Herself*
252	*decently behaved*	UVT Daybook, February 1933
	They would rather	ibid, 14 February 1933

253 *How are the mighty*	ibid, May 1933
Mabel Bourne!	ibid, October 1933
254 *There is always*	ibid, April 1933
The propaganda novel	RH *Novel Writing*, The Taylorian Institute, Oxford, 27 February 1933
255 *I am disgusted*	UVT Daybook, 26 August 1933
256 *grim outcome*	ibid, September 1933
It is her duty	ibid, November 1933
257 *I shall not be present*	ibid, 7 November 1933

SAME HEART

29 The intolerable load

262 *John was obviously*	Evguenia Souline, autobiographical notes, undated, c. 1957 (Monica Still)
I can see	RH to ES, 3 March 1939 (Texas)
May I take off	ibid
There was something	ES, autobiographical notes
263 *I fought like*	ibid
I am really	RH to ES, 17 July 1934
Meet me at	ibid, 20 July 1934
Darling, Yes	ibid, 24 July 1934
264 *And your darling*	ibid, 29 August 1934
I am tormented	ibid, 27 July 1934
265 *After a scene*	ibid, 31 July 1934
And when she	ibid
267 *I want you*	ibid, 13 August 1934
I resented it	ES, autobiographical notes
congenital invert	RH to ES, 19 August 1934
I asked if	ibid, 2 September 1934
268 *I love you too much*	RH to ES, 7 August 1934
Now listen Souline	RH to ES, 29 August 1934
269 *I haven't*	ibid
I found you a virgin	ibid, 7 June 1934
all crumpled	ibid, 30 December 1934
Very often	ES, autobiographical notes
270 *You woke me*	RH to ES, 8 December 1934
271 *She might have made*	ibid, 5 October 1934

30 A trois

272	*I feel crazy*	RH to ES, 27 November 1934 (Texas)
	I am not	ibid, 4 December 1934
273	*All that I did*	UVT Daybook, 13 November 1934 (Texas)
274	*I feel as though*	RH to ES, 22 November 1934
275	*Una wants to come*	ibid, December 1934
	I am perpetually	UVT Daybook, 4 March 1935 (Texas)
276	*Her mind never*	ibid, March 1935
277	*But how can I*	ibid
	So there is another	ibid, January 1935
	You're quite right	ibid, 20 March 1935

31 How long O Lord, how long

279	*Please, oh, please*	RH to ES, 1 April 1935 (Texas)
280	*I scarcely dare*	UVT Daybook, 12 April 1935 (Texas)
	I wonder how	RH to ES, Easter Sunday 1935 (Texas)
	If she was	UVT Daybook, April 1935 (Texas)
	Lord how every	ibid
281	*grieved thinking of*	UVT Daybook, April 1935 (Texas)
282	*Pull yourself together*	RH to ES, 19 May 1935 (Texas)
283	*Oooh I hate*	UVT Daybook, 24 June 1935 (Texas)
	I am always	ibid, 22 June 1935
284	*John looked upon me*	ES, autobiographical notes
285	*Why are we not*	UVT Daybook, October 1935 (Texas)
286	*Just now*	quoted in RH to ES, 7 November 1935 (Texas)
	You belong to me	RH to ES, 3 November 1935 (Texas)
287	*My poor old mother's*	ibid, 18 October 1935
	drag on	ibid, 26 October 1935
	Me she so hates	ibid
	The Warrens	UVT Daybook, 1 December 1935 (Texas)

32 His name was Father Martin but she called him Henry

289	*common as dirt*	UVT Daybook, 9 January 1936 (Texas)
	I have noticed	ibid, 18 January 1936
290	*with an enchanting*	ibid, 4 January 1936
	And much pleasant	ibid, 17 January 1936
	For my poor sake	RH to ES, 31 January 1936 (Texas)
291	*And here we are*	UVT Daybook, March 1936 (Texas)
292	*With Ladye's help*	ibid, April 1936
294	*In the two years*	ibid, 15 July 1936

	We cannot allow	ibid, July 1936
295	*I could do not much*	ES, autobiographical notes
	We shall be apart	UVT Daybook, 8 March 1936 (Texas)
	What a woman	ibid, August 1936
296	*It is not*	UVT Daybook, 7 October 1936 (Texas)
	She sneered	ibid
297	*Fascist anti-*	ibid, 5 November 1936
	It may shock	ibid, 24 December 1936

OUR THREE SELVES

33 An empty fiction

301	*The teaching*	UVT Daybook, 18 March 1937 (Texas)
302	*I pointed out*	ibid, 29 June 1937
303	*I cannot*	ibid, May 1937
	I think of what	RH to ES, 16 July 1937 (Texas)
304	*Don't you think*	ibid, 21 July 1937
	The cottage looks	ibid, 15 July 1937
	Oh Evguenia	ibid, 16 July 1937
305	*She seemed incapable*	ibid, 17 July 1937
	a grim horror	UVT Daybook, 8 August 1937 (Texas)
306	*Thank you good*	RH to ES, 25 August 1937 (Texas)
307	*She finds fault*	UVT Daybook, 10 September 1937 (Texas)
	When I have	ibid, 1 October 1937
	I seem to get	ibid, 23 October 1937
308	*Whatever she is*	ibid, 20 December 1937

34 Never mind Una

309	*Of course this 'study'*	UVT Daybook, 15 May 1938 (Texas)
	that way you would	ibid, 23 June 1938
310	*Every task*	ibid, 31 July 1938
311	*Horrified recipients*	ibid, 25 February 1938
312	*I would like*	RH to ES, 28 June 1938 (Texas)
313	*Can we never*	ibid
	Then my nerve	UVT Daybook, July 1938 (Texas)
314	*I should not like*	ibid, 24 July 1938
	It was all to me	ibid, 21 August 1938
	You aren't going	ibid
	I shrink under	ibid, 3 September 1938
315	*Lord what a jam*	ibid, 30 August 1938

	He is an hysteric	RH to ES, 13 September 1938 (Texas)
317	the pain of her	UVT Daybook, 15 November 1938 (Texas)
	In the weeks	ibid, 23 December 1938
	a brown saucer	ibid, 24 December 1938

35 The rain pours down, the icy wind howls

318	The fat	UVT Daybook, 11 January 1939 (Texas)
	Una won't	ibid, 21 January 1939
	Johnnie would	ibid, 22 January 1939
319	You have held	RII to ES, 3 March 1939 (Texas)
	Something very	ibid, 5 February 1939
	unless you do	ibid, 9 February 1939
320	Jews, Yes	ibid, 22 March 1939
	We are clear of	UVT Daybook, March 1939 (Texas)
321	that slug of	UVT Daybook, 2 July 1939 (Texas)
	He told me	Sandra Tealdi to Evguenia Soulina, 27 May 1939 (Monica Still)
322	I refuse in	UVT Daybook, 16 May 1939 (Texas)
	What's the good	RH to ES, 9 July 1939 (Texas)
	The flat is in	ibid, 19 July 1939
	Oh Piggie	ibid, 6 June 1939
323	I suspect	UVT Daybook, 24 July 1939 (Texas)
	I knocked	ibid, 26 August 1939
325	But for Mr Eden	ibid, 11 September 1939
	alias Florence	ibid, 20 September 1939
326	You fool	ibid, 7 October 1939
327	The rain pours	ibid, 30 October 1939
	My suspicions	ibid, 17 October 1939

36 At the Wayside

328	horrible spectacle	UVT Daybook, 7 January 1940 (Texas)
	I may despise	ibid, 5 February 1940
329	languidly served	ibid, 15 January 1940
	Suppose you had	RH to ES, 28 April 1940 (Texas)
331	As Evguenia	UVT Daybook, 10 May 1940 (Texas)
	The implication	ibid, 26 February 1941
	Are you a nurse	ibid, 22 September 1941
332	This woman has	ibid, 14 February 1941
	So there goes	ibid, 19 April 1941
	We demurred	ibid, 12 June 1941

333	*After all,*	ibid, June 1941
	Henceforward	ibid, 22 June 1941
	I advised John	ibid, 15 August 1941
334	*I write daily*	ibid, 29 August 1941
	I am sorry Miss	ibid, 24 September 1941
335	*I was happy*	ES, autobiographical notes (Texas)
336	*we Bolshevists*	UVT Daybook, 27 October 1941
	May I ask	ibid, 6 November 1941
	Then follows	ibid, 10 November 1941
337	*She sat there*	ibid, 17 November 1941
	I simply prayed	ibid, 1 December 1941
	so as to avoid	ibid, 9 December 1941

37 John's Calvary

338	*The bitch*	UVT Daybook, 15 January 1942 (Texas)
339	*I told her*	ibid, 29 January 1942
	She is terribly	UVT to ES, 5 February 1942 (Texas)
	These are grim	RH to ES, 6 February 1942
340	*Don't you remember*	ibid, 30 March 1942
	Oh how weary	ibid, 21 February 1942
	the dreadful creature	UVT Daybook, 6 April 1942 (Texas)
	I think it only right	UVT to ES, 6 April 1942 (Texas)
342	*And all because*	UVT Daybook, 12 August 1942 (Texas)
	I have had very many	RH to ES, 24 December 1942
343	*There a veritable*	UVT Daybook, 25 February 1943
	The memory of	ibid
344	*I sealed my mouth*	ES, autobiographical notes (Monica Still)
345	*When you began*	UVT Daybook, 30 December 1945
346	*I saw your eyes*	ibid, 25 December 1943
347	*My John is dying*	ibid, 29 September 1943
	You must be friends	ES to UVT, 29 July 1950 (Monica Still)
	You'll be good	UVT Letters to John, 27 March 1944
348	*There was never*	UVT Daybook, 9 March 1943
	She looked up	ibid, dated 21 June 1943, but written four months later
	I said that she had	Naomi Jacob, *Me and the Swans* (Kimber 1963)
	Ivory clear and pale	UVT Daybook, 7 October 1943
349	*resting together*	ibid

MY JOHN, MY JOHNNIE

38 Mine for ever

353	*would have the strength*	UVT Letters to John, May 1944
	I feel I must	ibid, 27 January 1944
354	*Such a decision*	*The Life and Death of RH*
	There is nothing	UVT Letters to John, 18 January 1949
	My diary shows	2 January 1944
355	*You are with Him*	ibid, 6 February 1944
	It won't matter	ibid, 23 June 1944
	Cards on the	ibid, 27 February 1944
356	*after all my precious*	ibid, 6 February 1944
	It's all horrible	ibid, 28 March 1944
	grave provocation	UVT, statement to the executors of her will, 23 September 1944
357	*Your letter*	Harold Rubinstein to Horatio Lovat Dickson, 14 February 1975
	I would only be	UVT Letters to John, 3 November 1944
358	*I wear your poplin*	ibid, 12 January 1944
	nothing ever for a	ibid, December 1944
359	*nothing can hurt*	ibid
	She showed me	Maria Visetti to Jane Caruth, 13 October 1943
	all these years	ibid
360	*If I comply*	ibid, 11 February 1944
361	*Truly your mantle*	UVT Letters to John, 6 March 1945
	darling little	ibid, 1 February 1944
	will never in this	ibid, 23 June 1945
362	*I think such solemn*	ibid
	The answer of course	ibid, zz February 1945
363	*I certainly don't*	ibid, 21 March 1945
	I have done for	ibid, 14 April 1945
	on a larger scale	ibid, June 1944
364	*I will not have*	ibid, October 1944
	That is a result	ibid, August 1945
	I hung on to	ibid, 14 September 1945
365	*It was all settled*	UVT Letters to John, 5 July 1946
	This marriage	ibid, 14 August 1946

39 *He* is my occupation

366	*I can't remember*	UVT Letters to John, April 1945
367	*a ghastly wreck*	ibid, 26 January 1944
	I will not let her	ibid, 27 January 1944
	They want *me*	ibid, 25 January 1944
368	*I am not really*	Peter Davies to Sir Oscar Dowson, 15 June 1946 (PRO)
	the impression that	memorandum from Chuter Ede to F. H. Logan, 19 June 1946 (PRO)
	From the Home Office	memorandum from F. H. Logan to Chuter Ede, 22 June 1946 (PRO)
369	*in case the priest's*	UVT Letters to John, December 1946
	If only she didn't	ibid, 25 June 1948
	I simply can't	ibid, 5 May 1948
	I am not rising	ibid, 31 August 1948
371	*I am deeply*	ibid, 14 May 1948
	I beg of you	ES to UVT, 12 April 1950
	She can't be	UVT Letters to John, 15 April 1950
372	*My dear Evguenia*	UVT to ES, 4 August 1950
374	*When we were alone*	UVT Letters to John, February 1957
	He looks so beautiful	ibid, 29 January 1956
375	*Nika asked me*	ibid, February 1956
	There is the usual	ibid, 11 October 1956
	Her decision that	ibid
376	*After all, the money*	ibid, 3 February 1957
	I am willing	ibid, 6 September 1957
377	*I think that being*	RH to ES, 7 September 1934
	My poor sweet	UVT Letters to John, 6 October 1957
378	*It would not even be*	UVT Daybook, February 1944

INDEX

NOTE: Writings by Radclyffe Hall appear directly under title; works by others appear under author's name